Sounds of Apocalypse

Eastern European Studies in Musicology

Edited by Maciej Gołąb

Editorial board
Mikuláš Bek (Brno)
Gražina Daunoravičienė (Vilnius)
Luba Kyjanovska (Lviv)
Igor Savchuk (Kyiv)
Adrian Thomas (Cardiff)
László Vikárius (Budapest)

Volume 25

Katarzyna Naliwajek

Sounds of Apocalypse

Music in Poland under German Occupation

Bibliographic Information published by the Deutsche Nationalbibliothek
The Deutsche Nationalbibliothek lists this publication in the Deutsche Nationalbibliografie; detailed bibliographic data is available online at http://dnb.d-nb.de.

Library of Congress Cataloging-in-Publication Data
A CIP catalog record for this book has been applied for at the Library of Congress.

This publication was financially supported by the University of Warsaw.

Cover illustration: Author's personal collection.

ISSN 2193-8342
ISBN 978-3-631-88170-5 (Print)
E-ISBN 978-3-631-89066-0 (E-PDF)
E-ISBN 978-3-631-89068-4 (EPUB)
DOI 10.3726/b20224

© Peter Lang GmbH
Internationaler Verlag der Wissenschaften
Berlin 2022
All rights reserved.

Peter Lang – Berlin · Lausanne · Bruxelles · New York
Oxford · Warszawa · Wien

All parts of this publication are protected by copyright. Any utilisation outside the strict limits of the copyright law, without the permission of the publisher, is forbidden and liable to prosecution. This applies in particular to reproductions, translations, microfilming, and storage and processing in electronic retrieval systems.

This publication has been peer reviewed.

www.peterlang.com

For my parents

Table of Contents

Introduction 11
    Silence versus sound memory 25
    State of research 36
    Methods, questions, and goals 44

Chapter One: Music as a manipulative tool in Nazi cultural and political domination 55
    1.1. Nazi propaganda of German cultural supremacy and racial hatred .. 55
    1.2. Racial pseudo-aesthetics as the ideological background of cultural policies 64
    1.3. Nazi administration and racial jurisdiction versus Polish culture 72
    1.4. Racial segregation and ghettoization 81
    1.5. Nazi propaganda towards different social and ethnic groups 84
    1.6. The appropriation of Chopin by the Nazi propaganda 87

Chapter Two: Musical life in the General Government and annexed territories 97
    2.1 Music in the General Government 99
        2.1.1. Germans for Germans 112
        2.1.2. Music by Poles for Poles 115
        2.1.3. Music by Jews for Jews: The Warsaw Ghetto 117
        2.1.4. Appropriation, destruction, genocide: Three facets of Nazi cultural policy in Krakow 124
        2.1.5. Control of the symbolic spaces 127
        2.1.6. Clandestine music as protest, resistance, and quest for freedom 135

2.2. Music in Reich-annexed territories: *Aufbau* in the *Warthegau* 142

2.3. Soundscape of occupied Poland in witnesses' testimonies 158

    2.3.1. Trauma-related sounds of violence 160

    2.3.2. Traumatic sound as creativity inception factor 166

    2.3.3. Sounds of being shot at 168

    2.3.4. Music as a tool of counteracting traumatic sounds 169

    2.3.5. Singing as method to counteract traumatic warfare sounds . 171

    2.3.6. Imagined music: Musical memory as survival technique 172

    2.3.7. Sounds of the ruined city 174

Chapter Three: The functions of music within the Nazi system of genocide in occupied Poland 177

3.1. Psychopathology of the ritual 179

3.2. Music as torture and as deception 183

3.3. Music and management in Treblinka 190

3.4. Sadistic domination: forced music-making 194

3.5. Music as entertainment for the guards 199

3.6. The interrelationship of torture and music from a psychoanalytical perspective 203

3.7. Mass Killings and the Sound of Music 205

3.8. Music as self-defense, resistance, survival, and mourning 209

Acknowledgments 221

Epilogue 225

List of abbreviations 231

    Bibliography 232

Appendix 251

Appendix to Introduction 251

Appendix to Chapter one 261

Appendix to 1.6. 266

Appendix to Chapter two 271

Appendix to 2.1.1. Poles for Poles 280

Propaganda through music for Poles as presented by the German media 283

Appendix to 2.1.2. Germans for Germans 285

Appendix to 2.1.3. Music by Jews for Jews 290

Appendix to 2.1.6. Clandestine music as protest, resistance, and quest for freedom 306

Appendix to 2.1.5. Control of the symbolic spaces 313

Musicians killed during the German occupation of Poland – a few portraits 317

    Marian Neuteich 321

    Singer Helena Ostrowska 322

    Looted Chopin memorabilia from the collection of Leopold Binental (1886–1944), the Polish-Jewish chopinologist murdered by the Germans 324

    The Plunder of the Binental Collection 328

List of items related to Chopin lost or stolen during the German occupation of Poland 330

History of the Fryderyk Chopin Institute Collection 332

Index of Names 341

Introduction

The utter disruption of musical life in Poland during its occupation by the Third Reich is analogous to mechanisms that ravaged all other spheres of life and culture. The destruction and plunder of Poland's infrastructure, industry, multicultural heritage, architecture, monuments, instruments, libraries, education, and state institutions with their staff, was unparalleled, just as the casualty rate in Poland, which constituted 18 per cent of the whole pre-war population, while in Germany it was 7.4 per cent, in Russia – 11.2 per cent, in Great Britain – 0.9 per cent.[1] These fundamental differences between the ravaged Polish state and other European countries were further aggravated by post-war impoverishment and the undermining of Poland's political position due to the decisions made jointly by the Allies and the Soviets. Musing over the Bundesarchiv photograph documenting the distribution of the spoils of war, decided on without the participation of those who had been despoiled, a bitter travesty comes to mind: "Poland as the Politicians' Blooded Playground."[2] In his seminal work, Norman Davies explained for the first time facts unknown in the West and until 1989 unknown in Poland itself, and he pointed out that "Poland became the killing-ground of Europe, the new Golgotha. Still, even in 1945 peace was not fully restored."[3]

The liberation of Polish territories from German occupation went hand in hand with the implementation of Soviet political control and the radical change of pre-war borders according to Stalin's plan, ratified in August 1945 at the Potsdam Conference (17 July – 2 August) by the United States, the United Kingdom, and the Soviet Union. This legitimized the transfer of power over Poland to the Soviet Union, as the puppet communist government created by the Soviets (Provisional Government of National Unity) was recognized by all three partners, thereby ending the recognition of the legitimate London-based Polish government-in-exile. Alongside British and American foreign ministers, an important role was played by the Russian foreign minister Vyacheslav Molotov, who just six years

---

1 Norman Davies, *Heart of Europe. A Short History of Poland* (Oxford: Clarendon Press, 1984), 64.
2 Bundesarchiv, Bild 183-R67561. I am refering here to the two most notable and influential books on Polish history: *God's Playground* (New York: Columbia University Press, 1982) by the famous British historian Norman Davies and *Bloodlands: Europe Between Hitler and Stalin* (New York: Basic Books, 2010) by Timothy D. Snyder.
3 Davies, *Heart of Europe*, 64.

earlier had signed a secret Pact with Nazi foreign minister Ribbentrop – a pact which divided Polish territories into "two spheres of influence" and set the stage for the attack on Poland in 1939, on September 1st and 17th respectively. The Soviets used all possible propaganda methods either to deny it, despite the blatant evidence (see Appendix and section 1.3. of this book), or argue that "the intervention" was justified.

The disappearance of Poland from the map of Europe between 1939–1945 was all the more natural for its neighbours since just twenty years before it hadn't existed either, being partitioned for 123 years (1795–1918) between Russia, Prussia, and Austria. The situation of Poland as a state, with borders shifting due to pacts signed by other countries, was thus – euphemistically speaking – unstable and this strongly influenced its cultural identity, its musical and non-musical realities and ideologies.

The time between September 1, 1939, and May 1945 constitutes not only the most tragic period in Poland's history, but also the most difficult one to investigate. In contrast to most of the other Nazi-occupied countries, the whole structure of musical life was shattered, and the very existence of musicians was imperilled. Soviet and German occupiers – for more than a century aggressively seeking to control Poland, trying to Russify and Germanize it – knew that the only continuity that held together the very idea of this non-existent state was contained in its culture, language, and intellectual power. This is why the occupying powers agreed that liquidating the Polish elites was necessary. And indeed, it was a task they scrupulously and eagerly effectuated when they seized Poland's territories again in 1939. Even though Chopin's piano at the Zamoyski palace in Warsaw was smashed to pieces, when the Russians threw it out of the window on 19 September 1863 in revenge for the unsuccessful attempt of Polish insurgents to kill the Russian governor Teodor Berg, it was immortalized in the visionary poem *Fortepian Szopena* (1863–4) by Cyprian Kamil Norwid and became an indestructible symbol of spiritual resistance. The number of pianos and other instruments destroyed and plundered in occupied Poland is impossible to evaluate. Also, the numbers of musicians killed on this "killing ground," into which Polish territories had been transformed, cannot be precisely established. In the process of effacing the identity of Shoah victims, documents recording the deaths of victims – among them established and less well-known musicians, young talents murdered in German death camps – were effectively destroyed by the functionaries of the Third Reich. Oral repertoires, as those of Roma, Jewish and other traditional musicians, were lost forever behind the gates of extermination camps. We are left with slivers of memory retained by the survivors and the debris of evidence the perpetrators were unable to destroy. And we are left with questions, trying to go back on the blood trails, trying to understand the function of music in the lives and deaths of the victims and survivors. Their identities as human beings devoted to music were much less important than their "racial status" and "usefulness" – categories which served to determine whether they were killed or kept alive. On August 24, 1944, in block 28 at KL Auschwitz, between 40 and 50 of the strongest and healthiest young prisoners – mostly Hungarian Jews – were selected for pseudo-medical experiments by a young Wehrmacht doctor. Samuel Stern, who was forced to assist during the experiments as an inmate-medic, remembered Szigetthi, an 18-year-old boy from Budapest, who "in spite of horrific pain never complained and notated from memory the most beautiful Mozart's compositions on the planks of the highest bunk."[4] This was his method of keeping his identity and resisting the unbearable suffering. In October, he was selected by the same doctor for the gas chamber with three other prisoners.

To the well-educated perpetrators who often held doctorates from famous universities, such criminal actions, mass murder included, were "justifiable." If they were not sentenced to life in prison or given the death penalty, they continued their academic, professional, and political careers unhindered in postwar Germany. Prof. Dr. med. Karl Gebhardt, Consulting Surgeon of the Waffen SS, Major General in the SS and President of the German Red Cross who was sentenced during the Nuremberg Trials did not show any remorse. To the contrary, he justified his experiments with sulphanilamide on Polish resistance fighters in Ravensbrück (the youngest was 16, the oldest 48) by claiming that it was a response to the assassination of Reinhard Heydrich, Deputy Reich Protector of Bohemia and Moravia, which took place on 27 May 1942 in Prague. When Polish witnesses were introduced to the court by the Prosecutor's medical expert, neurologist and psychiatrist Leo Alexander, the manipulatory cynicism of Gebhardt reached its apex. He became the prosecutor himself, accusing Alexander

> of being "filled with a hate against each and every German," to the point of "collapse." The four Polish women, he continued, had him, Gebhardt, to thank that they could

---

4   The man responsible for suffering and death of the victims of experiments, a Wehrmacht doctor Heinz Kaschub, continued his medical career after 1945 and died in 1977. Ernst Klee, *Auschwitz. Medycyna III Rzeszy i jej ofiary*, translated from German (*Auschwitz, die NS-Medizin und ihre Opfer*, Frankfurt am Main: Fischer Verlag, 1997) to Polish by Elżbieta Kalinowska-Styczeń (Krakow: Universitas, 2009), 199. Klee quoted here the testimony of prisoner medic Samuel Stern (*Die Schrecken von Auschwitz. Internationaler Suchdienst Arolsen: Pseudo-Medizinische Versuche im KL Auschwitz, Phlegmone-Versuche*, 15.05.1973. Annex I).

appear in Nuremberg to testify against him, because it was he who had secured permission for "60 experimental persons" to leave Ravensbrück for Sweden. This distortion of reality is typical of the accused as a whole. It is based essentially on a mechanism for perception which views the environment, totally disregarding other people and views, and structures it exclusively from the perspective of the self.[5]

Gebhardt's pseudo-scientific megalomaniac ebriety as extension of his narcissistic ego,[6] his sense of supremacy, nurtured by the profound disdain and hatred for the *Untermenschen*, and his omnipotence – both imagined and real since he was indeed "the lord of life and death" to the prisoners – made this conceited representative of German science absolutely immune to any empathy towards his victims. He did not perceive the women he mutilated in Ravensbrück as human individuals and thus it did not matter whether she was a young Polish girl or a maimed French conductor – they were treated as "experimental persons," bodies to be used and disposed of.[7] However, the psychoanalytical interpretations do not seem sufficient for explaining those Nazi attitudes towards their victims. The Italian philosopher Roberto Esposito states in his chilling analyses of what he called the Nazi *thanatopolitics* that "the overall role that medicine played in Nazi ideology and practices" is precisely what should be investigated:

---

5 Angelika Ebbinghaus, "Introduction: Reflections on the Nuremberg Medical Trial," in: Johannes Eltzschig, Michael Walter (eds.), *The Nuremberg Medical Trial 1946/47. Guide to the Microfiche Edition* (München: K.G. Saur Verlag, 2001), 28, 34–37, 50. The physician Zofia Mączka, deported to Ravensnbrück from prison in Krakow on September 13, 1941, as a political prisoner, worked in the camp hospital between July 1942 and July 1943 and stated in her detailed affidavit: "Many of the [purposefully] infected patients were ill for months and almost all of them became cripples. Why did Prof. Gebhardt, with his education, carry out these experiments? To test the new drugs of the German pharmaceutical industry. (…) The results of the treatment were not checked, or if they were, it was done in such an inadequate and superficial manner, that it was of no value." *The Nuremberg Medical Trial*, 33.
6 Jacques Lacan used the term "megalomaniac ebriety" after Michael Balint in his *Écrits. A Selection*, translated by Alan Sheridan (originally published in French by Éditions du Seuil, 1966), first published in the United Kingdom in 1977 by Tavistock Publications, here quoted from the Taylor & Francis edition (London, 2005), 105.
7 R.V., a French conductor, arrested by the Gestapo and tortured in prison, was transported in a tragic state to Ravensbrück on 4 July 1944. When in pain she defecated on the floor, Professor Gebhardt mutilated her as "punishment" with phosphorus, leaving her perineum permanently disfigured. He did so with other women prisoners. Ernst Klee quoted a medical raport on the condition of this person, whose identity is protected under initials (Klee, *Auschwitz*, 154).

We know that the Reich knew well how to compensate its doctors, not only with university professorships and honours, but also with something more concrete. (...) the surgeon Karl Brandt, who had already been commissioned in operation "Euthanasia," became one of the most powerful men of the regime, subordinate only to the supreme authority of the Führer in his subject area, which was the unlimited one of the life and death of everyone (without dwelling on Irmfried Eberl, promoted at thirty-two to commandant of Treblinka).[8]

The future "head of Zyklon-B distribution in Auschwitz, Joachim Mrugowski, spoke of 'the doctor's divine mission,' and 'the priest of the sacred flame of life'" in his 1939 publication.[9] And thus,

> It is no coincidence that the doctor, even before the sovereign or the priest, was equated with the heroic figure of the "soldier of life." In corresponding fashion, Slavic soldiers who arrived from the East were considered not only adversaries of the Reich, but "enemies of life." It isn't enough to conclude, however, that the limits between healing and killing have been eliminated in the biomedical vision of Nazism. Instead, we need to conceptualize them as two sides of the same project that makes one the necessary condiction of the other: it is only by killing as many people as possible that one could heal [*risanare*] those who represented the true Germany.[10]

Musical abilities, however, were so useful for the Nazi genocide system that they could counterbalance the "biological impurity" and redeem (at least temporarily) some chosen "enemies of life." Another Ravensbrück prisoner, a young singer and Polish resistance member, Zofia Ryś, was treated better, because her singing was noticed, so that her work as forced labourer was much lighter than in the case of other prisoners. In her report, Ryś admits that she could work in the Hohenlychen sanatorium's garden, embracing a special function: "she had to sing for the head of the Hohenlychen kitchen."[11] Born in 1920, she was arrested

---

8   Roberto Esposito, *Bíos: Biopolitics and philosophy* (translated by Timothy Campbell, "Posthumanities" 4, Minneapolis, London: University of Minnesota Press, 2008), 114–115. This philosopher analyses how the Nazi usage of notions such as *Rassenhygiene*, euthanasia and cleaniness motivated genocide by conceptualizing it as pest extermination. He quoted the words of Himmler addressed to the SS stationed at Kharkov according to which "Anti-Semitism is like disinfestations. Keeping lice away is not an ideological question – it is a question of cleaniness," 117.
9   Esposito, *Bíos*, 114. Esposito quotes from Joachim Mrugowsky's "Einleitung," in *Das ärtzliche Ethos* (The physician's ethos), ed. Christoph Wilhelm Hufeland (Munich and Berlin: J. F. Lehmann, 1939).
10 Ibid., 115.
11 "Hohenlychen, part of the spa town of Lychen, lies 12 kilometers (7.5 miles) to the northeast of the Ravensbrück concentration camp. During the National Socialist era,

in the aftermath of a daring Polish underground action to liberate the courier Jan Karski, emissary of the Polish government-in-exile, from hospital, where he was held after an attempted suicide in a Gestapo prison. This action was skilfully organized by Zofia's brother, Polish underground courier Zbigniew Ryś on July 28, 1940. She was arrested on April 29, 1941, in Warsaw, where she studied singing with Professor Stefan Belina-Skupiewski, was involved in the clandestine Institute of Theatrical Art and lived in the apartment of her sister Wanda and her brother-in-law, conductor Olgierd Straszyński, an important figure in the Polish underground. She knew she would be arrested, but did not go into hiding, so that she could take the blame for her sisters and mother, arrested earlier, to be released. From the Pawiak prison she was sent to Nowy Sącz, where she used to live and where the liberation of Karski had taken place. During cruel interrogations by Obersturmführer Heinrich Hamann[12] she did not denounce anyone. She was the prisoner of Ravensbürck for four years, from September 1941, where she also took part in clandestine activity. However, the Germans, who applied

---

Hohenlychen was the location for a well- known clinic for sport and work injuries headed by Professor Dr. Karl Gebhardt, a specialist in reconstructive surgery and a confidant of Heinrich Himmler. From 1936 onward, Gebhardt was a member of the SS Medical Corps and then the Waffen-SS, where, by the end of World War II, he had reached the rank of SS-Gruppenführer and Generalleutnant. Even before the war, he established a special clinic for SS members in his sanatorium. (…) Among his patients were members of various European royal families, diplomats, politicians, sports people, industrialists from various countries, as well as high-ranking members of the National Socialist political and military leadership. The sanatorium was officially known as the Red Cross Sanatorium Hohenlychen." Judith Hahn, "Hohenlychen," translated by Stephen Pallavicini, in: Geoffrey P. Megargee (ed.), *Ravensbrück Subcamp System* in: *The United States Holocaust Memorial Museum Encyclopedia of Camps and Ghettos, 1933-1945*, Vol. I: *Early Camps, Youth Camps, and Concentration Camps and Subcamps under the SS-Business Administration Main Office (WVHA)* (Bloomington: Indiana University Press, 2009), 1206–1207.

12 Heinrich Hamann (1908–1993), NSDAP and SS member since 1931, from December 1939 to August 1943 chief of Außendienststelle der Sicherheitspolizei – Grenzpolizeikommissariat Neu Sandez, where he personally murdered at least 100 people, among others the judge Wilhelm Miklaszewski (during the trial 77 killings were proven), in August 1943 transferred to Jasło and then Krakow. He went into hiding after the war under the name Hossfeld in West Germany, and was sentenced to life in prison only in 1966 during the trial in Bochum, released in the mid-1980s and lived in Bad Neuenahr. Partial information is contained in E. Klee, *Das Personenlexikon zum Dritten Reich: wer, war, was vor und nach 1945* (Frankfurt am Main: S. Fischer, 2007), 222.

the principle of collective responsibility, sentenced to death and subsequently executed the elite of Nowy Sącz as punishment for this successful underground action. The day before her transport to Ravensbrück she was given a sign through the window of her cell from the window of the Court, which was on the opposite side of the street, to sing that day at 7 pm Gounod's *Ave Maria*. It turned out that this was planned by her sister Stanisława and a court employee that she should sing for fellow prisoners who were to be executed the next day: her teacher of theatre, Bolesław Barbacki, her brother's friends, the priest Tadeusz Kaczmarek and several others.[13]

Rena Anisfeld from Nowy Sącz – who was one year older than Zofia Ryś, and lost her father, Mojżesz Guttreich, her mother Lea and all her brothers: Arie, Joel, Chanina, Jecheskiel, Aron, Icchak, Chaim – gave a haunting record of Hamann's murderous actions and of his use of music both for the amusement of the perpetrators and for the torture and degradation of the victims, to strip them of human dignity and transform them into his puppets:

> Immediately after the Gestapo appeared, some devilish ideas were set in motion: actions, shooting Jews, hangings. Hamann used to say: "All belongs to me, your lives also, actually it's all mine!" Obersturmführer Heinrich Hamann had the title of doctor. It was said he was an attorney, but I don't know how much of this is true. He was exceptionally beautiful. He was tall, blonde, with blue eyes. He had a wife and two sons. It was said that he came from Berlin.
>
> In the beginning, Hamann liquidated the Polish intelligentsia. He would transport them in cars to Marcinkowice, and execute them there. The pharmacist, Jarosz, the merchant, Górka, the doctor's son, Kozaczko, the judges, Smolik and Barbacki, all died in this manner. Hamann, the chief of Gestapo, was a natural born killer. (...)
>
> In April 1942, in the Court archives, Hamann accidentally discovered a list of the members of the Maks Rosenfeld Library. Before the war all the Jewish inhabitants of Nowy Sącz had used the library. Hamann ordered all who were on the list to be brought to him. There were about 400 people on the list, all the youth, the most beautiful children. "These are all communists!" – Hamman said.
>
> In the prison, he would then arrange a show with them. An orchestra would play for the whole night in the prison court. The young ones were forced to dance. On the

---

13 Katarzyna Naliwajek and Andrzej Spóz, *Okupacyjne losy muzyków* (Warsaw: Towarzystwo im. Witolda Lutosławskiego, 2015, Vol. 2), 233–235; Zofia Rysiówna, "Wspomnienia," *Rocznik Sądecki* (9) 1968, 443–444; *Zbigniew Ryś – Wspomnienia kuriera*, ed. by Feliks Kiryk et al. (Nowy Sącz: Prezydent Miasta Nowego Sącza, Polskie Towarzystwo Historyczne), 2013.For the sake of consistency, all the bibliographical information concerning my name is presented as "Naliwajek," even if a given work was published under a double surname.

gallery, the wives of the SS-men would sit together with their children and watch. "This is your dance of death!" – Hamann kept saying to the Jews.

In the morning they were carried handcuffed to the cemetery and shot. (…) After murdering the 400, SS-men got drunk and with drunken singing they entered the Jewish streets, entering the apartments and murdering. 80 people lost their lives that time. The corpses were found in the morning, in the apartments. There were dead mothers lying in their beds with their children by their side. (…) The action was called the "May action" because it was carried out in the beginning of May 1942.[14]

Already in these testimonies by two young women who came from the same town, we can delineate several functions of music which are typical of this period of genocide on occupied Polish territories. The omnipresence of the sadistic usage of music by the perpetrators, as demonstrated in this book, is a symptom of their systemic character. Because music linked with torture was used by the Nazis along the lines of a similar scenario, it is necessary to investigate how such patterns were instilled in German functionaries so that it became not only acceptable, justifiable, or even praiseworthy to kill to the sound of music and to make the victims play and dance before their death. The reasons of this profound need of music as a decorum of genocide for the perpetrators have to be understood in order to contextualize the Nazi use of propaganda through classical music played in concert halls and opera houses throughout occupied Poland. It is also important to explain why musical abilities of certain human beings constituted a decisive factor for their survival.

Thanks to the musical abilities of Zofia Ryś her life was spared. She became a famous, respected actress after the war (known under her name Rysiówna). The famous Viennese conductor, Alma Rosé (1906 Vienna – 1944 KL Auschwitz), from a prestigious musical family (Gustav Mahler was her uncle), was transported from Drancy to Birkenau because she was Jewish. She was allowed to live because she was admired for her music by German guards and needed as a professional conductor of the women's *Kapelle* there. Thanks to this function she could save some women who played an instrument, because they were more useful for the camp authorities and their status was higher than that of an average, disposable KL prisoner. For this multi-ethnic ensemble she arranged her version of *In mir klingt ein Lied*, based on Chopin's E major Etude Op. 10 No. 3.[15] They

---

14 Rena Anisfeld, *Gevies Eydes* ("Bearing Witness"), translated by Maciej Krol, edited by Renee Miller, Yizkor Book Project, 850–860, https://www.jewishgen.org/yizkor/Nowy_sacz/now850.html. She was born in Nowy Sącz in 1919. In her testimony, she gave a harrowing description of Hamann's beatings and murders.

15 In her biography by Richard Newman and Karen Kirtley (*Alma Rosé: Vienna to Auschwitz*, Portland: Amadeus Press, 2000), the story of the song is described.

played it for themselves inside their barrack, just as the male orchestra in Birkenau. The significance of this music will be discussed in greater depth in chapter three in the context of usage of Chopin's music as an element of propagandistic appropriation. It might be tempting to think of this song as bringing comfort to the prisoners, appeasing conflicts, and forming a sense of unity. In *Remnants of Auschwitz*, Giorgio Agamben went even as far as imagining that a soccer match played by SS and Sonderkommando members could constitute a "moment of normalcy."[16] Helena Dunicz-Niwińska, who played violin in the *Kapelle*, towards the end of her life suggested reconstructing Alma Rosé's arrangement to honour this heroic conductor on the 70th anniversary of her death.[17] When, according to her wish, the recording was produced and she read the draft of my commentary to it, she warned me against any such naïve and superficial ideas, stressing that playing the Chopin Etude in a Birkenau barrack did not, after all, contribute to any sense of community.[18]

---

16 Giorgio Agamben, *Remnants of Auschwitz. The Witness and the Archive*, translated by Daniel Heller-Roazen (New York: Zone Books 1999), 26.
17 *Chopin in Birkenau*, CD recording produced by Renata Koszyk in 2016 with her foreword. The orchestration for instruments used in the Birkenau women's orchestra was prepared by the composer Joanna Szymala. The ensemble which recorded it was put together by the conductor Szymon Bywalec. As he wrote in his commentary, he managed to combine "instrumentalists of the highest order, including lecturers at the Karol Szymanowski Academy of Music in Katowice, and their students. The group also included students of the Secondary School in Katowice. Thus, the level of performance was quite varied, much like in the original women's orchestra. After bringing together the entire ensemble, we began rehearsals which culminated in the recording of the piece in the beautiful new concert hall of the Academy of Music in Katowice on February 8, 2013." The soprano part was sung by Katarzyna Moś. It is just by coincidence that this young singer, coming from a musical family, had the same surname as the mandolin player from the Birkenau orchestra, Maria Moś-Wdowik. The musicians participated in the project *pro bono*.
18 Shirli Gilbert has already perspicaciously analysed and questioned the notion of "spiritual resistance," stating that "it has often relied on a tacit assumption of solidarity between Nazism's victims. Correspondingly, it has avoided discussion of less agreeble dynamics within inmate communities. (…) Primo Levi's concept of the 'Grey Zone' is a useful starting point in this regard." S. Gilbert, *Music in the Holocaust: Confronting Life in the Nazi Ghettos and Camps* (Oxford: Oxford University Press, 2005), 8. This discussion was further developed by Michael Beckerman in his article *Listening in the Grey Zone*, in: Fanning, David, and Levi, Erik (eds.), The Routledge Handbook to Music under German Occupation, 1938–1945. Propaganda. Myth and Reality, London / New York: Routledge, 2020, 451–458.

Nonetheless, numerous accounts demonstrate that specific songs and music had the power of uniting and uplifting their spirits even at the threshold of death – it represented the victims' dignity and identity. As Rena Anisfeld remembered from Auschwitz: "One time I saw a truck filled with naked men. They were going to a gas chamber. They were singing *Hatikwa*" (a traditional Zionist song which later became the national anthem of Israel). This testimony corresponds with the account by a former member of the *Sonderkommando* who reported that the song was spontaneously sung by Czech Jews at the entrance to the Auschwitz-Birkenau gas chamber in 1944. While singing they were beaten by Waffen-SS guards.[19] This ethical power of music is why German functionaries filled the mouths of the condemned with lime before their execution to prevent them from singing the Polish anthem at the last moment before their death, especially if the execution was taking place in the city streets, so that it would be unheard by witnesses. They did not take such great pains over French women transported in an open truck to the gas chamber in Auschwitz who were singing *La Marseillaise*. In several other sources, we find information that camp prisoners were killed or beaten by the guards for singing songs about hope such as the *Hatikvah* and the Polish anthem.[20]

The multicultural character of inter-war Poland, after it regained independence in 1918, is reflected in demographic data. Musicians' sensibilities and the repertoires they created were forged in this melting pot, enlivened by various, sometimes conflicting, cultural, ideological, and political currents. Therefore, musical and poetic expression contained in anthems – the symbolic representation of national identity – of persecuted nations such as Poles, Jews and Ukrainians naturally bear similarities, as they shared the same geopolitical space, similar fates, and their traditional music has so many themes and melodies in common that often it is impossible to narrow down their identity to one single source.[21]

According to the 1931 census, the Polish language was spoken by 68.9 per cent of the population; 8,6 per cent spoke Yiddish and Hebrew; 10,1 – Ukrainian; 3,8 – Ruthenian; 3,1 – Belorussian; 2,3 – German; 0,4 – Russian; other – 2,8. In

---

19 Gilbert, *Music in the Holocaust*, 154.
20 See Katarzyna Naliwajek: "Music and its Emotional Aspects during the Nazi Occupation of Poland," in Sarah Zalfen, Sven Oliver Müller, Iris Törmer (eds.), *Besatzungsmacht Musik. Zur Musik- und Emotionsgeschichte im Zeitalter der Weltkriege (1914–1949)*, Histoire, Vol. 30 (Bielefeld: transcript Verlag, 2012), 207–224.
21 For the discussion of the melodic prototypes of the Polish anthem and its filiations see: Maciej Gołąb, *Mazurek Dąbrowskiego. Muzyczne narodziny hymnu*. Warsaw Narodowy Instytut Fryderyka Chopina, 2021, 46 ff.

the cities the major languages were Polish (68,3); Yiddish and Hebrew (24,3), whereas in the countryside the majority spoke Polish (69,1), Ukrainian (13,1), Ruthenian (4,9) and Belorussian (4,1). Yiddish and Hebrew were spoken in the countryside by only 2,6 per cent of the population. 70,5 per cent of Varsovians spoke Polish, 28,5 per cent spoke Yiddish and Hebrew. In the towns of the Łódź region only 80,1 per cent were Polish speakers, 16,6 – Yiddish and Hebrew speakers, and 5,9 – German speakers. In the countryside of the Łódź region – 92,7 spoke Polish, 3,9 spoke Yiddish and Hebrew and 4,9 were German speakers. In the towns of the Lublin region – 61,8 per cent spoke Polish, and 37,5 – Yiddish and Hebrew. In the East, in the towns of the Białystok region – 56,9 per cent spoke Polish and 38,0 – Yiddish and Hebrew. In the tows of the Vilnius region 63,0 per cent spoke Polish and 28,9 – Yiddish and Hebrew, 5,5 – Lithuanian, 3,7 – Russian, 3,0 – Belorussian, while in the countryside – 58,8 per cent spoke Polish, 27,8 – Belorussian, 3,3 – Yiddish and Hebrew and 6,6 – Lithuanian. In the Volhynia region, only 16,6 per cent of the population spoke Polish, 68 per cent – Ukrainian and 9,9 per cent – Yiddish and Hebrew; and in the town: 27,5 per cent, 16,1 per cent and 48,6 per cent respectively. In the Lvov region 57,7 – spoke Polish, 18,5 – Ukrainian, 15,6 – Ruthenian and 7,4 – Yiddish and Hebrew. According to the same census the religious affiliation of the inhabitants of Poland was as follows: 64,8 per cent – Roman Catholic, 10,4 – Greek Catholic, 11,8 – Orthodox, 9,8 – Judaic, 2,6 – Evangelical, other Christian – 0,5, unspecified – 0,1. A comparison of census data in 1939 and in 1950 tells us more about what happened with the population within the borders of Poland. It was estimated at 35.1 million in 1939. The first post-war census took place in 1946, during mass forced displacements of the population. According to the 1950 census, treated as more reliable, there were 25 million inhabitants of the Polish state. These figures demonstrate that Poland as a result of the Second World War lost about 10 million inhabitants, due to population losses, territorial changes, and displacements. Given the natural increase of the population between 1939–1950, the actual losses should be regarded as even higher. The population of Warsaw decreased by 63 per cent (1 289 000 in 1939 vs. 479 000 in 1946), whereas in Krakow the population actually increased, because the city's infrastructure was largely undamaged and many of those who fled from other places or were liberated from the camps settled there (259 000 vs. 299 000). In Białystok, only 53 per cent of the pre-war population remained (107 000 vs. 57 000).[22]

---

22 Data in this paragraph are quoted from: Andrzej Jezierski (ed.), *Historia Polski w liczbach. Ludność. Terytorium*, Warsaw: Główny Urząd Statystyczny, 1994, 132–139;

Nazi German and Soviet invaders – after having disposed of local intelligentsia through extermination, in the case of the Nazis, and through deportations in the case of the Soviets – skilfully used all propagandistic, administrative, and legal means to undermine the traditional values which allowed for coexistence of the multicultural inhabitants in Polish territories for centuries. Most importantly, however, they introduced the *divide et impera* strategy they had already effectively used against the citizens of their own countries. In the 1930s, they had managed to apply mind control techniques to master social engineering, to manipulate and terrorize their own respective societies in order to establish the tight control of one party. Both Nazi and Communist parties trained their members to become not only docile but also internally motivated, in order to transform them into the absolute believers and unhuman functionaries of the system. The indoctrination was so efficacious that it crushed the traditional moral values and superseded them with the immoral ethos of party goals. Animosities which constitute an intrinsic part of any multicultural community were deftly used to play one group against another. In the Eastern territories which first went under the Soviet and then under the German occupation, these methods incited local populations to genocide, with its most extreme form in Volhynia. It happened not because of the conflicts of different ethnic groups having their own different political interests, but because the two totalitarian systems, which had annihilated the Polish state along with its judiciary system, subjected these groups to complex manipulation techniques in order to attain their goals and to save on ammunition and military effort. This is why the new jurisdiction was introduced first and then the lists of those who broke these immoral laws (for example, by trying to protect the Jews from death) and were "punished" by death were publicly displayed, printed on frivolous pink posters in order to humiliate the victims (See Appendix). This is also the reason why music was needed to enhance the differences in the status of different divided groups. Thus, concerts and opera performances for German or Ukrainian audiences in Lvov were also marketed on posters in appropriate language versions (See Appendix). The voices of the victims were to be annihilated just as the victims themselves.

The victims, however, responded to the persecutions with their own songs. As Ruth Rubin (1906–2000), a Canadian singer and scholar of Yiddish music, wrote in her 1963 book entitled *Voices of a People*, these songs memorialized and condemned the Nazi-German power and its personnel, which for six years engaged in sadistic expropriation of Jewish possessions (...) and then physically destroyed them when they were still alive. This macabre program of a military might organized in a brutal war against an unarmed civilian population of millions is revealed in hundreds of songs written by men, women, and children, old and young, in a desperate struggle to survive.[23]

As she wrote, the songs constituted a chronicle of the tragic experiences. According to her, they were also "one of the important weapons" that were "often flaunted courageously in the face of the invaders."[24] Ruth Rubin quoted from song collections published just after the war, mainly the one by the Yiddish poet, musician and resistance fighter from Vilna, Shmerke Kaczerginski (1908–1954), entitled *Lider fun di getos un lagern*.[25] She described and quoted their texts and music and enumerated several psychological and social roles of these songs:

Laments, dirges, topical ballads were created by the people, in which they described the terrible torture inflicted upon them by the German invaders. One such song chronicles the German attack on June 21, 1941, "at five o'clock in the morning," and before the sun rose "infants were slaughtered before their mothers' eyes," people were driven from their homes and buried alive, and Jewish maidens brought to shame.

This tragic period was marked by a new though brief burst of anonymous song creativity among the people, and the following lament, reminiscent of the seventeenth- and eighteenth-century martyrologies when the Ukrainian Haydamak hordes overran Jewish communities with fire and sword, is an eye-witness account of a young woman who was "married on Tuesday and on the following Sabbath, early in the morning, the *hitsls* were leading us to our death and the river ran red with our blood." Here are two stances of this topical ballad:

---

23 Ruth Rubin, *Voices of a People: The Story of Yiddish Folksong*, 2nd edition, New York: McGraw-Hill Book Company, 1973, 432.
24 Some Yiddish songs recorded by the survivors are presented at the United States Memorial Museum webpage: https://www.ushmm.org/collections/the-museums-collecti ons/collections-highlights/music-of-the-holocaust-highlights-from-the-collection/ music-of-the-holocaust. The Museum also published a CD recording *Rise Up and Fight! Songs of Jewish Partisans* performed by Theodore Bikel, Frieda Enoch and the Noble Voices Ensemble conducted by Rober DeCormier in 1996. It contains such important Jewish resistance songs as the *Shtey Oyf Tsum Kamf (Rise Up and Fight)*, *Partizaner-Marsh (March of the Partisans)*, *Yid, Du Partizaner (The Jewish Partisan)*, *Varshe (Warsaw)*, *Zog nit Keynmol Az Du Geyst Dem Letstn Veg (Never Say That You Have Reached the Final Road)*.
25 Shmerke Kaczerginski, *Lider fun di getos un lagern*, New York: Tsiko Bicher Farlag, 1948.

Me hot nit geshoynt nit kayn al, nit kayn jung,	They spared no one, old nor young,
Bam foter aroysgerisn hot men di tsung,	They tore out my father's tongue,
Di muter derdushet in hoyf afn mist	They smothered my mother in a pile of garbage
Un opgehakt dort ba di shvester di brist.	And chopped off my sisters' breasts.
Mayn man hot men shpiln genoyt auf der fleyt,	They forced my husband to play on the flute
Me hot im bagrobn, oy, lebedukerheyt,	And then he was buried, oh, alive.
Der malech-hamoves hot choyzek gemacht,	The Angel of Death did mock at us,
A mise-meshune hot er undz gebracht.	Bringing a horrible death to us.[26]

She also described several other categories of songs of this time: "lullabies, work songs, satirical songs and ballads, prayer songs, songs of pain and anguish, shame and humiliations, songs of ghetto life, concentration camp and death camp songs," stressing that the songs of normal times such as love, marriage, children, and merriment are almost entirely absent, whereas the "occasional drinking and dance song has the macabre quality of the seventeenth-century dance of death."[27] Among songs spontaneously created to "bolster the courage of the fighters, at the front, in the rear," she quoted one of the songs she termed as "Soviet Yiddish" and which certainly sounds utopian, but at the same time consists an attempt to somehow build a sense of larger, international community united against the perpetrators:

---

26 Rubin, *Voices*, 418. It was quoted from the 1944 Moscow edition by S. Kupershmid, *Folkslider fun der foterlendisher milchome* (Moscow: Meluche Farlag *Der Emes*, 1944), which uses in its title the Soviet term "Patriotic War" (*foterlendisher milchome*). See the article by Bret Werb, scholar of Yiddish song, "Fourteen Shoah Songbooks," *Musica Judaica* 20 (2013), 39–116.

27 Ibid., 424.

Yidn, rusn, ukrainer,
Poyln, totern, gruziner,
Nemt farkatshet bede net,
Schlogt dem daytsh vi vayt ir kent.
Alte layt un yunge kinder,
Kegn katsev, kegm shinder,
Kegn hitlern dem hunt –
Shanevet nit dos gezund.

Jews, Russians, Ukrainians,
Poles, Tartars, Georgians,
Roll up both your sleeves,
Hit the Germans with all you've got.
Old men and young children,
Against the butcher and the skinner,
Against Hitler that dog –
Do not spare your health.[28]

These and other functions of the vast repertoire of songs, invented and sung by the persecuted population of occupied Polish territories, in order to fulfil their different psychological, social, and political needs, are discussed mainly in chapter three.

Silence versus sound memory

At the end of the war the Soviet NKVD, which had infiltrated the Polish underground and had already been carrying out effective, extremely harmful actions during the war, continued their criminal activity with no restraints and "in the name of law" after the Red Army liberated the Polish territories from the Third Reich. At the same time the communists spread mischievous propaganda in Poland and abroad to discredit the most important resistance movement, the Home Army (Armia Krajowa, AK), because of its allegiance to the Polish government-in-exile in London. After the communists rigged the Polish parliamentary elections of January 1947, their control had tightened until Stalin's death. As a result, most outstanding individuals who had fought for Poland's cultural survival, organizing crucial clandestine networks not only for the purpose of military[29]

---

28 Ibid., 417.
29 An example of such biography is the one of Leopold Okulicki (1898–1946) who was denounced and arrested by the NKVD secret service for the first time in January 1941 in Lvov. Interrogated and tortured in Soviet prisons, he was released in August 1941 thanks to the agreement Sikorski-Mayski, signed shortly after the June 1941 attack of Germany on the Soviet Union. He took part in negotiations between General Anders, Stalin, and Molotov in March 1942. As the last commander of the AK he dissolved it on January 19, 1945. Kidnapped by the NKVD with other Polish politicians and taken to Moscow, he was accused of collaboration with Nazi Germany, sentenced in June 1945 in the staged "Trial of Sixteen" and died in Butyrki prison on Christmas Eve

and civil resistance[30] but also education, and who managed to survive the Nazi occupation despite the extreme danger involved in underground activity (punishable by death or, at the very least, imprisonment in a concentration camp), were relentlessly persecuted after the war, the purpose of which was to eliminate the leaders and crush the morale of the intelligentsia.[31]

Several musicians who were placed under intense surveillance of the Security Service (Służba Bezpieczeństwa, SB) were AK-affiliated or they were in contact with former members of the underground. In some cases, they were imprisoned, but most often threatened and blackmailed in various ways. That is why they kept silent and why testimonies were rarely gathered or written down. Silence was imposed by the "new order" and the new persecutions. The negative impact of the post-war persecution of musicians on documenting the history of music during the occupation is impossible to assess. Today the actions of musicians involved in conspiracy can be reconstructed only fragmentarily.

The strict post-war censorship, political manipulation and control constituted an unsurmountable hindrance to a broader historical investigation and interpretation of pre-war Poland's cultural diversity and its influence on music. For decades, until 1989, an in-depth research on the extremely complex topic of music in occupied Polish territories was thwarted, as was the discussion of the combined Nazi and Soviet occupation of Poland. Musicians and witnesses of the musical life under occupation as well as historians themselves were in many cases involved in underground activities during the war. This put them in danger

---

1946. The letter of protest sent by the Polish government-in-exile sent to American and British governments was dismissed by the Russians as a bluff of the "Fascist Polish government."

30 Eminent historian Władysław Bartoszewski (1922–2015), prisoner of Auschwitz, instrumental in creating the Żegota, the Home Army Council for Aid to the Jews, was falsely accused of being a spy, arrested on November 15, 1946, released on April 10, 1948, rearrested on December 14, 1949, then released again in August 1954 on a year's parole.

31 See Marci Shore, *Caviar and Ashes: A Warsaw Generation's Life and Death in Marxism, 1918–1968* (New Haven, London: Yale University Press, 2006). For the history of postwar music politics in Poland see: Sławomir Wieczorek, *On the music front: socialist-realist discourse on music in Poland 1948 to 1955*, translated by Robert Curry (Peter Lang, Berlin, 2020); Lisa Jakelski, *Making new music in Cold War Poland: the Warsaw Autumn Festival, 1956–1968* (Oakland, California: University of California Press, 2017).For the musical repertoire of political protest see the pathbreaking book by Andrea Bohlman, *Musical Solidarities: political action and music in late twentieth-century Poland* (New York: Oxford University Press, 2020).

also after the war, as the communist regime persecuted the former Home Army resitance members.

Other causes of silence were of socio-psychological nature: survivors, both Polish and Polish-Jewish, were in many cases unable to speak about that extremely traumatic time. It sometimes took them thirty years or more, if they lived that long, to cope with the trauma and verbalize those experiences. This anguish was clearly expressed by Miriam Akavia: "I had the feeling that silence was killing me over again. I was afflicted. I suffered from constant headaches and felt a great tension inside me." After thirty years of silence, she published her first text in 1975.[32] Survivors were forced not only to carry the enormous burden of haunting memories which were conscious, but also had to somehow find their individual ways of overcoming posttraumatic amnesia which had enabled their survival. Sometimes it led them towards a creation of new selves, towards an invention of new lives which would somehow encompass but also protect them from their wartime experiences. This was the case of the Warsaw Ghetto survivor and Warsaw Uprising fighter Halina Paszkowska-Turska (1927–2017) whose sonic memories are discussed in the second chapter, and her husband, Marian Turski, the Łódź ghetto and Auschwitz survivor who eventually became a historian, creator of the Museum of Polish Jews Polin and since 2021 president of the International Auschwitz Committee.

For the majority of witnesses, it was their sense of responsibility that made them overcome their mournful silence in order to testify in their own name and in the name of those who perished. However, far too often their testimonies fell on deaf ears and their importance was not recognized. A disillusionment in postwar international politics and system of justice due to political and economic interests of groups holding power, made them realize that they were unwanted witnesses, to the point that they ultimately silenced themselves. Their work was indeed being ignored, marginalized, or willingly misunderstood, especially by Nazi scholars who were still employed in the academia after the war, but also due to other political reasons. A good example is one of the first historians of Shoah, Józef (Joseph) Wulf (1912–1974) who was himself a Polish-Jewish survivor.[33]

---

32 Quoted in A. Czocher, Dobrochna Kałwa, Barbara Klich-Kluczewska, Beata Łabno (eds.), *Is War Men's Business? Fates of Women in Occupied Krakow in Twelve Scenes* (Krakow: Muzeum Historyczne Miasta Krakowa, 2011), 42.
33 He came from a Hasidic family from Krakow and took part in the Jewish underground. Arrested in 1943, he was deported to Auschwitz-Monowitz. For a precise description of Wulf's biography and the difficulties he faced in the post-war years see Klaus Kempter,

He was a friend of Mordecai Gebirtig (1877-1942), the author of popular folk songs, such as the *Arbetsloze marsh* (*The March of the Unemployed*, which is still being played at some manifestations in Warsaw). To commemorate the poet who was murdered on June 4, 1942, when German soldiers were shooting people in the streets and houses of the Krakow Ghetto, Wulf published in 1946 a collection of songs by Gebirtig, *S'brennt (1939-1942)*. He divided the songs into three categories: those "of the early war period; songs of the 'resettlement' (when the poet and his family were removed to the Krakow suburb of Łagiewniki); and the songs of the Krakow ghetto."[34] Wulf later moved to Germany where he devoted himself to collecting and publishing the documentation on different aspects of history of the Third Reich, music among other topics.[35] He took his life in 1974 after unsuccessful attempts to bring to life and institutionalize research on Nazi crimes.[36] The post-war political situation also led to silencing survivors' voices

---

"'Objective, not neutral:' Joseph Wulf, a documentary historian," *Holocaust Studies*, 21(2015): 1-2, 38-53. I am indebted to Bret Werb for the information on this article.

34 Gebirtig, Mordecai, Michał Borwicz, Nella Rost, and Józef Wulf, *S'brent: (1939-1942)*. Krakow: Wojewódzka Żydowska Komisja Historyczna, 1946. Quoted in Werb, *Fourteen Shoah Songbooks*, 52.

35 Joseph Wulf, *Musik im Dritten Reich: eine Dokumentation*, Gütersloh: Sigbert Mohn Verlag, 1963.

36 In first post-war decades, the lack or insufficient feeling of responsibility for participating in the Nazi regime on the part of musicologists and musicians, as well as their prominent academic, administrative, and political positions, had an impact on the research of musical culture in Nazi Germany and the occupied countries. Pamela Potter devoted several fascinating publications to these and related topics. See P. Potter, *Trends in German Musicology 1918-1945: The Effects of Methodological, Ideological and Institutional Change on the Writing of Music History* (Ann Arbor, 1991); "Musicology under Hitler: New Sources in Context," *Journal of the American Musicological Society* 1996 (49, 1), 70-113; "The Arts in Nazi Germany: A Silent Debate," *Contemporary European History* 2006 15 (4), 585-599. "Dismantling a Dystopia: On the Historiography of Music in the Third Reich, *Central European History* 2007 (40), 623-651. See also the debate on H. H. Eggebrecht published in *German Studies Review* 2012 (35/2) by Anne C. Shreffler ("Musicology, Biography, and National Socialism: The Case of Hans Heinrich Eggebrecht," 290-298), Boris von Haken ("How Do We Know What We Know about Hans Heinrich Eggebrecht?," 299-309) and Christopher R. Browning ("An American Historian's Perspective," 310-318), who concluded that "Eggebrecht was frequently in Kerch to guard prisoners and accompany their transport to Feodosia. Then in July Eggebrecht gave two radio concerts of Mozart and Beethoven sonatas that were broadcast to the troops, after which his Crimea service in the Feldgendarmerie came to en end" (315) and concluded his article stating that this musicologist was

in many other ways: Szymon Laks (1901–1983), who gave his testimony from Auschwitz early on after the war,[37] later, overwhelmed by the experience of postwar anti-Semitism, was no longer able to compose.

The immensity of Nazi genocide is overwhelming. Thanks to long-term efforts of such devoted collectors as Kaczerginski at least some of the precious testimonies of survivors could be gathered. Several people who have worked for the state institutions established in Poland, such as the camp museums, kept collecting testimonies and searching for information on the victims. However, there was not always sufficient care for the preservation of individual legacies, as in the case of another survivor Aleksander Kulisiewicz (1918–1982) who devoted all his postwar life to gathering and documenting poems and songs created by camp prisoners. He memorized himself several songs by his fellow prisoners who had not survived and performed them after the war in a poignant manner which reflected their mournful origin.[38] Two examples from his archive are discussed in chapter three.

The influence of trauma on the life of the survivors and their creativity has been analysed both from psychological[39] and musicological

---

an "NS-Täter, a Nazi perpetrator" and that the evidence is "beyond any reasonable doubt" (317).

37 Szymon Laks and René Coudy, *Musiques d'un autre monde* (*Music from another World*), Paris: Mercure de France, 1948. In November 1947, the manuscript received Prix Vérité from the jury presided by Georges Duhamel, who in the introduction quoted one of the perpetrators, an SS man; "The witnesses, even if there are any left and if they speak," said SS Unterscharführer Wolff one day, "will not be trusted by anyone..." ("Les témoins, s'il en reste et qu'ils parlent," déclarait un jour le SS Unterscharführer Wolff, "ne seront cru de personne...").

38 His unique archive, which was described already in 1984 (Konrad Strzelewicz, *Polskie wiersze obozowe i więzienne 1939–1945 w archiwum Aleksandra Kulisiewicza*, Krakow: Krajowa Agencja Wydawnicza, 1984) is now kept at the United States Holocaust Memorial Museum in Washington. Thanks to the research by Barbara Milewski and Bret Werb, these previously more widely unknown repertoires and interpretations could be published on CD and further discovered. See Barbara Milewski, "Remembering the Concentration Camps: Aleksander Kulisiewicz and his Concerts of Prisoners' Songs in the Federal Republic of Germany," in: Tina Frühauf and Lily Hirsch (eds.), *Dislocated Memories: Jews, Music, and Postwar German Culture* (Oxford: Oxford University Press, 2014).

39 See Dori Laub, "From Speechlessness to Narrative: The Cases of Holocaust Historians and of Psychiatrically Hospit alized Survivors," *Literature and Medicine* 24, 2 (2005)., B. A. Van der Kolk, and Fisler, R., "Dissociation and the fragmentary nature of traumatic memories: Overview and exploratory study," *Journal of Traumatic Stress*, 8/4 (1995).

perspectives.[40] This trauma was not only long-lasting, but also multi-layered, thus it was even more complex. The ordeal of war time was in many cases preceded by a past which was already painful, due to political, social, and personal reasons (as, for example, in the case of Witold Lutosławski, who at an early age lost his father, executed by the Russians).[41] The wartime trauma was also followed by new devastating experiences and suffering caused, as mentioned above, by the post-war political persecution of Polish citizens by the Polish state controlled by the Soviet Union. That is why their silence was becoming even deeper.

Musicians were not only spied on by the SB, but their international careers, which could still be rebuilt, were purposefully destroyed. They were not given the right to leave Poland and could not tour abroad.[42] The Polish Institute of National Remembrance (IPN) holds documentation produced over the decades by the SB, which brings proofs of the surveillance of musicians.[43] Among many others, this was the case of the eminent violinist Eugenia Umińska (1910 Warsaw – 1980 Krakow). She was known for her uncompromising attitude towards the occupiers: she refused to play for the Germans, which is why she ultimately had to go into hiding. The string quartet she had established in occupied Warsaw continued to play with a different first violinist, Irena Dubiska – until the death of the viola player, Henryk Trzonek, killed in a street execution in 1943 (see Appendix). The second violinist, Roman Padlewski, was killed during the Warsaw Uprising.[44] Many years after the war, she wrote of the fear caused by the post-war

---

40 The influence of trauma on composers is described in the book by Maria Cizmic: *Performing pain: music and trauma in Eastern Europe* (Oxford: Oxford University Press, 2012).
41 See: K. Naliwajek, "Witold Lutosławski in Occupied Warsaw," in: Lisa Jakelski, Nicholas Reyland (eds.), *Lutosławski's Worlds*, The Boydell Press, Suffolk, 2018, 141–163.
42 For documentation of these facts see K. Naliwajek, "Muzyka jako metoda przetrwania i oporu w mieście dwóch powstań i Zagłady" ("Music as survival and resistance ploy in the city of two uprisings and Shoah"), in K. Naliwajek, A. Spóz, *Okupacyjne losy muzyków*, 8–23.
43 E.g. AIPN BU 0296/254, Vol. 1; AIPN BU 0722/1, Vol. 15. See also K. Naliwajek, "Konstanty Regamey – muzyka na rozdrożach historii i polityki" ("Konstanty Regamey – music at the crossroads of history and politics") in Beata Bolesławska-Lewandowska, Jolanta Guz-Pasiak (eds.), *Twórcy – źródła – archiwa, Muzyka polska za granicą* (Warsaw: Instytut Sztuki PAN, 2017, Vol. 1), 72–76.
44 For detailed biographical information and extensive documentation on losses of music, musicians and music composed and performed in occupied Warsaw see the two volumes of *Okupacyjne losy muzyków, Warsaw 1939–1945*; vol. 1 ed. by Elżbieta Markowska and Katarzyna Naliwajek (Warsaw: Towarzystwo im. Witolda Lutosławskiego,

surveillance and persecution by the Security Service. This is evidenced by a letter she sent in 1975 to her friend Kiejstut Bacewicz, in which she emphasized the importance of reconstructing the musical life from the period of the occupation and wrote: "It is a pity that we did not have the opportunity and time to record certain memories – facts, names – 30 or 25 years ago. But then you still lived in a partial conspiracy, with the fear of endangering someone by writing his name next to other names, etc., etc.!!"[45]

This internal and external censorship, as well as political persecutions, stymied historical research and publications related to former Polish territories. Thus, musicians who came, for example, from Lvov could tell their entire stories only after 1989. This is the case of Helena Dunicz-Niwińska (1915 Vienna – 2018 Krakow) and Leopold Kozłowski-Kleinman (1918 Przemyślany – 2019 Krakow) whose testimonies on music in German camps are quoted in chapter three devoted to this topic. Helena Dunicz was arrested in Krakow by the SB in 1946, exactly a year after she was liberated from the Neustadt-Gleve camp on May 2, 1945, after being prisoner of Auschwitz-Birkenau. The Gestapo arrested her with her mother in their native Lwów on January 19, 1943. They were transported to Auschwitz on October 4 that year and branded with numbers 64118 and 64119. Her mother died there, whereas her brother died in the Mittelbau-Dora camp in April 1945.[46] In the "Epilogue" to the book, which she decided to write when

---

2014) and vol. 2 ed. by K. Naliwajek and Andrzej Spóz (Warsaw: Towarzystwo im. W. Lutosławskiego, 2015).

45 Quoted from Naliwajek, *Muzyka jako metoda przetrwania*. Danuta Gwizdalanka reconstructed the activities of the SB and determined that it was decided to "work out the contacts of Umińska, Hoffman, Lefeld, Szamotulska and Wiechowicz until 15 June 1954 – to recruit Umińska's housekeeper and control the mail until 20 June 1954," and later "to continue to observe, who comes to the apartment of Umińska Eugenia and on what topics the talks are conducted." Danuta Gwizdalanka, "Element podejrzany nr 1," *Ruch Muzyczny* 10 (2012).

46 Jan Józef Dunicz (1910 Lvov – 1945) – violinist, musicologist (Ph. D. in 1937) at the Jan Kazimierz University in Lvov. He took part in the clandestine documentation of historical monumets (Centralne Biuro Inwentaryzacji Zabytków) directed by profesor Jerzy Szablowski in Warsaw. He was also a courier and transported underground publications and materials, e.g. resistance songs written by Lvov composers to Warsaw, or money sent from Warsaw to support musicians in Lvov. Since 1943 he prepared analysis of Chopin's chamber works for the clandestine Polish Music Publishing Assosiaction (Towarzystwo Wydawnicze Muzyki Polskiej). He attended clandestine concerts and performed himself. All his scentific work was destroyed when was arrested by the Gestpo and taken to Pawiak prison, and then to Gross-Rosen camp (where he was

she was 96, she said the following: "One thing is certain: without my violin I would not have survived. (…) The difficult life after the war unfolded around me in the versions known by the names of Stalin, Gomułka, and Gierek."[47] She was detained for the first time during arrests in the streets of Krakow after patriotic observances on May 3, 1946, which

> (…) were not to the liking of the communist authorities. I did not take part in them, but I was punished nevertheless. I was detained along with a friend near Oleandry as we were returning from a walk up the Kościuszko Mound. They loaded as into a truck that was already overcrowded and kept us locked up for the next three or four days, during which time we also underwent interrogation in the barracks at Zakrzówek and in the cellars of the Security Bureau on Freedom Square (now once again named Disabled Veterans Square). I was arrested again several months later. It happened during the Christmas of 1946 (…)[48]

It was the NKVD that was searching for her cousin, Leonard Dunicz, a member of the anticommunist Freedom and Independence organization:

> Leonard received a gunshot wound while trying to escape and remained in their clutches for a long time. I was not imprisoned for long, only seven days. That was the new Poland. When I looked at my dossier in the Institute of National Remembrance archives in the nineties, I learned that the communists never lost interest in me. This was a complete waste of time because I was never engaged in any political activity.[49]

In the case of Polish Jews, who had survived the Holocaust, many of them were intimidated and even attacked, as they were in the Soviet Union itself.[50] As Bret Werb wrote, Shmerke Kaczerginski addressed it in his 1949 tract *Tsvishn*

---

branded number 2669). Four of his letters sent from Gross-Rosen reached his sister in Birkenau. Transferred to Bunzlau (Bolesławiec) on November 11, 1944, and then to Dora camp, where he died of exhaustion after the "death march" on 3 April 1945. Helena Dunicz-Niwińska, "Jan Józef Dunicz (1910–1945)," *Muzyka* 2005 (2), 121–125.

47 H. Dunicz-Niwińska, *One of the Girls in the Band. The Memoirs of a Violinist from Birkenau*, transcribed by Maria Szewczyk, translated from the Polish by William Brand, Oświęcim: Auschwitz-Birkenau State Museum 2014, 163. Her memoirs were published a year earlier in Polish, also by the Museum.

48 Ibid., 163–164.

49 Ibid.

50 Ruth Rubin wrote bitterly about the Stalinist post-war extinction of Jewish culture in the USSR: "with the tragic destruction of Yiddish cultural institutions and of many prominent Jewish men during the dire years of 1948–1953, this phase of Yiddish song may also have been brought to an abrupt end." Ruth Rubin, *Voices of a People: The Story of Yiddish Folksong* (New York: McGraw-Hill Book Company, 1973, 2nd edn.), 420.

hamer un serp: tsu der geshikhte fun der likvidatsie fun der yidisher kultur in sovetn rusland (*Between Hammer and Sickle: On the history of the liquidation of Jewish culture in Soviet Russia*).[51]

Several thousands of Jews, who had returned to their fatherland from the East or from the camps, left Poland by the beginning of 1947.[52] Those who had not left their country after the pogrom in Kielce which took place on July 4, 1946, were again "strongly encouraged" to leave Poland during the vociferous anti-Semitic campaign of 1968. Leopold Kozłowski, pianist and accordionist, suffered from a sudden paralysis, when he was fired from his post of military orchestra conductor at that time. Twenty-two years earlier, he changed his name from the Jewish- or German-sounding "Kleinmann" to standard Polish "Kozłowski." He was the only person of his klezmer family who had survived the Second World War.[53]

Nevertheless, Leopold Kozłowski stayed in Poland, as did Władysław Szpilman, who was constantly persecuted by the communists between 1948–1986, in

---

51 Werb, "Fourteen Shoah Songbooks," 65. As he wrote, it was the eminent Soviet Ukrainian music folklorist Moshe (Moise) Beregovski (1892–1961), who "was arrested in 1950, he was tried, convicted, and exiled to the eastern Siberian forced labor camp at Taishet the following year. Beregovski's prison term was belatedly commuted in 1955, two years after Stalin's death, and he returned from the Gulag determined to resume his research and hopeful of bringing several abandoned projects to press. Yet the authorities persisted in ascribing a 'Jewish-nationalist agenda' to his work, effectively assuring that no manuscript he submitted would pass the censor during his few remaining years." (Ibid., 94–96).

52 "By February 1947, no less than 70,000 Jews had left Poland – between a quarter and a third of the country's total Jewish population and the biggest exodus of the post-war era. (…) Altogether, between 1944 and 1947, some 130,000 Jews – or 40% to 50% of the community – left Poland, mostly via illegal or semi-legal outlets." Dariusz Stola, "Jewish Emigration from Communist Poland: The Decline of Polish Jewry in the Aftermath of the Holocaust," *East European Jewish Affairs* 2017 47 (2–3), 172.

53 He was the grandson of Pesach Brandwein, who together with his sons ran Galicia's most renowned klezmer orchestra. The band played for Marshall Józef Piłsudski and Emperor Franz Joseph among others. Kozłowski's father, Hermann Kleinman, was also an eminent violinist and ran his own klezmer orchestra. Leopold studied piano at the Lvov Conservatory with composer Tadeusz Majerski. With the help of Tadeusz Klimko, a Polish partisan fighter from Lvov, Leopold and his brother escaped from the camp and became part of a Polish partisan group. His biography was written by Jacek Cygan in 2010. See: *Klezmer. Opowieść o życiu Leopolda Kozłowskiego-Kleinmana* (Klezmer. A Tale of the Life of Leopold Kozłowski-Kleinman, Krakow–Budapest: Austeria, 2010).

particular around 1968, when a forged case against him was concocted, aimed at proving that he was an Israeli spy (together with his long-time music partner and friend, violinist Bronisław Gimpel), but ultimately failed. His name appears in the case file concerning "primarily persons of Jewish nationality" (!) and in the materials from the files of the Capital City Civic Militia concerning people who "found themselves in the operational interest in the years 1967–1971 due to their 'pro-Israeli attitudes.'" However, communist methods were all too well known to those who worked at cafés on both sides of the Ghetto wall, as they were analogous to the methods employed by the Gestapo. Ironically, documents of Szpilman's invigilation by the Ministry of the Interior, Department III, only testify to his dignified sense of Polish-Jewish identity:

> Classified. Note. Concerns: Szpilman Władysław, son of Stanisław and Edwarda Rapaport, born 5.12.1911 in Sosnowiec, Jewish nationality, Polish citizenship, artist-musician, employed in "PAGART", address Warsaw, Gimnastyczna 12 appt. 1.

During the period of Israel's aggression against Arab countries, he stood in solidarity with Israel's policy. In a private conversation on 8.06 this year at the 'Brystol' Café [spelling of the original; proper spelling 'Bristol'], he stated that Poland should not officially take any position on the conflict in the Middle East, let alone a position supporting the Arab states. In his opinion, the government of the People's Republic of Poland did the wrong thing when it issued a statement condemning Israel's aggression. At the same time, he praised the bravery of the Israeli army. The Israeli Army is strong and achieves such successes because its core is made up of former officers of the Polish Army and the Soviet Army, who have received excellent combat training.[54]

A few other examples of the persecution of musicians taken from the files of the Institute of National Remembrance: composer Piotr Perkowski (1901–1990) was under "operational surveillance as a former associate of the Polish government-in-exile during the war and director of the Krakow Philharmonic after 1945";[55] composer and conductor Andrzej Markowski (1924–1986) was under "operational surveillance concerning foreign business trips and maintaining contacts with foreigners",[56] whereas cellist and conductor Kazimierz Wiłkomirski (1900–1995), a "professor of music in Warsaw", was "suspected of

---

54 AIPN I – 0102/ / 67. All translations, if not stated otherwise, are by the author.
55 AIPN Kr 010/3635, documents of the Voivodeship Office of Internal Affairs (Wojewódzki Urząd Spraw Wewnętrznych) in Krakow, start date: 1950, end date – 1951.
56 AIPN Kr 010/7039/DVD. Start date: 1961, end date: 1963.

attending a rally during the events of March 1968."[57] All these three outstanding musicians were active in the underground during Nazi occupation. Perkowski was active in the Clandestine Music Council and organized, among other things, help for Władysław Szpilman and other musicians of Jewish descent. Markowski was the author of Home Army songs and took part in the Warsaw Uprising, and then was deported by the Germans to Stalag 344 Lamsdorf (Łambinowice), and later to Murnau. Together with his brother Jan, who had composed several of the best-known Warsaw Uprising songs, he participated in the cultural life of the prisoners there. His wife Bogusława was a prisoner of the Stalag in Lamsdorf, and then later of Stalag IV B. On May 2, 1945, she gave birth to their daughter in the camp.[58] Kazimierz Wiłkomirski also protected people of Jewish descent in occupied Warsaw. The rally he was suspected of attending took place on March 8, 1968, at the University of Warsaw and on March 9 at the Warsaw University of Technology – it was for freedom of speech (after Adam Mickiewicz's play *Dziady*, directed by Kazimierz Dejmek, was banned) and against anti-Semitic and anti-intelligentsia attacks of the communist authorities.[59]

For several years after the war heterogenous identities of Polish musicians could not be discussed freely and publicly due to strict censorship, which actively removed these topics both from the media and the educational curriculum. At the beginning of the 1980s, when underground publications during the Solidarity movement started appearing, such as the journal *Karta*, discussion of Polish-Jewish identity could finally take place, although the texts were often published under pseudonyms.[60]

57　AIPN BU 0423/2403.
58　After the war, Markowski studied at the Trinity College of Music in London (1946–1947) and then continued his composition and conducting studies in Warsaw (1947–1955). He made his debut in 1954 in Poznań and became conductor of the Silesian Philharmonic in Katowice (1955–1959), of the Krakow Philharmonic (1959–1964). In 1961, he performed Witold Lutosławski's *Venetian Games* during the Venice Biennale with the Krakow Philharmonic Chamber Orchestra he established. As director of the Wrocław Philharmonic he created the Wratislavia Cantans festival. He was the second conductor of the National Philharmonic (1971–1977) and a member of the programme committee of the Warsaw Autumn Festival (1971–1981), where he often performed as conductor. He was also the artistic director of the Łódź Philharmonic since 1982. He is the author of music to films by Andrzej Wajda and other eminent Polish directors.
59　See Marci Shore, 355 ff.
60　For example in the underground *Karta* (4) January 1987 texts: "A Pole who tries to be a Jew" by Małgorzata Niezabitowska (Polak, który próbuje być Żydem, 55–65) and "My Jewishness" by Marian Rudzisz (pseudonym, Moje żydostwo, 66–71).

State of research

Because of all of the above-mentioned reasons and because of its extreme complexity, the subject of music in occupied Poland has not been as extensively researched until now as the aspects of musical life in Western Europe – both in the Third Reich and in the countries under its occupation.[61] Recently, however, a more balanced view that takes into account the countries of the former "Eastern bloc," began to emerge. It is due to the efforts by eminent scholars, such as David Fanning and Erik Levi who initiated and edited a huge volume of *The Routledge Handbook to Music under German Occupation, 1938-1945. Propaganda. Myth and Reality*. This book presents the state of research in different countries and makes future comparative studies possible.[62] As Pauline Fairclough wrote in her review of this collection of essays, it "fills major gaps in the Anglophone musicological record," "covering eighteen national territories occupied by Nazi Germany or in a "neutral" relationship with it."[63]

In spite of political control in communist Poland, musicians and musicologists, together with other scholars, historians, and archivists, tried to document and publish as much as possible, taking advantage of moments when censorship restrictions were loosened. In the three or four transition years after the war, when the social realist political control was not yet enforced in the musical domain, short descriptions of concert activity and of music composed during that time were published in the newly founded journal *Ruch Muzyczny*, with lists of losses and commemorations of musicians who perished.[64]

---

61 Among books on music in the Third Reich see e.g. Michael Haas, *Forbidden Music: The Jewish Composers Banned by the Nazis* (Yale University Press, 2014); Lily E. Hirsch, *A Jewish Orchestra in Nazi Germany: Musical Politics and the Berlin Jewish Culture League* (Ann Arbor, Michigan: University of Michigan Press, 2010). Michael H. Kater, *The Twisted Muse: Musicians and their Music in the Third Reich* (Oxford: Oxford University Press 1997); *Composers of the Nazi Era: Eight Portraits* (Oxford: Oxford University Press, 2000). Among important books on music during the Second World War, see also Harvey Sachs, *Music in fascist Italy* (London, Weidenfeld and Nicolson, 1987).
62 David Fanning, Erik Levi, eds. *The Routledge Handbook to Music under German Occupation, 1938-1945. Propaganda. Myth and Reality* (London, New York: Routledge, 2020).
63 Pauline Fairclough, Review of the *The Routledge Handbook to Music under German Occupation* in *Music and Letters* 101 (4), November 2020, 799. 799-802.
64 S. K. [Stefan Kisielewski], "Życie muzyczne pod okupacją," *RM*, No. 1 (1945), 12-13; "Polska twórczość muzyczna pod okupacją," *RM*, No. 1 (1945), 14-16; "Śmierć Romana Padlewskiego," *RM* No. 4 (1945), 14, 15; M. Kwiek, "Wojenne dzieje zbiorów Warszawskiego Towarzystwa Muzycznego," *RM* No. 17-18 (1946), 24-26; Bronisław Rutkowski, "Konserwatorium Muzyczne w Warszawie w latach okupacji," *RM* No.

First publications of a wider scope appeared only at the beginning of the 1970s: an article concerning concert life in Warsaw during the war, with testimonies collected by Ewa Kopeczek-Michalska,[65] was followed by the most comprehensive text on musical life in occupied Warsaw published to date, authored by Elżbieta Dziębowska (1929–2016).[66] This eminent musicologist, who for many years had been editor-in-chief of the multi-volume *Encyklopedia Muzyczna* (Encyclopaedia of Music) published by PWM, lived as a young girl in occupied Warsaw and took part in the famous, successful attack by the AK on Franz Kutschera, SS Police Chief of the Warsaw District (*SS-Brigadeführer und Generalmajor der Polizei*), which took place on February 1, 1944. However, her family considered her too young to attend concerts in occupied Warsaw at that time.[67] In the ghetto, anybody involved in the underground would jeopardize the organisation by attending a concert, because cafés and venues which served the role of theatres or concert halls, were infiltrated by agents. This was the answer Marek Edelman gave me when I asked him about his experience of music in the ghetto.[68] Thus, he did not attend concerts or go to cafés. This is confirmed by secret German circulars distributed among Nazi authorities in occupied Poland, which stated that musical activity should be allowed in the cafés, because they are easier to infiltrate and control than clandestine gatherings in private apartments (see Appendix).

Attempts by Polish musicologists to study the topic around 1980, the time of the Solidarity movement (with its accompanying liberalization and expansion of civic freedoms), were thwarted by the imposition of martial law in December 1981, resulting in even tighter control of publications. Just a few months earlier,

---

24 (1946), 3, 4; "Egzekucje w Operze, Protokół nr 19/II," in *Biuletyn Głównej Komisji Badania Zbrodni Niemieckich w Polsce (I)*, Poznań: Wydawnictwo GKBZNP, 1946; Mieczysław Idzikowski, "Straty wojenne w portretach Fryderyka Chopina," *RM* No. 20 (1962).

65 Krystyna Kopeczek-Michalska, "Życie koncertowe w Warszawie w latach okupacji," *Muzyka* No. 3 (1970), 47–64.

66 Elżbieta Dziębowska, "Muzyka w Warszawie podczas okupacji hitlerowskiej," in Krzysztof Dunin-Wąsowicz, Janina Kaźmierska, Halina Winnicka (eds.), *Warsaw lat wojny i okupacji 1939–1945* (Warsaw: Państwowe Wydawnictwo Naukowe, 1972, Vol. 2), 31–71.

67 This was her answer to a question I asked her, in a private conversation we had at her home in Jurgów in the Tatra mountains, about her experiences of music in occupied Warsaw.

68 Information he gave me in a private email correspondence.

in April 1981, the Warsaw Musical Society (WTM) together with the Institute of Musicology at the University of Warsaw, managed to organize a conference on musical culture in Warsaw during the occupation, and excerpts from the papers presented there were published in *Ruch Muzyczny*.[69] In addition, testimonies of witnesses (Witold Lutosławski and Władysław Szpilman among others) were gathered by Maria Stanilewicz-Kamionka and stored in typescript at the WTM Library curated by Andrzej Spóz, himself a witness to wartime music in Warsaw. Mentions of musical activity in Warsaw were included in general publications on cultural life,[70] on theatre and literature, and on the role of the radio during the Warsaw Uprising in 1944.[71]

---

69 The conference *Kultura muzyczna Warszawy w latach okupacji hitlerowskiej* ("Musical Culture in Warsaw during Nazi Occupation"), was held between April 2 and 3, 1981. Among articles published in *Ruch Muzyczny* (1981) are: Maria Stanilewicz, "Muzyka w okupowanej Warszawie," *RM* No. 10, 5; *Muzyczny ruch wydawniczy*, No. 19, 14–15; Marian Fuks, "W dzielnicy zamkniętej," *RM* No. 16, 16; Alina Żurawska-Witkowska, 'Straty wojenne,' *RM* 1981 No. 14, 4–7; Maciej Józef Kwiatkowski, "Muzyka w Polskim Radiu w czasie II wojny światowej," *RM* No. 12, 3–4. The testimonies then gathered by M. Stanilewicz were published only recently, in Naliwajek, Spóz (2015). They were combined with illustrations and documents from the period, as well as information on composers' fates and their works.

70 Czesław Madajczyk (ed.), *Inter arma non silent Musae. Wojna i kultura 1939–1945*, Warsaw: Państwowy Instytut Wydawniczy, 1982. In this volume, Aleksander Gieysztor (1916–1999) proposed in his article ("Wojna a kultura: propozycje badawcze," 208–209) that for a better understanding of the occupation period the scope of investigation regarding war and culture should be widened and encompass daily-life culture and the ideological actions of the occupiers. This eminent historian himself played an important role in the underground in occupied Warsaw.

71 The first of such studies focused on culture as a means of resistance: Wiesław Głębocki and Karol Mórawski, *Kultura walcząca 1939–1945. Z dziejów kultury polskiej w okresie wojny i okupacji* (Warsaw: Wydawnictwa Szkolne i Pedagogiczne, 1979, 2nd corrected edition, Warsaw: Wydawnictwo Interpress, 1985). An earlier book by Bogusław Drewniak, *Kultura w cieniu swastyki* (Poznań: Wydawnictwo Poznańskie, 1969) is one of the first books in Poland that addresses the topic of culture under Nazi totalitarianism. Jerzy Święch, *Literatura polska w latach II wojny światowej* (Warsaw: Wydawnictwo Naukowe PWN, 1997); Stanisław Marczak-Oborski, *Teatr czasu wojny: polskie życie teatralne w latach II wojny światowej (1939–1945)* (Warsaw: Państwowy Instytut Wydawniczy, 1963); M. J. Kwiatkowski, *"Tu mówi powstańcza Warsaw" ... Dni Powstania w audycjach Polskiego Radia i dokumentach niemieckich* (Warsaw: Państwowy Instytut Wydawniczy, 1994).

By 1989, new efforts by Polish musicologists to revive music cast away and forgotten due to political reasons resulted in another conference and a publication,[72] and more complete lists of artists and musicians who were victims of Nazi occupation of Poland were published.[73] An important monograph on music in occupied Krakow, documenting the musical activities of Jewish musicians confined in the ghetto, was published in 1988.[74] Subsequently, important studies on the topic of war and culture in occupied Poland appeared,[75] as well as musicological publications researching the topic of music and politics, and reconstructing biographies. Prominent among those was the chapter "Modernism enslaved" in Maciej Gołąb's book on musical modernism, a monograph on Józef Koffler (1896–1944), the first Polish dodecaphonist and victim of the Holocaust.[76]

---

[72] Krystyna Tarnawska-Kaczorowska (ed.), *Muzyka źle obecna* (Ill-Present Music), Warsaw: Sekcja Muzykologów ZKP, 1989.

[73] Maria Rutowska, Edward Serwański, *Straty osobowe polskiego środowiska muzycznego w latach 1939–1945*, Warsaw: GKBZH, 1977. GKBZN (Main Commission for the Investigation of German Crimes in Poland (Główna Komisja Badania Zbrodni Niemieckich w Polsce) was set up in 1945 to document German crimes committed during the Second World War. It conducted investigations and published the results of its activities. See also: Maria Rutowska, Edward Serwański, *Losy polskich środowisk artystycznych w latach 1939–1945: architektura, sztuki plastyczne, muzyka i teatr: problemy metodologiczne strat osobowych* (Poznań: Instytut Zachodni, 1987).

[74] Stanisław Lachowicz who at the 1981 conference gave a paper on musical life in Krakow published the book *Muzyka w okupowanym Krakowie 1939–1945* (Krakow: Wydawnictwo Literackie, 1988).

[75] Piotr Matusak, *Edukacja i kultura Polski Podziemnej 1939–1945* (Siedlce: Siedleckie Towarzystwo Naukowe, 1997); Piotr Majewski, *Wojna i kultura. Instytucje kultury polskiej w okupacyjnych realiach Generalnego Gubernatorstwa* (Warsaw: Wydawnictwo Trio, 2005).

[76] Maciej Gołąb, *Musical Modernism in the Twentieth Century. Between Continuation, Innovation and Change of Phonosystem*, Eastern European Studies in Musicology, Frankfurt am Main: Peter Lang, 2015, Vol. 6, originally published as *Muzyczna moderna XX wieku*, Wydawnictwo Uniwersytetu Wrocławskiego, 2011; *Józef Koffler*, Krakow: Musica Iagellonica, 1995. English translation by Maksymilian Kapelański, Marek Żebrowski and Linda Schubert, Los Angeles: Polish Music Center, 2004. See also: Danuta Gwizdalanka, *Muzyka i polityka* (Krakow: PWM, 1999) and Andrzej Tuchowski, *Nationalism, Chauvinism and Racism as Reflected in European Musical Thought and in Compositions from the Interwar Period*, The Arts Series: Eastern European Studies in Musicology, Vol. 14 (Berlin, Bern, Bruxelles, New York, Oxford, Warsaw, Wien: Peter Lang, 2001); Iwona Lindstedt, *Kazimierz Serocki. Piszę tylko muzykę* (Krakow: PWM, 2020).

The research initiated by Professor Michał Bristiger which led to the the creation of the online journal *Muzykalia Judaica* made possible an international conference Polish-Jewish music in the twentieth century at the Polin Museum and the publication of important research results such as the one by Hanna Palmon, a descendant of Polish-Jewish pianist Artur Hermelin, who perished in the Holocaust,[77] as well as by Frank Harders-Wuthenow.[78] Some aspects of musical life and the destruction of musical institutions in occupied Warsaw were explored further,[79] also, as part of specific broader topics such as the history of the Warsaw Ghetto.[80]

Some of the works composed and preserved through the war were published by Polskie Wydawnictwo Muzyczne in the early post-war years, thanks to the determination of Tadeusz Ochlewski (1894–1975), its passionate and energetic director, who was himself a musician, active as a performer and editor of ancient music before the war. The fascinating *Quintette* for clarinet, bassoon, violin, cello and piano, written in occupied Warsaw between 1942 and 1944 by Konstanty Regamey, was published by PWM in 1946, despite the fact that Regamey had Swiss citizenship and had lived in Switzerland since 1944, having been sent there by the Germans from Stutthof where he was deported after the fall of the Warsaw Uprising. *Three Warsaw Polonaises of an unknown author from the eighteenth century*, reconstructed and orchestrated by Szymon Laks for the prisoners' *Kapelle* at Auschwitz-Birkenau, when he was a prisoner-conductor there, were published in 1950 with an astounding note that they are destined for a salon

---

77 Hanna Palmon, "The Polish Pianist Artur Hermelin," https://demusica.edu.pl/muzyka lia-xiii-judaica-4/ (Warsaw: Stowarzyszenie De Musica, 2012). She also published another important article, "Jewish Musicians of Lwów," *The Galitzianer. The Quaterly Research Journal of Gesher Galicia* (23 / 2) 2016, 10–15. Muzykalia Judaica which used to be edited by Michał Bristiger as chief editor, in company of Halina Goldberg (Indiana University, Bloomington), Antoni Buchner (Berlin), Michał Klubiński (Warsaw).
78 Frank Harders-Wuthenow, *Fate and Identity – Polish-Jewish composers in the 20th Century*, https://demusica.edu.pl/muzykalia-xiii-judaica-4/ (Warsaw: Stowarzyszenie De Musica, 2012).
79 Marian Fuks, "Filharmonia Warszawska w latach okupacji niemieckiej (1939–1945)," in *100 lat Filharmonii w Warszawie. 1901–2001*. Warsaw: Fundacja Bankowa im. Leopolda Kronenberga, Filharmonia Narodowa, 2001); Anna Frołów, *Życie muzyczne w okupowanej Warszawie w latach 1939–1945* (Warsaw: Akademia Muzyczna im. F. Chopina, 2004).
80 Barbara Engelking, Jacek Leociak, *Getto warszawskie. Przewodnik po nieistniejącym mieście* (Warsaw: Wydawnictwo IFiS PAN, 2001).

orchestra (which might have been conceived as a bitter joke and / or as a smoke screen for Stalinist censorship).[81] The significance of this musical reconstruction is discussed in chapter three.

Quite surprisingly, some of the underground (AK) songs composed during the occupation in Warsaw by Witold Lutosławski and Andrzej Panufnik (alongside other composers) were published around that time (1948) as well.[82] This is striking since it not only constituted a continuation of clandestine publications of this resistance repertoire from before 1944, but it also propagated the famous songs of the Warsaw Uprising.[83] Later, much broader collections of clandestine songs were gathered, along with descriptions of the circumstances of their creation and performance.[84] The topic of resistance and protest through music is discussed in chapter 2.

Musical life in Warsaw and Krakow,[85] which became the most important centres of music in the General Government, is better known and researched than the one in smaller cities in Polish territories incorporated into the Reich, such as Poznań and Łódź, although some partial information can be found in more general historical accounts or in detailed studies on history and culture of that period. Different aspects of music in the ghettos have already been described in books by Gila Flam (1992) and Shirli Gilbert (2005).[86] A new book on Nazi

---

[81] Szymon Laks (ed.), *3 polonezy warszawskie nieznanego autora z XVIII wieku* na orkiestrę salonową (Krakow: PWM, 1950). For the history of this piece and its reconstruction, see Naliwajek, *Three Warsaw Polonaises – a musical reconstruction in the world of Shoah* (*Trzy polonezy warszawskie – muzyczna rekonstrukcja w świecie Zagłady*) and the following text by Szymon Bywalec, author of the musical reconstruction of the orchestral score and conductor of the recording, at https://forbiddenmusic.info/en/polonaises/.

[82] Famous songs sung during the Warsaw Uprising, such as Panufnik's *Warszawskie dzieci* were published in Andrzej Panufnik, *Pieśni walki podziemnej 1939–1945*, No. 3 (Krakow: PWM, 1948).

[83] See: Barbara Milewski, "Hidden in Plain View: The Music of Holocaust Survival in Poland's First Post-war Feature Film." In: *Music, Collective Memory, Trauma, and Nostalgia in European Cinema after the Second World War* ed. Michael Baumgartner, Ewelina Boczkowska (New York: Routledge, 2019), 111–137.

[84] Tadeusz Szewera, Olgierd Straszyński, *Niech wiatr ją poniesie.* Łódź: Wydawnictwo Łódzkie, 1970 (2nd edition, 1975); Szewera, *Za każdy kamień Twój Stolico* (Łódź-Tarnobrzeg: Biblioteka Tarnobrzeskich Zeszytów Historycznych, 1999).

[85] For documentation on music in Krakow ghetto, see J. Wulf, et al, Gebirtig, Mordecai, *S'brent* (Warsaw, Wojewódzka Żydowska Komisja Historyczna, 1946).

[86] Gila Flam, *Singing for Survival: Songs of the Lodz Ghetto, 1940–45* (Urbana and Chicago: University of Illinois Press, 1992); S. Gilbert, *Music in the Holocaust*.

cultural policies in Reich-annexed Polish territories provides substantial information, especially on German musical life there.[87] One of the of the first publications that mentioned the topic of music in occupied Poland as part of the Nazi empire, was Fred K. Prieberg's (1928–2010) *Musik im NS Staat*. The enormous documentation gathered by him is contained in his *Handbuch Deutsche Musiker 1933-45*.[88]

The number of publications on music in camps on the territory of occupied Poland (mainly Auschwitz-Birkenau)[89] and in camps in Germany, such as Sachsenhausen,[90] has also considerably grown in the last twenty-five years. Guido

---

87 Sylwia Grochowina, *Cultural policy of the Nazi occupying forces in the Reich District Gdańsk-West Prussia, the Reich District Wartheland, and the Reich District of Katowice in the years 1939-1945* (Toruń: Foundation of General Elżbieta Zawacka, 2017).
88 Fred K. Prieberg, *Musik im NS Staat* (Franfurt am Main: Fischer Taschenbuch Verlag, 1982). I am thankful to Harvey Sachs for kindly letting me "steal" this book from his library shelf some years ago. The impressive amount of information collected by him from written and oral sources was edited as *Handbuch Deutsche Musiker 1933-45*, CD-R (Kiel 2004). I would like to thank Professor Michael Custodis from Münster University for his help in accessing this database.
89 The crucial study concerning musical ensembles in Auschwitz-Birkenau is by Jacek Lachendro, published first in Polish ("Orkiestry w KL Auschwitz," *Zeszyty Oświęcimskie* 27, Wydawnictwo Państwowego Muzeum Auschwitz-Birkenau w Oświęcimiu, 2012) and then in English: "The Orchestras in KL Auschwitz," *Auschwitz Studies 27* (Auschwitz-Birkenau State Museum in Oświęcim, 2015). The above-mentioned memoirs by H. Dunicz-Niwińska, provide important new evidence. Hubert Szczęśniak investigated the music collections at the Auschwitz-Birkenau Museum in his article "Muzykalia w zbiorach Państwowego Muzeum Auschwitz-Birkenau," *Kwartalnik Młodych Muzykologów UJ* 1 (2017), 125–175. See also the article by Krzysztof Bilica, *Muzyka w obozie według Szymona Laksa i innych, Muzykalia XI, Judaica 3*, https://demusica.edu.pl/wp-content/uploads/2019/07/bilica_muzykalia_11_judaica3. pdf). Already in 1996 Gabriele Knapp in her book *Das Frauenorchester in Auschwitz. Musikalische Zwangarbeit und ihre Bewältigung* (Hamburg: von Bockel Verlag, 1996) included interviews with some members of the women's orchestra in Birkenau to critically investigate multiple falsifications contained in the controversial book by Fania Fénelon on this topic. A new book by Susan Eischeid (*The Truth about Fania Fénelon and the Women's Orchestra of Auschwitz-Birkenau*, Department of Music, Valdosta State University, Georgia: Palgrave Macmillan, 2016) provides a critical evaluation of earlier publications, arguing that Fénelon's book should not be treated as actual source material.
90 Juliane Brauer, *Musik im Konzentrationslager Sachsenhausen* (Berlin: Schriftenreihe der Stiftung Brandenburgische Gedenkstätten Vol. 25, 2009).

Fackler in his important book entitled *Des Lagers Stimme* described several functions of music in German concentration camps.[91] Because of several similarities in the camp organization, these functions are in part similar to the ones in death camps. They are described in chapter three.

Biographies of Polish-Jewish musicians, who almost all perished in the Holocaust, were reconstructed first of all by Isachar Fater (1912 Drobin – 2004 Tel Aviv). He took part in the interwar musical life in Poland, where he studied music with well-known composers and pedagogues, Stanisław Kazuro and Tadeusz Mayzner. Fater personally knew most of the musicians about whom he wrote, and this is also why his book has the quality of a profoundly touching testimony.[92] Publications in dictionary or encyclopaedic form provided extensive information on individual musicians – especially the one by Leon Błaszczyk on Jewish musicians,[93] while published memoirs brought personal perspectives and source material.[94] Archives and libraries documented their severe losses and the ways of preserving those precious materials which could be saved.[95] Nevertheless, immeasurable losses to Polish music due to Shoah have not yet been fully described and it will probably never be possible to assess them.

---

91 Guido Fackler, *Des Lagers Stimme. Musik im KZ. Alltag und Haftlingskultur in den Konzentrationslagern 1933 bis 1936* (Bremen: Edition Temmen, 2000).
92 Isachar Fater, *Muzyka żydowska w Polsce w okresie międzywojennym*, translated into Polish by Ewa Świderska (Warsaw: Oficyna Wydawnicza Rytm, 1997). This seminal book was published earlier in Yiddish: *Yiddishe muzik in Polyn tsvishn beyde velt-milhomes* (Tel Aviv, 1970) and in Hebrew: *Muzika Yehudit B'Polin Bein Shtei Milchamot Haolam* (Tel Aviv, 1992) and partially translated by Ada Holtzman into English: *Jewish Music in Poland between the World Wars*. Available at: https://www.jewishgen.org/yizkor/musicians/Musicians.html.
93 Stanisław Dybowski, *Słownik pianistów polskich* (Warsaw: Selene, 2003); Tomasz Lerski, Syrena Record. Pierwsza polska wytwórnia fonograficzna 1904–1939, (New York – Warsaw: Editions "Karin", 2004); Leon Tadeusz Błaszczyk, *Żydzi w kulturze muzycznej ziem polskich w XIX i XX wieku* (Warsaw: Stowarzyszenie Żydowski Instytut Historyczny w Polsce, 2014).
94 E.g. Mary Berg, *Dziennik z getta warszawskiego*, tr. Maria Salapska (Warsaw: Czytelnik, 1983).
95 See for example Mariola Nałęcz, "Chopiniana z dawnej kolekcji Breitkopfa i Härtla w zbiorze Biblioteki Narodowej w Warszawie;" "Fragmenty korespondencji Fryderyka Chopina," in Małgorzata Kozłowska (ed.), *Ocalone przez BGK: katalog wystawy* (Warsaw: 2014). This topic was further documented in Naliwajek, Spóz, *Okupacyjne losy muzyków*.

Methods, questions, and goals

This study was originally mainly historically orientated. The methodology consisted in the analysis of archival sources of different types (photographs, concert programmes and posters, films, recordings, written sources such as official and clandestine press of the period, and published and unpublished memoirs)[96] in combination with oral history data. Five main territorially defined topics were chosen, allowing for a comparative analysis of research into music in the General Government and in the territories annexed into the Third Reich. Warsaw and Krakow, as the main urban centres of the General Government, were juxtaposed with the main cities of the so-called Warthegau province, Poznań and Łódź. However, because many musicians from these cities became prisoners and victims of different types of camps, the research had to be extended to the analyses of the roles music played in places of detention and death.

An extensive study encompassing various realms of life in such extremely different conditions as urban centres and camps in occupied Poland has not yet been conducted. The investigation of this topic, undertaken by the author of this book in several articles which are quoted below, led to the assumption that music was subjected to similar racial segregation and ghettoization as the population itself.[97] Thus, further research stemmed from a conviction that – in contradiction to German policies and propaganda – one should attempt to encompass all the three segregated musical, cultural and socio-political spheres (Jewish, Polish, German) in one broader view, to find out what were the roles of music in each of

---

96 This research was conducted among others thanks to a project grant financed by the Polish National Science Centre between 2015 and 2018. The documentation was earlier gathered for the exhibition *Music in Occupied Poland. 1939–1945* (2010) organized in cooperation with Frank Harders-Wuthenow. I was honoured with the Hosenfeld/Szpilman-Gedenkpreis for this exhibition at the University of Lüneburg in 2011. More recently it was presented in a Polish-German version at the Krzyżowa Foundation (2017) and in Oświęcim in January 2018, when it was inaugurated by the 102-year-old Helena Dunicz-Niwińska, in the presence of other Auschwitz survivors and was accompanied by a concert of German junior high school students, as it took place during musical meetings of Polish and German youth in Oświęcim, to commemorate the anniversary of the liberation of the camp.

97 Katarzyna Naliwajek, "The Racialization and Ghettoization of Music in the General Government" in Pauline Faircloug (ed.), *Twentieth-Century Music and Politics* (Farnham: Ashgate, 2013), 191–210; Katarzyna Naliwajek, "Nazi Censorship in Music: Warsaw 1941," in Erik Levi (ed.), *The Impact of Nazism on Twentieth Century Music* (Vienna: Boehlau Verlag, 2014), 151–173.

them. This approach seemed to me the only method which would lead me to my primary goal – to understand how and why extreme Nazi cruelty was so systemically combined with music. It was nevertheless extremely difficult to find a way to combine such extremely different spheres and circumstances in which music was present, for several reasons.

First of all, because of the nature of contexts in which the sound of music appeared on the "killing ground" into which the Third Reich transformed Poland. The city of Warsaw was the site of two uprisings, mass murder and mass destruction. The rest of occupied Poland was covered with a dense net of Nazi detention and genocide sites. The immensity and denseness of this net can be seen on the map representing it, with concentration and extermination camps, such as Auschwitz-Birkenau, Treblinka, Sobibor, Stutthof, forced labour camps, POW camps and prisons (see Appendix).

The second source of difficulties is a result of the extreme differences between the conditions of musical lives in different parts of the racially segregated population. It is very challenging to combine these threads into one narrative. That is why they are usually discussed separately.

Third, the unbearable immensity of the Holocaust and of the genocide of the non-Jewish population of Poland, as well as the complexity of the socio-political reality of that time, makes these difficulties even more daunting.

The following question arises then: what kind of methodologies could be used to talk about music being played in between the sounds of killing? The traditional methods of historical musicology are by no means sufficient in this case. Symphonic music played between 1939 and 1945 on these territories, even if played in most ceremonial settings, with the best performers and solemn Nazi speeches, always has to be heard against the background of the sounds of the apocalypse which was simultaneously taking place. While the documentation, enumeration and comparison of the repertoires performed for and by Germans, Poles and Jews in these circumstances all constitute an important part of this picture, it is necessary in my view to understand first of all the context in which these concerts were taking place.

That is why this book focuses more on the questions of propaganda and its effects, and rather on soundscapes than on musical compositions and the repertoires being performed in the urban centres. The latter issues will be addressed in another book which is under preparation.

Thus, the first chapter is devoted to analysing ideological reasons and motivations of the Nazis which led to the destruction, plunder, and appropriation of Polish and Polish-Jewish musical culture. The second chapter describes the effects of Nazi jurisdiction, i.e. the segregation of musical life in occupied Polish territories, according to Nuremberg "laws," and the attempts of Polish and Polish-Jewish musicians to counteract it and to survive. The third chapter describes and discusses the final, murderous effects of Nazi policies. Various functions of music in German camps are discussed in order to understand the sociopsychological motives for using music during genocide.

This book brings together the effects of several years of research by bringing together findings presented at conferences and published in the form of book chapters and articles between 2006 to 2021. Historical research, such as gathering of biographical information, documentation of musical life and reconstruction of the repertoires, constitutes an important part of these studies. It is evident, however, that without investigating some, more or less hidden, sociopsychological motivations of those involved in the genocide, it is impossible to analyse such complex and challenging topics as the presence of music in death camps.[98]

The complexity of the subject is only paralleled by its extremities, presenting a fragmented whole of sometimes a seemingly contradictory or paradoxical nature, with the following main questions which lie at its core. What are the reasons of the coexistence of music and genocide, how and why a phenomenon considered quintessentially beautiful, subtle, even sacred in its essence, considered for ages as the most profound expression of human ideals, could be placed in sites of planned mass murder? Is music itself responsible, as Pascal Quignard would have it?[99] Is it another embodiment of Apollo's narcissistic cruelty clothed in aesthetic and cultural superiority versus Marsyas's inferiority doomed to lose and be "punished" in a most torturous way? How could a notorious, sadistic, murderous functionary of a Nazi death camp[100] have been visibly touched while

---

98 For a discussion of the role of music in preparatory stages of genocides see: M. J. Grant, Mareike Jacobs, Rebecca Möllemann, Simone Christine Münz, and Cornelia Nuxoll, "Music, the 'Third Reich', and 'The 8 Stages of Genocide'" in Wojciech Klimczyk, Agata Świerzowska (eds.), *Music and Genocide*, 'Studies in Social Sciences, Philosophy and History of Ideas' Vol. 9 (Frakfurt am Main: Peter Lang Edition, 2015), 83–103. See also the literature on Rwandan hate songs broadcast by the Radio Télévision Libre des Mille Collines between July 1993 and July 1994, which prepared the genocide, e.g. Darryl Li, "Echoes of Violence: Considerations on Radio and Genocide in Rwanda," *Journal of Genocide Research*, 6/1 (2004), 9–27.
99 See Anna Chęćka for her brilliant polemic with Quignard, in her *Ucho i umysł: szkice o doświadczaniu muzyki* (Gdańsk: Wydawnictwo Słowo/Obraz Terytoria, 2012) and other publications.
100 One of the many examples of such criminals is SS-Hauptscharführer Gerhard Palitzsch responsible for the killings of thousands of prisoners at the Auschwitz-Birkenau camp.

hearing music played by a prisoner whom he could at any time kill in the most cruel and ruthless way? How could a well brought up man, playing piano with dexterity and culture, be devoid of any "human" sentiments, of any sense of pity toward the victims, even if they were children? Psychiatrists and psychologists have come a long way toward understanding and accepting the truth that Nazi perpetrators in the vast majority were not psychopaths.

The examination of the critical question of why the perpetrators needed music in places of mass killing demonstrated the necessity of reconstructing the logic of associations linked with music in the imagination of the perpetrators. The process of uncovering specific Nazi "values" and "ideals" in this context, taking the last SS commandant of the Treblinka death camp, Kurt Hubert Franz (1914 Düsseldorf – 1998 Wuppertal), as a primary example, led to inquiries into two main fields of study.

The first of these fields devoted to investigating the usage of music as an instrument of torture, brings up the psychoanalytic notions such as "messianic sadism."[101] Salman Akhtar defines it as a "facet of extreme ethnoracial and religious prejudice" and a "cruelty towards others that in the internal world of the perpetrators seems morally justified."[102]

The second field of study stems from the question of how this cruelty involving music could become an important ritual in the death-camp system. It led me to the consideration of sociological and aesthetic components of Nazi identity.[103]

These factors resulted in the need of expanding the research, previously meant as a predominantly historical one, with a more diverse approach and required implementing methods of social psychology, ethnomusicology, and anthropology.

See his description in Rudolf Höss, *Wyznania spod szubienicy: autobiografia Rudolfa Hössa komendanta KL Auschwitz spisana w krakowskim więzieniu Montelupich*, translated by Wiesław Grzymski, annotated by Andrzej Pankowicz (Warsaw: Oficyna Wydawnicza Mireki, 2012).

101 Salman Akhtar, "From Unmentalized Xenophobia to Messianic Sadism: Some Reflections on the Phenomenology of Prejudice," in H. Parens, A. Mahfouz, S. W. Twemlow & D.E. Scharff (eds.), *The Future of Prejudice: Psychoanalysis and the Prevention of Prejudice* (Lanham: Rowman & Littlefield 2007), 7–19; Salman Akhtar, *Comprehensive Dictionary of Psychoanalysis* (London: Karnac Books, 2009).

102 Cf. ibid.

103 Naliwajek, "The Functions of Music within the Nazi System of Genocide in Occupied Poland," in: Klimczyk, Świerzowska (eds.), *Music and Genocide*, 83–103.

My initial hypothesis held that actual realities of life under German occupation were so full of ambiguities and complexities that only the witnesses could shed light on this topic. It proved valid in the process of juxtaposing their testimonies with evidence contained in written or iconographic sources.

The critique of oral history according to which witnesses are partial in their testimonies and thereby give a falsified image of the realities they describe has lost its primacy in recent years, especially in sociology and anthropology. To the contrary, it is recognized that the subjective character of witnesses' memories and their personal experience of the historical past is precisely what makes their evidence so valuable.[104] The anchor points provided by written sources are only ostensibly stable. Excessive reliance on such documents may lead to misinterpretation while referring to personal memories may help to find the grey zones which otherwise would be difficult to notice. Thus, it is the juxtaposition of different individual narratives with various source material that helps to elucidate the complex structures of history.

The tissue of personal testimonies in the form of autobiography, although more susceptible to deliberate falsifications, is obviously as strongly affected by the subjective filter as the oral narratives. Autobiographies of the perpetrators bring important insight into the process of molding their specific psyche in order to create a human "automaton" who reiterates sentences containing expressions such as: "I needed to" and "liquidate," "dispose of". Such euphemisms and technical terms were used to replace the simple and explicit but ethically contemptible word "kill."

Autobiographies of mass murderers such as Rudolf Höss provide evidence of the effective mechanisms providing multiple filters that rendered genocide possible. Victims are being killed by an individual who no longer perceives them as truly human beings, but rather as inferior, deindividualized, non-human and a harmful "pest" to be exterminated. Analyzing Höss's autobiography, *Meine Psyche, Werden, Leben und Erleben* (*My psyche, becoming, living and experiencing*), written in prison in January and February 1947, one discovers the momentum of the process described by the eminent British anthropologist Anthony Cohen who analyzed the replacement or take-over of an individual

---

104 It is interesting to note that from the point of view of the soundscape theory written archival material may be even treated as inferior. See a review of such discussions in: Carolyn Birdsall, *Nazi Soundscapes. Sound, Technology and Urban Space in Germany, 1933–1945* (Amsterdam: Amsterdam University Press, 2012), 13.

self-identity by corporate identity. The former is gradually displaced and dissipated in the collective goals and responsibilities of the latter.

Höss and many other Nazi Reich functionaries were formed in their adolescence, when – as in his case – they took part in the First World War and killed for the first time as teenagers, being brutalized and at the same time desensitized by this experience. The lack of parental affection in childhood, an authoritative, fanatic, and disciplining father, and a strict religious education which turned Höss into an obedient future cog of corporate identity, prepared the psychological ground for him to become a perfect, conscientious member of an organisation. The effect an organization has on an individual can be described as a "psychic prison." This term has been coined by Gareth Morgan in his influential book of 1986. It was meant as a metaphor referring to Plato's cave and presenting organisations as "socially constructed realities that emerge out of the unconscious preoccupations of its members" and become unconscious traps for them.[105]

This corresponds, on a more philosophical than sociological level, to the otherwise disputable and, in some passages, disappointing short essay *Heidegger and Nazism* by Giorgio Agamben. There he recalls the moment when in 1966 during a seminar on Heraclitus in Le Thor he asked Heidegger whether he had read Kafka.[106] Heidegger allegedly replied that although he had read a little, he was nevertheless impressed by the unfinished short story *Der Bau* (translated to English as *The Burrow*). Kafka wrote the story six months before his death in 1924 and it was published by his friend Max Brod in *Beim Bau der Chinesischen Mauer* (Berlin, 1931). An anthropomorphic animal, unnamed but similar to a mole, badger, or a fox, and obsessed with the fear of the unfamiliar, is building a burrow as his safe home. But eventually it turns out to be a trap. This leads Agamben to the conclusion that national states built as safe homes became similar deathtraps. Heidegger's fascination with Kafka's self-defeating idea of *Der Bau* and Morgan's concept of a "psychic prison" bring us to the diagnosis given by Anthony Cohen. He claimed that "the deterministic power of the organisation is regarded as inhering not in any penal sanctions which it may be able to impose, but in the organisation's assumed capacity to confer identity on its members." In the chapter "Organisational Membership" from his book *Self Consciousness: An*

---

105 Gareth Morgan, *Images of organisation* (Beverly Hills: Sage, 1986). Quoted in Anthony P. Cohen, *Self Consciousness: An Alternative Anthropology of Identity* (New York: Routledge, 1994), 92–93.
106 Giorgio Agamben, "Heidegger e il nazismo," in *La Potenza del pensiero. Saggi e conferenze* (Vicenza: Neri Pozza Editore, 2005), 321–331.

Alternative Anthropology of Identity, Cohen described contemporary management strategies which aim at enticing an individual "into identifying with the organisation so completely as to create an identity of aspiration and absolute loyalty."[107]

However, in the manufacturing of an ideal Nazi or a devoted member of any criminal organisation, this process of grafting and stitching various elements together would be incomplete without a hidden driving force which animates them into an acting body. It is *jouissance*, the zealous enjoyment which is linked with gratifying feelings, as described by Slavoj Žižek in his *Plague of Fantasies*. They appear when one begins to feel a part of a bigger, meta-individual body governed by a collective Will.[108] The satisfaction is being brought in by fulfilling some higher necessity, often called "duty" and hypocritically used as an excuse. Žižek gives the example of a Stalinist politician who "loves mankind," but it is his "Duty to the Progress of Humanity" to carry out executions, and comments:

> What we encounter here is the properly *perverse* attitude of adopting the position of the pure instrument of the big Other's Will: it's not my responsibility, it's not me who is effectively doing it, I am merely an instrument of the higher Historical Necessity... The obscene *jouissance* of this situation is generated by the fact that I conceive of myself as exculpated from what I am doing: isn't' it nice to be able to inflict pain on others in the full awareness that I'm not responsible for it, that I am merely fulfilling the Other's Will... *this* is what Kantian ethics prohibits. This position of the sadist pervert provides the answer to the question: How can the subject be guilty when he merely realizes an "objective," externally imposed necessity? By subjectively assuming this "objective necessity" – by finding *enjoyment* in what is imposed on him.[109]

He also analyzed the concept of surplus-obedience: "when the subject did things which went beyond his own modest survival, and brought him excessive material and professional gains or power." He also explained why Hannah Arendt's famous idea of the "banality of Evil" is inadequate, arguing that its purely *symbolic* bureaucratic logic should be supplemented with two other components:

> (...) the *imaginary* screen of satisfactions, myths, and so on, which enable the subjects to maintain a distance towards (and thus to "neutralize") the horrors they are involved in and the knowledge they have about them (telling themselves that Jews are only being transported to some new Eastern camps; claiming that just a small number of them were actually killed; listening to classical music in the evening and thus convincing

---

107 Cohen, *Self Consciousness*, 92.
108 See S. Žižek, *The Plague of Fantasies* (London, New York: Verso 2008), 72.
109 Ibid., 286–7.

themselves that "after all, we are men of culture, unfortunately forced to do some unpleasant, but necessary things," etc.); and, above all, the *real* of the perverse (sadistic) *jouissance* in what they were doing (torturing, killing, dismembering bodies…). It is especially important to bear in mind how the very "bureaucratization" of the crime was ambiguous in its libidinal impact: on the one hand, it enabled (some of) the participants to neutralize the horror and take it as "just another job"; on the other, the basic lesson of the perverse ritual also applies here: this "bureaucratization" was in itself a source of an additional *jouissance* (does it not provide an additional kick if one performs the killing as a complicated administrative-criminal operation?)[110]

Hannah Arendt analyzed *in vivo* the reality of the narcissistic and perverse *jouissance* while observing Nazi functionaries being tried for their crimes committed in Auschwitz:

> The clinical normality of the defendants notwithstanding, the chief human factor in Auschwitz was sadism, and sadism is basically sexual. One suspects that the smiling reminiscences of the defendants, who listen delightedly to the recounting of deeds that occasionally make not only the witnesses but the jurors cry and faint; their incredible bows to those who bear testimony against them and recognize them, having once been their helpless victims; their open joy at being recognized (though incriminated) and hence remembered; and their unusually high spirits throughout: that all this reflects the sweet remembrance of great sexual pleasure, as well as indicating blatant insolence. Had not Boger approached a victim with the line of a medieval love song, "Thou art mine" (Du bist mein / Ich bin dein / des solt du gewiss sein) – a refinement of which such almost illiterate brutes as Kaduk, Schlage, Baretzki, and Bednarek would hardly have been capable? But here in the courtroom they all behave alike. From what the witnesses describe, there must have been an atmosphere of black magic and monstrous orgies in the ritual of "rigorous interrogation," in the "white gloves" they put on when they went to the bunker, in the cheap bragging about being Satan incarnate, which was the specialty of Boger and the Romanian pharmacist Capesius.[111]

These insightful observations explain further the mechanisms, which made music an additional stimulant, enhancing the excitement aroused by torture and killing of victims. It increased the sense of enjoyment, injecting additional musical delight into the veins of the perpetrator. Indeed, the survivors very often use the word "orgy" to describe situations when they were forced to make music for those who had the power to decide who will live and who will die. Orgy certainly

---

110 Žižek, *The Plague of Fantasies*, 69. This paragraph and reference to Žižek's and Arendt's books were inspired by Andrzej Leder's observations in his *Prześniona rewolucja. Ćwiczenie z logiki historycznej* (Warsaw: Wydawnictwo Krytyki Politycznej, 2014), 20–25.
111 Hannah Arendt, *Responsibility and Judgment* (New York: Schocken Books), 252–253.

involves *jouissance* and thus a musician is needed, even if he or she will be debased, sexually abused, tortured, and eventually killed – even more so in this case, as the narcissistic domination over a defenseless victim makes the whole sensation much more gratifying.

The reactions of these criminals in court show that the perpetrators not only intensely relished their memories, but also that they perceived the trial itself as a present moment of glory. In fact, this was another type of violence and an assertion of their power to inflict pain on new victims, those who had to listen to their accounts in court. This process of expressing the atrocities they commited in the language of a judiciary account, was clearly gratifying for them, as it was for the other perpetrators whose memories will be discussed in the last chapter of this book.

Biographers who have access to "insider information" are able to investigate data unavailable to those who do not belong to a particular family or a certain milieu. Niklas Frank's painful and bitterly ironic narrative possesses the power of a testimony and an accusation written by a witness who spent the rest of his life trying to grasp and analyze the reality he had lived in as a child and as a young man. The poignant *Epilogue* of his book *Meine deutsche Mutter* is devoted to the "poisonous conspiracy of silence," imposed by Nazi elder women after the war, the "Nazi grannies", as he called them. In order to portray the emotional condition of women who, like his own mother, willingly acted as the feminine backup of the Nazi system, he described their sense of morbid excitement, combining euphoria and self-pity:

> (…) you wanted to live because thanks to Hitler life became more beautiful. We also loved highways, our husbands finally got a job. Oh, my dear grandson! With shovels and lewd chants on their lips that glorified the greatness of the race and of Germany, they went first to build roads, and then went to war to kill with these shovels. Why should we scream? Was it our own offspring that wailed? We were the victims, we had to be strong (…)"[112]

In his typical Nazi biography, Höss, betrayed and bitterly disappointed by the church, had to abandon the symbolism of church rituals, which had shaped his imagination in childhood, and needed to have it replaced with another type of ritualistic para-, supra- or meta-reality, with something that Morgan would call a "socially constructed reality." This is why Nazi public rituals needed music to offer their members a sense of communal worship, pompous imagery, and

---

[112] Niklas Frank, *Moja niemiecka matka*, translated to Polish by Jadwia Wolska-Stefanowicz, *Epilog "Straszne babunie"* (Warsaw: Bellona, 2006), 420.

narcissistic boost, all in one powerful product supplemented with a perfectly designed soundscape.

Furthermore, this was precisely crafted to produce, boost and fulfill the needs of members of such organisations as, among others, Deutsches Jungvolk, Jungmädelbund, Hitlerjugend, Bund Deutscher Mädel, Schönheit der Arbeit, Kraft durch Freude (KdF – "Strength Through Joy"), which was part of the Deutsche Arbeitsfront ("German Labour Front"), as well as the Nazi Party itself (NSDAP, *Nationalsozialistische Deutsche Arbeiterpartei*) with its paramilitary wing SA (*Sturmabteilung*, "Storm Detachment"), Wehrmacht, the paramilitary organisation SS (*Schutzstaffel*, "Protection Squadron" and its combat branch Waffen-SS), Luftwaffe, Kriegsmarine and so forth. In all these and other Nazi organisations music was needed, as it was justly considered the perfect method of integrating and indoctrinating their members. This is why such a vast Nazi musical repertoire was created, also by adopting earlier German songs, folk songs, marches, and military music. Countless songbooks destined for all these organisations were edited and published by specialists, with the goal of instilling and strengthening absolute loyalty to Nazi values and the Nazi state, and of fomenting militant, nationalistic, racist, and anti-Semitic sentiments. Nazi musicologists and musicians, for the most part members of the Party, were deeply invested in this work of indoctrination. As the editors of *Lieder in Politik und Alltag des Nationalsozialismus* point out, this musical persuasion which involved a smooth transformation of pre-existing singing practices and repertoires, was an important factor in making possible Nazi rule. According to witnesses whom they quoted, it was "a singing dictatorship" which "injected" these *Lieder* like a narcotic, but "while the heroin stays only one year in the blood, the Nazi lieder stay for twenty-thirty years in the brain."[113]

---

113 See Gottfried Niedhart, George Broderick (eds.), *Lieder in Politik und Alltag des Nationalsozialismus* (Fankfurt am Main: Peter Lang, 1999), 5, 133.

Chapter One: Music as a manipulative tool in Nazi cultural and political domination

1.1. Nazi propaganda of German cultural supremacy and racial hatred

Nazi ideologues designed and enforced a strategy aiming at total domination over occupied Poland. This was implemented first through military control, the annexation of Polish territories, the physical elimination of Poland's elites and of those members of pre-war Polish society deemed pernicious by the Third Reich from racial and ideological points of view: Jews, Gypsies and those involved in any patriotic activity linked with Polish nationality, thus also activities of a cultural nature. However, it was the use by the Nazi Germans of an elaborate array of methods involving complex propagandistic measures that was crucial in preparing the ground for genocide and its realization.

In occupied Poland, music – among other domains – was not only politicized by the Nazi authorities, which is typical of any totalitarian system, but also treated as another means of implementing their racial policy. This stemmed from their conviction that the control of access to cultural goods was as important as the racial segregation of the newly conquered ethnic groups. Whereas the territories of Poland were envisioned as part of the planned Greater German Colonial Empire,[1] cultural expansion constituted an important counterpart to military aggression. The Nazi authorities, imposing a new administrative and legal organisation, regarded matters of higher spiritual order, such as art, literature and especially music, as crucial to this process; the more so that Nazis had used arguments of this kind to legitimize their political actions long before they came to power. Since Hitler and other prominent Nazi ideologists believed in the cultural supremacy of Germany, they wanted to establish a system which functioned as effectively as possible to secure the position of the "master race" in the conquered territories.

The music policies in occupied Polish territories undoubtedly echoed the statements of principal Nazi ideologists and were a direct expression of Nazi

---

1   See Diemut Majer, *'Non-Germans' under the Third Reich. The Nazi Jurisdiction and Administrative System in Germany and Occupied Eastern Europe, with Special Regard to Occupied Poland, 1939–1945* (Baltimore: John Hopkins University Press, 2003), 187.

beliefs. Therefore, the investigation of Nazi writings throws light upon the motivation for, and the methodology of, musical racialization and ghettoization. The interconnection between the immoral Nazi doctrines and the atrocity of the criminal acts subsequently committed is easier to understand when observed from the perspective of the racialization of access to culture, specifically to music, and how it was applied to various groups divided according to the racial dogma.

Before the attack on Poland and especially during the first months of the war, German Nazi scientists and ideologues prepared ground for the segregation policies and genocidal actions that were to unfold in the occupied eastern territories. Propagandistic products were then further marketed by the German media, which we can observe in phoney "documentary" films and published sources such as the press, containing engineered photographs, and books commissioned by the authorities. Still, the ideologically biased research of historians, historians of art, etc., was used in secret actions – not only to plunder art collections, musical instruments, etc., as in other occupied countries,[2] but also for the physical extermination of the intelligentsia, quite correctly seen by the Nazis as custodians who took care of the preservation of objects of art, but first and foremost, bearers of national identity, responsible for conveying to subsequent generations this sense of identity and cultural belonging. This is why so many teachers, artists and priests were executed or sent to various detention sites as soon as the German troops entered a new territory. It was the all-pervasive effort to cripple and belittle everything which was deemed Polish and Jewish, and to transfer all that was considered valuable into the field of *Deutschtum* ("Germanness"). It has already been well documented that this constituted part of a meticulously planned attack on Polish culture, which was either totally rejected or in a few exceptional cases appropriated as Germanic in essence.

Several key ideological components constituted the foundation of the dogma of the Third Reich's supremacy over the vanquished population in all realms. One of them, the concept of *Lebensraum*, was coined mainly as an expression of German territorial expansion, but had a much broader character, not only

---

2   See research on Nazi music plundering by Willem de Vries, author of the book *Sonderstab Musik: Music confiscations by the Einsatzstab Reichsleiter Rosenberg under the Nazi occupation of Western Europe* (Amsterdam: Amsterdam University Press, 1996), by Berkley researcher Carla Shapreau (*Lost Music project: the Nazi-Era Plunder of Music in Europe*, www.carlashapreau.com) and papers presented during study day *La musique spoliée. Sources et méthodes de recherche*, at Centre d'histoire de Sciences Politiques, Paris, 31 January 2020, https://akadem.org/sommaire/colloques/la-musique-spoliee/la-rafle-des-instruments-28-02-2020-119402_4895.php.

ideological and racial but also pseudo-aesthetic. Stephen G. Fritz explained the development of the notion of *Lebensraum* in Hitler's mind by the mid-1920s as "the key link between the destruction of Jewish-Bolshevism and the acquisition of *Lebensraum* in the east, both of which were necessary in order to secure Germany's existence."[3] Fritz compellingly described the earlier evolution of this and other convictions that formed the core of Nazi beliefs. These ideas were developed and applied by specially established institutions in the Reich. As Grochowina pointed out:

> The plans of a campaign against Polish culture were prepared both by central authorities of the Third Reich and German science and research institutions. Osteuropa-Institut (the Eastern Europe Institute) in Wrocław was particularly active in this sphere. Its director, Professor Hans Uebersberger even stated that the "national-political and cultural" issues of Poland were dominating their researchwork. The studies in the Cultural Section (from 1942 Historical and Political Section) were mostly conducted by professors Albert Hesse and Manfred Laubert. A propaganda action against Polish culture (*Kulturpropaganda*) was carried out through different publications. It stressed the alleged primitiveness and deficiency of Polish culture, which supposedly had no eminent authors, traditions and works of its own (...). It forced the idea that all the products of Polish culture that had any value were a direct result of German influences. It also strove to find "historical evidence" of presence and cultural domination of Germans on Polish lands. Disparagement of Polish cultural achievements was not only an end in itself as the German cultural influences in Polish lands were an argument supporting the demands to redraw the German-Polish border. It was argued that any land reached by the influence of German culture was German land. The plans of the campaign against Polish culture were therefore a part of general plans of expansion and extermination connected with implementing the concept of *Lebensraum*.[4]

---

[3] Stephen G. Fritz, *Ostkrieg: Hitler's War of Extermination in the East* (Lexington, KY: University Press of Kentucky, 2011), 8: "In the desperate period following World War I, this potent combination of nineteenth-century notions of social Darwinism, imperialism, racism, and anti-Semitism provided a seemingly plausible explanation for Germany's current quandary and a prescription for action to save and renew the nation. Once established, the quest for *Lebensraum* and the final reckoning with Jewish-Bolshevism remained the cornerstone of Hitler's life's work: only the conquest of living space could make good the mistakes of the past, preserve the racial value of the German *Volk*, and provide the resources to lift Germany out of its economic misery. Just a few days after becoming chancellor, Hitler announced unequivocally to his startled generals that his aim was «to conquer and ruthlessly Germanize new living space in the east.»"

[4] Grochowina, *Cultural policy*, 80. See also Ingo Haar, *Historiker im Nationalsozialismus. Deutsche Geschichtswissenschaft und der "Volkstumskampf" im Osten*. Göttingen: Vandenhoeck & Ruprecht, 2000.

Music was treated as a useful manipulative tool not only by the main propagandists such as Goebbels, but also – as discussed in the Introduction – by Nazi musicologists who prepared the ideological ground before and during the time of the German attack on Poland.[5] Driven by their deep ideological engagement, Nazi musicologists and musicians managed to build, organize and shape a powerful machine of persuasion and indoctrination, which, from an early age, reached all members of the society. A consideration of activities engaged in by those individuals wholeheartedly committed to Nazi goals allows us to comprehend how this machinery was developed and how it prepared ground for genocide.

One of the core ideas of Nazi propaganda about Polish music was the superiority of German culture, which legitimized the attack on Poland on ideological and cultural grounds. In accordance with the new regulations introduced in Poland, ideological attacks on Polish culture – including its music – were enforced. Evidence can be found, for instance, in the texts published in *Die Musik*, which became the "organ for the supervision of the entire intellectual and ideological training and education of the NSDAP" ("Organ der Hauptstelle Musik bei Beauftragten des Führers für die Überwachung der gesamten geistigen und weltanschaulichen Schulung und Erziehung der NSDAP"). Its editor-in-chief, Dr. Herbert Gerigk, was not only a member of the Nazi party since 1932, member of the SS since 1935, and co-author the infamous *Lexikon der Juden in der Musik* (*Lexicon of Jews in Music*, 1940), but he also became head of the Music Office in Einsatzstab Reichsleiter Rosenberg, which plundered cultural property in occupied countries.[6]

Thus, the journal *Die Musik* became the organ of implementation of the "25-point program of the NSDAP," signed in Munich on February 24, 1920, which stated that one of the goals of the Party was to continue "artificially increasing the discontent of the masses."[7] Propaganda techniques, which served to persuade

---

5 See Naliwajek, *Nazi musical imperialism in Poland*, in David Fanning, Erik Levi, (eds.), *Routledge Handbook to Music under German Occupation*, Routledge: Oxon–New York 2020, 63 ff. I am very indebted to the editors of this chapter for their commitment, patience, hard work and support. This paragraph and two of the songs described here are contained in that text.
6 Although Gerigk was personally involved in the persecution of Jewish musicians, he was not sentenced for his crimes after the war. See Ernst Klee, *Das Personenlexikon zum Dritten Reich. Wer war was vor und nach 1945*, 2. (revised) edition (Frankfurt am Main: Fischer Taschenbuch, 2007), 180; and Prieberg, *Handbuch*, 2015–2023.
7 The preamble in the original: "Das Programm der Deutschen Arbeiterpartei ist ein Zeit-Programm. Die Führer lehnen es ab, nach Erreichung der im Programm

the society of the necessity of implementing the 25 points, were realized through precise strategies including songs which could be effectively used even on very young children. Civic rights were to be reserved for the *Volksgenosse*, "national comrades" who, because of their "German blood," were members of the race (point 4). By reiterating these words in multiple songs, these concepts could be instilled even in those who were not brought up in an atmosphere of anti-Semitism. Point 23 – "Newspapers that violate the common good shall be prohibited. We demand the legal struggle against an art and literary genre that exerts a corrosive influence on our popular life, and the closure of events that violate the above demands" – legitimized the implementation of these regulations in the future.[8] Already in point 3 colonial expansion was planned: "We demand land and soil (colonies) to feed our people and to settle our surplus population."[9]

Nazi articles published in *Die Musik*, clothed in para-musicological analysis, served as a potent tool of indoctrination, rendering the imagery of killings of civilians as righteous and heroic action against the enemies, executed with a pure heart and joy, though with some self-pitying sentiment. The lyrics of Nazi songs painted a derogatory image of the enemy, namely Jews and Poles, and included explicit images of killings. The analysis of these songs supplies useful evidence to help explain the process of the dehumanization of the "enemy." This preliminary stage – the propaganda of racial hatred – prepared the soldiers psychologically for mass killings of civilians.

---

aufgestellten Ziele neue aufzustellen, nur zu dem Zwecke, um durch künstlich gesteigerte Unzufriedenheit der Massen das Fortbestehen der Partei zu ermöglichen."

8 Cf. the entry of 5.7.1938 by Goebbels in his *Tagebücher*: "Yesterday: (…) Jews in Sachsenhausen are treated too badly. I order to stop this [news]. The order for Dr. Bömer to address the Polish ambassador regarding 'Kurier Krakowski'. This is the most inflammatory newspaper of all world journalism. Lipski is constantly explaining that it is an opposition newspaper. But it won't help him much." Quoted from the Polish translation: Joseph Goebbels, *Dzienniki, t. 1: 1923–1939*, translated to Polish and edited by Eugeniusz Cezary Król (Warsaw: Świat Książki, 2013), 472.

9 "3. Wir fordern Land und Boden (Kolonien) zur Ernährung unseres Volkes und Ansiedlung unseres Bevölkerungsüberschusses; 4. Staatsbürger kann nur sein, wer Volksgenosse ist. Volksgenosse kann nur sein, wer deutschen Blutes ist, ohne Rücksichtnahme auf Konfession. Kein Jude kann daher Volksgenosse sein. (…) 24.d. Zeitungen, die gegen das Gemeinwohl verstoßen, sind zu verbieten. Wir fordern den gesetzlichen Kampf gegen eine Kunst und Literaturrichtung, die einen zersetzenden Einfluß auf unser Volksleben ausübt, und die Schließung von Veranstaltungen, die gegen vorstehende Forderungen verstoßen."

In the article from September 1938 entitled *Verbotene Lieder der Bewegung in der Kampfzeit*, Hans Bajer praised "beloved" SA songs and proudly quoted the fourth stanza of as *War einst ein junger Sturmsoldat* (There once was a young stormtrooper): "We are from Gausturm Greater Berlin / and have joyful courage. / When the Jew's blood splashes from the knife / then once again everything is great" ("Wir sind vom Gausturm Groß-Berlin / und haben frohen Mut. / Wenn das Judenblut vom Messer spritzt / dann geht's noch mal so gut.")[10]

Another author, Gerhard Pallmann, in his numerous articles, held in the style of an objective "scientific" description, such as *Das Kriegserlebnis im Spielgel des Soldatenliedes* ("The experience of war in the mirror of soldiers' songs") published in November 1939, enthusiastically presented the genocidal imagery contained in some of the Nazi songs.[11] One of the songs he quoted, *Wir stossen unsre Schwerter nach Polen tief hinein*, which opens with words inducing pitilessness ("We push our swords deep into Poland / The hand becomes hard and harder, / The heart becomes hard as stone"), carries omnipresent images of blood "on our tracks" ("Das Blut auf unsren Bahnen") which is permeating the sand of Poland. Another one, an "unknown war song of the Eastern Front," *Zwischen Krasnik und Lublin* ("Between Kraśnik and Lublin"), described as "the song of the new knights" and quoted by Pallmann in his article, contains lyrics of explicit brutality written by the "poet" Peter Scher:

> Ihr Reiter, auf, an den Pollack, die hellen Schwerten blitzen,
> Gebt's ihm, was er verdient, dem Pack, und jeder Hieb muss sitzen.
> Nichts andres ist uns ja so lieb, als wild darein zu schlagen;
> Es soll der Schall von jedem Hieb den Brüdern Gruss besagen.
> Ihr Brüder all in Ost und West, heiho! Jetzt geht's im Ganzen!
> Drauf, Reiter, drauf! Und wie die Pest! Der Pole, der muss tanzen.
>
> You riders, up, to the Pollack, the bright swords flash,
> Give him what he deserves, the pack, and every blow must be well struck.
> Nothing else is so dear to us than to strike wildly into it;

---

10 Hans Bajer, "Verbotene Lieder der Bewegung in der Kampfzeit," *Die Musik* 30/12, September (1938), 800–804.
11 Gerhard Pallmann, "Das Kriegserlebnis im Spielgel des Soldatenliedes," *Die Musik* 32/2, November (1939–1940), 41–49. In his commentary he speaks of the "igniting" character of the song during the attack on Poland ("Naturgemäss steht hier einstwielen die Ostfront im Vordergrund. Ich erwähnte bereits, dass das Lied von Walter Flex ,Wie stossen unser Schwerter nach Polen tief hinein' im Jahre 1935, als ich es das erstemal mit der Truppe sang, wenig ansprach. Dagegen zündete es sofort in den Herbstagen 1939.)"

Let the sound of every blow be a greeting to the brothers.
You brothers all in th east and west, heiho! Now it's really on!
On it, riders, on it! And like the plague! The Pole, he must dance.[12]

"The plague of Jews in Poland, which our soldiers now learn about" is only mentioned somewhat in passing, in the context of a song presented as a "traditional" one, coming from the time of the First World War. The lyrics are poking fun at Yiddish pronunciation, presenting Jews as evil-intentioned cheaters adding lime ("Mauerkalk") to cake ("Strüdelach") and water in which someone washed his feet ("Fussbadwasser") to tea ("Tschai"). At the same time it serves as an incitement to violence, encouraging to snap Sara ("Reiss ihr a Watschen!") and her husband. Pallmann adds in his commentary an additional boost of German civilizational superiority, sighing "No wonder that our dear soldiers long from their hearts for the old German cleanness" ("Kein Wunder, das sich unsere lieben Soldaten von Herzen nach der alten deutschen Sauberkeit zurücksehnen").[13] One of the songs he quoted, *Wir stossen unsre Schwerter nach Polen tief hinein*, opens with words inducing pitilessness ("We push our swords deep into Poland / The hand becomes hard and harder, / The heart becomes hard as stone"), and carries omnipresent images of blood "on our tracks" ("Das Blut auf unsren Bahnen") permeating the sand of Poland.

The lyrics of another Nazi song, *Der Führer hat gerufen* ("The leader has called"), open with a typical pompous imagery and mention its sonic counterpart: "Das Banner fliegt, die Trommel ruft, vom Schritt der Heere dröhnt die Luft" ("The banner flies, the drum calls, the air roars when the armies march") and end with a sickening image of destroying the enemy ("wir gerben ihm sein lüstern Fell" – literally: "we are tanning his lecherous fur"). It was originally written in 1915 by Rudolf Alexander Schröder (who despite his involvement with the Nazi regime was nominated for the Nobel prize after the war). The music was composed by a musicologist and composer Heinrich Spitta (1902–1972) who replaced "Kaiser" with "Führer" in the Nazi era. Tanning the skin of "the other" covered with "lascivious" fur carries genocidal connotations, corresponding not only with anti-Semitic propaganda and the actual persecution of Jews, but also with the ruthless exploitation of the victims' bodies, to the point of using the hair of the women killed in gas chambers for the German textile industry.[14]

---

12 Pallmann, "Das Kriegserlebnis," 48.
13 Pallmann, "Das Kriegserlebnis," 49.
14 One of most severe moments of the organized plundering of Jewish property was the sudden order to surrender all fur coats to the German authorities under the threat of

The violence contained in the songs created by the Nazi musicians and musicologists is obvious. However, they also employed more sophisticated musicological tools to prove that all valuable qualities of Polish musical history were either of German origin – through the educational lineage traceable to German composers and teachers – or just purely German. These methods were typical of aggressive Germanizing policies enforced in the nineteenth century.

In September 1939, Gerigk's article hailing the "liberation of Danzig" preceded Kurt Hennemeyer's article "Vom deutschen Geist in der polnischen Musik" ("On the German Spirit in Polish Music").[15] Hennemeyer claimed that the development of Chopin and Moniuszko as major figures in Polish music could not have happened without the efforts of their German composition teacher, Joseph Elsner. He detected predominantly Germanic impulses in the music of Karłowicz and Szymanowski, while questioning the notion of Polish folk elements in their music.[16]

Other articles in this vein followed in subsequent issues, arguing that Chopin was "German" in the sense that he had a German teacher, Joseph Elsner. Characteristically, similar arguments were used in the article *Von Heinrich Fink bis zu Joseph Elsner. Deutsche Musiker in Polen* by Dr. Herbert Drescher in official German press in the General Government, *Krakauer Zeitung* in July 1940. The author concludes that all Polish musicians, including the most famous ones such as Chopin and Moniuszko, "take their beginning just like the stream from a source – from Elsner" as their "spiritual father". Drescher argued that

> German nature and German style have not only left their mark on the stone fortifications of past centuries in Poland, but also found their expression in a considerable number of Polish melodies. What the German sword conquered in the East, the German peasant colonized, and the German merchant brought to prosperity; the Polish land had

---

death. This plundering was described in several diaries of witnesses. See Yitzhak Arad, *Plunder of Jewish Property in the Nazi-Occupied Areas Of the Soviet Union* (https://www.yadvashem.org/articles/academic/plunder-of-jewish-property-in-occupied-areas-of-soviet-union.html), who quotes from the *Diary of the Vilna Ghetto* by Hermann Kruk (New York: YIVO, 1961, 102–103) a German report about 35 freight cars with furs and fur coats, which were sent in December 1941 (Nuremberg Doc., L-18) and the harrowing description by Leib Garfunkel, *The Destruction of Kovno's Jewry* published in Hebrew (Jerusalem: Yad Vashem, 1959), 58–61.
15 *Die Musik*, 31 (1939–1940), 786–797.
16 Kurt Hennemeyer, "Vom deutschen Geist in der polnischen Musik," *Die Musik* 31 No. 12, September (1939–1940), 786–97.

the German artist, and not least the German musician, who filled it with his spirit, in the past and now.[17]

Who were the authors of these "musicological" articles? The answers are given by Fred K. Prieberg in his monumental *Handbuch deutsche Musiker* which provides extensive data on Nazi songbooks, their authors, and recipients. He proves that this repertoire was enormous, while the biographies of Nazi musicologists and musicians were often similar to each other; most of them joined NSDAP in 1933. An example of such a typical biography is the one of Gotthold Frotscher (1897–1967). He earned his doctorate on the aesthetics of the Berlin Lied in the eighteenth century (Lepzig, 1922) and later his habilitation in 1934 in Danzig where he became Professor of Musicology and leader of the Collegium Musicum. Between 1935–45 he worked as Professor at the Universität Berlin where he stayed after 1945. He authored three musicological books on organ music, Bach and "Goethe und das deutsche Volkslied," published respectively in 1934, 1939 and 1941. A member of NSDAP since May 1, 1933 (No. 2 844 274), he performed different functions: *Fachgruppenleiter Musik* in Kampfbund für deutsche Kultur in Danzig; since 1935 collaborator and Referent der Hauptabteilung Musik im Kulturamt der RJF; President of the Organ association (*Orgelarbeitsgemeinschaft*). He gave numerous indoctrinating lectures on music and race (*Musik und Rasse*, among others in Berlin, January 27, 1937, at the Reichstagung für Musik); he served as instructor at The National Socialist Teachers League (Nationalsozialistischer Lehrerbund, NSLB; again in Bayreuth in April 1938; in Wiedenhof near Breslau, in November 1938, at the Silesian Gaumusiklager des NSLB). He also gave lectures on tasks, directions and problems of the musical racial style research (e.g. *Aufgaben und Probleme der musikalischen Rassestilforschung* at the Tagung der Reichsmusiktage, Düsseldorf, May 28, 1938), which he published as *Aufgaben und Ausrichtung der musikalischen Rassestilforschung* (in "Rasse und Musik", ed. G. Waldmann, Amt der RJF, Berlin, 1939, 102–112), *Volksbräuche und Volkslieder der Deutschen in Polen* (*Musik in Judend un Volk* 1939 No. 2, 399–415), *Die Bedeutung der deutschen Musik im Osten* (MiJuV 1941 No. IV/1, January, 2–3), *Hitlerjugend musiziert* ("Jahrbuch der deutschen Musik" 1943, 59–60). Among the several songbooks he edited are *Neue Soldatenlieder*,

---

17 Herbert Drescher, *Von Heinrich Fink bis zu Joseph Elsner. Deutsche Musiker in Polen*, Krakauer Zeitung Nr 159 7/9 July 1940, 9–10, on the first and second page of column entitled *From Time and History. Cultural Contributions for the East – in Collaboration with the Institute for German Eastwork* (*Aus Zeit und Geschichte. Kulturbeiträge für den Osten – in Zusammenarbeit mit dem Institut für deutsche Ostarbeit*).

destined for Hitlerjugend (1940) and SS (1941), *Lieder der Luftwaffe* (1942), *Wir Mädel singen* for Bund Deutscher Mädel (the first edition came out in 1936) where the song is described as "the expression of our being," "giving shape to our daily routine."[18]

Pallmann was one of the most active Nazi musicologists and author of several songbooks, among others *Kriegslieder des deutschen Volkes* (1939).[19] It was Dr. Gerigk however, described by Prieberg as "der Denunziant" of Jewish musicians, who "embodied the absolute bureaucratic ruthlessness against people and values."[20] We will return to him later.

Products of ideologically biased, pseudo-scientific "musicological" research were promulgated from more specialized journals such as *Die Musik* to the everyday German press in occupied Polish territories. Further examples from the official press for the Polish-speaking readers prove that this kind of propaganda was also aptly replicated there. These strategies demonstrate the importance of such cultural propaganda in a broader ideological totalitarian plan. It seems crucial, however, before moving on to the propagandistic abuses of musical culture in occupied Poland, to discuss the pseudo-aesthetic foundations of these core Nazi beliefs concerning the need of establishing total Germanic cultural hegemony over the conquered world.

1.2. Racial pseudo-aesthetics as the ideological background of cultural policies

Music was widely used by the Nazis as a means of boosting the triumphalist ideology of Aryan race domination. In this realm, the role of music was to prove the superiority of German culture, whose identity was composed of such elements as: the German nation itself, the German race, German art, and so forth. This endless, self-serving enumeration reverberated in Nazi books, articles, and speeches. The omnipresent attempts at proving this racial and cultural superiority went hand in hand with attempts to prove the inferiority of the cultures to be dominated.

The racialization of musical aesthetics begun by Richard Wagner in his notorious essay *Das Judenthum in der Musik* (1869), was further developed by his followers. One in particular stands out: Alfred Rosenberg, editor of the virulent Nazi

---

18 See F. K. Prieberg, *Handbuch deutsche Musiker*, 1715–1725.
19 Prieberg, *Handbuch*, 5082–5126.
20 Prieberg, *Handbuch*, 2015–2016.

newspaper *Völkischer Beobachter*, founder of the Militant League for German Culture and of the Institute for the Study of the Jewish Question, and author of the pseudo-philosophical *Der Mythus des zwanzigsten Jahrhunderts* (*The Myth of the Twentieth Century*, 1930). His Nazi career led him to occupy significant positions and gave him executive power to shape cultural life according to his racial beliefs; he became Commissar for Supervision of Intellectual and Ideological Education of the Nazi Party, founder of the above-mentioned *Sonderstab Musik* (Special Task Force for Music), the function of which was to loot the best instruments and scores in the conquered territories owned by Jews, as well as libraries and museum collections. He then rose to the post of Reich Minister for the Occupied Eastern Territories.

The second book of his *Mythus*, entitled *Wesen der germanischen Kunst* (*Nature of Germanic Art*), opens with a chapter titled *Das rassische Schönheitsideal* (*Racial Ideal of Beauty*), which hails the beginning of an epoch when works of overwhelming intellectual power and – more importantly – of cultural and racial superiority, are being produced, while "alien works" are rejected.[21] The essence of all Nordic Western art – its ideal of beauty, its inner will and heroic honour, linked with inner truthfulness – has been revealed, so Rosenberg argues, in Richard Wagner's music. Rosenberg's favorite rhetoric device is to invoke the "two million dead German heroes who gave their lives for nothing other than the honour and freedom of the German people" which is "the sole source of our spiritual rebirth" and the "heroic" in music. The long-awaited German poet "will, with his strong hand, drive out the worms from our theatres; he will make the musicians fruitful with new heroic music, and guide the chisel of the sculptor."[22] This uplifting belief equating the honor of the heroic German nation with heroic German music is harshly contrasted with the contemptible vision of Jews who, according to the author, are not only devoid of such noble qualities as honor and

---

21 Alfred Rosenberg, *Der Mythus des zwanzigsten Jahrhunderts: eine Wertung der seelisch-geistigen Gestaltenkämpfe unserer Zeit* (*The Myth of the Twentieth Century. An Evaluation of the Spiritual-Intellectual Confrontations of Our Age*), München: Hocheneichen Verlag, 1934. The ideological pattern was set in the first chapter *Race and Race Soul*. I discussed this topic in *The Functions of Music within the Nazi System of Genocide in Occupied Poland*, in: W. Klimczyk, A. Świerzowska (eds.), *Music and Genocide*, "Studies in Social Sciences, Philosophy and History of Ideas", Vol. 9 (Frankfurt am Main: Peter Lang Edition 2015,) 83–103.
22 "Dieser deutsche Dichter wird dann auch mit starker Hand das Gewürm von unseren Theatern verjagen, er wird den Musiker zu einer neuen Heldenmusik befruchten und dem Bildhauer den Meißel führen." Ibid., 450.

heroism, but also lack true artistic creativity.[23] Rosenberg posits a dichotomy between the Germanic "right path" and the "fall from the right path" due to Jewish influence in art: "When, as in our time, Jewish 'artists' take a prominent place in artistic life, this is an unmistakable sign that we had strayed from the right path: that within us – let's hope temporarily – an essential spiritual power has been buried."[24]

The purpose of the pseudo-arguments employed, among others, by Hitler in *Mein Kampf* and by Alfred Rosenberg in his *Myth of the Twentieth Century* was to make readers understand how detrimental for German culture were the influences of inferior races (with the Jews presented as the main danger) and how the idealized German culture, already brimming with the highest artistic standards, could regain this greatest distinction by getting rid of those who corrupted art and society. Alfred Rosenberg provides in his *Myth of the Twentieth Century* a striking metaphoric comparison of Nazi usurpations to a mystic chord: the Germanic conquest of the world is not a boundless expansion, but an enhanced

---

23 The original reads as follows: "Aus dieser Seelenstimmung erklärt sich bis auf heute die Gier des jüdischen Volkes, zugleich auch sein fast vollständiger Mangel an echter seelischer und künstlerischer Schöpferkraft. (…) Deshalb wird jüdische 'Kunst' niemals persönlicher aber auch niemals wirklich sachlicher Stil sein, sondern bloß technische Geschicklichkeit und subjektive, auf äußerliche Wirkung ausgehende Mache verraten; meistens mit grobsinnlichen Einschlägen verbunden, wenn nicht ganz und gar auf Unsittlichkeit eingestellt. (…) Sie weckt also weder aesthetische Selbstvergessenheit, noch wendet sie sich an den Willen, sondern bloß (im besten Fall) an das technische Urteil oder an subjektive Gefühlserregung. (…) man prüfe die jüdischen Wunderkinder am Klavier, an der Geige, auf den Brettern: Talmi, Technik, Mache, Effekt, Quantität, Virtuosität, alles was man will, nur keine Genialität, keine Schöpferkraft. Und in ursprünglicher Fremdheit europäischen Wesens machte sich das gesamte Judentum zum Förderer der Nigger 'Kunst' auf allen Gebieten. (…) Die heutigen verzweifelten Versuche jüdischer bildender Künstler, durch Futurismus, Expressionismus, 'neue Sachlichkeit' ihre Begabung zu beweisen, sind ein lebendiges Zeugnis für diese alte Tatsache. Einzelne Ansätze zu höherem streben sollen nicht geleugnet werden (Juda Halevy), aber es fehlte beim Judentum, als ganzes betrachtet, das Fluidum, aus dem wirklich große Werke geboren warden." Ibid., 364–536.

24 "Wenn wie in unserer Zeit die jüdischen 'Künstler' einen hervorragenden Platz in unserem Kunstleben einnahmen, so ist es ein untrügliches Zeichen dafür, daß wir vom rechten Wege abgeirrt waren, daß uns – nur zeitweilig hoffentlich – eine nicht zu missende Seelenkraft verschüttet worden ist." Ibid.

forcefulness – that is, a willed action – the "sweet sacred chord," to which Schubert attributed omnipotence.[25]

This expression, meant as highly poetical, yet in fact highly ambiguous, characteristic of Rosenberg's style, reveals a telling component of the Nazis' forcefully aestheticized ideology: an imaginary mystical communion between their criminal *Lebensraum* project and the presupposed sacred dimension of music. The aim of this line of reasoning was to sanction their anti-Semitic and anti-democratic actions, and to give such a legitimization of the Nazi ideology that could satisfy both pseudo-religious and narcissistic needs. The music of the great German masters, as they called them, was the most appropriate legitimization of all policies to be undertaken. Thus, the "Germanic conquest of the world" became the embodiment of the Schubertian sweet sacred chord – the persecution first of their fellow citizens and later of the conquered nations was aestheticized to the extreme. In the pseudo-aesthetic philosophy of Rosenberg, it acquired the status of a sacred ideal symbolized by music. The dream of omnipotence, characteristic of narcissistic Nazi psychology, was perhaps subconsciously sought for along the lines of the Jungian and Freudian process of *Übertragung* or 'transference.' The desire of power and domination was transferred onto Schubert and his idea of a sweet, sacred chord.

Thus, in Rosenberg's text, Schubert almost became a porte-parole of Nazi beliefs about the necessity of the "Germanic conquest of the world," and provided a defensible justification. This tightly interwoven connection between the exalted Nazi power and the power of music could be considered as simple manipulation, typical of a totalitarian mode of thinking. However, the omnipresence of music in all important domains of the Nazi system, even in the most gruesome detention and genocide centres, was not linked with spiritual psychological needs (although it made use of them to associate these domains with the

---

25 A longer excerpt reads: "Die Musik Bachs und Beethovens ist nicht die höchste erreichbare Stufe der Verflüchtigung der Seele, sondernbeeutet gerade den Durchbruch einer Seelenkraft ohnegleichen, die nicht bloß stoffliche Fesseln abstreift (das ist nur die negative Seite), sondern etwas ganz Bestimmtes ausspricht, wenn dies auch nicht immer gleich schwarz auf weiß nachHause getragen werden kann. Die germanische Weltüberwindung ist nicht uferlose Ausweitung (was 'Verflüchtigung' wäre), sondern gesteigerte Eindringlichkeit (d. h. willenhafte Tat), der 'süße heilige Akkord', dem Schubert die Allmacht zuschrieb. Der Wille ist Seelenprägung für eine zielbewußte Energie, gehört also in die zielsetzende (finale) Betrachtungsweise, währendder Trieb mit der ursachenforschenden (kausalen) Denkweise verbunden ist." A. Rosenberg, *Der Mythus*, chapter: *Der aestethetische Wille*, 406.

sacredness of pure German art); it was treated as the taking over of symbolic spaces – the second stage after getting rid of unwanted non-German elements. Rosenberg's writings served as models, which were developed by Nazi musicologists in their efforts to explain that Jews had to be excluded from the *heiligen Angelegenheit* (Rosenberg's expression, "sacred matter") of German music and art. Over and over again they claimed that it was a matter of resisting foreign infiltration and the bastardization of German art: "jüdisch-destruktive Geist und die rassische Überfremdung und Verbastardierung im Musikleben des deutsches Volkes aus." This argumentation, later repeated in occupied Poland, was characterized by an obsession on *Aufbau*, presented as "the noble task" of cleansing the cultural institutions in order to return to the "simple values of blood and the racial soul and the German spirit." They have complained that, before Nazi came to power, the management of the State Academy of Music was entrusted to the "racial mongrel" Franz Schreker whose "perverted operas" were "contaminating the spirit of the nation (*Volksseele*).[26] The music of the Jew Arnold Schoenberg

---

26 Rudolf Sonner, "Aufbau und Kultur seit 1933," *Die Musik: Organ des Amtes Musik beim Beauftragten des Führers für die Überwachung der gesamten geistigen und weltanschaulichen Schulung und Erziehung der NSDAP*, 30 (7) April 1938, 435. In German original: "Nicht minder wirken sich der jüdisch-destruktive Geist und die rassische Überfremdung und Verbastardierung im Musikleben des deutschen Volkes aus. (…) Die Leitung der Staatlichen Hochschule für Musik lag in den Händen des Rassemischlings Franz Schreker, der mi seinen überspannten und perversen Opern die Volksseele vergistete. An dem von ihm geleiteten Institut unterrichtete der vom Kaufmann zur Musik hinüber gewechselte Jude Arnold Schönberg, der in seiner Musik alle Gesetze funktionsharmonischer Logik sowie alle Gestaltungsprinzipien leugnete. (…) Insbesondere war es der Jude Paul Bekker, der die deutsche Musikkultur mit seinem Frankfurter Pesthauch zu unterhöhlen verstand. Ihm zur Seite sekundierte der Berliner Jude Adolf Weissmann. 'Moderne Kammermusikfeste' brachten die irrsinnigsten, aber auch naivsten Produktionen der Juden und Judenbastarde Sekles, Schönberg, Weill, Křenek, Gâl, Milhaud, Lichtenstein, Korngold, Deutsch, Wolff, Mahler usw. Um den deutschen Hörer irrezuführen, wurden geschickt Richard Strauss und Hans Pfitzner in die Vortragsfolge eingeschmuggelt. Wer diese "Neutöner" ablehnte, galt als ungebildet, reaktionär und unmusikalisch." Rosenberg and Robert Ley are quoted on page 436, where Sonner wrote: "Demzufolge war die vornehmte Aufgabe dieser Kulturorganisation, die von dem bisher jüdischen Kunstbetrieb verschütteten Kraftströme wieder planmässig freizulegen und aufzufangen, die Kunst wieder auf die einfachen Werte des Blutes und der Rassenseele und des deutschen Geistes zurückzuführen, d.h. sie weltanschaulich auszurichten. Nachdem diese erste Etappe der Vormarsches erreicht war, galt es, das Volk wieder an die Kunst heranzuführen; den 'Arbeit und Kunst gehören zusammen. Sie kommen aus einer Wurzel: der Rasse. Wir begreifen die Sehnsucht des

who taught there "denied all the laws of functional logic and all principles of design." Those who rejected the insane and naïve "productions of Jews and Jewish bastards" were "considered uneducated, reactionary and unmusical." The aggressive denouncement of Jews, characteristic of such musicologists' prose is somewhat similar to the despiteful rhetoric used just two years later in the "reptile" propagandistic German press for Poles (Nowy Kurier Warszawski" among other newspapers and magazines). This time however, the denounced Jews were killed (Andrzej Włast, the author of lyrics to several pre-war hits, mentioned in such an article was shot in the Ghetto street).

The fact that Rosenberg's book lacked the premeditated simplicity of *Mein Kampf* apparently prompted a criticism from Hitler, who despised "placid aesthetes and blasé intellectuals" and considered them futile particularly in the field of propaganda.[27] However, the *quod erat demonstrandum* of German superiority

---

Arbeitenden nach Kunst und Kultur. Wir haben dem deutsche Arbeiter die Theater und Kunsttempel erschlossen' (Dr. Robert Ley)."

27 "Particularly in the field of propaganda, placid aesthetes and blasé intellectuals should never be allowed to take the lead. The former would readily transform the impressive character of real propaganda into something suitable only for literary tea parties. As to the second class of people, one must always beware of this pest; for, in consequence of their insensibility to normal impressions, they are constantly seeking new excitements. (…) The blase intellectuals are always the first to criticize propaganda, or rather its message, because this appears to them to be outmoded and trivial. They are always looking for something new, always yearning for change; and thus they become the mortal enemies of every effort that may be made to influence the masses in an effective way. The moment the organisation and message of a propagandist movement begins to be orientated according to their tastes it becomes incoherent and scattered. It is not the purpose of propaganda to create a series of alterations in sentiment with a view to pleasing these blase gentry. Its chief function is to convince the masses, whose slowness of understanding needs to be given time in order that they may absorb information; and only constant repetition will finally succeed in imprinting an idea on the memory of the crowd." Quotations from *Mein Kampf* are given in English translation by James Murphy first published in March 1939 by Hurst and Blackett Ltd., available online in A Project Gutenberg of Australia eBook.
In the German original: "Gerade auf dem Gebiete der Propaganda darf man sich niemals von Ästheten oder Blasierten leiten lassen: Von den ersteren nicht, weil sonst der Inhalt in Form und Ausdruck in kürzester Zeit, statt für die Masse sich zu eignen, nur mehr für literarische Teegesellschaften Zugkraft entwickelt; vor den zweiten aber hätte man sich deshalb ängstlich, weil ihr Mangel an eigenem frischen Empfinden immer nach neuen Reizen sucht. (…) Sie sind immer die ersten Kritiker der Propaganda oder besser ihres Inhaltes, der ihnen zu althergebracht, zu abgedroschen, dann wieder zu

in all possible domains, including art, is reiterated in Rosenberg's writings relentlessly, and conforms to the propaganda rule defined by Hitler in Chapter VI of *Mein Kampf* entitled "War Propaganda," according to which only constant repetition imprints an idea on the memory of the crowd. The urge to purify Germanic music of alien elements hailed in Alfred Rosenberg's writings was omnipresent in Nazi beliefs, writings, and propaganda. German culture was constantly exalted as superior and "alien" art as racially inferior, created by sub-humans who were incapable of producing a true masterpiece. Alien culture was considered an existential threat to Germanic civilization.

Hitler himself relentlessly voiced his anti-Semitic hatred and gave various "arguments" to fuel it and legitimize it; he also presented his ideas on the inferiority of Poles versus the dignity and nobility of the German race in "historical" perspective. He regarded the use of the German language by Poles as a threat to this sacred racial purity and the nobility of the German language and race; hence, Germanization was not the ultimate goal:

> Unfortunately, a policy towards Poland, whereby the East was to be Germanized, was demanded by many and was based on the same false reasoning. Here again it was believed that the Polish people could be Germanized by being compelled to use the German language. The result would have been fatal. A people of foreign race would have had to use the German language to express modes of thought that were foreign to the German, thus compromising by its own inferiority the dignity and nobility of our nation.[28]

During the decade after the publication of the *Myth* these views acquired a criminal, genocidal dimension. When on June 26, 1943, Joseph Goebbels delivered his speech about *Immortal German Culture* at the opening of the Seventh Great

---

überlebt usw. erscheint. Sie wollen immer Neues, suchen Abwechslung und werden dadurch zu wahren Todfeinden jeder wirksamen politischen Massengewinnung. Denn sowie sich die Organisation und der Inhalt einer Propaganda nach ihren Bedürfnissen zu richten beginnen, verlieren sie jede Geschlossenheit und zerflattern statt dessen vollständig. Propaganda ist jedoch nicht dazu da, blasierten Herrchen laufend interessante Abwechslung zu verschaffen, sondern zu überzeugen, und zwar die Masse zu überzeugen. Diese aber braucht in ihrer Schwerfälligkeit immer eine bestimmte Zeit, ehe sie auch nur von einer Sache Kenntnis zu nehmen bereit ist, und nur einer tausendfachen Wiederholung einfachster Begriffe wird sie endlich ihr Gedächtnis schenken. Diese aber braucht in ihrer Schwerfälligkeit immer eine bestimmte Zeit, ehe sie auch nur von einer Sache Kenntnis zu nehmen bereit ist, und nur einer tausendfachen Wiederholung einfachster Begriffe wird sie endlich ihr Gedächtnis schenken." *Mein Kampf*, 202–203.

28 Ibid., 219.

German Art Exhibition, Jewish artists and musicians were being relentlessly murdered in the territories of occupied Poland, while the Nazi Minister of Propaganda stated proudly:

> Never have the German people had such a drive toward intellectual and spiritual things as they do today. I am not speaking of the less pleasant manifestations of war, which are always there. One should see our theaters, concert halls, museums, art exhibitions. Day and night, summer and winter, tens and hundreds of thousands of Germans sit or stand there astonished at so much beauty. We have become richer, more fulfilled, and better as a result of the war. (…) The German people are not spending their money on art because there is no other way to spend it, as is sometimes said. The path to art is the path to their hearts.[29]

"The path to art is the path to their hearts" is no mere statement of grand propagandistic rhetoric, nor is it simply an expression of Nazi belief in the manipulative power of art. It is also the key to understanding their cultural policy towards non-German ethnicities in the former Polish territories, where various components of racial ideology motivated the establishment of new laws and rules in the field of music.

The omnipresent claim for German *Lebensraum* was used to legitimize the segregation and ghettoization of music, as well as the genocidal actions in occupied Poland. Similar perverted argumentation of the destructive "Jewish influence" was given in Nazi publications as the reason to control culture in occupied Polish territories. In 1942, Dr. Friedrich Gollert, assistant to the Chief of the Office and Head of the Office of Planning in the Warsaw District (*Persönlischer Referent des Chefs des Amtes und Leiter des Amtes für Raumordnung*), in his brochure *Warschau über deutscher Herrschaft. Deutsche Aufbauarbeit im Distrikt Warschau* (*Warsaw under German rule: German reconstruction work in the Warsaw District*), published by order of SA-Gruppenführer Dr. Ludwig Fischer, Governor of Distrikt Warschau, expressed this idea in a straightforward manner:

> Besides, the Jews, who accounted for one third of the entire population of Warsaw, exerted a strong influence on the intellectual, cultural, and political life, so that public opinion had been poisoned to a great extent throughout these years of Jewish influence. It was therefore obvious that in the interest of preventing a further incitement of the Polish population against Germanness, all the anti-German printed materials had to be discarded, just as all the new releases had to be verified beforehand. In addition, it

---

29 Joseph Goebbels, "Unsterbliche deutsche Kultur. Rede zur Eröffnung der 7. Großen Deutschen Kunstausstellung," in *Der steile Aufstieg* (Munich: Zentralverlag der NSDAP, 1944).

was necessary to monitor the cultural life of Poles as much as possible. (…) In view of the incitement of the population, it was still necessary to supervise the programs in the re-licensed entertainment facilities and to cleanse them of products of Jewish-Marxist mentality.[30]

1.3. Nazi administration and racial jurisdiction versus Polish culture

As a result of the Ribbentrop-Molotov Pact, Poland was divided into three parts: the USSR-annexed territories, the Reich-annexed territories, and the *Generalgouvernement für die besetzten polnischen Gebiete* (General Government for the Occupied Polish Territories), renamed in 1940 as the *Generalgouvernement* (General Government).[31] Areas annexed to the Reich were administratively

---

30 "Ausserdem hatten die Juden, die ein Drittel der gesamten Einwohnerzahl Warschaus ausmachten, einer sehr starken Einfluss auf das geistige, kulturelle und politische Leben ausgeübt, so dass die öffentlische Meinung durch diese jahrelange jüdische Beeinflussung außerordentlich vergiftet worden war. Es war daher selbstverständlich, dass im Interesse der Verhinderung einer weiteren Verhetzung der polnischer Bevölkerung gegenüber dem Deutschtum alle deutschfeindlischen Druck-Erzeugnisse ausgesondert werden mussten, genau wie alle Neuerscheinungen vorher überprüft werden mussten. Darüber hinaus galt es, das kulturelle Leben der Polen weitgehend zu überwachen. (…) Mit Rücksicht auf die Verhetzung der Bevölkerung war es weiter notwendig, die Programme in den wieder zugelassenen Unterhaltungsstätten zu beaufsichtigen und sie von Erzeugnissen jüdisch-marxistischer Mentalität zu saubern." Friedrich Gollert, *Warschau über deutscher Herrschaft. Deutsche Aufbauarbeit im Distrikt Warschau* (Krakau: Burgverlag Krakau GmbH, 1942), 271-272.

31 A detailed description of this partition is given in *Law Reports of Trials of War Criminals*, Vol. 14, 23: "In accordance with the German-Soviet Pact of 28th September, 1939, the Republic of Poland was partitioned as follows: Out of the entire territory of 150,486 square miles, with a population of 35,340,000, some 72,866 square miles, with a population of some 22,250,000 came under German occupation, and some 77,620 square miles, with a population of some 13,090,000 were taken over by Soviet Russia. From the beginning, the German-occupied territories were divided into two parts almost equal in extent:

(a) The territories of Western Poland with some additions of Central and Southern Poland, which, in accordance with the Decree of 8 October 1939, published in the *Reichsgesetzblatt*, but contrary to international law, were incorporated in the German Reich on 26th October, 1939; *(b)* Of the remainder of the Central and Southern Poland, including the cities of Warsaw, Krakow and Lublin, the so-called Government General was created. This area was intended by the Germans to be a kind of protectorate. It was originally called the "Government General of the Occupied Polish Areas" (*Generalgouvernement für die besetzten polnischen Gebiete*). On 18 August

divided into Reich provinces *Pommern, Danzig-Westpreussen, Ostpreussen* and *Warthegau.* The General Government was divided at first into four (Krakau, Radom, Lublin, Warschau). After the 1941 invasion of the Soviet Union, a fifth district, *Galizien* with its centre in Lvov, was established.[32]

The German invasion of Poland in September 1939 marked the beginning of the most disastrous years in the already deeply painful history of this country. This attack had an unprecedented character, as it mercilessly targeted civilians and cultural sites, while Nazi propaganda presented it by means of all available media, notably "documentary" films in 1940 (the notorious *Feldzug in Polen* directed by Fritz Hippler, with music by Herbert Windt and *Feuertaufe* directed by Hans Bertram with music by Norbert Schultze), not only as a justified military action against military targets, a "just" war, but also an aesthetically impressive one.[33]

1940, however, this terminology was changed, and thenceforth the territory was called "General Government" or *General Gouvernement des Deutschen Reichs*.

32 According to *Law Reports of Trials of War Criminals*, Vol. 14, 26, the "complex organisation of the German authority was being exercised only in the interests of the Reich and in complete disregard of the interests and rights of the local inhabitants, and was particularly directed at the extermination of the Polish and Jewish population." The "administration of the Government-General was organized in accordance with the *Füh="rerprinzip* and based on full co-operation and interdependence of the administrative and police authorities on all levels. It may be added that the Governor General was at the same time head of the N.S.D.A.P. of the territory and that the great majority of higher German officials there were members of the Nazi Party." For a precise description of Nazi administration and several other topics including a broader overview of the Nazi cultural policy, see: Grochowina, *Cultural policy*.

33 Cf. Hilmar Hoffmann, *The Triumph of Propaganda: Film and National Socialism, 1933–1945*, trans. John A. Broadwin and V. R. Berghahn (Providence, RI, 1997), 216 ff. The author observed that "Films like *Feuertaufe, Feldzug in Polen* and *Sieg im Westen* wage the battles for a second time, this time to win them also with aesthetic means. By compressing the battle, picking some scenes, and deleting others, constructing rudimentary contexts that never existed in reality in this density, these movies discard all that is undesirable from a propagandistic point of view. They show 'images of horrific beauty' instead of brutal horror pictures" (219). This could be observed also in some of contemporary war coverages in media, where more than dubious choices of background music accompany footages of attacks on civilians.

34 Cf. Mieczysław B. Biskupski, Piotr Stefan Wandycz, *Ideology, Politics, and Diplomacy in East Central Europe* (Rochester, 2003).

The Soviet invasion of Poland on Setember 17 paralysed Polish defence efforts and marked the beginning of the persecution of Polish elites in those territories under Soviet rule, such persecution having been earlier implemented in areas conquered by the Wehrmacht. The country was partitioned into German-Russian "spheres of interests," according to clauses contained in the "Secret Supplementary Protocol" (*Geheimes Zusatzprotokoll*) to the Ribbentrop-Molotov pact signed on August 23, 1939 (the existence of which was denied by the Soviet Union until 1989).[34] Another Secret Protocol supplemented to the *Deutsch-sowjetischer Grenz- und Freundschaftsvertrag*, signed by Molotov and Ribbentrop in Moscow on September 28, 1939, had an even greater importance, as it stated:

> Both Parties will tolerate in their territories no Polish agitation which affects the territories of the other Party. They will suppress in their territories all beginnings of such agitation and inform each other concerning suitable measures for this purpose.[35]

It was this statement which formalized the mutual agreement about the persecution of former Polish citizens with any means possible, both by Nazi Germany and the Soviet Union. Its intentionally generalized character "legalized" any action, directed mainly against the Polish intelligentsia, and permitted a tacit collaboration for purpose of annihilating Polish elites. The methods employed were in many respects similar. Germans "liquidated" those considered as inimical to their culture, mainly in executions led by *Einsatzgruppen*, or sent them to concentration camps – first those already established in Germany, such as Dachau, and later those established in former Polish territories, such as Auschwitz. The Soviets also executed many Polish officers (never admitting these crimes),[36] or

---

35 Zoltán Maruzsa, "The Molotov-Ribbentrop Pact and What is Behind," in Maruzsa (ed.), *Unknown Clauses: The Background Deals of Totalitarian Systems in the Face of World War II The Molotov-Ribbentrop Pact* (Budapest: Department of Modern and Contemporary Global History, 2010), 20. The German original reads: "Die unterzeichneten Bevollmächtigten haben bei Anschluss des deutsch-sowjetischen Grenz- und Freundschaftsvertrages ihr Einverständnis über folgendes festgestellt: Beide Teile werden auf ihren Gebieten keine polnische Agitation dulden, die auf die Gebiete des anderen Teiles hinüberwirkt. Sie werden alle Ansätze zu einer solchen Agitation auf ihren Gebieten unterbinden und sich gegenseitig über die hierfür zweckmäßigen Maßnahmen unterrichten."

36 See Claudia Weber, *Krieg der Täter. Die Massenerschießungen von Katyń* (Hamburg: Hamburger Edition, 2015) and the contemporary historical propaganda by the Russian and Belorussian states.

37 N. Davis, *God's Playground*, 441.

sent them to camps in Siberia, using them as forced labour workers who would eventually die of hunger, extreme weather conditions, and physical work.

The illegal jurisdiction imposed by the Nazis in occupied Polish territories stemmed from the Nazi doctrine of Nordic racial superiority and of the racial inferiority of Jews, Romani, and Slavic ethnicities. Polish national identity ceased to exist after September 1939 and consequently musicians, as other former citizens of the Republic of Poland, lost the protection of basic civil laws. As Norman Davis puts it:

> In neither case, whether inside the Reich or outside it, did the population enjoy the protection of the civil law. All the occupied territories were designated as lawless *Arbeitsbereich* (Work Areas) where martial law was in force and where "death" or "concentration camp" were the only two forms of stipulated punishment for any type of offence.[37]

Policies applied by the Nazi authorities in occupied Poland from September 1939 were directed against Polish culture, which embodied for them one of the inimical targets to be destroyed in the *Generalplan Ost*, the most extreme fulfilment of Hitler's *Lebensraum* concept and the *Drang nach Osten* ideology. Secretly prepared in 1939–1941 by the SS organ Reich Security Office (*Reichssicherheitshauptamt*, RSHA) and preceded by academic research conducted by the *Ostforschung*, this plan proposed the extermination, enslavement, Germanization or expulsion of Slavic nations, in order to Germanize the conquered territories thoroughly and to ensure that the ethnic groups living there would eventually vanish completely, just as Poland as a state disappeared from the maps through its division into the General Government and the areas annexed to the USSR or to the Third Reich.[38]

---

38 Haar thus described these facts: "First, those Polish and Jewish groups deemed unfit for integration into the German population were to be deported. These included all Polish citizens not considered to have an important economic function. Second, all members of the Polish intelligentsia, priests, teachers, scientists, and Poles of a national democratic orientation were selected to immediate liquidation. (…) In order to achieve these two goals, all agencies involved in the various aspects of the project – the central offices in Berlin as well as national branches operating in the areas projected for settlement – depended on expert research to facilitate the resettlement process". In conclusion of this chapter, the author added that "historians maintained an eloquent silence about their own roles during the National Socialist period. It is one of the most noteworthy problems of postwar German historiography that the same historians who helped plan deportations of Jews and Poles under National Socialism assumed responsibility for researching the deportations of Germans from East-Central Europe after 1945. The result is an apologist historiography that continues to exercise strong influence in

To realize this aim, Hitler considered the liquidation of Polish leadership necessary and expressed his intentions in unambiguous terms on numerous occasions, mainly during meetings with his subordinates.[39] Already by August/September 1939, different types of extermination policies towards leaders considered as potentially dangerous had been implemented, first, during the *Unternehmen Tannenberg* (Operation Tannenberg) and from May 1940 in *Außerordentliche Befriedungsaktion* (Special Pacification Operation). They were based on lists (*Sonderfahndungsbuch Polen*) which had been prepared before September 1939 and contained over sixty thousand names. Among Hitler's directives of October 17, 1939, next to such "logistic" regulations as "all Poles and Jews deported from Germany and from the incorporated territories shall be concentrated in the Government General," the following orders are found: "Polish intelligentsia shall not be allowed to lead the Polish nation", "all foundations and nuclei of Polish national consolidation shall be destroyed," "the Poles should be forced down to the lowest standard of living and be allowed only the minimum necessary for sustenance, so that they become a source of cheap labor for Germany." He also stressed that "no legal restrictions" should impede this national struggle."[40]

Polish culture perceived as the hotbed of "Polish nationalism" (a term used to describe all elements linked to Polish identity) was the target chosen for destruction also because cultural development, education, and science, hindered the plan for the degradation of the Polish population (*Polnische Bevölkerung*) and its transformation into a docile labour force.

Regulations concerning education were designed to ensure that a new elite could not be formed. Schooling was restricted to primary schools and secondary

---

German academic and public spheres to this day." Ingo Haar, "German Ostforschung and Anti-Semitism," in H**aar, Michael Fahlbusch (eds.),** *German Scholars and Ethnic Cleansing, 1920–1945* (New York: Berghahn Books, 2005), 16 ff.

39 According to the account given by General Fedor von Bock. On 22 August 1939, Hitler announced to his generals that after their military action, SS troops should undertake to exterminate Polish *Führerschicht*. According to General Wilhelm Keitl (chief of Oberkommando der Wehrmacht) Hitler named the liquidation of Polish intelligentsia as *politische Flurbereinigung* (political consolidation of land).

40 Quoted in *Law Reports of Trials of War Criminals*, selected and prepared by The United Nations War Crimes Commission (London: His Majesty's Stationery Office, 1949), Vol. 14, 24–25. For the rest of the document see Library of Congress Military Legal Resources, available online. Cf. also Majer, '*Non-Germans' under the Third Reich*.

41 Ibid.

schools that trained professionals in various specialities recognized as useful by the authorities (e.g. carpenter, dressmaker). This was outlined in the "Measures Against Polish Culture and Education" section of Josef Bühler's trial:

> Education was completely reorganized. It was controlled by a special department of the Governor-General's office in Krakow and by corresponding sections created under the district-governors. The officials of the school administration had to be Germans, although the educational councils could appoint Poles as school supervisors. Only trade and professional schools were re-established for Poles. This was in line with the general policy of preparing Polish youth for physical work and of developing technical skill in compliance with the general plan to use the Polish population mainly as a source of manpower. The Polish curriculum was substantially restricted.[41]

To prove that the occupied country had no culture or national identity, and in order to turn it into an "intellectual desert" (in the words of General Governor Hans Frank), regulations concerning education ensured that a new elite could not emerge: universities and higher schools of art were closed to Polish students and professors.[42] Independent Polish newspapers and periodicals were banned and replaced by German propaganda journalism in Polish; and musical and cultural institutions, such as orchestras, libraries, choirs, radio and music associations, as well as all other cultural associations, were closed. Still, contrary to all the decisions regarding cultural policy in Warthegau, cafes and restaurants for the Polish population were allowed on the grounds that they were easy to monitor and control.[43] By Frank's decree of March 8, 1940, all cultural activity in the GG was subjected to control by the Department of Education and Propaganda.

The importance of regulations concerning access to education and culture for non-Germans can be measured from the space devoted to it at a high-level conference conducted on October 31, 1939, when the Reichsminister of Propaganda Dr. Joseph Goebbels flew from Berlin to Łódź to meet Dr. Arthur Seyss-Inquart, administrative chief for the southern territories of occupied Poland,

---

42 Ibid., 29.
43 E. Wetzel and G. Hecht, *Treating of Poles and Jews in the remaining [part of] Poland* [i.e. General Government], passage in: *Die Frage der Behandlung der Bevölkerung der ehemaligen polnischen Gebiete nach rassenpolitischen Gesichtspunkten* [The question of treating the population of the former Polish territory from the racial-political point of view], 25 November 1939. Quoted in *Kultura walcząca*, 289–94.

Reichsamtsleiter Dr. Maximilian Freiherr du Prel,[44] and the newly appointed (on October 26) General Governor Hans Frank. Frank presented his views, stating that:

> Poles should be left only with such possibilities of education which will demonstrate to them the hopelessness of their national position. That is why they are entitled to watch solely films of low quality or such films that would present to their eyes the magnitude and power of the German Reich.[45]

His opinions were shared by Goebbels, who spoke against the establishment of Polish theatres, cinemas, and cabarets.[46]

Four days earlier (on October 26), Frank had assumed his function of General Governor, chose Krakow for his capital and the Royal Wawel Castle – renamed

---

44 Du Prel worked at the *Völkischer Beobachter* from 1933 on, from October 1939 until July 1940 was the chief of the department of press and propaganda at Franks' office and later ascended to the grade of SS-Sturmbannführer.

45 "Herr Generalgouverneur führte aus (…) Der Wawel in Krakau werde nur mehr die Bezeichnung Krakauer Burg tragen. (…) Einleitend führte Herr Generalgouverneur aus: Den Polen dürfen nur solche Bildungsmöglichkeiten zur Verfügung gestellt werden, die ihnen die Aussichtslosigkeit ihres völkischen Schicksals zeigten. Es könnten daher höchstens schlechte Filme oder solche, die die Grösse und Stärke des Deutschen Reiches vor Augen führen, in Frage kommen. Es werde nowendig sein, dass grosse Lautsprecheranlagen einen gewissen Nachrichtendienst für die Polen vermitteln. Reichsminister Dr. Goebbels sprach sich grundsätzlich in Übereinstimmung mit den Asuführungen des Herrn Generalgouverneurs gegen die Einrichtung eines polnische Theater-, Kino- und Kabarettbetriebes aus. es würden in den grösseren Städten undMärkten stationare Lautsprecheranalgen aufgestellt werden, die zu bestimmten Zeiten Nachrichten über den Stand der lage und Befehlsparolen für die Polen geben." See: *Tagebuch des Herrn Generalgouverneurs für die besetzten polnische Gebiete*, in: Stanisław Piotrowski, *Hans Franks Tagebuch* (Warsaw, PWN 1963), übersetzt von Katja Weintraub, 278.

46 "Einleitend führte Herr Generalgouverneur aus: Den Polen dürfen nur solche Bildungsmöglichkeiten zur Verfügung gestellt werden, die ihnen die Aussichtslosigkeit ihres völkischen Schicksals zeigten. Es könnten daher höchstens schlechte Filme oder solche, die die Grösse und Stärke des Deutschen Reiches vor Augen führen, in Frage kommen. (…) Reichsminister Dr. Goebbels sprach sich grundsätzlich in Übereinstimmung mit den Asuführungen des Herrn Generalgouverneurs gegen die Einrichtung eines polnische Theater-, Kino- und Kabarettbetriebes aus. Es würden in den grösseren Städten und Märkten stationare Lautsprecheranalgen aufgestellt werden, die zu bestimmten Zeiten Nachrichten über den Stand der lage und Befehlsparolen für die Polen geben." Ibid., 254.

"Krakauer Burg" – for his headquarters,[47] where music was to serve important propagandistic roles. This was a typical way of dealing with historic buildings – they were appropriated and transformed into symbols of the new state and new German order. In 1940, Frank, opening the *Institut für Deutsche Ostarbeit* (Institute for German Work in the East) on the premises of the closed Jagiellonian University, stated in his opening speech that "the establishment of the Institute means the resumption of the historical mission that Germanism is to fulfil in this place" and the "restitution of all that which the Poles took away from the German spirit and German influence in this territory."[48]

While in one decree the chief reason for confiscations and sequestrations was the "strengthening of Germanism," another decree issued by Frank stated that confiscation or sequestration could be ordered in connection with the carrying out of tasks "serving the public interest." For instance, private property could be seized because it was "financially unremunerative" or "anti-social." Through this decree, so-called "abandoned property," i.e., property belonging to people who left the country owing to the circumstances of war or had been deported, or simply belonging to Jews, was also seized.[49]

Goebbels strongly believed in the power of the radio as an important intermediary between the idea and the nation;[50] for that reason, he argued that the entire information system of the Poles had to be destroyed; they should have no radio sets and were to be entirely excluded from broadcasting. As far as the film industry was concerned, "Dr. Goebbels with particular joy took note of the fact that Polish movie theatres were already confiscated."[51] It was also stated during

---

47 On 29 October 1939, "Herr Generalgouverneur führte aus (…) Der Wawel in Krakau werde nur mehr die Bezeichnung Krakauer Burg tragen." Ibid., 278.
48 *Law Reports of Trials of War Criminals*, 29.
49 See Bühler's trial's description (Ibid.). Chopin's family portraits of 1829 painted by Ambroży Mieroszewski (1929) are one of many examples of lost paintings. Their reproduction preserved to this day only thanks to Leopold Binental, who published them in his books in the 1930. As his origin was Jewish, his collection was looted while he was still in Warsaw. Thanks to Paderewski he received a Swiss visa, but he was arrested in France and murdered in Auschwitz in 1944. Information on L. Binental was provided to me by Hanna Wróblewska-Strauss, to whom I extend my thanks.
50 He expressed on numerous occasions, cf. his speech *Der Rundfunk als achte Großmacht* [The Radio as the Eight Great Power], published in *Signale der neuen Zeit. 25 ausgewählte Reden von Dr. Joseph Goebbels* (Munich: Zentralverlag der NSDAP, 1934), 197–207.
51 "Reichsminister Dr. Goebbels führe aus, dass das gesamte achrichtenvermittlungswesen der Polen zerschlagen werden müsse. Die Polen dürften keine Rundfunkapparate

the meeting that the nationalism of Poles should be incessantly supervised and that all emerging nationalist aspirations would have to be quickly crushed again.[52] These decisions were immediately implemented in new laws.[53] The mere possession of a radio set by Poles and Jews soon became punishable by death.

Polish culture was targeted as the embodiment of "Polishness" as opposed to the Germanic ideal of "Germanness". In the General Government, which was the area of the concentration of Poles and Jews deported from the Reich-incorporated territories and all those who had lived there before, a special method of dealing with this mass of *Polnische und Jüdische Bevölkerung* had to be devised, so that they would become docile and willing to perform the subservient functions needed by the Reich. The manipulation and reduction of access to culture among other social goods was a method successfully used by the Nazis elsewhere (e.g., racialization and ghettoization of musical activities by creating and maintaining the Jüdisches Kulturbund in Germany). Parallely to these measures, the General Government was covered with a tight network of prisons, ghettos, and different types of camps, which were intended to exert total control and terrorize the non-German population.

---

und nur reine Nachrichtenzeitungen, keinesfalls eine Meinungspresse behalten. Grunsätzlich dürfen sie auch keine Theater, Kinos und Kabaretts bekommen, damit ihnen nicht immer vor Augen geführt werden würde, wa ihnen verloren gegangen sei. (…) Hinsichtlich des Filmwesens nahm Reichsminister Dr. Goebbels mit besonderer Freude davon Kenntnis, dass die polnischen Filmtheater bereits beschlagnahmt seien (…) die Polen seien dagegen ganz vom Rundfunk auszuschliessen." *Tagebuch*, 254.

52 "Man müsse überhaupt immer wieder prüfen, wohin sich der Nationalismus der Polen flüchte. Alle auftauchenden nationalistischen Bestrebungen müssten dann sofort wieder zerschlagen warden." Ibid., 255.

53 For instance, on 10 November 1939, soon before anniversary of Polish Independence Day (celebrated in 1918–1938 on 11 November), Hans Frank ordered to schoot one man out of every house on which a poster evoking 11th November would be found. "Herr Generalgouverneur emfing den Distriktschef Dr. Wächter, der das Ankleben von Hetzplakaten zum 11 November (polnischer Freiheitstag) in einigen Gegenden meldete. Herr Generalgouverneur ordnete an, dass in jedem Haus, in dem ein Plakat angehängt bleibt, ein männlicher Einwohner erschossen wird. Diese Anordnung wird durch den Polizeichef durchgeführt. Ferner ordnete Herr Generalgouverneur an, dass Festgttesdienste aus Anlass des 11. November selbstveständlich verboten bleiben. Distiktschef Dr. Wächter teilte mit, dass in Krakau 120 Geiseln vorsorglich festgenommen worden sind (…)." Ibid., 255.

1.4. Racial segregation and ghettoization

Nazi cultural policy in occupied Poland was in many respects similar to that in the territories incorporated into the Reich. Multidimensional cultural segregation guidelines were introduced. Just as Poles and Jews were not allowed to lead a normal life under the protection of civil law, they were also denied access to normal musical life.

A German "stark pulsierendes Kulturleben" ("strongly pulsating cultural life") – as one of the articles in the *Warschauer Zeitung* in 1941 was titled[54]– was one of the greatest ambitions of the Nazi authorities in occupied Poland, and music was a vital part of it.

In the fall of 1940, during the solemn celebrations of the first anniversary of the General Government proclamation, Hans Frank established a symphony orchestra in Krakow, as well as the Philharmonic of the General Government and the Theater der Stadt Warschau (Theatre of the City of Warsaw in the building of the closed pre-war Teatr Polski – "Polish Theatre"). This cultural institution was intended primarily for Germans, with Polish musicians playing in the orchestra under German conductors. Later, however, it was also directed to the Polish audience, primarily with an operetta repertoire, although symphonic concerts were also gradually introduced.

Frank himself explained his motivations to organize the 'artistic life' of the General Government during a meeting of the district and chief officers of the General Government NSDAP held at the Kings' Hall of the Wawel Castle on March 18, 1942:

> We are still cold-bloodedly continuing the fight to attain our goals. Gentlemen, you see how the state organs work, you see that we do not refrain from anything, and dozens of people are put up against a wall. It is necessary, just because the healthy mind shows that we cannot spare the blood of foreign nations while the best German blood is sacrificed. (…) That is why if any Polish leading forces appear, they should be relentlessly destroyed, and with ruthless energy.
> This should not be publicized; it should happen tacitly. And if we afford the Poles the luxury of attending … philharmonics, which we present to foreign journalists, it doesn't matter at all. People play music according to our wishes, and when they are no longer useful to us, we shall dissolve the institution.[55]

---

54 Title of an article in *Warschauer Zeitung* 1941, No. 260, 3 XI, 4.
55 *Arbeitstagung der Distriktsstandortführer und Amtsleiter des Arbeitsbereiches Generalgouvernement der NSDAP im Königssaal der Burg zu Krakau*, quoted in Piotrowski. It should be added that most important goals of the General Governor were effectuated at this time: "The persecution of the Jews was immediately begun in the General

Polish musicians could not perform in concert halls unless they chose to perform for the Nazis; otherwise, they had the possibility to perform exclusively in cafes or churches.

A report of the Warsaw district chief of September 30, 1941, stated that: "Since no radical solution to the problem of the Polish intelligentsia was carried out, an attempt had to be made to manage the difficulties and the political activity of the artistic circles in ways that enable us to carry out constant surveillance."[56]

A circular entitled *Kulturpolitische Richlinien* (Cultural-Political Guidelines) prepared in 1940 by the GG Propaganda Office forbade to the Poles "all serious plays or operas," "all concerts of high quality" allowing for "some forms of primitive entertainment," "operettas, revues, and light comedies," whereas the music repertoire meant to be played in the cafes also requires authorization on a daily basis and Polish artists can only play for Poles."[57] It was defined in detail:

> 3. Music. Polish musical presentations are to be permitted only if they serve as entertainment. Ones that offer any form of a higher-quality aesthetic experience are forbidden. Within Polish music, marches, national songs, as well as all classical pieces are banned. The music repertoires of the cafes are to be submitted [to the censorsip] for approval.
> 4. Theatre. (…) Performances of serious plays and operas are forbidden to Poles. (…)
> 5. Minor art (in other words: variety shows, revues). All performances representing Polish national traditions [*Volkstum*] are forbidden.[58]

Hans Frank furthermore stated in his instruction in March 1940: "Performances of Polish and German artists together are prohibited (…) As far as Polish artists are concerned, there are no obstacles to lower the level or imbue their

---

Government. The area originally contained from 2,500,000 to 3,500,000 Jews. They were forced into ghettos, subjected to discriminatory laws, deprived of the food necessary to avoid starvation, and finally systematically and brutally exterminated. On 16 December 1941, Frank told the Cabinet of the Governor-General: 'We must annihilate the Jews wherever we find them and wherever it is possible, in order to maintain there the structure of Reich as a whole.' By 25 January 1944, Frank estimated that there were only 100,000 Jews left'. *Law Reports*, Vol. 14, 35.

56 In *Zweijahresbericht des Distriktschefs in Warschau vom 30 IX 1941* it is stated that: "Da keine radikale Lösung des Problems der polnischen Intelligenz durchgeführt wurde, musste versucht werden die schwer kontrollierbare und zweifellos auch politische Tätigkeit der Künstlerkreise in Bahnen zu lenken die uns eine ständige Überwachung ermöglichen." C. Madajczyk, *Inter arma non silent Musae*, 129.

57 *Kultura walcząca*, 66–67.

58 Karol Marian Pospieszalski, *Hitlerowskie 'prawo' okupacyjne w Polsce*, Poznań: Instytut Zachodni, *Documenta Occupationis 5*, 1952.

programmes with erotic feeling. In any event, all performances representing the life of Polish nation are prohibited."[59] Thus, the only kind of music accepted by the German authorities to be played by Polish musicians, were cabaret songs and operetta arias.

It should also be emphasized that musicians lost their sources of income as music critics, teachers at conservatories, conductors, artistic directors, music editors or composers, because all of the institutions they worked for had been shut down. They had to support themselves and their families by any means possible, including attempts to trade on the black market, play in the streets or at funerals, etc.

The Nazi authorities effectively strove to create a debased view of the racially and spiritually inferior conquered population, a vilified image of a subhuman, incapable of higher emotions, devoid of honour, playing for money while his compatriots were being persecuted.[60]

This Machiavellian stratagem, meant to "infringe the status of Polish art,"[61] was immediately recognized by the Polish musicians. Nazi cultural policies set

---

59 See Zofia Polubiec (ed.), *Okupacja i ruch oporu w Dzienniku Hansa Franka 1939-1945* [Occupation and Resistance in Diary of Hans Frank], Vol. I, 1939-1942, trans. from German by Danuta Dąbrowska and Mieczysław Tomala, Warsaw 1970. Cf selected German edition: Werner Präg und Wolfgang Jacobmyer (eds.), *Das Diensttagebuch des deutschen Generalgouverneurs in Polen 1939-1945*, (Stuttgart 1975); second selected edition: Imanuel Geiss und Wolfgang Jacobmeyer (eds.), *Deutsche Politik in Polen 1939-1945: aus dem Diensttagebuch von Hans Frank, Generalgouverneur in Polen* (Opladen 1980).
60 This 'cultural policy' was well described by Richard C. Lukas in *The Forgotten Holocaust. The Poles under German Occupation 1939-1944* (Hippocrene Books, New York 1986, 105): 'German authorities allowed Poles to attend only third-rate theatrical productions, often pornographic in nature. Since the Union of Polish Stage Artists forbade its members to perform in German-controlled theatres, this meant that actors and actresses frequently became singers or gave recitations at coffee houses where people drank ersatz coffee and ate minuscule pastries. From time to time, some Polish actors violated the prohibition and appeared in performances that were propagandistic and anti-Polish; for this, the underground punished these offenders. The Nazis produced an anti-Semitic play, *Quarantine (Kwarantanna)*, which the Poles boycotted; nowhere did this play gain 'either recognition or spectators' among the Polish people."
61 Konstanty Regamey, "Muzyka polska pod okupacją niemiecką" ("Polish Music under German occupation"), *Horyzonty. Miesięcznik poświęcony sprawom kultury. Ilustrowane pismo polskie na emigracji - bezpartyjne i apolityczne* (Horizons. A monthly cultural review. Illustrated Polish Émigrés Review - nonpartisan and unpolitical), Freiburg 1946 (Year I), No. 1, 17.

out in 1940 were perceptively described in the clandestine Polish "Information Bulletin" of January 9, 1941: "Ultimately, Poles should even lose faith in Poland and in themselves. To attain this goal, the press of the General Government is pursuing an unremitting propaganda, which abuses our past, our culture, our national character, stating that Poland owes almost all of its civilization to Germans." On January 30, 1941, the same underground periodical commented:

> The city is divested almost completely of intellectual entertainment. In place of (…) symphonic concerts – we have concerts at the cafes, where it is not allowed to play Chopin, Paderewski, Moniuszko. Absolute uncertainty – as far as the most important goods of a human being are concerned: liberty and life. Every now and then random detentions are made, planned arrests – of individual people or en mass – continue, behind them the spectre of Auschwitz looms more or less distinctly.[62]

1.5. Nazi propaganda towards different social and ethnic groups

Nazi propaganda in Germany, aimed at shaping the minds of Nazis-to-be, managed to de-humanize future victims and to instil in the minds of the perpetrators the image of persecution and extermination as a justified fulfilment of duty. The German propaganda for Germans in the General Government was an extension of such propaganda introduced earlier in the Third Reich. At the same time, a victorious and triumphant image of the German state was demonstrated by numerous cultural events and military music played in the most important venues of the occupied cities.

The second important pillar of this scheme was propaganda destined for conquered societies, the role of which was to justify segregation policies. It consisted, for example, in presenting Jews to non-Jews either as detrimental from a political-economic point of view as adherents, paradoxically, of both Bolshevism and capitalism, or later – as life-threatening as carriers of dangerous diseases (typhus, etc.), to prepare subsequent stages of terror and the Holocaust. It should be noted how conscientiously German propaganda was spread in the "previously Polish territories" (in Nazi terminology, *ehemalige Polnische Gebiete*), where

---

[62] *Biuletyn informacyjny*, 30 January 1941, 3. The anonymous author of the article – as the underground press was cruelly persecuted by the Nazis – stresses also: "All higher schools are closed, as well as scientific institutes, archives, libraries, all secondary schools offering general [not professional] education, condemning professors, scientists and the youth to forced unemployment."

ethnically diverse populations posed a special challenge. Dr. Friedrich Gollert described it very clearly:

> Whereas in the Reich propaganda was applied to those of the same blood, in the General Government the ethnic structure ratios are thoroughly different. Here the propaganda is not only for German people, but it has to be also directed at Poles, Russians, Ukrainians, Jews, and its effect on the mentality within different types of individual ethnic groups must be taken into consideration.[63]

This propaganda was skilfully adapted to different ethnicities in an effort to revivify the prejudices against different ethnic groups in order to isolate them as the de-humanized "other." Consequently, the German press for Poles (e.g. *Nowy Kurier Warszawski*) abounded with various kinds of anti-Semitic propaganda even after the uprising in the ghetto and its subsequent liquidation. It was analysed in the book *Krakow under Enemy Rule*,

> The press was another means of propaganda. No sooner had the Germans made their entry into Krakow than they settled down in the printing works of the *Ilustrowany Kurier Codzienny* and began to publish the *Krakauer Zeitung*. Besides the daily news, this contained political and scientific articles brimming with threats and statements inimical to Poles. They poured forth the most contemptuous abuse on the past and present of Poland, and under the guise of pseudo-scientific theories they spread the most senseless inventions of the German propaganda. Almost at the same time, the *Goniec Krakowski*, issued in Polish, began to appear. From beginning to end it was an instrument of German propaganda, though presented both in Germany and abroad as an organ of the Polish public opinion.[64]

Thirdly, the propaganda directed abroad (both to the Allies and to collaborating countries) secured, under the cover of false reporting, the time necessary for the completion of genocidal policies. The name of the "*Generalgouvernement* for the occupied territories of Poland" is an example of such propaganda. The term was used:

---

63 Gollert, *Warschau über deutscher Herrschaft*, 271. The original reads: "Während sich aber die Propaganda-arbeit im Reich an Menschen gleischen Blutes wendet, liegen die Verhältnisse im Generalgouvernement infolge der volkstumsmässigen Struktur des Gebietes völlig anders. Hier wendet sich die Propaganda nicht nur an deutsche Menschen, sondern sie hat auch auf Polen, Russen, Ukrainer und sogar Juden ihre Wirkung auszuüben, wobei auf die verschiedenartige Mentalität der einzelnen Volksgruppen Rücksicht genommen werden muss."

64 Jan Dąbrowski et al., *Krakow under Enemy Rule* (Krakow: Drukarnia Uniwersytetu Jagiellońskiego, 1946), 6–7.

in the initial stage of the civil government which lasted until July 1940 when France was beaten. Germany was not yet sure of her military success, and kept a shred of Poland, thus termed; "a denomination in which special mention was made of Poland as something that could be an object of possible bargaining at the peace conference. As soon as France was beaten, those in authority in the state, the army and the party gave themselves to the conviction that victory was a certainty, and, what is more, that the end of the war was near. (...) All this was connected with the firm belief that not only those territories which had been directly incorporated in the Reich, would remain permanently under German rule but also the Generalgouvernment. The outward token of this was the elimination from the designation of the "Generalgouvernment" of the phrase "for the occupied territories of Poland." This was proclaimed by [Hans] Frank on July 30, 1940. And so what remained was an indefinite administrative appellation: "Generalgouvernment," with the complete exclusion of any mention whatever of Poland. The Nazi party was to organize the German element operating here as "Führerschicht", i.e. the class called upon to lead the Polish ethnic masses.[65]

---

65 Ibid., 27. Because different names applied to the conquered Polish territories constituted an important element of the Nazi politics and propaganda, a few remarks concerning terminology should be added here. The German administration terminology was often intentionally misleading. One example of this is *Generalgouvernement*, a term denoting certain administrative region of a governorate (*Verwaltungsgebiet eines Gouverneurs*). Its colonial coloring directly referred to the German administrative tradition of governorate from before 1918 when Poland was under partitions, so it did not exist as a state. Indeed, Poland after September 1939 ceased to exist again. Because of this essential difference between Poland and other countries occupied by the Third Reich which kept their status as states, the name "Poland" as such cannot be used to denote these territories between September 1939 and May 1945. Therefore, they should not be erroneously called "Poland" or "General Government Poland," as it has been often seen in the literature – for example to denote the location of death of the victims because these names are historically inaccurate in this context. They falsify the truth, suggesting that Polish state still existed during that time. In fact, the only legal political continuity of the pre-war independent state was the Polish Government in exile which was unable to protect the former citizens of Poland as well as the other victims of the genocide taking place on these territories then. Thus, the original term *Generalgouvernement* or "General Governement" is more appropriate and it should be further specified as Nazi or German just as by analogy the term "occupied Poland" has to be further specified by being supplemented with the name of one of the two occupying states: Germany or Soviet Union. See the mission of Jan Karski and *The Mass Extermination of Jews in German Occupied Poland*, note addressed to the Governments of the United Nations by the Polish government-in-exile on December 10th, 1942, with introduction by Edward Raczyński, published on behalf of the Polish Ministry of Foreign Affair (London – New York – Melbourne: Hutschinson & Co., 1942).

Music was aptly instrumentalized in each of these three pillars of Nazi propaganda, which served to illustrate and justify the ideological goals of the German Nazi authorities of the General Government. It constituted both an important field where these mechanisms were introduced and a tool that served to attain these goals.

1.6. The appropriation of Chopin by the Nazi propaganda

The case of Chopin is the most telling example of both segregation and appropriation, typical of Nazi policies. Chopin's music was not permitted to be played by Poles for Poles in the occupied Polish territories from the very beginning of the occupation. It was banned from the repertoire because it was recognized as a part of Polish cultural identity or "Polish nationalism." The famous expression in which Robert Schumann compared Chopin's music to "cannons buried in flowers," with the intention of highlighting its revolutionary power, was very well known by the Nazi musicologists. Poles were to be detached from that musical energy as well as from the memory of Chopin. In May 1940, Chopin's monument was destroyed in Warsaw's Łazienki park. His music, however, was still allowed to be played *nur für Deutsche* – for Germans only. What makes this image more complicated, though, is the fact that by 1942 and 1943, when the military situation was changing, the Nazi authorities began to use Chopin's figure to manipulate the Polish public opinion (more on that below). But first they had to Germanize the composer.

Just one month after the German invasion of Poland in September 1939, the *Reichsmusikkammer* issued a directive banning the performance of all music by composers from "enemy countries" in German concert halls. Beginning in June 1940, Paderewski's compositions were counted among "undesirable music" (*unerwünschte Musik*) and forbidden in Nazi Germany with the following statement:

> Undesirable music
> Based on the order for the protection of musical cultural property of 29 March 1939, the Reich music inspection authority officially pronounced the following musical works as unwanted and harmful.
> Publication [*Inverlagnahme*], which consists in the sale and performance of these works in the German Reich territories, is forbidden.[66]

---

66 *Die Musik* No. 9 (June 1940), 322–333. presents this somewhat strange list: "Unerwünschte Musik: Auf Grund der Anordnung zum Schutze musikalischen Kulturgutes dem 29. März 1939 hat die Reichs-Musikprüfstelle folgende musikalische Werke

While all of Paderewski's compositions were counted among this exotic mixture of "undesirable music," Chopin's works were surprisingly exempt from this order, and were indeed very often performed in German concert halls.[67] During the 1938–1939 concert season in Berlin, over a half of Chopin's works were performed (93), with many important works – the B-minor Sonata, F-minor *Phantasy*, the Waltz in A-flat, and C sharp minor Scherzo – being played five times each. In the season 1940–1941, 117 of his works were played 331 times (*Preludes Op. 28* four times; the B-minor Sonata eight times). In the season 1941–1942, 125 of Chopin's compositions were performed 476 times, among them the Ballade in A flat, eleven times. In comparison, only 56 of Beethoven's piano works were played 182 times, among them 29 Sonatas, 141 times.[68] One can clearly observe that the tendency to perform Chopin in Berlin was constantly growing between 1938–1942.[69]

How did the propagandists explain the inconsistency between the ban on performing "music of enemy countries" and the permission to perform Chopin? Nazi propaganda claimed that Chopin was a part of Germanic culture and strove to Germanize him by all means. These appropriation methods were somewhat similar to the "musicological analyses" applied by Nazi ideologues to all the great masters. As Michael Meyer observed in his article *The Nazi Musicologist as Myth Maker in the Third Reich*, whereas "Bach embodied German ideals (…). Chopin, the Pole, was largely Germanized and celebrated."[70]

---

für unerwünscht und schädlich erklärt. Die Inverlangnahme, der Vertrieb und die Aufführung dieser Werke ist im deutschen Reichsgebiet verboten: *Träumerei nach Schumann*, bearb. D. Kreuder. *Dann lächelst du* von Frank Filip (…), *Two left feet* von K. Gordon, *Frankie and Johny*, *Conga dans la nuit* von Grenet; *Flüterpropaganda* von S. Schieder, *Sämtlische Werke* von Ignatz Paderewski."

67 The Reichsmusikkammer acceptance to perform Chopin's music in Nazi Germany was issued in October 1939, see: *Amtliche Mitteilungen der Reichsmusikkammer* 6/19 (October 1939), 57–58.
68 *Die Musik* 33 (1942), 392.
69 These statistics are drawn from the subsequent *Die Musik* concert season descriptions: *Die Musik* No. 4 (January 1940), 59 (*Was brachte uns die vorige Spielzeit im Konzertsaal?*; season 1938–1939); No. 12 (September 1941), 423; (season 1940–1941), 1942 (season 1941–1942), 392.
70 Cf. Michael Meyer, "The Nazi Musicologist as Myth Maker in the Third Reich," *Journal of Contemporary History*, Vol. 10, No. 4 (Oct., 1975), 660: "It is interesting that racial determinism was emphasized repeatedly in apparent denial of notions of individual heroism, a problem which did arise in the application of racial nor to native musicians (…) Other difficulties arose: Beethoven's physical characteristics and ancestry suggested racial mixing, in spite of the fact that his music was said to have demonstrated

Nazi musicologists even attempted to simplify their task by including the composers they wished to Germanize into a single German lineage and inventing narratives which would show, for example, the influence of "German" Mozart on "Germanic" Chopin. Kurt Hennemeyer, in the previously quoted article published in the September 1939 issue of *Die Musik*, went so far as to claim that "the Polish people have always recognized and truly appreciated the greatness of the German people, the unrestricted power of the German spirit in its influence on the cultural development of Poland." Thus, the "dying Frederic Chopin," expressing his wish for Mozart to be played in his memory, paid tribute to the "noble people of Germany, to whom he himself and with him the whole of Poland, owed the advancement in all areas of their national life".[71]

Joseph Wulf in his documentation on music during the Third Reich included the article entitled *Kampf um Chopin* (*Battle for Chopin*) published by "Dr. E. K." in "Die Musik-Woche" on October 28, 1939. The author, Dr. Ernst Krienitz opened his text on the the "completely apolitical Pole" with the words:

> Sic transit gloria Poloniae – This is how one could modify a well-known quote and it is no less permissible to translate it freely: "This is how the glory of Poland passes away."
>
> The Eastern campaign is over – completely over. Nothing, absolutely nothing is left of the once so proud, oh so proud Pole, and what concerns us musicians – a man named François Frédéric Chopin died on October 17, 1849, exactly 90 years ago.

---

the essence of Nordic heroism in music (…) Walther Rauschenberger attempted to resolve the conflict by granting that Nordic souls could reside in dark Germans. Analyses of this sort were applied to all the great masters: Bach embodied German ideals (…). Chopin, the Pole, was largely Germanized and celebrated." Erik Levi in his book *Mozart and the Nazis: How the Third Reich Abused a Cultural Icon* (New Haven, London: Yale University Press, 2010) described these questions in depth.

71 Hennemeyer, "Vom deutschen Geist in der polnischen Musik," 286–287. The German original here reads: "Die Einsichtideen des polnischen Volkes – auch sie werden in Polen wieder zu Worte kommen können – haben immer in realem Sinn diese Grösse des deutschen Volkes, die unbregrenzte macht des deutschen Geistes in seinem Einfluss aud die kulturelle Entwicklung Polens, erkannt und gewürdigt. Und wenn der sterbende Frederic Chopins als sein musikalischen Vermächtnis den Wunsch an seine Frende richtete: 'Als Andenken an mich spielt Mozart!', dann entrichtete dieser stolze und zugleich edle Pole noch in seiner Todesstunde einen letzten Gruss und Dank an jenes nicht minder Stolze und gleichermassen edle Volk der Deutschen, dem er und mit ihm das ganze Polen auf allen Gebieten seines völkischen Lebens den Aufstieg verdankten."

The said Chopin, the only Polish musician who entered the Temple of Immortality, does he really represent Polishness?[72]

Krienitz continued in a vein similar to the tone of the articles being published in Nazi press in September 1939. From the Prieberg's documentation we learn that he also "explained Chopin" to the *Wahldeutschen* ("Germans by choice") on October 6, 1943. It was mentioned in the correspondence on Chopin's memorabilia exchanged between Nazi officials – among them Dr. Gustav Abb, the director of the former National Library of Warsaw renamed into Staatsbibliothek Warschau and Dr. Wilhelm Witte – while they were preparing the Chopin exhibition (see Appendix).[73] This exhibition, organized in Krakow in October 1943, was the most distinctive manifestation of the propagandistic appropriation of Chopin as a Germanic composer. It was organized by Nazi musicologists under the guidance of Hans Frank who bought Eduard Ganche's Chopin-related collection from France[74] as another attempt to fit Chopin into the Nazified view of culture.

---

[72] In the original: "Sic transit gloria Poloniae – So könnte man ein allbekanntes Zitat abwandeln und es ist nicht minder erlaubt ist, frei zu übersetzen: 'So ging das ruhmsüchtige Polen dahin.' Der Feldzug im Ostern ist aus – restlos aus. Nichts, rein gar nichts ist übriggeblieben von dem einst so stolzen, ach so stolzen Polen wäre da nicht, und das geht uns Musiker an – ein Mann namens François Frédéric Chopin gestorben übrigens am 17 Oktober 1849, also vor genau 90 Jahren. Besagter Chopin, der einzige polnische Musiker, der in den Tempel der Unsterblichkeit einging, repräsentiert er nun wirklich das Polentum? Der Frage nachzugehen, dürfte sich verloren und wir glaubten, dass es am besten und unter Führung eines Mannes aus unseren Reihen geschehen könne. So suchten wir also Johannes Strauß, den deutschen Chopin-Spieler auf? Was wir erfuhren, ist in zweifacher Hinsicht wichtig, um es hier festzuhalten."

[73] "Krienitz erklärt den Komponisten zum Wahldeutschen 6. Oktober 1943" – this is described in the "Anlage I zum Antwortschreiben von Wilhelm Witte an Gustav Abb, 9/X/43, mit der Liste von Dr. Julian Pulikowski. Quelle: Bibliotek der Universität Wrocław, Signatur: 156/IX, BAP, HV Bibliotheken, St. 1201 No. 25 c. 80. Provenienz: Willem de Vries." Prieberg, *Handbuch*, 884–885.

[74] Dieter Schenk in his *Hans Frank. Hitlers Kronjurist und Generalgouverneur* (Frankfurt am Main, S. Fischer Verlag GmbH, 2006) tried to resolve the extreme disparity between Hans Frank's murdering programme and cultural programme by referring to Harald Welzer diagnose in *Täter* that the Nazis managed to place the Polish intelligentsia destruction and the murder of Jews in the context which absolutized the "Führer's order" and thus the two programmes – the cultural one and the extermination one – did not collide anymore Quotation from Polish translation *Hans Frank. Biografia generalnego gubernatora*, published by Wydawnictwo Znak (Krakow, 2009, 183).

In all official newspapers of the GG, both in German and in Polish, there appeared an article entitled "The Chopin exhibition in Krakow – a monument of German magnanimity." The same title was given to the debunking article in the clandestine Polish *Cultural Review* [Przegląd Spraw Kultury], which unmasked this narrative in November 1943:

> By the end of October, Germans organized in the Jagiellonian Library in Krakow an exhibition of objects related to Chopin. The exhibits taken out of still extant remains of Polish collections in Warsaw and Krakow were gathered as well. Of course exhibits well known in Polish literature and frequently published are called "unknown and unpublished" works of art, the discovery of which – as always in German propaganda – is credited to the pioneering Germans. On the occasion of this event the occupational reptile press widely exalted German generosity, unskilfully disclosing the scheme behind the scenes. Here it is: From "reliable sources" it was recently heard that Chopin qualified as a Volksdeutsch, for his descent on his father's side is related to the German-Alsatian family Schopping. The crown of German reasoning is the assertion, "that nationalistic interpretations of Chopin's music should not delude, because under all ornaments, behind all decorative and constructive elements, lies the kernel of German music."

It is fascinating to observe that almost the same sentences were used in the official German and Polish-language press of the General Government. This also sheds light on the methods of conceiving and organizing the steady flow of propaganda related to such events in all relevant languages.

An article in the *Warschauer Zeitung* on October 28, 1943, entitled *Weitdenkende Kulturplanung im Osten. Die Chopinsammlung in Krakau von Generalgouverneur Dr. Frank der Öffenthlichkeit übergeben. Ein Denkmal deutscher Grosszügigkeit* ("Far-reaching cultural planning in the East. The Chopin Collection in Krakow is being presented to the public by Governor General Dr. Frank. A monument of German generosity"), reads as follows:

> As a figure he has gained significant allure, as we have recently heard from a credible source, that his paternal heritage has possible links to the German-Alsatian family of Schopping. The national aspects of Chopin's music, which are brought to the fore by all musicians and musicologists, ought not to distract from the fact that behind all the ornaments, behind all the decorative, colouring, and structural elements, it is a quintessence of German music, that can ultimately be traced to Chopin's German musical training.
>
> Seine Persönlichkeit gewinnt für uns noch einen besonderen Reiz..., wenn wir kürzlich aus berufenem Munde gehört haben, dass seine Herkunft väterlischerseits möglicherweise mit der deutsch-elsässischen Familie Schopping in Zusammenhang steht. (…) Die nationale Seite der Chopinischen Musik, die von allen Musikern und Musikwissenschaftlern betont wird, darf nicht darüber hinwegtäuschen, dass hinter allen Ornamenten, hinter den dekorativen, kolorierenden und konstruktiven Elementen ein Kern

deutscher Musik steckt, der im letzten Grunde auf Chopins deutsche Musikerziehung zurückgeht.

Thus, by Germanizing Chopin on thoroughly racial grounds, by claiming that his ancestry was "close" to German or almost German while simultaneously defining the "true" essence of his music as purely German, the highest "values" of Nazi ideology – blood and race – were confirmed.

Another example of the propagandistic abuse of Chopin's figure is the story of Chopin's heart during the Warsaw Uprising in 1944. The heart was kept in the church of Holy Cross, located in Warsaw's Old City, where severe clashes between Polish Home Army soldiers and the Wehrmacht were taking place. A priest named Schultze who served in the Wehrmacht suggested that the heart should be removed from the Holy Cross church when fighting during the Uprising intensified. It was thus removed with the approval of Polish priests and saved. This was propagandistically exploited by the SS General Obergruppenführer Erich von dem Bach, who officially handed over the heart to the archbishop Antoni Szlagowski on September 9, 1944; the whole ceremony was filmed. The event was staged during the Warsaw Uprising, in the midst of the mass murder of Polish civilians and the complete, deliberate destruction of the city.

Erich von dem Bach, SS-Obergruppenführer, General of Waffen-SS and Police, responsible for these and several other crimes,[75] gave back to the Polish

---

[75] He was appointed "Commissioner for the Strengthening of Germandom" in Silesia ['Kommissar für die Festigung deutschen Volkstums'] on 7 November 1939. At the beginning of 1940 he brought forth the idea of establishing the concentration camp in Auschwitz for Poles arrested in the 'AB-Aktion', which were sent to the camp in first transport on 14 June 1940. After the attack on the Soviet Union, he was nominated by Himmler General of SS and police and was in charge for the mass killings of Jewish population by the Einsatzgruppen mobile death squads in Vilnius, Grodno, Minsk, Lida, Riga Bialystok, Baranovichi, Mogilev, and Pinsk. The squads were responsible for the mass murder of 35,000 civilians in Riga and more than 200,000 Jewish civilians in Belarus and eastern territories of occupied Poland. In stalag 352 near Minsk over 100 000 Soviet prisoners of war died. 'Actions' in Belarusian villages and towns by von dem Bach and Otto Dirlewanger resulted in 345 000 victims, with only 15 percent belonging to ani-German partisan units. Victims were often burnt alive in barns, sometimes drowned, or sent to minefields. There were probably many more victims, whose disappearance was undocumented. During the Warsaw Uprising units under his command killed approximately 200,000 civilians, using methods he used in Belarus. He was never sentenced for these crimes. See Alexandra Richie, *Warsaw 1944: the fateful uprising*, London: William Collins – an imprint of HarperCollins Publishers, 2013.

clergy the urn with Chopin's heart. On September 9, 1944, he sent two officers to Milanówek near Warsaw to the elderly archbishop Antoni Szlagowski,[76] who was at that time in charge of Warsaw churches and brought him by car in the company of two priests to the Wola district, where a month earlier, between August 5–12, the mass murder of Polish civilians (the toll estimated between 40,000 and 50,000 victims) took place.[77] At the Räumungstab der Zivilverwaltung, occupying Społem cooperative buildings at Wolska street 84, Von dem Bach, the Governor of the Warsaw District Ludwig Fischer, and Deputy Governor Keller were present, with photographers and filming crew. Spotlights filled the room at the first floor; however, at the crucial moment of the ceremony, due to a sudden electric cut, they faded out. As attempts to repair the breakdown were unsuccessful, the relieved archbishop told the priests that this time the Germans would not be able to use the event for their propaganda. One of the high-ranking officers from von dem Bach's staff then presented the urn to the archbishop, saluting him with the Nazi salute and reportedly stating that in this war the Great Reich had always done everything possible to protect from annihilation the most precious cultural goods of universal humanity for future generations, and that the German soldier in the east defended the old Christian culture against extinction and barbarism:[78] "Carrying out the order of the Obergruppenführer and General of Police

---

76 Antoni Szlagowski (1864–1956) was 80 years old by that time. He was Professor and in 1927/8 Rector of the University of Warsaw. He was against the plans of the Warsaw Uprising but did not agree to Germans' request to write a pastoral letter to uprising fighters to lay down their arms nor to write a letter against Soviert Union. On 18 August, he visited Pruszków camp and the managed to obtain consent to free priests and elderly people. He was deported on 4 September to Milanówek where he organized temporary Warsaw Curia.

77 For the description of Wola massacres see Richie. She quotes memories of then eight-month pregnant Wanda Lurie, whose all three children aged 11, 6, and 3,5 years old were killed in shootings on 5 August at Wolska 55 street, whereas she was shot in her neck but survived lying among corpses for three days. She remembered that the German soldier before the killings hit her so that she fell, because she was trying to beg for her and her children lives speaking about officer's honour, and that he hit her oldest son shouting 'faster, faster, you Polish bandit.' After the killings the Germans were robbing corpses (they also took her watch, not noticing that she was alive), drank vodka, singing joyful songs and laughing.

78 According to Richie, ballet, classical music, opera, and cabaret were indeed important to general von dem Bach. In his Minsk time he organized special evenings at Minsk theatre for officers to relax after their daily service, and local artists were even offered more food rations in order to survive (ibid., 51), whereas Otto Dirlewanger, later cruel commander of Polish civilians' killings during the Warsaw Uprising, preferred

von dem Bach, I am handing his Excellency the bishop the urn with the heart of sacred Chopin, preserved by our soldiers." The bishop was then accompanied to Milanówek where the priests hid the urn fearing that this cynical "benevolence" might be temporary.[79]

A different aspect of the Polish musical tradition considered valuable from an aesthetical and, correspondingly, also from a racial point of view, was the Gorale culture from the Podhale region. In the fall of 1939, two Gorals, Henryk Szatkowski and Wacław Krzeptowski, cultivated the idea of a German descent of the Goralenvolk. With the encouragement of Nazi authorities, they created a Goralenverein which replaced the Goral's Association.[80] The Nazis were fascinated by the folklore and the nature of the region. Images of Gorals were omnipresent in the official Polish and German press, their art was presented at exhibitions and their music was performed. At the same time, in November 1939, the Gestapo established their seat ("Der Kommandeur der Sicherheitspolizei und des S. D. im Distrikt Krakau. Grenzpolizeikommissariat") at the "Palace" villa in Zakopane, on Tatra Strasse (which was renamed by the Germans from Chałubińskiego Street). This became one of the worst Gestapo interrogation prisons where several thousand Poles were cruelly tortured and executed, while

---

to organize cruel orgies called "evenings with comrades" (*Kameradenschaftliche Abend*) to gramophone music, especially his favourite song *Alle Tage ist kein Sonntag*, when young women prisoners were raped and often murdered. Ibid., 62. This song was by Carl Clewing who was, just as Dirlewanger, passionate of hunting, and since May 1933 member of NSDAP, SA and SS. He published *Musik und Jägerei* in 1937, in 1938 had a lecture on *Singen und Sprechen* during Reichsmusiktage, in 1939 he composed a *Cantata for the Birth of Edda Göring* and published *Volksausgabe 100 Jägerlieder* and *Liederbuch der Luftwaffe* ed. with Hans Felix Husadel) and in 1941 *Adlerliederheft*. *Feldausgabe des Liederbuches der Luftwaffe*; the last two were put on selected titles (*Liste der auszusondernden Literatur*) for the occupied territories in the East.

79 Events reconstructed by Andrzej Pettyn, *Chopin's Heart* in: Kazimierz Sztarbałło and Michał Wardzyński, (eds.), *Heart of the city: church of the Holy Cross in Warsaw*, trans. Joanna Holzman (Warsaw: Mazowiecka Jednostka Wdrażania Programów Unijnych, 2011), 148–50.

80 A similar attempt was the idea of Kaschobenvolk towards Kashubians. Despite the Nazi authorities' actions, this was unsuccessful and only 2–3% of Kashubians accepted the Kaschobenvolk List. After 1941, they were forced to accept the Volksliste and were forcefully taken into the German army.

others were sent to Auschwitz. The propagandistic and administrative efforts aimed at the appropriation of Gorale culture were ultimately unsuccessful.[81]

Another paradox of this period's politics is that while Chopin monument in Warsaw was destroyed in May 1940, one of the official banknotes (denomination of 10 zlotys) of the GG in 1940 featured this very same Chopin monument. In contrast, the banknote of the highest denomination (500 zlotys) bore the image of a Goral in his traditional dress.[82]

It is important to note that Nazi "logic" suppressed the same cultural heritage because of its relation to Polish national tradition, while simultaneously promoted it whenever the music could have proved useful for Nazi propaganda purposes. This specifically Nazi "musical reception" demonstrates its totalitarian abuses and comes close to the essence of Nazi biopolitical manipulative framework. Chopin's music, in order to be aesthetically valuable, needs to come from an individual that is acceptable from a racial perspective. Once it is proven to be so, it may be exploited for the greater glory of the Third Reich.

---

81 The Goralenverein was fought against by the Polish underground army and Krzeptowski was executed by the AK in January 1945.
82 I would like to extend my thanks to Professor Andrzej Olszewski, who brought this fact to my attention.

Chapter Two: Musical life in the General Government and annexed territories

In September and October 1939, musicians lost not only their rights as Polish citizens, but all their sources of income. They could no longer work as professors at conservatories and universities because they were closed, nor as music critics, because all Polish press was prohibited. Conductors, artistic directors, and philharmonic musicians could not perform anymore because all the philharmonic orchestras and other chamber ensembles as well as all other Polish institutions were liquidated. New compositions could no longer be published nor performed, so no music. The careers of numerous talented composers of popular music ended abruptly as well. The Polish Radio with its orchestras, ensembles, infrastructure, and broadcasting system, all the recording and film industries such as the famous "Syrena Record" company which had flourished in the interwar period, ceased to exist.

The situation in occupied Poland was extremely complex as the administrative status of its different regions and main cities was completely changed after September 1939. Polish territories were divided into three main parts. The Western part was annexed to the Third Reich as the *eingegliederte Ostgebiete*, with four administrative districts, namely the Reichsgau Wartheland (major cities of Poznań and Łódź), Reichsgau Danzig-West Preussen (major cities of Gdańsk and Bydgoszcz), Ost Preussen, and Ober Schlesien (major city Katowice). The central part of Poland, including the cites of Krakow and Warsaw, was transformed into the so-called *Generalgouvernement* under German rule (originally termed *Das Generalgouvernement für die besetzten polnischen Gebiete*, from 31 July 1940 – *Das Generalgouvernement*), whereas the Eastern part came under the jurisdiction of the Soviet Union under the terms of the Molotov-Ribbentrop pact.[1]

In the Reich-incorporated territories it was crucial for the Nazis to relocate Polish and Jewish population to the General Government. People were being thrown out of their houses and workplaces and forced to leave. In consequence, Polish composers from the most important musical centres, such as Poznań

---

1 A precise description of these administrative policies, see chapter 2, *German Culture under the Occupation System in Polish Lands incorporated into the Third Reich in the years 1939–1945* in Grochowina, *Cultural policy*, 75 ff.

(renamed Posen) and Łódź (renamed Lodz, then Litzmannstadt) which then belonged to Warthegau or other Reich provinces, headed for Warsaw or Krakow or hid elsewhere; in some instances they were arrested or interned in camps along with other members of the intelligentsia. The Jewish musicians, if unable to hide, were imprisoned in the ghettos. The official music life was monopolised by the Germans as a means of expanding their *Lebensraum*.

In contrast to the territories annexed to the Reich, musical activity for Poles was allowed in the General Government. Still, Hans Frank confined it to "some forms of primitive entertainment" in the cafes. This was a strategy applied in order to control Polish and Jewish cultural and intellectual milieus. This strategy is confirmed in the NSDAP document of November 1939, entitled *Die Frage der Behandlung der Bevölkerung der ehemaligen polnischen Gebiete nach rassenpolitischen Gesichtspunkten* (The Question of Dealing with the Population of the Former Polish Territory from the Racial-Political Point of View). In its section entitled *Treatment of Poles and Jews in the Remaining [part of] Poland* (that is General Government), the following guidelines are presented:

> Cafes and restaurants, although they were often the meeting points of nationalistic and intellectual circles in Poland, should not be closed, as control over them seems to be easier than over the private gatherings of conspirators, as would necessarily have happened and in which Polish history abounds.

The methods of control delineated in the NSDAP document quoted above were diligently applied. Cafes were closed if they broke censorship rules (as was the case with the Zachęta cafe, where a concert featured Polish compositions), or because at a certain point it was useful for the policy of terror and intimidation exercised by the Nazi authorities. At one of the first cafes, Arkadia, which opened in occupied Warsaw at the end of 1939 in what was left of the Warsaw Philharmonic building (most of which had been destroyed in bombing raids in September, along with the musical scores and instrument collections), and which was the centre of right-wing nationalistic underground activity, everybody present was arrested on December 5, 1940. Some of the cafe's visitors and employees were executed, others were sent to concentration camps. The composer and pianist Henryk Gadomski (1907–1941), although he had nothing to do with the clandestine activities there, was transported to Auschwitz on January 6, 1941, where he perished the same year. His compositions were destroyed during the war.[2]

---

2 He graduated from conducting class at the Warsaw Conservatory in 1931 and then earned his living as a composer of incidental music for several Warsaw theaters. His

2.1 Music in the General Government

In the *Generalgouvernement*, musicians could work but only under certain conditions. It was only allowed after obtaining a registered and renewable permission, the so-called *Erlaubniskarte*, and only having one's concert programme accepted by the Nazi censors. The *Erlaubniskarte* (see Appendix) was just a permission to perform as a musician. Yet another document, a proof of stable employment, was required in case of an inspection and also could be of help in the case of a roundup. That system allowed the Nazi authorities to gain control over the employment in the cafes, all the more so that the papers were "revocable at any time" ("jederzeit widerrufliche"). One such document was granted to Witold Lutosławski in 1940 by "Der Chef des Distrikts Warschau Abteilung für Volksaufklarung und Propaganda" who was signed as Hösl. It was probably Albert Hösl, a German composer, later appointed director of a secondary music school opened by the German authorities in the former building of the Warsaw conservatory.

After the Polish territory was divided and Krakow was established as the political center of the Nazi power over the *Generalgouvernement* (as they termed it), Warsaw became the most important centre of Polish musical activity and resistance. In spite of the terror and various forms of propaganda, the former capital of Poland remained a constant challenge for the German authorities.

On October 2, 1940, the city of Warsaw became divided. By his decree, *SA-Gruppenführer, Der Chef des Distrikts Warschau* (Warsaw District Governor) Dr. Ludwig Fischer, himself an amateur violinist, established a ghetto for those who were considered Jewish by the Nazi authorities. Already in 1939 numerous inhabitants of the city were forced to abandon their houses or flats which were given to German soldiers and civilians coming from the Reich).[3] Since October 1940 the inhabitants had to relocate from one part of the city to another and the three districts: Jewish, German and Polish were to lead separate existences, with different laws established for each of these groups. Waldemar Schön, who held

---

compositions for symphony orchestra were performed at the Polish Radio and Warsaw Philharmonic (*Tryptyk*) and Warsaw Opera House (*Ludowe Tańce*). He was also the author of songs and of music for piano. O.B., *Pamięci Henryka Gadomskiego* (To the Memory of Henryk Gadomski), *Ruch Muzyczny* 1946, No. 20/21, 30.

[3] See Tatiana Berenstein, Artur Eisenbach, Adam Rutkowski (eds.), *Eksterminacja Żydów na ziemiach polskich w okresie okupacji hitlerowskiej: zbiór dokumentów*, [Extermination of Jews on Polish territory during Nazi occupation: collection of documents] (Warsaw: Żydowski Instytut Historyczny, 1957), 95–96.

the post of Leiter der Abteilung Umsiedlung at Warsaw Disctrict Governonor's office, reported on January 20, 1941, on difficulties of this task.[4] Already by the end of 1941, on November 10, another decree followed, designating the death penalty for leaving the ghetto without permission (soon extended to those who helped people of Jewish origin). Thus, the absolute segregation consisted at first in the physical separation of Jews and, subsequently, in their extermination.

At the same time when ghettoization was instituted, malicious anti-Semitic propaganda was omnipresent in newspapers for Poles, posters, exhibitions, etc. Its guidelines were described by Dr. Friedrich Gollert, who had the function of "Persönlicher Referent des Chefs des Amtes und Leiter des Amtes für Raumordnung" and was the author of *Warschau unter deutsche Herrschaft* ("Warsaw under German rule," see Appendix), published in Krakow in 1942 on commission of Ludwig Fischer:

> There were several major actions undertaken to inform the whole population, among them "the anti-typhus campaign," the anti-Jewish Action" and "the V-action," with the aim of informing the public about the important things.

He also devoted a chapter on "the need for constituting a separate quarter for the Jews," who, he claimed, had lived in Warsaw in undescribably unhygienic conditions and were responsible for spreading infectious diseases such as abdominal typhus and dysentery. Thus, the establishment of the Jewish ghetto was justified by the argument, that only in this way German Wehrmacht soldiers and officers, as well as the Polish population, could be protected against major epidemics. Other arguments included the conviction that Jews must be confined to a separate space, or otherwise legislative measures adopted in order to resist the influence of Jews on cultural life and the economy would be ineffective. He added that after the implication of the measures and the resettlement of some 700 ethnic Germans, 113,000 Poles and 138,000 Jews, the "Jewish Wohnbezirk in Warsaw is a closed district, the area is closed off by walls, fences and the like

---

4 "Es war klar, dass dieser Gedanke bei den besonders gelagerten und äusserst komplizierten Verhältnissen der Stadt Warschau zunächst als undurchführbar anmuten müsste. Einwände wurden von verschiedenen Seiten, insbesondere von der Stadtverwaltung geltend gemacht (…). In ganzen gesehen wurde eine Umgruppierung von 113.000 Polen und 138.000 Juden bewältigt. (…) Die jüdische Wohnbezirk ist etwa 403 ha gross. Auf diesem Gebiet wohnen nach Angaben des Judenrates, der eine Volkszählung vorgenommen haben will, etwa 410.000 Juden, nach unseren Beobachtungen und Schätzungen, die von verschiedenen Seiten vorgenommen wurden, etwa 470–590.000 Juden." Ibid., 99–103.

against the surroundings, where people and goods are allowed only with special permission."[5]

Also in fall 1940, by the time the "Jewish residential district" was established in Warsaw, Hans Frank organized in Krakow the "Orchestra of the General Government," in order to celebrate the first anniversary of the General Governement's proclamation. Dr. Hanns Rohr was appointed as the orchestra's conductor, while Rudolf Erb was his deputy. Both came from Munich. The first solemn concert was advertised with Beethoven death-mask on the poster. An analogous ceremony advertised by analogous poster took place in Warsaw, at the Theater der Stadt Warschau (Theatre of the City of Warsaw), newly established in the building of the former Teatr Polski (see Appendix). The orchestras were formed of Polish musicians. *Nowy Kurier Warszawski* informed of the General Governement Philharmonic opening in a big article titled "Late fall in Krakow" (Późna jesień w Krakowie), adorned with a photograph. It proudly announced that concerts were held for the German and Polish audiences separately and combined it with information on other ceremonies organized for the occasion of the first anniversary of the General Government, during which "not even one Jew could be seen."[6]

These ways of limiting and segregating access to music are important as examples of countless violations of human rights. That is why the examination the repertoire itself is not a sufficient tool in dealing with this disastrous chapter in European history of music. These data have to be confronted not only with testimonies but also with other sources, such as the official German documents and jurisdiction.

Nazi musical policies, even if considered only with reference to the rebellious city of Warsaw, remain a complex issue for two reasons: first – because of the constant changes in policy of the Abteilung für Volksaufklärung und Propaganda according to their needs to manipulate the public opinion at different stages of the war, and secondly – because the city was divided by the Germans into three main separated areas with different laws and different rights regarding the access to music. Thus, music censorship guidelines, being an integral part of this policy, cannot be discussed separately from this context. Just as the population was segregated, the propaganda measures were applied accordingly – among others through specially designed press, destined at all the three groups, which was

---

5 Gollert, *Warschau unter deutscher Herrschaft*.
6 [Pikador], *Późna jesień w Krakowie* [*Late fall in Krakow*], NKW 1940, No. 258 of 2–3 November.

represented by the three main newspapers: *Warschauer (or Krakauer) Zeitung* for Germans, *Nowy Kurier Warszawski* for Poles, and *Gazeta Żydowska* for Jews. This official press, called "reptile" by the Polish public, brings information about the extremely varied landscape of venues where music was performed. However, several facts should be considered in the interpretation of this source.

First of all, the official press, was one of the most important tools of Nazi propaganda and the information included there should be read as such. This was already perceptively analysed by the clandestine press. In the most important underground biweekly *Biuletyn Informacyjny* of January 9, 1941, it is described as follows on page 1:

> The name of "reptile press" is given to newspaper-reptiles, which treacherously vest themselves in the skin of Polish language, to poison with their venomous content the organism of the Polish nation. The language used in these reviews is Polish, but the brain and hand which directs it is German. Its goal is the work for <u>Germany</u>. The biggest reptile newspaper of the "Government" is *Nowy Kurier Warszawski* (daily sales of over 150.000 copies, on holidays and Sundays – ca. 300.000). The monthly revenue of this daily amounts to over 300.000 zlotys). (…) All the enumerated reviews are not private property, but are created, directed and financed by special publishing institutions brought into being by the Propaganda Office of the General Government in Krakow. As a result, their considerable income goes directly to this German Propaganda Office. Conclusion: whoever buys reptile newspapers is by the same token financing German propaganda and absorbs a certain dose of propagandistic poison. And however healthy is the organism and the poison dose small – yet its systematic dosing must implicate a result. The scarcity of space does not allow us to present other interesting methods of the Nazi propaganda, which is able to make use of a seemingly quite innocent novel, an "impartially" written article and even of a photograph of the Polish army.

On the other hand, any involvement in, or even possession of, such clandestine publications as the *Biuletyn Informacyjny* which were the only source of exact information, was most cruelly persecuted by the Nazi authorities. *Biuletyn Informacyjny* delivered exact news from the front, informed the society about the tragedy of the Jewish population, about the death penalties for the denouncing of Jews, about the terror and extermination policies in different places of former Poland, about the losses to Polish science, culture, art etc. – it covered all the topics that were vital despite absent in the official propagandistic press. Thus, when such a clandestine publication was found, it resulted in investigation and tortures of its possessor. As in the case of those involved in the clandestine universities and schools, these people were sent concentration camps or executed. For the German Nazis, these methods were justifiable – due to the influence of the propaganda and the mind control, so crucial for the Nazi rule.

However, analyzing the content of the propagandistic *Nowy Kurier Warszawski* (*New Warsaw Courier*, NKW), whose "target-group" was the "Polnische Bevölkerung", makes it possible to find out what kind of music was officially allowed to be played by Poles for Poles. Because musicians, in order to earn their living, could play only in the cafes, their concerts had to be advertised somehow. There were two main forms of such advertisement – in propagandistic press addressed specifically to each of the *Bevölkerung* groups and in the form of posters. This is why this press constitutes a useful source; however, it needs to be considered that all the photographic and other "journalistic" material contained there represents pure propaganda.

The musicians who had no other source of income and had the required performance abilities, were forced to play at the cafes, even if they were eminent composers. Their new, original work, except for piano or chamber pieces, could not be performed, especially in the first year of the Nazi occupation. However, composers were most often pianists as well and they often performed as such. The piano duo offered quite a lot of colouristic possibilities to them. It was also very attractive for the cafés audiences consisting of music lovers who suffered from the lack of orchestral music. Among the two most famous musical phenomena present on both sides of the Ghetto wall in Warsaw there was the duo one formed by Witold Lutosławski and his fellow composer Andrzej Panufnik and – the one of Lutosławski's friend, Władysław Szpilman and Adolf Goldfeder, a lawyer who fought in the 1920 anti-Soviet war. Władysław Szpilman composed his Gershwinesque *Concertino* for piano and orchestra yet in 1940 (he managed to reconstruct from memory after the war). His *Mazurka*, composed later in the ghetto, remains a touching symbol of Szpilman's Chopinesque lineage, of his intelligence and sense of humour, which are all encapsulated in its allusive anti-censorship formula.

Lutosławski – after having returned to Warsaw from the front – was invited by the members of Chór Dana (Dan's Choir) to work as their musical director. This ensemble, founded in 1928 by Władysław Daniłowski and extremely popular in Poland in the 1930s, was modelled after the famous American quintet, "The Revelers." Lutosławski directed the ensemble, worked as accompanist and arranger. As he said in an interview given to the Warsaw Musical Society in 1980:

> At the beginning, searching to find an income, I worked with the Chór Dana. Because Daniłowski was abroad, one of the choir members, I don't know which one, turned to me with the proposition to direct this choir. I was also to arrange for the ensemble different settings of various pieces and to accompany during their performances. They took place at the "Ziemiańska" cafe and lasted a few months. Then I also performed at a few

other cafes – I don't remember which anymore – with this ensemble and a few soloists from former Warsaw revue theatres.

The most elaborate programme was performed at the "Lardelli" cafe, where a substantial orchestra (of ca. 60 musicians) was conducted by the collaborator Adam Dołżycki and where also Germans used to come. Some of the musicians (among them the soloists) probably did not consider it morally wrong to perform with him at the beginning, as Dołżycki, a man of Ukrainian origin married to a German woman, was a well-known conductor (mainly at the Warsaw Opera house) before the war. His connections with the Nazis became apparent only gradually. He signed the Ukrainian *Volksliste*. Clandestine organizations advised the soloists not to play in "Lardelli". Exceptions were made for those who were endangered and had no choice because of their Jewish origin, such as the famous singer Ada Sari, or others whose Jewish wife, husband or friend needed protection. (The same is true of those who performed in the other theatres, especially in the most important of them, Theater der Stadt Warschau, the Theatre of the City of Warsaw). Some testimonies offer evidence that Dołżycki forced fellow musicians to perform for the Germans. The reptile *Nowy Kurier Warszawski* advertised his concerts ("If one speaks about the Warsaw symphonic season, one thinks of the Lardelli."), whereas the underground *Biuletyn Informacyjny* of October 30, 1941, was advising the Polish public to boycott the concerts there.

For a certain time, there existed another chamber orchestra, albeit a smaller one, created by Zygmunt Latoszewski, which performed at the cafe "Gastronomia", as well as several other ensembles. The *Nowy Kurier Warszawski* published advertisements and even reviews of some of these artistic events, as always interspersed with propaganda. In No. 37 Dołżycki was advertised conducting Skriabin's *Symphony No. 2*, Schumann, Tchaikovsky, Puccini, Bach, Beethoven, Gluck, Mozart, and Paganini. In No. 43, a review of Latoszewski's concert at "Gastronomia" was placed next to an article entitled *Do not sell anything to Jews*. The programme included Bach's *Toccata and Fugue in d minor* orchestrated by Jerzy [sic[7]] Padlewski, Grieg's *Holberg's Suite Elegy*, *Burlesque* from Tchaikovsky's *Serenade Op. 48*, *Waltz* from Richard Stauss' *Rosenkavalier*, and Johann Strauss' *Waltzer*. Zofia Fedyczkowa performed with the orchestra *Hymn to the sun* from *The Golden Cockerel* of Rimsky-Korsakov, an aria from Mozart's *Entführung im Serail*, and *Waltz Caton* from opera *Casanova* by Ludomir Różycki.

---

7   It was Roman Padlewski, Jerzy's brother who was the author of the orchestration. Both brothers became victims of the Nazis.

A review of a concert at Lardelli's in No. 49 described a repertoire including Bach, Brahms, Mozart, Gluck, Paganini, Haydn, Mozart, Beethoven, Rimsky-Korsakov's *Scheherazade*, and fragments from operas *Rigoletto, Ballo di maschere, Madama Butterfly, Carmen* and Catalani's *Wally*. Józef Śmidowicz played there one of the Brahms *Piano Concertos*. The author [A. P.] states that "It should be recognized that the programmes at Lardelli's are gradually prepared in a more diligent way, and one should mention that a proper, good programme is difficult to realize nowadays because of the fire which destroyed the Philharmonic and Opera House libraries". In Nos. 53–58, the anti-Semitic propaganda became more intense and aggressive and there are no mentions of performances of serious repertory and for almost two weeks no information about the cafes (except for the night-club "Adria" advertisement in No. 63). On March 10, 1941, an explanation can be found in No. 58 in the first-page article entitled *How did Igo Sym die?*

After this actor, an important Nazi collaborator and Gestapo agent, appointed director of the Theater der Stadt Warschau by the German Propaganda Abteilung, was killed on the orders of an underground court, the cafes were closed for two weeks, ca. 180 people were arrested, twenty of them were executed, and famous theatre directors Stefan Jaracz and Leon Schiller as well as actors were sent to Auschwitz. *Biuletyn Informacyjny* of March 13 notes "the incommensurability between a killing of an actor, German agent, and the force of repressions" and brings an explanation that the affair served as a pretext to the authorities: "What is going on there? To answer this question, one should know that at a governors' briefing in the first days of January Fischer was reprimanded by Frank for the fact that the Warsaw district is the least controlled of all in the General Government. Fischer was cautioned among other matters to liquidate the Warsaw clandestine press within a month, and this is what he strived to achieve in the well-known January arrests."

NKW's No. 77 of 1 April 1941 brings news of the première of Lehar's operetta *Gipsy Love* at the Theatre of the City of Warsaw. In turn, No. 98 of April 27, 1941, features an article taken from the German press entitled *Obrazki z Warszawy* (*Images from Warsaw*, in a series *What do others write?*) in a mocking and threatening tone depicting the "degenerated" Polish intelligentsia in the cafes. Two days later a review discussed the recent musical repertoire in Warsaw:

> Dołżycki plays a lot of suites, that is, a musical form which is extraordinarily adequate for our times. We have lately heard Grieg's *Peer Gynt*, Spendiarov's *Crimean Sketches*, Bizet's *L'Arlésienne, Scènes pittoresques* and *Scènes Napolitanes* of Massenet, then the original suite *Hary Janos* of the talented Hungarian Kodály, full of grotesque thematic and instrumental ideas (…). The Friday all-Tchaikovsky concert featured the ever-fascinating

Piano Concerto played by Żurawlew (...). One of the most attractive events of this week was the Tuesday recital by Professor J. Śmidowicz at the "Art House" [Dom Sztuki], led by Professor Woytowicz and promoting in an uncompromising way the chamber music of the purest form (...). Among other pieces Schumann's *Symphonic Studies* was played.[8]

In No. 104, a concert of the General Governement's Philharmonic Orchestra (in Krakow) was announced on p. 3: Dvorak's *Cello Concerto* (young Józef Mikulski), *Overture* to Weber's *Oberon*, the *Romantic Suite* by the ardent Nazi Carl Ehrenberg, "contemporary composer, professor of composition and conducting master class at the Academy of Music in München", and Tchaikowsky's *Italian Capriccio*. On 4 May – a concert of the Ukrainian National Choir of the General Governement Orchestra at the Conservatory Hall. Also, in May (No. 112, 14 May 1941), in the article entitled "From cafes' stages. Concerts," we read about Ada Sari singing Rossini, Bellini, Donizetti, Verdi, Rachmaninov's *Georgian Song*, *The Rose* and *The Nightingale* of Rimsky-Korsakov, Reger's *Lullaby*, R. Strauss's *Serenade*, pieces by the Polish composer B. Wallek-Walewski, J. Strauss's waltzes, arias from the operas *Adrianna Lecouvreur* and *Mirella* by Gounod, *Mignon* by Thomas and Donizetti's *Linda*. We can observe that the Russian repertoire forbidden by the censor in the Spring of 1941 was still officially reported in the press. By the end of May, a Polish composition (Noskowski's *Step*) appears at Lardelli's alongside Smetana's *Vltava* and pieces by Wagner, Schumann, Tchaikowsky, Brahms, Beethoven, Schubert, Schumann, Rachmaninov, and Liszt.[9] Also in May, some Polish repertoire seems to have been performed at Bolesław Woytowicz's café, among others – Szymanowski's *String Quartet No. 1* and Jan Ekier's *Quartet*.[10]

Music institutions such as the GG Philharmonic and Theater der Stadt Warschau were meant to display the power and glory of the Nazi state and to testify to the superiority of German culture. Symphonic concerts were originally intended and advertised as concerts "for Germans only." The public was also entertained with light operettas, musical comedies by such authors popular with the Nazis as Ralph Bernatzky and ballets. Because German authorities considered it a powerful propagandistic tool, repertoires for Polish audiences were also prepared according to the guidelines of the time. In Warsaw, only operetta and comedy repertoire was accessible to Poles until 1942. In September of this year,

---

8   NKW 1941, No. 100, 29 IV, 3, 'Z kawiarnianej estrady' (From the cafe stage).
9   [A. S.] 'Z estrady. Koncerty,' NKW 1941, No. 127, 30 May, 3.
10 NKW 1941, No. 132, 6 June. A more complete image of these cafe scenes, even restricted to 1941, is beyond the scope of this article and will be presented in a broader study.

however, symphonic concert matinées were introduced at the Theatre of the City of Warsaw for Polish audiences. They were conducted by the collaborationist Adam Dołżycki, who earlier gave symphonic concerts at the Lardelli cafe.

The reasons of the changes in Nazi politics toward Poles and in their music censorship guidelines were strictly linked with the increasingly difficult military situation of the Third Reich after Operation Barbarossa. Music was a particularly sensitive domain in which these changes were evident, as it was conceived as a perfect tool for the manipulation of the public opinion and was organized by the Propaganda Abteilung. With the invasion of the Soviet Union in June 1941, despite the intensification of the unremitting terror,[11] a distinct shift in Nazi cultural policies in the GG can be observed. In fact, Nazi "cultural policy" was nothing more and nothing less than one of propaganda tools. Thus, changes in the permissible repertoire followed, or sometimes anticipated, changes on the fronts and the configurations of the Third Reich's allies and enemies.

The marketing of German benevolence toward Polish culture in the propagandistic press for Poles went hand in hand with the aggressive anti-Semitic and anti-Soviet propaganda. Already in 1941, the performance of some Polish music was permitted in Krakow. In 1942, the ban to play Chopin was not only lifted, but Nazi authorities encouraged collaborationists and exerted pressure on other Polish musicians to perform this previously forbidden music. Characteristically, this repertoire was not played at non-collaborationist cafes.

The first of the symphonic concerts for Polish audiences at the *Theater der Stadt Warschau* (named in Polish "Teatr Miasta Warszawy"), with Mozart's Symphony in E flat major, Chopin's E minor Concerto and Schubert's *Unfinished Symphony*, took place on September 20, 1942. The concert is described in review entitled "Pierwszy koncert symfoniczny" (First Symphonic Concert) in the series *From the Theatre of Warsaw City* (Nowy Kurier Warszawski 1942, No. 224 of 22 September, 3). An author hidden under pseudonym "Sympleks" wrote in the typical kitschy style of this newspaper: "A recollection of the times when life revolved quietly and blissfully, as wheels of a beautiful porcelain clock, was brought to listeners with the smoothness and volatility of this Symphony."[12]

---

11 'The order of 2 October 1943 concerning the "combating of attempts against the German work of reconstruction" permitted all: executions, tortures, plunder, as it was punished only by death or deportation to concentration camps'. (*Law Reports of Trials and War Criminals*, 28).
12 *Nowy Kurier Warszawski* 1942, No. 224 of 22 September, 3).

By 1940 Poles were forbidden to perform music by Jewish authors. All the cafe programmes, lyrics of songs and arias had to be submitted to the censor in German translation. This can be observed in a preserved programme (discovered in a private collection) of February 1941, which belonged to the singer Zofia Zeyland-Kapuścińska, with annotations by a Nazi censor from the Abteilung für Volksaufklärung und Propaganda residing with other German authorities in the Brühl palace. It provides evidence which allows us to evaluate what repertoire was banned by the Nazi regime at that time in Warsaw.[13]

On the front page we read that it is approved by the censor and see the following "remark": "It should be noted that only compositions approved in this programme can be performed. As a matter of principle, any Jewish compositions in Aryan enterprises should basically be removed."[14]

There are also stamps of the office: on the top the number (814) given to this document, below the date (February 8, 1941), and the stamp "GENEHMIGT [approved]. Der Chef des Distrikts Warschau. Abteilung für Volksaufklärung und Propaganda, Warschau", with a handwritten date (6/3 41) and an illegible signature or number. It means that it took almost a month before the programme was "corrected" by the censor. This page, covered with numerous brown-reddish stains, is signed at the bottom by the singer, "zur Kenntnis genommen" ("I accept the above conditions").

The table of contents is divided into "Opern-arien", "Lieder italienisch gesungen" and "Lieder polnisch gesungen". From 12 enumerated operas, all the Puccini repertoire was left by the censor, as well as the arias by Gounod, Mascagni, Strauss and Catalani, whereas both Wagner arias (from *Lohengrin* and *Tannhäuser*) were crossed out. Not surprisingly, all seven lighter lieder sung in Italian, such as *Torna Amore*, *Mal D'Amore* and *Lolita* by Buzzi Peccia, *La Folleta* by S.

---

13 My warmest thanks go to the owners of this document, Bożena and Jacek Wójcik, who kindly gave their permission to publish it, when I discovered it by case in their collection of scores. Biographical details of this singer are unavailable. I published these findings in the article 'Nazi Censorship in Music: Warsaw 1941,' in Erik Levi (ed.), *The Impact of Nazism on Twentieth Century Music* (Vienna: Boehlau Verlag 2014), 151–173.

14 "Zur Veröffentlichung zugelassen. Auf Grund dieses Programms, ist der Geschäftsunternehmer verpflichtet, eine Benachrichtung über die Aufführung dieses Programms in sinem Lokal zu übersenden." Below, a "Vermerk": "Es wird darauf hingewiesen, das nur in diesem Programm genehmigten Kompositionen zur Auffürhung gebracht werden dürfen. Jüdische Kompositionen fallen in arischen Unternehmungen grundsätzlich fort".

Marchesi and *Stornellatrice* by Respighi, as well as the *Serenata* by E. Toselli and *Estrellita* by M. Ponce were accepted.

All the songs sung in Polish, with their German translations provided, were analyzed in depth by the censor. Those referring to love were accepted, both by German composers, such as Carl Bohm's (1844–1920) *Still wie die Nacht* (*Cicha jak noc*), and Polish ones: Witold Friemann's (1889–1977) *Cudne oczy* (*Wunderschöne Augen*), Jan Gall's (1856–1912) *Serenade*, Napoleon Rutkowski's (1868–1931) *Mów do mnie jeszcze* (*Sprich noch zu mir*, to a poem by the famous Polish author Kazimierz Przerwa-Tetmajer), *Są takie chwile* (*Es gibt Augenblicke*) by Aleksander Wielhorski,[15] *Boston* by Władysław Walentynowicz,[16] *Casanova* and the infantile *Laleczki moje* (*Meine Püppchen*) by Ludomir Różycki (1883–1953), as well as the light-hearted *Karuzel* (*Das Karussel*) by Stanisław Nawrocki (1894–1950, student of Paderewski),[17] and such popular songs as *Kochaj a cały świat jest mój* (*Lieb mich und die Welt ist mein*) by Ernest R. Ball[18] and *Wiosna* (*Der Frühling*) by Charles Gounod. Both *Ständchen* by Schubert and *Traum durch die Dämmerung* by R. Strauss, referring to corporeal love, were left by the censor, whereas *Morgen* by the latter was crossed out. This leads one to speculate as to whether the reasons for this were due to the artistic level of this song and its importance for German culture (just as Wagner was not allowed for the *Untermenschen*) or because of its optimistic vision and hope contained in the words "this earth again breathing with sun"?

---

15 Born in 1890, this Chopinist and composer, was active during the war as pianist in cafes and at clandestine concerts and as pedagogue. He was arrested and although he was among the hostages that were to be executed by the Nazis, he survived. He died in 1952. Most of his compositions were burnt in the Warsaw Uprising. Cf. Stanisław Dybowski, *Słownik pianistów polskich* (Warsaw: Selene, 2003), 727.
16 Born in 1902 in Yaransk in Russia, he died in 1999 in Sopot in Poland, pianist, composer, music critic and pedagogue; he played popular music in the cafes during the war (Cafe Club, Kolorowa, Złoty Ul). His pieces for the radio trio composed of Rachoń, Hoherman and Szpilman and other works were lost during the war. Ibid., 712–714.
17 The titles are quoted here in their Polish and German versions, as in the original source. Most of the Polish composers in this list (except for Różycki) were known mainly for their song repertoire and were after the war largely forgotten, e.g. Polish conductor and composer Jan Karol Gall (1856 Warsaw – 1912 Lvov) or Witold Friemann (1889 Konin – Laski near Warsaw 1977), conductor, pianist, composer, and pedagogue, who worked in the Polish Radio in Warsaw before the war and took part in clandestine concerts during the war.
18 The Polish title means: *Love Me, and the Whole World is Mine*.

All of the numerous songs by Grieg (Łabędź / Ein Schwann, Pierwiosnek / Mit einer Primula veris, Pierwsze spotkanie / Erstes begegnen, Sen / Ein Traum, Na łodzi / Im Kahne, Małgorzatka / Margaretlein, Kocham Cię / Ich liebe dich) were accepted by the censor, while the entire Russian repertoire was rejected. Were such guidelines introduced because Operation Barbarossa was soon to commence? The Nazi attack on the Sviet Union was originally planned for May 1941, so not surprisingly the Propaganda Office might have found it inappropriate for Russian music to be played as the *Kampf gegen Bolschevismus* was about to be waged. It was probably for this reason that such repertoire was banned, the more so since the texts were quite innocent as exemplified in Grechaninov's *Kołysanka* (Wiegenlied), Rachmaninov's *Bzy* (Flieder), Nikolai Tcherepnin's *Ciebie bym ucałowała* (Einen Kuss möcht ich dir geben), although one could argue that Tchaikovsky's *Ten kto tęsknotę zna* (Nur wer die Sehnsucht kennt) and Grechaninov's *Na pola złote* (*Auf Felder goldig gelb*), evoking longing and suffering, even if again linked to love, could have sounded a little less innocent from the lips of a Polish artist. On the other hand, the same theme of longing and, in this case, typically Polish "żal" ("das Leid"), although caused by the death of the beloved, constituted perhaps the reason for rejecting Herman Bemberg's *Indisches Lied*.[19] Or was it rather because the composer was French despite his parents being of German-Argentinian origin?

Of all these interventions of the Nazi censor, one is tragically telling. It concerns a waltz that was extremely popular before and after the war, entitled *François*, composed by Adam Karasiński in 1907, popularized by Tola Mankiewiczówna and Mieczysław Fogg with lyrics written in 1934 by Andrzej Włast.[20] And it is precisely the name of this poet, librettist, author of over 2000

---

19 H. Bemberg (ca. 1861, Buenos Aires or Paris – 1931 Berne) studied under Massenet. His music was influenced by Massent and Gounod and his output consisted of songs and piano repertoire, cantatas and operas.

20 It was the composer's son, Zygmunt Karasiński (born on 2 May 1898 in Warsaw, left Poland in 1968 due to the anti-Semitic campaign of the Communist regime and died on 20 June 1973 in Copenhagen), who arranged this song in this new version and is often quoted as its author. He also created most of the famous Polish songs of the inter-war period with Andrzej Włast's words. Zygmunt Karasiński, violinist, pianist, clarinettist, saxophonist, composer, and arranger studied with his father, then violin with Jerzy Jarzębski at the Warsaw Conservatory. He accompanied silent films, then played in the first Polish jazz band (with Szymon Kataszek, Jerzy Petersburski, piano, Sam Salwano, percussion). In Warsaw, Karasiński and Kataszek's Jazz Tango was one of the most popular dance orchestras. In 1941, he founded in Białystok the ensemble

lyrics that prompted the censor to reject the whole song since he was perfectly aware that Włast (orig. Gustaw Baumritter, born March 17, 1895 in Łódź) was of Jewish origin. Neither the waltz *François* nor its author were able to slip through the net. Around the beginning of 1943 the poet's friends attempted to take him out of the Warsaw ghetto, but at the sight of the guards, he panicked, started running away and was shot.[21]

His text for the song which was not permitted to be performed in spring 1941 in Warsaw is an evocation of the charming past. Although it was written before the war, the old waltz could serve in fact as a nostalgic symbol of the popular Polish song repertoire history ("Among old scores of grandma / This waltz was preserved / I recollect this soirée at her place / I see it in my dreams. / Musicians at the piano / Visitors all around," and the expression of the poet's wish in its refrain: "If only once / That time returned / If the hearts of evil men / were awaken by charm of the old waltz *François* ").[22]

The censor's choices offer immediate evidence that there was a strict application of several different categories: political (Russian music banned, although as we shall see below, this is contradicted by other sources), purely ideological, based on the belief of the supremacy of great German art (Wagner not for Poles) and racist (compositions by authors of Jewish origin cannot be performed by Poles). Furthermore, any repertory which was related to nostalgia, grief, the past and hope for a brighter future was off limits for the Poles. On the other hand, we can observe how the censor followed the guidelines of a confidential circular sent in 1940 by the Department of Education and Propaganda of the General Gouvernement, which allowed the Poles some forms of primitive entertainment[23] and of the General Governor himself ("as far as Polish artists are concerned, there are no obstacles to lower the level or imbue their programmes

---

Białoruski Jazz (Belorussian Jazz) and played in a revia-jazz group in Lvov. After the war he worked for the Polish Radio as a composer and arranger.

21 Among his most famous songs are: *Całuję twoją dłoń, madame* (I am kissing your hand, Madame*)*, *Ja się boję sama spać* (I fear to sleep alone*)*, *Rebeka*, *Tango Milonga*, *Titina*, *Warszawo ma* (My Warsaw), *Zapomnisz o mnie* (You will forget me), *Już nigdy* (Nevermore), *Ostatnie tango* (Last Tango). After Dariusz Michalski, *Powróćmy jak za dawnych lat... Historia polskiej muzyki rozrywkowej w latach 1900–1939* (Warsaw: Iskry, 2007).
22 "W starych nutach babuni / Walc przechował się ten, / Pomnę wieczorek u niej, Widzę go jak przez sen. Grajek przy fortepianie, Goście snują się w krąg"; "Gdyby jeszcze raz / Wrócił tamten czas, / Gdyby zbudził serca złych ludzi / Czar modnego walca *François*."
23 See Lachowicz, *Muzyka w okupowanym Krakowie*, 12–13.

with erotic feeling. Nonetheless, all performances representing the life of the Polish nation are prohibited").[24]

How could the censor know so well who was who and what was to be banned? It is interesting to note that at least for a certain period there was no "imported" German censor of music in Warsaw, as it was probably required of such an official to understand all the subtleties and have a good command of Polish. Here is a passage from a testimony of the singer Janina Godlewska, who was tasked with contacting the censor by the Polish charity organization Rada Główna Opiekuńcza (Main Care Council) and by one of the most important music cafes SiM, "Sztuka i Moda" ("Art and Fashion", where Panufnik and Lutosławski, among others, performed):

> This task was given to me, since the censor residing at the Brühl Palace, whose name was Bartz-Borodin, knew me from the time before the war (we performed together at SiM). When the war began, Bartz-Borodin signed the Volksliste and became a censor. In our programme propositions we always planned to perform more Polish music. Bartz-Borodin crossed out two-thirds, and the rest was what we needed. Later on, the censor was changed, and the post was taken by a German with a Czech name – Janeczek or Janaczek – I also managed to deal with him somehow.[25]

2.1.1. Germans for Germans

Classical music concerts and opera performances in the Theater der Stadt Warschau (former "Polish Theatre" ["Teatr Polski"]) were organized at first by Germans for Germans only: soldiers, civilians who worked in numerous offices and their families. Mostly German artists coming from the Reich performed there. Probably due to the costs of transportation and wages of German musicians, and also because they had been in part mobilized, Polish musicians were also asked to, or forced to, play there. Some of the operettas and revues performed by Poles

---

24 Zofia Polubiec (ed.), *Okupacja i ruch oporu w Dzienniku Hansa Franka 1939–1945* [Occupation and Resistance in Diary of Hans Frank], Vol. I, 1939–1942, trans. from German by Danuta Dąbrowska and Mieczysław Tomala (Warsaw: Książka i Wiedza, 1970).
25 She was the wife of Andrzej Bogucki who also played at the cafes in Warsaw and created numerous cabaret shows. After her arrival from Lvov to Warsaw in May 1940, she had performed at first with Władysław Szpilman in the Dorys cafe up to the moment when he could not no longer leave the ghetto. Later on (13 February 1943), it was the singer and her husband who helped Szpilman escape from the ghetto (although she does not mention this information in her testimony, we know it thanks to Szpilman himself and the composer Piotr Perkowski, who also helped the pianist).

were also available to the Polish public. Working there was seen as collaboration and frequenting these concerts was deemed inappropriate, as in the case of other German-controlled theatres.[26] Among several newspapers for Germans, the *Warschauer Zeitung* brought information about cultural events "nur für Deutsche" in the GG and other parts of the Reich.

German musical activity in occupied Poland was gradually more and more thriving, according to Goebbels's guidelines, which stated that the Polish cultural life should not be in any way supported, and that the only goal was the development of a programme that was indigenously German.[27] The culmination of this were two important festivals in November 1941 – the "Deutsche Kulturtage" and "Mozart Tage," which took place in territories of occupied Poland, as well as in the Reich.[28] This was advertised and enthousiastically described in German press in articles such as *Stark pulsierendes Kulturleben, Glanzvoller Anschluss der Kulturtage in Warschau* (WZ of November 6, 1940, 5). Among operas staged at that time was *Iphigenie in Aulis* by C. W. Gluck – it took place on November 1 at the Staats-Theater des Generalgouvernements.[29] Several other concerts and other events took place in Warsaw in November 1940, which were described in several articles in *Warschauer Zeitung*: "Beethoven-Abend im Theater der SS und Polizei" (Beethoven evening at the Theater of the SS and Police), "Elly Ney in Warschau, Klavierabend im Palais Brühl" (Elly Ney in Warsaw, Piano evening at the Brühl palace, WZ No. 265, November 9, 1940, 3), "Der Weg der kulturellen Arbeit. Geistige 'Bodenständigkeit' im GG Hausmusik für Front und Heimat. Ein Aufruf Hermann Abendroths" (The path of cultural work. Intellectual "down-to-earthness" in the GG Hausmusik for the front and homeland. An appeal by Hermann Abendroth, WZ, No. 267, 12 XI, 4), *Dank an die volksdeutschen Frauen*: "Warschaus deutsche Frauen versammelten sich im Theater der Stadt Warschau, um von der Beauftragten der NSDAP für den Fraueneinsatz im Generalgouvernement" (Thanks to the ethnic German women: "Warsaw's German women gathered in the theatre of the city of Warsaw to be informed

---

26 The most important clandestine journal, *Biuletyn Informacyjny* of 30 January 1941 in an article entitled *Zabawa* (*Entertainment*, 1–2) explains why the frequentation of cinemas, theatres and cabarets is a not a proper behaviour, when thousands of families mourn the loss of those who fell on the front, murdered in prisons and camps.
27 These guidelines were presented at a conference for the Ministry of Propaganda departments' directors on 2 November 1939, cf. C. Madajczyk, *Polityka III Rzeszy*..., 128.
28 See Levi, *Mozart and the Nazis*.
29 WZ 1941, No. 258, 1 Nov., 9. The opera started at 7.30 pm and finished at 10.20 pm according to this advertisement.

by the NSDAP commissioner about the women's work in the *Generalgouvernement*"). The article "Zwei Jahre Warchauer Kulturleben im Zeitungsspiegel" (Two years of Warchau's cultural life in the newspaper mirror) mention the next performance of *Iphigenie in Aulis*, 12 XI (WZ, No. 262, 6 Nov., 5 and 6). "Wieder 'Deutsche Kulturtage' in Warschau. Zahlreiche Veranstaltungen vom 26–30. November – Künstler aus dem Reich wirken mit and Deutsches Theater im Ostraum. Mittelalterlische Mysterienspiele in Krakau – Deutsche Ensembles in Warschau – Frontbühnen in Zahlen" (German Culture Days again in Warsaw. Numerous events from 26–30 November – artists from the Reich are involved in the German Theater in the East (*Ostraum*). Medieval Mystery Plays in Krakow – German Ensembles in Warsaw – Front Stages in Numbers), both long articles, No. 268, 13 Nov., 5); "Elly Ney spielte in Warschau. Beethoven – Mozart – Schubert, Mozarttage des Generalgouvernements vom 8. bis 14. Dezember"(Elly Ney played in Warsaw. Beethoven – Mozart – Schubert, Mozart Days of the Generalgouvernement from 8 to 14 December).[30] On November 22, the Stadt Theater performance of *Wiener Blut* operette was advertised in *Warschauer Zeitung*. Several other articles followed: "Der Auftrag des deutschen Kulturschaffens im Kriege. Warschaus 'Deutsche Kulturtage' feierlich eröffnet – Gouverneur Dr. Fischer gab kulturellen Leistungsbericht" (The Mission of German Cultural Work during the War. Warsaw's "German Cultural Days" Ceremoniously Opened – Governor Dr. Fischer Gave Cultural Efficiency Report No. 280, 5), "Kulturelle Förderung der Volksdeutschen. Eine Hauptaufgabe der Partei – Distriktsstandorttagung der NSDAP als Abschluss der Warschauer Kulturtage" (Cultural Promotion of the Ethnic Germans. One of the main tasks of the party - district meeting of the NSDAP as the conclusion of the Warsaw Culture Days, No. 283), "Ausklang der Mozartwoche. Das "Requiem" als Staatsakt" (Conclusion of the Mozart Week. The "Requiem" as an act of state).

On December 9, 1940 (No. 290, 4–6), the following articles appeared, informing of a "congress of musicologists": "Stand der Mozartforschung. Kongress der Musikwissenschaftler," (State of Mozart research. Congress of Musicologists programme of *Warschauer Mozarttage*, advertisement of the festival). On December 11, the following concerts were advertised: *Eine kleine Nachtmusik, Der Schauspieldirektor, Les Petits riens* and the Mozart-Abend at the Staats-Theater des Generalgouvernements, 12 December, under the *Musikalische Leitung* (musical direction) of Albert Hösl, and "Kammermusik auch in Warschau" (Chamber

---

30 WZ 1941, No. 270, 15 Nov., 4.

music also in Warsaw, at the Palais Brühl, No. 294, 13 Dec., 4). This documentation is extremely vast, and it will be presented in another volume.

2.1.2. Music by Poles for Poles

As in the rest of the GG, shortly after September 1939 concert and operatic life was prohibited by the Nazi regime to former Polish citizens in Warsaw. This situation was aggravated even further by the fact that the Opera House and Warsaw Philharmonic buildings with instruments and libraries were destroyed during the September bombardments. Polish cultural institutions (such as the Polish Radio) were dissolved, as well as all orchestras and ensembles. Music by Poles for Poles retreated to cafes or churches or took the form of clandestine concerts in private apartments, since official concert life was controlled.

Major streets and squares were renamed with German appellations, such as the central Adolf Hitler Platz, while concert halls and theatres, if not destroyed in the September bombings, were taken over by the Germans – the most striking example in Warsaw was the above mentioned Teatr Polski (Polish Theatre), transformed into the Theater der Stadt Warschau.

The situation in the first months of the occupation was succinctly described by the eminent Polish writer, Zofia Nałkowska, who wrote in her diary already on December 31, 1939:

> It becomes clear to me what previously was inconceivable: that whole cultures can be extinguished, now known only to archaeologists from excavations. Press, radio, cinema, theatres, lectures, concerts, books – there is nothing. Life develops in silence. Monuments, paintings, artistic materials, scientific instruments – things that survived the fire have been taken away (…) All universities, associations and societies are shut down. Only innumerable cafes exist. The only published journal [*Nowy Kurier Warszawski*] is continuous scoff and insult. (…) Apartments plundered for furniture, people for clothing: whole herds have been chased from one city to another. Executions.[31]

The efforts by the Nazis to make impossible the continuation of a normal concert life in the occupied city made it impossible for musicians to continue work in conditions which were a far cry from Warsaw's thriving pre-war musical life. Some forms of musical entertainment, albeit only in cafes and in the streets, were permitted in the General Government by November 1939. For example, Zygmunt Latoszewski, a conductor from Poznań, primarily concerned with opera, conducted a small orchestra at the "Gastronomia" cafe in Warsaw.

---

31 Zofia Nałkowska, *Dzienniki 1939–1944* (Warsaw 1996).

It was in general understood by Poles that to work at legal theatres under German administration and to attend them meant accepting and legitimizing the functioning of the criminal German authorities, who wished to present themselves as cultured and civilized *Kulturträger*. Thus, it was seen as a form of collaboration. The Clandestine Council of Musicians granted the permission to perform there only in special cases. Most musicians declined, when they were given "offers" to perform at such venues, which were often presented in the form of blackmail by agents of the Third Reich, of whom the most active, the most effective and best known was the actor and singer Igo Sym (1896–1941), who gained popularity before the war playing in Austrian, German, and Polish films and in Warsaw revue theatres. For his highly pernicious activity he was sentenced to death and killed by the Polish underground. The German authorities responded with terror and mass arrests of musicians and actors.[32]

In this context, especially in the first years of the occupation, it became an act of resistance towards Nazi policies to perform in places run independently by private owners, although subjected to Nazi censorship, and to play there the standard repertoire – not only works by Beethoven or Mozart, but also Polish music – from works by the representative figures of Chopin and Szymanowski to the most recent compositions.

A rare allusion to it can be found in one of early musical advertisements in the official press in January 1940. The following capitalized text: "TRADITION DEFINES THE CULTURE OF THE NATIONS" is placed alongside information about concerts at the Lourse cafe (Krakowskie Przedmieście 13), where thirty Warsaw Philharmonic musicians gave concerts every day (starting on January 20, 1940) under direction of "the outstandingly talented young Kapellmeister Bolesław Lewandowski between 4 and 7 PM. On Thursday great symphonic concerts. Performances by outstanding soloists."[33] Another venue advertised on the

---

32 Sym died on 7 March 1941. Cafes and theatres were closed, 118 hostages were taken; among them 21 were executed on 11 March 1941 in Palmiry. Others, such as prominent actors and directors Leon Schiller and Stefan Jaracz were sent to Auschwitz. Schiller was ransomed by his sister Anna Jackowska for 12 thousand zlotys she acquired selling her jewels. Jaracz was also released, on 15 May, but he had not recuperated and died in August 1945. This actor was also director of the famous Ateneum theatre before the war, which during the occupation, on 28 October 1943, was transformed into one more theatre for German soldiers and policemen. Cf. Ludwik Landau, *Kronika lat wojny i okupacji*, Vol. 3 (Warsaw, 1963), 356.

33 NKW 1940 No. 16 of 20 January, 4: "Wieczór Szubertowski, orkiestra pod dyr. Olgierda Straszyńskiego, zaś od 20 stycznia 1940 r. codziennie filharmonicy warszawscy (30

same page was "Adria" at Moniuszki Street 10 – the pre-war elegant dancing club next to the building of the Philharmonic. There, some well-known musicians appeared, who until September 1939 performed mainly at the Warsaw Opera House, such as the outstanding singer Edward Bender, who performed a "Schubertian evening" with orchestra conducted by Olgierd Straszyński.

2.1.3. Music by Jews for Jews: The Warsaw Ghetto

In the first stage of the Warsaw ghetto's operation, in 1941, its reality was most succinctly described by Emmanuel Ringelblum, who wrote that "all cultural life is in ruins." He further explained:

> After the establishment of the ghetto, the authorities allowed internal cultural activity without restrictions. The commissar of the Jewish district, attorney Auerswald, did not care much what Jews were doing in the ghetto, he cared about one thing only: Jews should die of hunger (...)
> The regulations of the German Propaganda Office forbidding the performance of Aryan composers are not observed in the ghetto; "freedom" reigns here. They play what they want, not paying attention to the censorship which allows only a very restricted number of musical compositions. Some of the more eminent musicians were hired in schools, where they trained children's vocal ensembles, whose performances were very much appreciated by the public.[34]

The orchestra, despite the lack of important instruments and several other difficulties, performed indeed in 1941 under the direction of such outstanding musicians as Szymon Pulmann and composer and conductor Marian Neuteich (1890 or 1906–1943), who "shortly before the uprising in the Warsaw ghetto was deported by Germans to the camp and weapon factories in Poniatowa and was killed there"[35] (or, according to other sources, in Trawniki camp). However, the

---

osób pod dyrekcją wybitnie utalentowanego młodego kapelmistrza Bolesława Lewandowskiego). Koncertują od 16 do 19 u L. Lourse'a Krak. Przedmieście 13. TRADYCJA STANOWI O KULTURZE NARODÓW. W czwartki wielkie koncerty symfoniczne. Występy wybitnych solistów." Bolesław Lewandowski (1912 Kharkov – 1981 Warsaw) – graduated in composition (1935) and conducting (1937) at the Warsaw Conservatory and worked as conductor of the Warsaw Opera House until the war. And resumed his operatic conductor's career after 1945, meanwhile worked at cafes. He died after conducting Mussorgsky's Boris Godunov at the Opera House in Warsaw. After *Almanach sceny polskiej* 1980/81.

34 Ringelblum 1948, 597. English translation by the author.
35 Andrzej Kempa and Marek Szukalak, Słownik biograficzny Żydzi dawnej Łodzi (Łódź 2001).

orchestra was later dissolved by German authorities arbitrarily, because of the previous noncompliance to the repertoire rules imposed by the new laws. Thus, the policy of initial indifference toward cultural activity in the ghetto constituted a perfidious manipulation, which preceded the ultimate extermination of the ghetto's inhabitants. It should be stressed that as in the case of other large ghettos, especially the one in Łódź, musical performances were needed by the Nazi propagandists to show that Jews were well treated there, even better than their non-Jewish neighbors, to further divide and incite anti-Semitic hatred.

The chronology is as follows: On November 16, 1940, the ghetto was sealed off. Just 9 days later the first concert of the Jewish Symphony Orchestra took place at the Central Judaic Library in Tłomackie Street. On June 1, 1941, the Great Synagogue was reopened there. On October 1, 1941, elementary schools were permitted to open in the ghetto, while a month later the construction of the extermination camp in Bełżec began, and Fischer's decree on the death penalty for leaving the ghetto without permission was followed by the opening on December 7, 1941, of the extermination camp in Chełm (Kulmhof) on the Ner River. Earlier, numerous cafes operated, with eminent musicians forced to play there or in the streets; for example, on February 2 the propagandistic *Gazeta Żydowska* informed its readers that Władysław Szpilman and Artur Gold were to play at the Nowoczesna cafe (Modern Cafe), and in Issue No. 51 it was mentioned that "the only theatre of the district playing in Polish is open."

In an article published in *Gazeta Żydowska*, entitled "Inter arma musae non silent," we read the following account:

> Adam Furmański (...) was heard in Kiev by Emil Młynarski, and then sponsored by Baron Kronenberg, gave concerts in Warsaw, graduated with distinction from the Conservatory, encouraged by his sponsor to go to Italy under one condition, to change his religion, Furmański stayed, was accepted at the Warsaw Philharmonic and created his own orchestra. He is a pioneer and propagator of great art; he is the first to arrive in small towns and cities and is the initiator of children's concerts.
>
> Ten years ago, he celebrated his silver jubilee. From many parts of the world colleagues and students arrived to celebrate their master. Among them Mieczysław Horszowski. (...) 1941. Adam Furmański in the Jewish district (...) just as throughout his entire life (...) puts all his energy, faith and enthusiasm into the new, hard work. With a young musician H. Stromberg, and other musicians he creates an institution of enormous cultural value – the Jewish Symphonic Orchestra.

Adam Furmański (1883–1943, probably murdered in Treblinka) also created a street orchestra, which played, as Ringelblum reported, on the corner of Pańska and Żelazna, on Sundays at 3 pm., next to the barbed wire fence, which separated the ghetto from the rest of the city. Hundreds of Poles came there to listen to "the forbidden music." A Polish policeman gathered money from the crowd and gave it to the orchestra, "thus it lasted all the afternoon, until the curfew..."

Gazeta Żydowska published a lot of information on different musical performances, for example in No. 73 in the article "Artistic chronicle. Musical Impressions," where a symphonic concert conducted by Marian Neuteich is described; the review points out the enormous popularity of Tchaikovsky and the "unfortunately unavoidable" effect resulting from the use of a saxophone instead of a horn in the second movement *Andante cantabile* in his *Fifth Symphony*. In No. 78, on page 2 more information about missing instruments was included: "A few instruments (horn, bassoon, oboe) had to be replaced with other instruments. That is why some works were prepared by Pullman for chamber orchestra." As in other articles, the repertoire is enumerated (Vivaldi, Bach, Haydn, Mozart, Beethoven, Schubert, Tchaikovsky, Brahms, Verdi, Bruckner, Beethoven's *Grosse Fuge*). However, in the light of Emanuel Ringelblum's words, its analysis is not genuinely relevant in relation to music censorship – as the real goal behind this "liberal" smokescreen and the "liberty" to play (with neither proper instruments, nor scores) was the physical extermination of both musicians and their listeners, and the racial laws in music were used only as pretexts in this criminal plan. A quotation from the memoirs of Stanisław Różycki of 1942 offers an image of the reality in which all intellectual and artistic values were in fact banned for the ghetto population:

> In the cruel fight for a piece of bread, for a few metres of space to live, for maintaining health, strength and life, one cannot devote much energy nor energy to spiritual matters. Another thing are the German restrictions and bans. One cannot publish anything, teach, learn, associate, exchange cultural values. We are cut off from the world: libraries (...), schools, scientific institutions etc. are banned. There are no cinemas, no radio, no contact with global culture. Nothing reaches us, no product of human soul reaches us. Not only comestible and industrial merchandise must be smuggled, but also products of the mind.[36]

Thus, if we describe the repertoire played in the ghettos, not only the conditions of this activity have to be described, but also the circumstance of the killings that took the lives of almost all of the Jewish musicians mentioned in *Gazeta Żydowska*.

The ban on performing music by Polish musicians labelled "Jewish" was introduced in parallel with the ban on performing "Aryan" music by Jewish musicians. In the first stage of the Warsaw ghetto's operation, throughout 1941, some

---

36 Quoted in *Extermination*..., 137.

of the artists of Jewish origin managed to work in the ghetto, but in spite of these attempts their cultural life was ruined, as noted by Emanuel Ringelblum. Though officially only music by Jewish composers was permitted – and a limited number of compositions at that – the regulations of the German Propaganda Office forbidding the performance of Aryan composers were not strictly observed,[37] and works by Beethoven, Brahms, Tchaikovsky, Mozart, Grieg, Chopin, and other composers were performed. Later, however, this regulation was used as a pretext to disband the orchestra.

In the history of the Warsaw ghetto, the heroism of musicians who tried to make their living by playing in an orchestra which lacked various instruments, the innumerable images of musicians who played in the streets of the ghetto (such as the violin professor from the Leipzig Conservatory, described in her Diary by Mary Berg),[38] the overwhelming losses in the field of music, attest to the most tragic manifestation of music ghettoization in the history of mankind. The essence of this was perfectly understood inside the ghetto, and was perhaps best grasped – and denounced – in the bitter poem by Władysław Schlengel, who was murdered there:

Mam okno na tamtą stronę,	I have a window to the other side,
bezczelne żydowskie okno	an impudent Jewish window
na piękny park Krasińskiego,	on the beautiful Krasiński park,
gdzie liście jesienne mokną...	full of wet autumn leaves...
A mnie w oknie stanąć nie wolno	And I am not allowed to stand in the window

(bardzo to słuszny przepis),	(a most appropriate ordinance, indeed),
Żydowskie robaki... krety...	Jewish worms... moles...
powinni i muszą być ślepi.	should and have to be blind.

Pod wieczór szaroliliowy	Towards the greylilac evening
składają gałęzie pokłon	branches make a bow
i patrzą się drzewa aryjskie	and Aryan trees stare
w to moje żydowskie okno...	into my Jewish window...

| Niech siedzą w barłogach, norach | Let them sit in their pits, burrows |

---

37 Emmanuel Ringelblum, *Kronika getta warszawskiego: wrzesień 1939 – styczeń 1943*, translated from Yiddish by Adam Rutkowski, Warsaw: Czytelnik, 1988.
38 Edited by S. L. Schneiderman, New York 1945.

w robotę z utkwionym okiem i wara im od patrzenia i od żydowskich okien...	eyes fixed on work and away from staring and from their Jewish windows away...
A ja... kiedy noc zapada... by wszystko wyrównać i zatrzeć, dopadam do okna w ciemności i patrzę... żarłocznie patrzę...	And me... when the night is falling... to balance all things and efface them, I stand in the window in darkness and stare... voraciously stare...
i kradnę zgaszoną Warszawę, szumy i gwizdy dalekie, zarysy domów i ulic, kikuty wieżyc kalekie...	and I am stealing the extinguished Warsaw, its distant rustles and whistles, outlines of streets and houses, stumps of its crippled towers...
Kradnę sylwetkę Ratusza, u stóp mam plac Teatralny, pozwala księżyc Wachmeister na szmugiel sentymentalny...	I am stealing the City Hall's silhouette, the Theatre Square at my feet, the Wachmeister moon tolerates a little bit of sentimental smuggling...
Wbijają się oczy żarłocznie, jak ostrza w pierś nocy utkwione, w warszawski wieczór milczący, w miasto me zaciemnione...	My voracious eyes penetrate, like blades, the bosom of night, the silent Warsaw evening, my city blackened throughout...
A kiedy mam dosyć zapasu na jutro, a może i więcej... żegnam milczące miasto, Magicznie podnoszę ręce... zamykam oczy i szepcę: – Warszawo... odezwij się... czekam...	And when the stock is sufficient for tomorrow and maybe more... I bid farewell to the silent city, Magically I raise my hands... I close my eyes and whisper: – Warsaw... speak... I am waiting...
Wnet fortepiany w mieście podnoszą milczące wieka... podnoszą się same na rozkaz ciężkie, smutne, zmęczone...	Soon pianos in the city lift up their silent lids... raising themselves to the command heavy, somber and tired...

i płynie ze stu fortepianów	and from a hundred pianos there drifts
w noc... Szopenowski polonez...	into the night... Chopin's polonaise...
Wzywają mnie klawikordy,	The clavichords are calling me,
w męką nabrzmiałej ciszy	in anguished swollen silence
płyną nad miastem akordy	chords float over the city
spod trupio białych klawiszy...	from under the dead-white keys...
Koniec... opuszczam ręce...	The end... I lower my hands...
wraca do pudeł polonez...	the polonaise returns to the boxes....
Wracam i myślę, że źle jest	I turn and think that it's bad
mieć okno na tamtą stronę...	to have a window to the other side...

Among the outstanding pianists who were murdered by the Nazis were: Janina Familier-Hepner (1896–1942), who was one of the best Polish pianists before the war, appreciated for her Chopin and Liszt performances, and who continued to perform in the ghetto in the "Femina" theatre and during some charity events; Leon Boruński (1909–1942), who won the seventh prize at the Second Chopin Piano Competition in 1932; Róża Etkin-Moszkowska (1908–1945), the youngest participant at the First Chopin Competition in 1927 and recipient of the third prize; Halina Kalmanowicz (ca. 1910–1942) from Vilnius; Ryszard Szpiro; Kazimierz Gelernter and Ignacy Rosenbaum (see Appendix).

This tragedy was unfolding in the same city where the "Aryan for Aryans" music was featured during the cultural events for the German public (soldiers and civilians) such as, for instance, the above-mentioned "Deutscher Kulturtage" festival in Warsaw in November 1941. A German cultural life was one of the greatest ambitions of the Nazi authorities and music played a vital part of it. The Jews, the *Untermenschen*, were divested of everything, music included. Just as food, music was allowed exclusively on the order of the *Übermench*, for his entertainment.

Janina Brandwajn-Ziemian, a survivor of the Warsaw ghetto, in her memoir gave a following account of the time when she, along with other Jews, served as slave workers under the command of two SS-men, Willy and Otto:

> After some time, we got an additional German, Otto, a 20-year-old brute, who tormented the workers in different ways. He announced that none of us was allowed to eat breakfast ahead of him. He would leave the house after breakfast and only the second breakfast was prepared by a worker chosen by Willi for a cook. We would leave the house at 6 am and we could not eat until 11, the violation of this ban was being punished by whipping.

Among the workers there was a musician well-known in the ghetto, Jakub Kagan.[39] Our German Willy considered himself a great music admirer, so he commanded him to play for us every day for half an hour on the piano that was stolen from one of the flats. We had to [obey] and it gave us an extra half an hour of inactivity every day, but we were forced to pay a small sum of money to Jakub, which for many of us was a great burden. Strange thing: I was taught as a child that somebody, who loves music and animals, was a good person, and here the SS-man Willi – not the worst one of them, but who knows his past – forces us to listen to the music. He listened to it with emotion, while other Germans, who have bred and caressed dogs, were killing small children. Meanwhile, we have completed the cleaning the apartments. And we moved to the shops, from which the Germans were hauling all the goods. One of these shops was a perfumery. There Otto grabbed an intensely red lipstick, smeared with it his mouth, as well as mine and those of a few other girls, and started to shout: "me whore and you whore", laughing his head off. He found in the yarn warehouse some old spool shaped like a penis. He offered it to the most beautiful girl in our group, shouting: If your groom is killed, you can make use of it. We realized he was a sexual deviant. A few days later, when we started to clear things and garbage that had been thrown out of the windows onto the ruins on the other side of the street, he set a pile of wood on fire and commanded a girl to jump through the flames.[40]

Janina Brandwajn was later nearly killed by the SS-man Otto – she replied "Jawohl" and began to laugh hysterically after he pressed his new revolver to her head and asked "Kann ich dich erschiessen?" ("Can I shoot you?") – this unusual reaction saved her life, while an older Jew, who begged for his life, saying he had a wife and children, was shot.[41] She dedicated her book to the memory of the members of her family: her father, doctor Hieronim Brandwajn, who was mobilized to the Polish Army in August 1939 and was murdered in May 1940 in Katyń, to her grandmother Leja Fliederbaum, who was shot by the Germans on her hospital bed on September 12, 1942, and to her grandfather Zygmunt Brandwajn who died on January 21, 1942, of pneumonia after he had to give away his only fur coat to the Germans.

Marcel Reich-Ranicki who used to write concert reviews for the propagandistic "Gazeta Żydowska" under the nickname Wiktor Hart, in an interview given at the end of his life, described yet another instance of a deeply instilled interconnectivity between Nazi hatred of the Jews and the sadistic actions of young German soldiers which involved music:

---

39 More on this musician in chapter 2.
40 Janina Brandwajn-Ziemian, *Młodość w cieniu śmierci* (Youth in the shadow of death, Łódź: Oficyna bibliofilów, 1995), 70.
41 Ibid., 72.

We now had to start marching, and of course we did not know where and for what purpose. It was not far away; the destination of our march was about twenty or thirty minutes away. Only the soldiers who led us, mostly young guys, about twenty-five years old, had fun on the road by forcing us to do what they could think of. Suddenly they ordered us to run fast, then we had to run back again. If there was a big puddle, then of course we had to go through the middle of it. Then we were forced to sing songs. So, of course, we sang Polish songs. But they disliked this, and they demanded Jewish songs. Then they commanded chants [*Sprechchöre*; speaking choirs], saying: "We are Jewish pigs. We are dirty Jews. We are subhumans."[42]

2.1.4. Appropriation, destruction, genocide: Three facets of Nazi cultural policy in Krakow

The move to create German *Lebensraum* in the case of Krakow – as in Warsaw and other cities – consisted ininitially in the physical eviction of Jews and Poles from the centre of the city.

Krakow – a city smaller than Warsaw and much easier to control – was the first target of the Germans. It was selected to "carry out the scheme, long since worked out, of depriving the Poles of the heritage of their forefathers." Based on a thoroughly considered plan, Krakow was chosen to be the capital of the *Generalgouvernement* and was "the first which was to be converted into a German city not only in name and outward appearance, but also in the composition of its population – the Poles were to be speedily removed to make room for Germans."[43] The Nazi authorities[44] proceeded systematically to carry out the plan, which had long before been elaborated for the complete break-up and absorption of the Polish nation by the German element – a fate previously shared by those Slav peoples that lived between the Elbe and the Baltics. This began already in 1939, when hundreds of thousands of Poles had been evicted from Greater Poland, Silesia, and Pomerania and penned up in the *Generalgouvernement*.

Coinciding with the process of removing Poles from Krakow, was of course the simultaneous process of Germanizing the city both in appearance, by giving it the outward aspects of a German city, and in reality – by constantly increasing the number of Germans living within its bounds. Krakow had been selected to become the centre from which the German spirit was to radiate throughout the Polish territories. The idea was to become firmly rooted in the heads of both

---

42 Marcel Reich-Ranicki, *Zwischen Diktatur und Literatur: ein Gespräch mit Joachim Fest*, Frankfurt am Main: Fischer Taschenbuch, 1993, 50.
43 Jan Dąbrowski et al., *Krakow under Enemy Rule...*, 4.
44 Ibid.

Germans and Poles that Krakow was a "German city from time immemorial," based on the general claim of the autochthony of Germans on Polish soil and of their later inflow at the time of settlement, defined as the "return" of Germans to their abandoned homesteads. And so, an energetic propaganda was generated, at first in the press and then in pseudo-scientific publications, the source of which was the German Institute for Work in the East (*Institut für Deutsche Ostarbeit*). It was established by governor-general Frank on April 19, 1940, and its seat became the venerable building of Krakow's ancient university, the Collegium Majus and the neighbouring buildings.[45]

The goals of the GG authorities for the Germanization of Krakow were clearly described in the above-quoted *Krakow under Enemy Rule* of 1946:

In 1940, some of the streets were given German names and from 1941 onward the process assumed a general character. The town's arms were altered, the swastika replacing the white eagle. The Market Square was called "Adolf Hitlerplatz" and the use of its Polish name was banned. Likewise, the Wawel Castle was officially named "Burg" and the use of the appellation Wawel was prohibited. (...) No Polish press and no Polish theatre were allowed to exist. At the close of 1939 the Słowacki Memorial Theatre became a German "national theatre." The Germans' next move was aimed at clearing Krakow of its Polish population. This was accompanied by fierce propaganda in which it was demonstrated that Krakow owed all of its cultural possessions gathered in the past exclusively to the Germans (...) This propaganda, which was carried on in the press, in pseudo-scientific publications, in lectures and over the wireless, included among the Germans whoever could be considered as such by the origin of this surname, by his Christian name or by whatever trifling pretext offered itself. (...) The ground being thus prepared, by means of the propaganda, the work of de-Polonizing of Krakow went on all the more briskly. (...) It was put into effect at an increasingly rapid pace, especially after 1940. (...) A detailed scheme was evolved whereby Krakow was divided into three zones – one purely German, one mixed, and the third Polish. (...) Freedom of movement also came to be restricted for Poles. First the Polish children were deprived of Jordan Park, which was reserved for the exclusive use of Germans. Next it was Park Krakowski, then it was the swimming bath on the Błonia. Finally, a considerable part of the benches on the "Planty" were provided with the inscription "Nur für Deutsche." In 1942 the Poles were confined to the use of the back end of tram cars and a similar division was made on the railways.[46]

Nazi *Lebensraum* goals, which were strongly rooted in pseudo-philosophical beliefs, could be achieved through appropriation and control not only of physical,

---

45   Ibid., 8, 25–26.
46   Ibid., 15–17, 22.

but also of symbolic spaces. This was executed on several planes, from appropriation to destruction to genocide.

To de-Polonize the conquered territories, appellations linked to geographical regions were used, such as "the Vistula region" instead of "Poland." In Krakow, the same methods were adopted as in the case of Warsaw. Krakow as the capital of the General Government had to acquire a German character by a similar and even more intense and rapid process. Monuments linked with Polish national identity and culture were pulled down – for example, the Grunwald monument to the victory over the Teutonic Order in November 1939. (In Warsaw, the Chopin monument was destroyed in May 1940.) By the same token, "the equestrian statue of [military hero Tadeusz] Kościuszko and the bust of [the playwright Aleksander] Fredro, and also commemorative plaques to [the writer and painter Stanisław] Wyspiański, [poet Adam] Asnyk and [composer Władysław] Żeleński" were removed,[47] and in some cases replaced with German ones. The centrally located statue of the national bard Adam Mickiewicz was also destroyed. In a text written in the first years after the war, Dora Agatstein-Dormont, described how Jewish monuments, theatres (Teatr Żydowski on Bocheńska Street), associations, private collections, schools, libraries, orphanages and hospitals and synagogues were looted and destroyed. The Jewish Academic House on Przemyska Street was turned into a brothel for the German military.[48]

The stages of genocide against Jews in Krakow were described thus in a 1946 publication:

> Initially the German policy towards the Jews tended to exclude them from the rest of the population and to divest them of their possessions. In its further evolution, from 1942 onwards it tended to their complete extermination. (…) after the defeat of France, the Germans proceeded to the systematic realization of their programme, long since prepared as the solution of the Jewish question. It fell into two stages. The first consisted in the 'restraint' of the Jewish population so as to deprive it of freedom of movement and submit it to complete supervision by the German police. The Jews were forbidden to leave their places (…) Subsequent to the 'restraint' of the Jews came the removal from the city to more or less remote parts of the provinces of those who were recognized

---

47　Ibid., 14.
48　In the article documenting the process of pauperisation and murder of Jews in Krakow, Dora Agatstein-Dormontowa, "Żydzi w okresie okupacji niemieckiej," in: *Krakow w latach okupacji 1939–1945. Studia i materiały, Rocznik Krakowski*, Vol. 31 (1949–1957) (Krakow: Nakładem Towarzystwa Miłośników Historii i Zabytków Krakowa), 222–223.

superfluous or non-working. (...) Next, in summer 1941, a ghetto was arranged in Krakow (as in other Polish towns), for which purpose the eastern part of Podgórze was allocated, the Christian population being displaced of it. In the first place the Kazimierz district was evacuated of Jews, whereupon the Christians from Podgórze were transferred there, and the greater part of those dislodged from the German zone (...) In it, squalor, hunger and sickness reigned supreme. (...) This state of affairs, however, was not of long duration. The second stage soon followed. (...) The final liquidation of the ghetto took place on 13 and 14 March 1943. The great majority of the Jews, except a small number who were kept at Płaszów labour camp, were – among atrocities and savagery – convoyed beyond the bounds of Krakow, mostly to the gas chambers of Oświęcim (Auschwitz). The Jewish hospital and orphanage were "liquidated" off-hand – children, patients and medical staff, all were murdered. All the possessions of the Jewish population were pillaged or aimlessly destroyed. It took months to clear the houses and streets of the heap of smashed furniture. The objects of value, in particular the silver plate, were brought together and plundered by the German police. The 55.000 Jews that Krakow numbered in 1939, had melted down to less than 1000.[49]

In a terrifying account of persecutions and plunder, the macabre scenes of slaughter of women, children and the elderly, which also described the activity of the Jewish underground and of the Council of Aid to the Jews (*Rada Pomocy Żydom*), Dora Agatstein-Dormontowa, herself a Holocaust survivor, saved with her daughter Karolina by a Polish couple,[50] detailed the "action" of June 1942 in the Krakow ghetto. It was conducted by the Head of SS and Police of the Krakow district Julian Scherner; among more than 5,000 victims were the Jewish poet and singer Mordecai Gebirtig (in Agatstein's text, spelled as diminutive *Mordche*) and the painter Abraham Neumann.[51]

2.1.5. Control of the symbolic spaces

Whereas in the Reich, as a German witness quoted in Carolyn Birdsall's study described it, "The state-subsidised radio sets (*Volksempfänger*) had the purpose of keeping the people acoustically under control,"[52] in the General Government

---

49 J. Dąbrowski (1946), 30–33.
50 Ludwika (1891–1970) and Zygmunt Szostak (1886–1972), who lived in Warsaw's Żoliborz quarter, took care of them from August 1942, when Dora Agatstein escaped from the ghetto in Lvov a month before its liquidation. On 13 November 2012, Yad Vashem recognized them as Righteous Among the Nations. Agatstein with her daughter and Karolina lived in Krakow, which they left in 1950 to go to Israel. Information retrieved from the webpage of Yad Vashem.
51 D. Agatstein-Dormontowa, (1957), 211.
52 Birdsall, *Nazi Soundscapes*, 11.

non-Germans (Jews and Poles) were prohibited from using the radio and by January 1940 all sets had to be deposited at the nearest police station. In Krakow, by order of Mayor Ernst Zörner in late 1939, all "Polish and Jewish owners" also had to declare that they owned mechanical vehicles. By his order of January 11, 1940, they had to give away their radio sets.[53] However, the first order confiscating radio sets had been issued on December 15, 1939, and even earlier, on October 10, 1939, a ban on listening to foreign radio stations had been issued.[54] This regulation permitted Nazi German authorities to achieve at least four goals: (1) dispossessing former Polish citizens of valuable objects such as radio sets, which was one of many examples of ruthless looting; (2) acquiring these objects now permitted them to be passed on to Germans; (3) Poles and Jews were cut off from any uncensored source of information or other radio content, including music; (4) in the case of radio sets now kept illegally, this constituted a pretext for imprisonment, interrogations and even sentencing to imprisonment in camps or execution. In this context, media theorist Marshall McLuhan was right insofar as he argued that the radio in Nazi Germany created this *Lebensraum* as "fountains of auditory space", which made Hitler's appeal more powerful and attractive, "retribalizing" individuals in the realm of National Socialist ideology.[55] Those who were not part of the "tribe" were excluded and their access to information was limited to propaganda spewed from loudspeakers in the streets.

These measures, which served to Nazify the landscape and soundscape of Krakow, were explained as early as 1946 in a study co-authored by Polish professors and archivists who were witnesses of that period:

> Most clamorous and glaring was the propaganda carried on by means of processions, party celebrations and sporting fixtures. On every occasion of this kind, principally in the first years of the occupation, the town – particularly the Market Square and adjoining thoroughfares – sank in a sea of red bunting and swastikas. Bands and marches of party formations and Hitler Youth would fill the town with a blatant din. Restaurants and cafes would swarm with throngs of victors sated with glory and craving food and drink of which the non-German population was deprived. (...) Any business in the

---

53 Ibid., 194.
54 S. Lachowicz (1988), 14.
55 Quoted in Birdsall, who – criticizing this theory – wrote: "This discourse mystifies radio as an oral medium and perpetuates a post-war tradition that explained National Socialism in terms of the irrational or a return to ancient barbarism." C. Birdsall, *Nazi Soundscapes...*, 12.

gastronomic line which could boast good equipment had been seized for the exclusive use of the German population.[56]

Likewise, the reasons for not only economic but also intellectual control of the Polish population were explained in *Krakow under Enemy Rule*:

> In Krakow, just as in the rest of the country, the Polish population was kept from the very start under a rule of bloodshed and terror. Here also certain stages can be discerned, dependent upon the general run of the war (…).
>
> Hitlerism in Poland, once faced with the impossibility of either exterminating or displacing all the Poles, applied itself to its basic aim, that of depriving the nation of its leading classes both intellectual and economic, of replacing these by the German element, and of degrading the Poles to play the role of passive manure – the role to which their compatriots had already been degraded in East Prussia. The Polish intellectuals, Polish trade and industry, even the more lucrative crafts, were to die away in the normal course and at a pace quickened by persecution. The Poles within the limits of their country were to be mere serfs, to work for the Germans, to provide the latter with labor and in future with conscripts; then, when the time came and the process of Germanization had done its work, to supplement the higher class. The first step towards the realization of this scheme was to obliterate Polish intellectual culture or at least to check its growth, or better still, not to allow it to even vegetate. The Poles were to become a nation deprived of an intellectual class. None but Germans were to be intellectuals either in the professions or in the sphere of learning and art. The existing circles of Polish intellectuals were to melt away by natural death at a rate accelerated by oppression and, the war once over, by compulsory or voluntary emigration.[57]

As in Warsaw, official Polish musical activity was allowed only in cafes and only with special permission. The Władysław Żeleński Music School was closed and its building was taken over by the Germans on Feberuary 5, 1940, at the same time as the Conservatory of the Music Association. The Żeleński School began to function clandestinely, directed by Kazimierz Krzyształowicz. Among its teachers were Halina Ekier and Kazimiera Treterowa who described the history of this school. One of the teachers – Nora Jolles – perished in one of the camps, another – Jadwiga Kopycinska – in Auschwitz. Illegal events, however,

---

56 Jan Dąbrowski et al., *Krakow under Enemy Rule*…, 28. Jan Konstanty Dąbrowski (1890–1965) was history professor at the Jagiellonian University, who was among the arrested in the Sonderaktion Krakau. Co-authors of the book included: Feliks Kopera, director of the National Museum in Krakow, Kazimierz Buczkowski, curator of the National Museum in Krakow, Marian Friedberg, Head of the Ancient Archives of the City of Krakow, Kazimierz Piwarski, professor at the Jagiellonian University, Wacław Skrzywan, Department Head at the Chamber of Commerce.

57 J. Dąbrowski (1946), *Krakow under Enemy Rule*…, 3, 8.

were organized in private apartments. As Kazimiera Treterowa wrote in her typeset account held at the National Archive in Krakow,

> The inhabitants of Krakow were deprived of stage music. You didn't go to German concerts at the Philharmonic, you listened to the radio only clandestinely to get information about the events of the war. In this period of shocking, tragic experiences, the desire to divert one's thoughts from the nightmare of war was so strong that private concerts began to be organized.[58]

While on October 14, 1940, the Philharmonic of the General Government was solemnly inaugurated, with speeches by Hans Frank and his deputy Joseph Bühler, manhunts in the streets of Krakow and executions in the vicinity of the city continued relentlessly, directed mainly against the intelligentsia.

One example is the action at the musical cafe for Poles in Krakow, "U plastyków" or "Kawiarnia Plastyków" at 3 Łobzowska Street. This cafe, between February 13, 1941, and April 16, 1942, presented about a hundred recitals, both vocal and instrumental, including pianists Jan Ekier and his sister Halina.[59]

As the authors of *Krakow under Enemy Rule* wrote:

> That terror wave reached its climax in the spring moths of 1942 which preceded the renewed offensive in the east. According to the instructions received by the heads of German offices in the *Generalgouvernement* in February 1942, that same year was to witness Germany's decisive effort for achieving victory. The Gestapo was preparing to harass the population of the town by means of arrests and deportation. A start was made on 19 April 1942, when almost all who were present in the "Plastyków" cafe were seized. About 200 men, for the most part belonging to the intellectual circles of Krakow were arrested and sent to Oświęcim, where the majority of them paid the usual penalty of their lives, among them Dr. Ottmann, secretary in the Jagiellonian University, M. Rubczak, Adademician, M. Puszet [Ludwik Puget], sculptor, Professor Weiner, M. Ekielski, civil engineer.

---

58 Cf. a rare photograph documenting an illegal concert at Janina Stolfowa's apartment at Retoryka Street 1, with Halina Ekier at the piano from the Archiwum Państwowe in Krakow, published in: Anna Czocher, *W okupowanym Krakowie. Codzienność polskich mieszkańców miasta 1939–1945* (Gdańsk: Wydawnictwo Oskar, 2011). Lachowicz (127) writes about Olga and Jadwiga Stolfowa's musical salon.

59 Lachowicz, 103–109, gave the full list of musicians who performed at this cafe, based on information from *Goniec Krakowski*. He also quoted the article by Adam Rieger published in *RM* 1945 in October, enumerating artists who performed there: Dobrowolski, Drabik, Dubiska, Dzieduszycki, Ekier, Ekierówna, Gaczek, Ilnicka, Madeja, Madeyska, Markiewiczówna, Mikuszewski, Morbitzerowa, Platówna, Bilińska-Riegerowa, Rosnerowie, Stefańska, Syrewicz, Szlemińska, Żmudziński and others.

In the course of the following days, several hundred officers of the reserve were arrested (2,000 of them were taken in the district of Krakow) and with very few exceptions they were done to death at Oświęcim shortly after (...). From then on, till the end of June, every night people were arrested and the greater part of them sent at once to Oświęcim (...), and almost everyday round-ups were carried out in the streets. Parts of the "Planty" and whole streets were cordoned off, combed, and most of the men were, particularly the young, were carried off (...) Only a small part of those taken were ever released, the others used to be despatched to concentration or labour camps or were executed. In those months, Krakow's losses in manpower amounted to between ten and twenty thousand men who were carried away and for the most part massacred.[60]

Only 30 men survived out of the 200 arrested at that time (first arrests happened there on March 8, 1942).[61] Most of them died in Auschwitz the same year. Ludwik Puget (1877–1942) – who organized the concerts at the cafe together with Hanna Rudzka-Cybisowa – was executed on May 27 in Auschwitz. He was a sculptor, painter, historian of art, a descendant of an aristocratic family (he was a baron). He was famous also for his handsome appearance and had created the cabaret "Under the Pink Cuckoo" in Poznań, popular among intellectual circles in the interwar years.

Concerts in private apartments continued however, with such artists as Irena Dubiska, Halina and Jan Ekier, Zbigniew Jeżewski, Irena Lewińska, Irena Meyerowa, Franciszek Łukasiewicz, Włodzimierz Obidowicz, Zdzisław Roessner, Andrzej Wąsowski, and Tadeusz Żmudziński, among others. Halina Ekier and another teacher, Halina Czarkowska took care of musicians and children who were displaced after the Warsaw Uprising. The Żeleński School as private institution was liquidated in 1950.[62]

---

60 Ibid., 35–6. Edward Kubalski (1872–1958), in his memoires written between 1 September 1939 and 18 January 1945, wrote on 16 April 1942 that "in 'Plastyków' cafe, reopened after a few days yesterday evening, all guests were arrested." On 18 April, he wrote that this round-up was the beginning of arrests of reserve officers, which happened during the night of 16 to 17 April. At that time his only son Stanisław was arrested and died the same year in Auschwitz. E. Kubalski, *Niemcy w Krakowie*, Jan Grabowski, Zbigniew R. Grabowski (eds.), Krakow – Budapest: Wydawnictwo Austeria, 2010, 206. On 30 June, he mentions the information on death of Ludwik Puget (Puszet) in Auschwitz, which "moved everybody" (223).
61 S. Lachowicz, *W okupowanym Krakowie...*, 16–17.
62 Kzimiera Treterowa, typescript, National Archive in Krakow.

Kazimierz Wiłkomirski[63] quoted a recollection by percussionist Józef Stojka who said that Hans Rohr, the appointed conductor of the GG Philharmonic, came to the Lardelli cafe to look for musicians, explaining that if the summons was boycotted, even performances in the cafes would be forbidden and all the musicians would remain jobless. The history of this orchestra will be described elsewhere; it is worth noting, however, that the orchestra, clearly used by Hans Frank as an instrument of propaganda, was at the same time an institution which permitted the survival of Polish musicians and those in hiding because of their Jewish background, such as first violinists Otto Teutsch and Artur Nachtstern. This orchestra was also a place where the segregation policies within the city were blurred. The fact that the first violinist Fritz Sonnleitner and the conductors were German, while all the other musicians were Polish, can be interpreted as an effort to keep Polish musicians in the position of "serfs" within the German hegemony.

However, the actual relations between German and Polish musicians were good. In an interview conducted by the author, a witness who played in the orchestra stated that musicians from both sides respected each other for their artistry.[64] In the fall of 1941, Sonnleitner created his Fritz Sonnleitner-Quartett der Philharmonie des Generalgouvernements with Polish musicians (Józef Salacz, Tadeusz Szulc and Józef Mikulski), which gave concerts until April 12, 1943.[65] The above-mentioned witness stated that one of the orchestra's conductors, Rudolf Hindemith, saved two musicians from a street round-up, which took place close to the building where rehearsals and concerts were taking place.[66] This

---

63 K. Wiłkomirski, *Wspomnienia* (Krakow: Polskie Wydawnictwo Muzyczne, 1971), 550–551. For the history of the orchestra see also A. Woźniakowska, *60 lat Filharmonii im. Karola Szymanowskiego w Krakowie. 1945–2005* (Krakow: Filharmonia im. K. Szymanowskiego w Krakowie, 2004), 22–28.
64 This person wanted to remain anonymous.
65 Cf. S. Lachowicz, 76–77.
66 To be sure, this type of relations was extraordinary in the middle of cruelty and persecutions; S. Lachowicz, who was also witness of the time, makes it clear in the attempt of evaluation which closes his book: "Music did not alleviate the Hitlerite customs. I remember one good Jewish musician who for a few months gave accordion lessons to Gestapo chief in Tarnów. He praised his pupil that he offered sometimes a piece of bread and ersatz coffee; he saw in this a guarantee for his own survival. Soon, however, on the order of the latter he was murdered in the street, when he was coming back home after a lesson. I remember the corpse lying next to the kerb, with head covered with a newspaper. But these are questions pertaining to domain of psychopathology,

person also recalled the moment when Sonnleitner was called into active Wehrmacht service and had to leave Krakow.

Nazi propaganda focused on the Germanization of Krakow tried to make use of the most important symbols of this city, also of the parts of its auditory landscape. Thus, not only did they rename Wawel Castle as *Krakauer Burg* and tried to posthumously Germanize Fryderyk Chopin, but also intended to appropriate the traditional bugle call (*Hejnał*) played from the steeple of St. Mary's Church in central Krakow. The latter intention can be read in nine letters exchanged between the mayor (*Stadthauptman*) Karl Schmid and his collaborators in late 1940.[67] Schmid sent his first letter on September 30 to Magistratsdirektor Dusza, asking that "on the tower of St. Mary's Church before the war, a trumpeter blew a certain melody every day. I would like to know if this practice was resumed after the war, and on what this practice was based. On what occasion was the music introduced? Who ordered the bugler and, on whose instructions did he act?"

Dr. Kurtz from the Abteilung Volksauflärung und Propaganda sent a letter on October 10 to Schmid (delivered to the Stadthauptman on the 12th) on the letterhead of the Abteilung Volksauflärung und Propaganda of the Amt des Generalgouverneurs für die besetzten polnischen Gebiete, in which he responded that the bugle call had no political meaning.[68] On November 12, Schmid replied that the call could serve German interests without any military associations: "As can be seen from the 5 enclosures, the tower blowing, which is common here, could be resumed. This would be a peculiar game, which would certainly also meet the interest of the Germans. Before I make a final decision, please let me know soon if there are no objections from the military side."[69] After receiving the

---

which seem to exceed the competences of the author, although they seem to be so unambiguous…" Ibid., 132.
67 Preserved in National Archive in Krakow, under signature SmKr 213. "Auf dem Turm der Marienkirche wurde vor dem Kriege durch einen Trompeter täglich eine bestimmte Melodie geblasen. Ich bitte um Mitteilung, ob diese übung nach dem Kriege wieder aufgenommen wurde, und ausserdem, worauf sich diese übung gründer. Aus welchem Anlass wurde die Musik eingeführt? Wer hatte den Bläser bestellt und auf wessen Weisung handelte er?"
68 "Dieses Signal ist früher über alle polnischen Sender als Mittagszeichen gegangen und sogar Anlass für verschiedene Novellen usw. Gewesen. Ich würde es für richtig halten, das Turmblasen wieder inzuführen, da e seine schöne Sitte ist und tatsächlich keinen politischen Hintergrund hat."
69 "Wie aus den 5 Beilagen ersichtlich ist, könnte das hier übliche Turmblasen wieder aufgenommen warden. Es ware dies ein eigenartiges Spiel, das sicherlich auch dem Interesse der Deutschen beggegnen würde. Bevor ich eine endgülgige Entscheidung

declaration that the call had no military significance, at a meeting he convened on December 17 with Director Schmidt of the Department of Nation Enlightenment and Propaganda, Schmid signed the document *Aktenvermerk betr. Turmblasen*, in which he "pointed out that St. Mary's Church was created by Germans and was only accessible to Germans for the last hundred years. He presumed that the bugle call [*Turmblase*] was especially cultivated by the Germans, and that we should not, on our part, have any reservations about the reintroduction."[70]

The exchange ends with the letter of December 17, sent by Schmid to the Krakow Fire Department, which before the war had performed the bugle call, ordering its reinstatement, with its first sounding on December 24 at 7 PM.[71]

Based on evidence gathered to date, one can argue that similarities were considerable in Nazi German policies in Warsaw and Krakow: Germanization and de-Polonization. Control over inhabitants and resettlements of the pre-war citizenry appear to have been even more pronounced in Krakow, the capital of the General Government. Music was used to attain these goals; the scope of propagandistic measures involving music still requires further examination. Actions taken against such an outstanding independent Polish cultural centre as the Plastyków cafe were ruthless; similar actions were also taking place in Warsaw.[72] The

---

treffe, bitte ich um baldgefl. Mitteilung, ob militärischerseits keine Bedenken bestehen."
"As can be seen from the 5 enclosures, the tower blowing, which is common here, could be resumed. This would be a peculiar game, which would certainly also meet the interest of the Germans. Before I make a final decision, please let me know soon if there are no objections from the military side."

70 "Am 17.12. 1940 habe ich mit Herrn Präsident Schmidt von der Abteilung für Volksaufklärung und Propaganda wegen der Wiedereinführung des Turmblasens Rücksprache genommen und ihn namentlich von dem Shreiben von Herrn Dr. Kurtz vom 10.10.1940 unterrichtet. Präsident Schmidt begrüsste sehr lebhaft die Wiedereinführung allen Stellen gegenüber zu vertreten. Er wies besonders noch darauf hin, dass die Marienkirche ja von Deutschen erstellt sei und jahrhundertelang nur für Deutsche zugänglich war. Er vermute, dass das Turmblasen namentlich auch von den Deutschen gepflegt wurde und deshalb von unserer Seite keinerlei Bedenken gegen die Wiedereinführung bestehen sollten."

71 An die Städt. Feuerwehr, Krakau. Ostring': "Auf den Bericht vom 6.11.1940 ordne ich hiermit an, dass das Turmblasen in der alten Wise wieder aufgenommen wird. Zunächst wird das Spiel aber auf mittags 12 Uhr und abends 7 Uhr beschränkt. Zu diesen Zeiten ist es in der früheren Weise auszuführen. Das Spiel beginnt erstmals am 24. Dezember um 19 Uhr. Für den Fall, dass irgendwelche Zweifel besteigen, wolle bei mir umgehend Rückfrage gehalten werden."

72 The case of "Arkadia" cafe which was opened at the beginning of 1940 or the end of 1939 in the preserved part of Warsaw Philharmonic building, already after the opening

whole idea behind restricting independent musical activities among Poles presupposed further forms of vigilance and control. German control of the musical repertoire and access to it, the planned manipulation of auditory spaces and, most importantly, the physical extermination of musicians and their audiences dictated by the racial Nuremberg Laws, resulted in the most extreme realizations of *Lebensraum* concept which resulted in massive losses to Polish musical culture. Thus, the symbolic spaces created in illicit, clandestine music-making were vitally important in all spheres of occupied Poland, from cities and urban spaces to detention sites such as prisons, ghettos, and the massive system of German concentration camps.

2.1.6. Clandestine music as protest, resistance, and quest for freedom

In Nazi occupied Poland, music played a significant role both as a method of protest against the occupiers and as a way to express personal freedom. The ban on Chopin's music at the beginning of occupation and the destruction of his statue in Łazienki Park in May 1940 made his figure only more symbolic as the representation of freedom of thought, of independent music making and of safeguarding national identity. The Polish society reacted to these policies not only by playing his music clandestinely, but also with irony. A card placed on the ruin of Chopin's statue declared: "I don't know who destroyed me, but I know why: so that I won't play the funeral march for your leader." Three months later, on August 30, 1940, when during the Nazi ceremony of renaming the Piłsudski Square in Warsaw to "Adolf-Hitler Platz", the statue of Prince Józef Poniatowski was concealed behind a red screen, the next day at the statue's pedestal a card appeared with the following warning: "Joseph, if you want to avoid my fate declare yourself

---

of such cafes as "Bristol", "Lira" by Piotr Perkowski and the most famous one, "Sztuka i Moda" (SiM) cafe which was inaugurated on 16 December 1939. This musical cafe, where the underground activity was strong and not perfectly organized, operated until 4 December 1940, when Gestapo arrested everybody present there. As described by W. Bartoszewski, (1974), some of the arrested, who were kept in Pawiak prison, were executed in Palmiry near Warsaw on 12 June 1941 (29 persons, 14 women among them). Others were sent to concentration camps; the wife of Stanisław Piasecki who was the editor of right-wing underground journal *Walka*, medical doctor Irena Piasecka was sent in a *Sondertransport* of 274 women to Ravensbrück. W. Bartoszewski, (1974). *1859 dni* Warszawy, 209, 225–226.

Volksdeutsch – Chopin." This was quoted by the underground weekly *Biuletyn informacyjny* as an audacious joke.[73]

Within the specific conditions in which Polish culture was systematically destroyed, Poles could only play music in cafes or in German-controlled halls, and music making was censored. More serious undertakings were attempted by Polish underground organizations, which aimed at counteracting the Nazi "cultural policy." Music became the actual means of maintaining dignity and identity in these conditions, performing Polish music became a form of protest against the lack of freedom, inhumane Nazi policies and Germanization.

In attempting to define such music, three main types can be discerned. The Clandestine Council of Musicians (Tajna Rada Muzyków) undertook organization of concerts in private apartments where ambitious programmes were performed, and a network of support for musicians in hiding was developed, which among other things was aimed at fundraising during concerts to pay for food and other necessities for those musicians. The most famous case of a musician supported in this way was Władysław Szpilman, who was supported in hiding with money earned from concerts organized by Witold Lutosławski or the singer Janina Godlewska-Bogucka, even though such activity could be punished by the Nazis with the death penalty. Also, several private individuals organized clandestine concerts. Playing Chopin and Polish music such as Szymanowski's was thus itself a form of protest against the occupiers' policies. The scores were copied by hand, as they were otherwise unavailable

Warsaw's suppressed musical life became quite intense in 1940 in numerous artistic cafes and in clandestine form in private apartments. Already by November 1939, the first "artistic" cafes emerged. Zygmunt Latoszewski from Poznań, who specialized in opera conducting before the war, conducted a small orchestra at the "Gastronomia" cafe in Warsaw. At the same time, musicians, many of whom were linked to different resistance movements, responded to the terror by creating underground musical institutions (one of the main organizers was composer Piotr Perkowski, later instrumental in saving Władysaw Szpilman's life)

---

73 In original Polish version: "Józiu, jeżeli chcesz uniknąć mego losu – podaj się za volksdeutscha – Szopen," *Biuletyn informacyjny*, 6 September 1940, 6. Two days later, on 8 September such eminent personalities of Polish cultural life as singer Mira Zimińska and writer Adolf Nowaczyński were arrested among others. Interestingly, Prince Poniatowski's statue, with its classicist form not so far removed from Nazi aesthetic ideals, survived longer than the Chopin monument; it was blown up only in December 1944, during the desrcuction of Warsaw effectuated on the orders of General Erich von dem Bach.

that served various aims: the organization of musical clandestine life, planning of the reconstruction of musical life after the war, support for musicians and people in hiding, and the commissioning of special songs for the Home Army (such songs were composed, for instance, by Witold Lutosławski). Clandestine performances of new compositions and of music by Chopin, Szymanowski and other censored composers were constrained to the restricted space of the private apartment (see a clandestine concert programme in the Appendix).

When Warsaw was divided by the Nazis, and the ghetto was established, playing music there in spite of the tragic conditions was in itself a form of protest. The protest against dehumanization was a constant fight for dignity and freedom in art. The singing by the "Ghetto nightingale," Marysia Ajzensztadt, and her death at Umschlagplatz, where she was shot by German soldiers, symbolize the lot of many artists who with their music refused the degradation planned and realized by the Nazis. Such heroic endeavours as Jacob Glatstein's childrens' choir give us an idea of the way in which music functioned as a form of protest and gave people hope (see a photograph of Jacob Glatstein's children choir and a music programme from the Warsaw Ghetto).

When discussing protest music, one should mention the repertoire of new songs written by such outstanding composers as Witold Lutosławski and Andrzej Panufnik on commission from the underground Information and Propaganda Office of the Home Army (Armia Krajowa). This type of music was designed to express the will to struggle against the occupiers and fight for independence. These songs, known in Poland to this day, were written mainly for people trained to be soldiers in the underground in anticipation of an uprising. In October 1942, the most important clandestine paper, *Biuletyn Informacyjny*, announced a competition for texts of three types of songs, strictly defining their character. Prospective authors had only a month to send their work, using the same illegal channels through which the bulletin was distributed.

The first type, defined as "The Song of Underground Poland" (Pieśń Polski Podziemnej) was to be rhythmical, and constitute a form of "hymn, inducing an atmosphere of power and perseverance." The second type, a "Soldier's March," "will lead the soldiers of the uprising in battle and will be played through loudspeakers in days of freedom. The words should express ideas of Freedom of the Great and Righteous Poland, which will deal out punishment to the criminals." The third category, another type of a soldier's song, was "to recreate the mood of the soldier, who is fighting in difficult uprising conditions, but is still animated by high spirit, enthusiasm and a specific sense of humour." The outcome of the competition was published again in *Biuletyn Informacyjny* and the new lyrics were transmitted to the musicians. Already in December 1942 the first song was ready, to the words by the winner of the competition, Stanisław Ryszard Dobrowolski (1907–1985, pseudonym "Goliard") and music by Jan Ekier (born in 1913, pseudonym "Janosik"). Titled *Szturmówka*, which could be translated as "Assault Song", this song quickly gained popularity and was performed during clandestine concerts, underground boy and girl scout meetings and later, during the Warsaw Uprising, it was also published clandestinely. There followed other songs, for example one written by a very talented poet Tadeusz Gajcy (under the pseudonym "Witold Orczyk"), who received the second prize during the competition, with music by Jan Ekier – *Attack* (*Uderzenie*, 1942). The poet took part in the Warsaw Uprising and was killed. Third and fourth stanzas read as follows:

Na broni naszej chmurnej i ostrej	On our weapon, turbid and sharp
Ojczyzny nowy uniesiemy kształt,	We will carry the new shape of our Homeland
Ciosem na cios, Ciosem na cios,	
Za krzywdę celny mówić będzie strzał.	Strike for a strike, Strike for a strike,
Tylko uderzyć zawzięcie i mocno	For injustice the unerring shot will speak.
Tylko pod pięścią rozpędzony marsz	
Serce jak grom, Serce jak grom,	Just hit fiercely and firmly
Wrogowi czujnie stanąć twarzą w twarz.	Under the fist a rushing march
	Heart like thunder, heart like thunder,
	Stand alert to face the enemy.

Another author of such songs was Krytyna Krahelska (1914–1944) who later – as one of many women paramedics during the Warsaw Uprising – was killed by Nazi snipers, even though she wore on her clothing the sign of the red cross.[74]

Finally, a huge repertoire of songs of dissent was created in cities (these were among other street songs) and in places of detention, persecution, and mass-killings, such as prisons, ghettos, and different types of camps. Many of these songs were for the most part anonymous because of the danger from the occupiers, the names of the authors were in some cases established after the war.

Singers and musicians who sang in the cities before the war became even more numerous during the war, there were whole bands of impoverished musicians that played in the streets, but singers in particular constantly faced arrest, prison, internment in camps or death. This applied even to children, especially if they sang songs with some patriotic or anti-German content. Apart from the

---

74 Krystyna Krahelska, *Smutna rzeka...* (London: Koło Byłych Żołnierzy Armii Krajowej, 1964).

traditional Polish song repertoire, street singers performed new songs, some of which were written clandestinely or invented by anonymous authors; in several cases new words were added to well-known melodies. They were often set in the folk song style, with some satirical elements. The history of these new songs was described in the preface to a clandestine collection of songs entitled *Songs of Arms* ("Pieśni zbrojne"). It was published by the Clandestine Military Publishing ("Tajne Wojskowe Zakłady Wydawnicze," see Appendix). On the cover we can also see the intentionally false date: 1938. This simple trick could save somebody's life during a hasty round-up by the Germans, which often took place in the streets. Only inside can we see the actual date, which is April 1942. The preface reads as follows:

> Neither September 1939 nor the beginning of German-Soviet occupation of the Country favoured singing. The course of events was so breathtaking, the catastrophe so terrible, conditions of new life engulfed in such terror and suffering – that, in these monstrous times, all song in Poland went silent. (…) However, already in mid-1940 this silence was broken (…) by… spontaneous folk song. Just as in the time of Tatar raids [on Poland], or in times of [the Swedish] Deluge – unknown authors appeared from nowhere, simple people, who within their hearts found words and melodies telling of the suffering (…) and who prophesied the advent of a new, great Tomorrow. Hundreds of singers, male or female, street, train, or road singers, wandering from house to house, from town to town, from village do village, carried these words of suffering, heroism and hope throughout Polish lands.
>
> We all know very well with what an avid heart one listened to these first, courageous songs. (…) When the first important English bombing of the Reich began – a carol about the joyous news was created: Berlin crumbles, Hamburg burns, it gets on Hitler's and Goering's nerves.

Songs and words were published inside, such as the above-mentioned *Assault Song* [*Szturmówka*] or *The Attack* [*Uderzenie*].

Songs created in prisons and other detention sites were also often written to well known pre-war melodies. Thus, the guards, who did not know Polish, could not understand the true content of the songs, the goal of which being primarily to uplift the morale of prisoners and express their protest. Prison guards usually forbade singing, but prisoners often quietly sung in their cells. One known example is the *Prisoners' Anthem* by female prisoners of the Pawiak prison which was infamous in Warsaw because of the abominable torture inflicted on men, women, and youngsters by SS functionaries. The hymn's melody was taken from the well-known tune *He died, poor thing, in the army hospital* (*Zmarł biedaczysko w szpitalu polowym*) from the pre-war popular film *Ten from Pawiak* (*Dziesięciu z Pawiaka*). One version of the words added to this melody was created by Józefa

Radzymińska in 1941, tortured during interrogations in the Gestapo prison at the Szucha Alley where Pawiak prisoners were interrogated. It begins in the following way: "Proud, perseverant, we are sitting behind bars, / our hearts won't be won over by time. / We will laugh under their whizzing whips, / nothing will defeat us." ("Dumne, zacięte siedzimy za kratą, / nie zmoże serc naszych czas. / Śmiać się będziemy pod świstem ich batów, / nic nie zwycięży już nas.").[75] As described in the memoirs of another female prisoner of Pawiak, Janina Dunin-Wąsowicz, this song was sung very low, after the roll call. An interesting example of a prison song was provided by another witness, Henryk Strzałkowski, arrested in January 1943 with his three elder brothers, tortured by the Gestapo to prove that they had helped resistance fighters. He was kept in a prison in Białystok, in the eastern part of the Polish territories, then transported to the Stutthof concentration camp, and afterwards to the Mauthausen-Gusen camp. According to his testimony regarding the Białystok prison, a song with new words was sung to a melody of the great hit of the 1930s: *Tango notturno* with music by Hans-Otto Borgmann, popularized in Poland by Pola Negri, a Polish actress who had become a Hollywood star:

---

75 Józefa Radzymińska, *Dwa razy popiół: wspomnienia z lat 1939–1949* (Krakow: Wydawnictwo Literackie, 1970), quoted in Tadeusz Szewera: 1999, 30. She wrote that at women's division at Pawiak prison called "Serbia," the prisonners sang a lot, because "nothing alleviates sadness better than a song."

Teraz jest wojna, piosenek nikt nie tworzy,	It is war now, nobody creates songs,
to zmarnowanie naszych młodych lat.	It is a waste of our young years
Dzisiaj piosenkę nową z podniesioną głową,	Today a new song with your head lifted up
zaśpiewaj bracie zza niemieckich krat.	Sing brother from behind German bars
Niewolnicze tango wspomnień i cierpienia,	Slave tango of memories and torment
niewolnicze tango sześcioletniego więzienia.	Slave tango of six-years-long imprisonment
Polak batutę weźmie w swoje ręce,	The Pole will take in his hands a baton,
na saksofonie zagra Rumun, Czech,	Rumanian and Czech will play saxophone,
Anglik i Francuz niech zanucą trele,	English and French will sing along,
a bas z bandżolą to wolności śpiew	And bass with banjola, it is freedom song
Niewolnicze tango wspomnień i cierpienia,	Slave tango of memories and torment
niewolnicze tango sześcioletniego więzienia.	Slave tango of six-years-long imprisonment
Lecz przyjdzie chwila i kajdany zerwę,	But the moment will come when I'll break my chains,
wtedy usłyszysz głos piosenki, zew.	You will then hear the voice of song, a call,
Usta me zanucą niewolnicze tango,	My lips will hum the slave tango,
niewolnicze tango to wolności śpiew.	Slave tango is freedom's song.
Niewolnicze tango wspomnień i cierpienia,	Slave tango of memories and torment
niewolnicze tango sześcioletniego więzienia.	Slave tango of six-years-long imprisonment[76]

This satirical strain in camp and prison repertoire was there for an obvious reason: again, to support the morale of prisoners, for example in the Stutthof camp. When prisoners from Pawiak prison were brought there in June 1944, the inmates sang satirical verses to the traditional Polish melody *Szły dwa dziady* commencing with the words: "It is an unpleasant affair air air / Warsaw is in

---

76 "Byłem numerem za kolczastym drutem," in: Andrzej Alicki, Marek Kietliński, Dariusz Kloza, Barbara Świętońska, Anna Żuk (eds.), *Pieśń ujdzie cało* (Towarzystwo Opieki nad Majdankiem, Zarząd Oddziału w Białymstoku 2004).

Stutthof today ay ay" ("Nieprzyjemna dla nas sprawa wa wa wa, / Jest w Stuttho-
fie dziś Warszawa wa wa wa").

The Polish response to the policy of destruction of higher education was clandestine coursework organized either in schools, where pupils were taught a Polish program instead of through textbooks approved by the Germans, or in private apartments. Often two kinds of teachers were employed; those who were official (for instance, specialists in tailoring), to prepare for the frequent German inspections, and those who taught history, Polish literature, and other subjects. On the university level clandestine courses in various specialties were taught in private apartments. These educational actions were brutally repressed. Professors and directors of schools were arrested by the Gestapo, and after interrogation they were executed or sent to concentration camps. The students at these clandestine universities were subjected to similar persecutions.

Things were better in the field of musical education, for music naturally offered more possibilities for conspiracy and required no specific textbooks, which could be later used by the Gestapo as incriminating proof. The *Staadtlische Musikschule* opened in the former Warsaw Conservatory building and was intended officially as a vocational school for future orchestra musicians. Its director was a German musician, Albert Hösl, who was not a fanatical supervisor; in fact, the vice-director, Kazimierz Sikorski, the distinguished Polish pedagogue and composer, who was designated by the clandestine Polish Musicians Association to fulfill this task, took care of the school himself. There, Polish teachers illegally taught composition and conducting. Witnesses only noted one intervention of the Gestapo at the school and a single student arrest. The students were partly protected in case of roundups by a document stipulating that they studied in this official school.

A substantial song repertoire was created in the ghettos and other detention and genocide sites in response to the tragic reality. The numerous functions of this music were documented and explained un the above-quoted books: by Gila Flam in her book *Singing for Survival. Songs of the Łódź Ghetto, 1940–45* and by Shirli Gilbert's book *Music in the Holocaust*. Most of these songs were written in Yiddish; they often functioned as street songs and were satirical in tone. These topics will be addressed in chapter 3.

2.2. Music in Reich-annexed territories: *Aufbau* in the Warthegau

The situation in the Reich-annexed territories, such as the region of Poznań and Łódź, being parts of *Reichsgau Wartheland*, resulted from Hitler's assumption that this area should become entirely German as soon as possible. Thus, the authorities of the Warthegau aggressively sought to banish all traces of Polish culture by: "(1) closing down or destroying all Polish scientific and cultural institutions, the entire press, the wireless, cinemas and theatres; (2) closing down and destroying the network of Polish schools both elementary, middle and high, and closing down all Polish collections, archives and libraries; (3) destroying many of the relics and monuments of Polish culture and art or transforming them so as no longer to serve Polish culture."[77] The above-quoted NSDAP document *Die Frage der Behandlung der Bevölkerung der ehemaligen polnischen Gebiete nach rassenpolitischen Gesichtspunkten* ("The question of treating the population of the former Polish territory from the racial-political point of view") of November 1939 gave the following instructions concerning the population in the *Eingegliederte Ostgebiete*:

> Polish restaurants and cafes – as centres of Polish national life – should be forbidden. Poles are not allowed to frequent German theatres, cabarets and cinema-theatres. Polish theatres, cinema-theatres and other places of cultural entertainment should be closed. There will be no Polish daily newspapers, no Polish books or reviews will be published. For the same reason the Poles are not allowed to own radios and gramophones. (…)

In the same document it is also ordered that

> The whole of the Polish intelligentsia [from the Reich-incorporated territories] should be immediately transported to the remaining territory (the notion of Polish intelligentsia encompasses, first of all, Polish priests, teachers [higher schools included], doctors, dentists, veterinarians, officers, clerks of higher rank, important merchants and landowners, writers, editors, as well as all persons who graduated from high schools or universities).[78]

These plans were quickly carried out. Already on October 25, 1939, Goebbels could observe in his diary after a meeting with Warthegau Governor Arthur Greiser that "Poles are slowly deported in the remaining rump state. Of the intelligentsia not much is left."[79] Poles who could be useful for the Reich were not

---

77 *Law Reports of Trials of War Criminals*, Vol. 13, 73–4.
78 Ibid.
79 'Greiser berichtet mir über Theaterfragen in Posen, deren ich mich nun…. annehmen will. Er erzählt mir auch von den dortigen Zuständen. Es geht noch immer hoch her. Die Partei kann noch nicht recht durchgreifen, solange das Militär ihr dauernd in den Arm fällt. Aber das hört ja nun bald auf. Die Polen werden langsam in den übrigbleibenden Reststaat abgeschoben. Von der Intelligenz ist nicht mehr viel übriggeblieben.' Elke Fröhlich (ed.), *Die Tagebücher von Joseph Goebbels. Sämtliche Fragmente*, München (K. G. Saur), 1987, Vol. 3, 620.

deported. This corresponded with Greiser's attitude towards Poles and Jews, which Catherine Epstein has aptly characterized as "an inconsistent mixture of racial hatred and pragmatic concern."[80] Greiser's attitude was expressed among others in his article "Zur Volkstumsfrage" published in *Völkischer Beobachter* on April 29, 1942, where he stated that Polish intelligentsia, middle class and clerics always produced great "haters of Germany," and quoted his own book *Der Aufbau im Osten* (Jena: Fischer, 1942, 8): "The Pole also has a whole different attitude toward the things of daily life and to the culture in Europe... For Poles it is the best satisfaction, the utter height of feeling, when he can drink and gorge himself like an animal."[81]

To exclude any possibility of a Polish-German coexistence, Greiser introduced a strict segregation system, which Epstein notes, underscoring his vision of German-Polish relations, voiced in his phrase: "The German is the master in this area, the Pole is the serf!"[82] In guidelines issued in September 1940, he ordered that the Germans should be educated in "the necessity of absolutely reserving a personal distance from Polish nationals" and that friendly relations were unacceptable.[83] Segregation measures were introduced in all realms; playgrounds and park benches, public baths, and even recreational boats were "for Germans only." Poles lost property rights and were not allowed to visit museums, libraries, theatres, and concert halls.[84]

As documented in "Measures against Polish Culture and Science," Greiser's subsequent regulations were as follows:

> This war began with the liquidation of the intelligentsia and clergy: the entire Warthegau was denuded of Polish professors, scientists, teachers, [j]udges, advocates, doctors, engineers, and other representatives of the classes that constituted the greatest hindrance to the Germanization of the country. The cultural centre of Poznań University was closed immediately on the entry of the Germans, and most of the professors were arrested and either sent to concentration camps, or imprisoned, or else held as hostages, or deported to the General Government. In December 1939, some of the professors were released from prison and deported to the General Government, being deprived not only of their private property, but even of their manuscripts and scientific works. Altogether,

---

80 Catherine Epstein, *Model Nazi. Arthur Greiser and the Occupation of Western Poland* (Oxford, Oxford University Press, 2010), 231.
81 Ibid., 195.
82 Ibid.
83 Ibid., 198
84 Ibid., 199.

as a result of these measures, there perished 24 professors, 15 supernumerary professors, 26 assistants, and 20 university officials.

The buildings of Poznań University and all cultural institutions were taken over by the Nazi authorities and used for various purposes (...). On April 27, 1941, a German university was opened in Poznań, which came under the authority of Greiser, as he became its president; all teaching came under the German rector, Dr. Carstens, and he from the beginning laid down that 'in this university of the East there will be no place for scientists dealing with problems only from the objective point of view (Law Reports of Trials of War Criminals 1949, 82–83).

Books, archives, museums and art collections, scientific periodicals and newspapers were confiscated (ca. 30 public museums and over 100 private collections) or destroyed.[85] It was also forbidden to print any kind of books in Polish and from April 1940 – the sale of all French- and English-language books, as well as the sale of the music of Chopin and other Polish composers, was banned. Libraries were closed and towards the end of 1940 the Propaganda Office published a list of forbidden Polish books that comprised ca. 3,000 titles. On November 21,1941, Greiser ordered the removal of all bells from Polish churches, including those protected by the law as historic monuments. By order of October 15, 1944, all church organs were sequestered.[86] The buildings and all the equipment of Polish cultural institutions, which were all closed, were put at the disposal of German

---

85 The same text gives the following details: "Gauleiter Greiser laid upon the members of the Hitlerjugend the special duty of destroying all the libraries of the Society for People's Libraries, which premises were demolished, and the books burned and destroyed. Similarly school libraries were destroyed." Book Collecting Point (*Buchsammelstelle*) was organized in the church of St. Michael in Poznań, where almost two million volumes from public and private libraries of the Warthegau were sorted and either distributed to various German institutions or sent to paper-mill for pulping. See *Law Reports of Trials of War Criminals* (1949, 82–83).

86 "The churches were despoiled completely. A memorandum from the Gestapo submitted to Greiser, No. II b.l of 21 March 1942, informed him that in the action taken for security reasons against the Polish churches at the beginning of October 1941, money, foreign exchange, script, church books, documents, libraries, and other important written material was removed from the Church offices and from the houses of the priests, while chalices, monstrances, candlesticks, candles and linen were removed from the churches. The candles – about 20 tons – were handed over to the army, and the linen – about 6 tons – to the German Red Cross. The memorandum drew Greiser's attention to the fact that many articles of value, such as pictures, furniture and carpets, still remained in the churches and recommended that they should be taken over." (Law Reports of Trials of War Criminals 1949, 82).

institutions. This policy affected theatres (in Poznań, Łódź and Kalisz), cinemas, and the Opera House and the Music Conservatory in Poznań. Regretfully, the document continues: "Even choral societies were closed, and the famous Poznań Cathedral Choir that was known all over Europe was disbanded and its director, Father [Wacław] Gieburowski [1878–1943], imprisoned" (he was later released and transported to the General Government).

The broadcasting stations in Poznań and Łódź became German stations; all wireless receiving sets belonging to Poles were confiscated and listening to foreign stations, especially London, was punishable by death (*Law Reports of Trials of War Criminals* 1949, 84).

An extraordinary effort was made toward the destruction of Polish memorials which, as the document foregrounds, "were destroyed in an especially insulting manner and the destruction was accompanied by mockery and ridicule. These acts were given great emphasis in the German Press."[87] Among those destroyed in Poznań were the Chopin and Moniuszko statues. A case study that demonstrates the strategies employed is the Wielkopolskie Museum (Museum of Greater Poland, before 1919 the Kaiser Friedrich Museum) in Poznań. In place of its director, the historian of art Dr. Nikodem Pajzderski, who was arrested in October 1939 and killed on January 6, 1940, in Fort VII camp in Poznań,[88] a German director, Dr. Rühle, was appointed, and the museum solemnly reopened on January 24. The General Government's German-language press relayed with satisfaction that the museum – instead of being an exponent of "Polish Kitsch" – had

---

87 What is more, the Order of 17 April 1940, which was published in the *Ostdeutscher Beobachter* under the aegis of Gauleiter Greiser, required the removal of all Polish inscriptions by 15 May 1940. (Law Reports of Trials of War Criminals 1949, 84). It should be mentioned that a similar approach towards Russian culture was later manifest while the invasion on Soviet Union, as was stated on 20 November 1945 during Nuremberg trials: "The Germans destroyed 427 museums, among them the wealthy museums of Leningrad, Smolensk, Stalingrad, Novgorod, Poltava, and others. (...) They broke up the estate of the poet Pushkin in Mikhailovskoye, desecrated his grave, and destroyed the neighbouring villages and the Svyatogor monastery." (Trial of the Major War Criminals 1947, 66, 67). Orthography of Polish names as well as punctuation was corrected in fragments quoted above and below.

88 The first commandant of Fort VII camp was Herbert Lange, who was member of Einsatzgruppe VI in September 1939, later organized mass killings of patients of mental asylums in occupied Poland, in December 1941 he was appointed as the first commandant of the Chełmno on Ner River extermination camp, a post he held until 1942. The second commandant of the Fort VII camp was SS-Oberführer Erich Neumann.

finally become the executor of such lofty endeavour as an exhibition of the region's purely German character.[89] The collection of monumental sculptures by Wacław Szymanowski known as "The Procession to the Wawel" was among the works of art which were destroyed. Characteristically, every possible effort was made to demolish all the existent copies of this sculptor's most famous work, the Chopin monument in Warsaw's Łazienki Park, the plaster replicas of which and a wooden copy donated by the artist were also destroyed in the Poznań museum.[90]

According to Hitler's views on the ultimately detrimental effects of Germanization of the Poles, the education rules in Warthegau stated that Poles were to learn German, yet poorly enough to testify that "the German is also the master in terms of language."[91]

Nonetheless, in ordering to establish and bolster German cultural superiority in occupied Poland, the Nazis faced two major problems. The first was to create an effective programme of resettlement to increase the number of Germans that

---

89 "Posen, 24. Januar. In einer schlichten Feierstunde wurde in Unwesenheit des Reichsstatthalters Gauleiter Greiser, und führende Vertreter aus Partei und Wehrmacht, des Staatlichen und kulturellen Lebens das alte, 1894 gegründete Kaiser-Friedrich-Museum in Posen nach seiner Reinigung von polnischem Kitsch und polnischer Verfälschung der Oeffentlichkeit übergeben. Ebenso wie auf anderen Gebieten hat auch in diesem Landesmuseum die polnische Kulturleistung der letzten 20 Jahre einzig und allein darin bestanden, dass man hochtrabend seinen Ramen in 'Grosspolnisches Museum' änderte und alle Beweise für die den geschichtlich deutschen Charakter des Warthe-Landes aus uhm verschwinden liess. 'Heute ist', wie Museumsdirektor Dr. Kühle in seiner Eröffnunfsansprache erklärte, 'das Kaiser-Friedrich-Muzeum wieder seiner ursprünglichen Aufgabe zugeführt worden, nämlich in seinen volksstundlichen, kunstlerischen und naturwissenschaftlichen Sammlungen und Austellungen den germanisch-deutschen Charakter von Land und Leuten des Warthe-Gaues zu zeigen'." *Warschauer Zeitung* 1940, 4.
90 However, one of the employees of the Museum managed to hide a copy of the statue's head in the cellar. As a result of this Nazi undertaking it was extremely difficult to reconstruct the statue after the war. It was finally reconstructed and unveiled in May 1958.
91 Ibid., 201. Epstein quoted here a Polish historian, Czesław Łuczak (from his *Dyskryminacja Polaków w Wielkopolsce w okresie okupacji hitlerowskiej: wybór źródeł*. Poznań: Wydawnictwo Poznańskie, 1966, 321–233) and added: "In the guidelines for schooling, Viktor Böttcher, president of Posen district argued that 'the teaching of fundamental beliefs (German language instruction in a deeper sense, history instruction) is not to take place. It must always be prevented that Poles gain so much education that they could pass for Germans. Priority value is attached to the teaching of order, cleanliness, discipline, and decency.'"

resided in Poland. To ensure there were sufficient numbers of Germans living in the various regions, the authorities had to draw upon two distinctive types of Germans: firstly – former citizens of the Reich (*Reichsdeutsche*), and secondly – ethnically German people from areas outside the Reich such as the Baltic states (*Volksdeutsche*). Hand in hand with this resettlement programme, there was the need to establish the most effective means for dealing with former Polish citizens. In spite of reinforcing a defined ideological position with regard to the Poles, the methods of implementation strongly depended upon the political status of the given area.

Whereas former Polish citizens constituted the majority of the population in the GG, the proportion of former Polish citizens in the territories annexed to the Third Reich varied considerably according to the different administrative districts. Nevertheless, the ultimate objective of the authorities controlling all these areas was to uphold the policy of Germanization combined with the absolute exclusion and destruction of Polish culture and its representatives. Those former Polish citizens who were allowed to stay in the new regions were not expelled, but only because they were needed as a working force to serve the Germans. They faced segregation, dire living conditions and were deprived of education opportunities beyond the primary school level.[92]

The political, ideological, and pseudo-aesthetic arguments used in favour of Germans residing in these areas remained similar to those applied to Germans in the GG. It could be summarized in the favourite rhetorical expression, often used in titles of articles and books: the German cultural 'build-up' or 'development' (*Aufbau*), which consisted in clearing culture of "contaminating" Jewish elements and forging it into an imagined purely German unity.[93] However, in the areas cleared almost completely of Poles and Jews, it placed greater emphasis on the notion of a greater spiritual German community (*Gemeinschaft*). Such an idea was more likely to be realized in the Warthegau province, whereas in the GG the German authorities still had to deal with the unwanted presence of Jews and Poles.

---

92 Catherine Epstein, *Model Nazi: Arthur Greiser and the Occupation of Western Poland*, (Oxford: Oxford University Press, 2010), 201. Further documentation on this topic may be found in Czesław Łuczak: *Dyskryminacja Polaków w Wielkopolsce w okresie okupacji hitlerowskiej: wybór źródeł*, (Poznań: Wydaw Poznańskie 1966); and Karol Marian Pospieszalski, *Hitlerowskie 'prawo' okupacyjne w Polsce* (Documenta Occupationis, Vol. 5, Poznań: Instytut Zachodni, 1952).

93 For a typical example in the area of music see Günter Haußwald, "Kulturaufbau im deutschen Osten," *Zeitschrift für Musik* 108/3 March (1941), 191–92.

The appointment of Arthur Greiser as Governor of the newly created Warthegau Province in 1939 unleashed arguably the most extreme attempt at Germanization in all the occupied territories of the East. As early as September 2, 1939, Greiser stated his intentions in an unequivocal language as he addressed the population of Poznań, the city which now became the central headquarters of the new region:

> All Polish influences, whether in the sphere of politics or culture or economy, will be eliminated once and for all. We Germans came here as masters, and the Poles are to be our servants (…). Our most important task is to settle this land with people to whom the concept of Poland will be in the future merely a historical memory.[94]

The population statistics of the Warthegau starkly illustrate the nature of the task that he was to face. In 1939, only 325,000 individuals, or 6.6% of the population in what would become the Warthegau, could consider themselves German. To remedy this situation Greiser spearheaded what historian Catherine Epstein has described as "one of the most dramatic and sustained Nazi demographic experiments." In his effort to "Germanize" his Gau, Greiser initiated the first mass gassings of Jews in Nazi-occupied Europe. Furthermore, he adopted an array of cruel measures: resettlement, deportation, and murder; segregation and anti-church policies; and the transformation of the Gau's natural and cultural environment. Due to the influx of re-settlers and Reich Germans, the ethnic cleansing and expulsion of Poles, and the murder of Jews, Greiser raised the percentage of Germans in the Warthegau to 22.9% by April 1944.[95]

One direct manifestation of Greiser's Germanization policies was that the capital city of the Warthegau, Poznań, was renamed to Posen, the name it had held during the earlier German occupation of this area following the second Prussian partition of Poland in 1793 and before the only successful Polish uprising at the turn of 1919 – the Greater Poland uprising (*Powstanie Wielkopolskie*) instigated by the arrival of Ignacy Jan Paderewski in Poznań. From the outset, several Nazi offices operating in Posen and other cities and towns of Warthegau took care of policies whose goal was to make this area German.[96] Former Polish citizens were

---

94 "Das Programm für Posen," *Posener Tageblatt*, 22 September 1939, 3.
95 Catherine Epstein, *Model Nazi*, 161. For a more in-depth analysis of German population in Warthegau see Grochowina, *Cultural Policy*, 117–118, where the author precisely explained the Nazi terminology and the fundamental division of German population to local Germans (*Volksdeutsche*), Germans who had arrived from the Reich (*Reichsdeutsche*) and the resettled people (*Umsiedler*).
96 To name just a few: Generaltreuhänder für die Sicherstellung deutsches Kulturgutes in den angegliederten Ostgebieten, Der Dienststelle Reichsgau Warthegau, Kulturamt,

thrown out of their homes, which were appropriated by German newcomers, as were Polish institutions that were commandeered for the sake of the German *Gemeinschaft*. Already in September 1939, a special division directed by Professor Peter Paulsen from Rostock University (*Einsatzkommando Paulsen*) was established by the Reich's Ministry of Inner Affairs and the Prussian government in order to confiscate Polish art collections.[97]

Polish musicians, teachers, and intellectuals in Poznań and Łódź, the other large city in the Warthegau, were targeted by Greiser as dangerous "geistige Oberschicht" (intellectual / spiritual upper class).[98] A substantial number had to move to the GG, whereas several others were imprisoned. Marian Sauer – professor of piano at the Music Conservatory in Poznań was arrested and shot by the Nazis. Other Polish intellectuals were murdered in Fort VII, the first Nazi concentration camp in Poznań. Among them, in December 1939, was Witold Noskowski, journalist, music and theatre critic, who worked for the newspaper *Kurier Poznański* and was co-founder of the cabaret Green Balloon ("Zielony Balonik"), famous in inter-war Poland. Most often false reasons of death were given, such as suicide or in the case of the music teacher Mieczysław Kaszak, who died on June 2, 1943, "weakness after quinsy." Some of the intellectuals who were not executed in the first months of the occupation or were arrested later, were transferred to Dachau, Auschwitz, Mauthausen-Gusen and other camps.[99]

Deutsche Umsiedlungs-Treuhand GmbH, in Posen, Deutsche Kulturpropaganda GmbH, + 'Wochenspruch d. NSDAP', 'Parole der Woche' Werbestelle Ost, Buchhandlung für Universitäts u. Fachliteratur Kohl und Bielenstein, etc.

97 *Mitteilungsblatt der Preußischen Archivverwaltung*, 1940, Bd. I, 8, quoted in the article on the role of Polish museums and museologists in saving and restitution of lost cultural heritage in the twentieth and twenty-first centuries by Dariusz Matelski, "Rola muzeów i muzealników polskich w ratowaniu i restytucji utraconego dziedzictwa kultury w XX–XXI wieku (część I – do 1945 r.)" "The (part I – until 1945)," *Rocznik Muzeum Wsi Mazowieckiej w Sierpcu* (2), 2011, 65–106. See also the catalogue of looted works of Polish art "secured" by the Germans in the General Government, *Sichergestellte Kunstwerke im Generalgouvernement* (Breslau: Wilh. Gottl. Korn, ca 1940).

98 On extermination on Polish intelligentsia, as well as on destruction and plunder of Polish cultural heritage, monuments of Chopin and Moniuszko among others, see: Grochowina, *Cultural Policy*, 83–104.

99 Stanisław Nawrocki, "Losy inteligencji poznańskiej podczas okupacji," *Kronika Miasta Poznania* 66/2 (1998). In the long list of victims killed in different parts of occupied Poland or camps in Germany, contained in this article, one finds other journalists of the *Kurier Poznański* and professors of the Poznań University, such as Konstanty Troczyński, literary critic and lecturer at the Poznań University, who worked at the

Although the documentation was destroyed by the Nazis at the end of the war it is known that the killers included Herbert Lange who from November 1939 was in charge of the Gestapo in occupied Poznań as SS-Untersturmführer (in 1940 promoted to SS-Obersturmführer and in 1941 to SS-Hauptsturmführer as commander of the Chełmno extermination camp by SS-Standartenführer Ernst Damzog, head of the Sicherheitspolizei (SiPo) and Sicherheitsdienst (SD) in Posen), responsible for the extermination of the mentally ill in Wartheland (5408 patients in Owińska, Kościan and Działdowo), and Poles at Fort VII where a gas-chamber was used. His unit, Kommando Lange, later (April 1942) renamed to SS Sonderkommando Kulmhof, was to exterminate 100 thousand Jews from the Warthegau brought to Chełmno (Kulmhof) from the Litzmannstadt (Łódź) Ghetto.

Meanwhile the German press, supported by numerous articles in brochures and books, combined with other media transmitted enthusiastic reports about the fervent development of German culture instilled by the Reich's personnel brought to occupied Poland. A typical example of such propaganda is the journal entitled *Wartheland, Zeitschrift für Aufbau und Kultur im deutschen Osten*, published in Posen, or the article "Kultureller Aufbau im Wartheland" by Oberregierungsrat Dr. Peter Gast (Posen), published in *Ostland Kalender 1941* as the 56th Yearbook of the *Baltic Calendar* (a reference to the huge influx of Baltic Germans that settled in the region). In clear terms, Gast explained the basis of Gauleiter Greiser's programme of Germanization and the crucial role culture had to play in the realization of this task. According to him, "the *Aufbau* work in the East could have long-lasting results only when in-depth action is involved." Thus, to "ground the German spirit and culture in this region, to make it autochthonic there" was far more essential than, for example, the development of a transport system. Gast outlines the reasons why music and all the pompous aura created around it by the Nazis was so important in occupied Poland and justifies the huge efforts and considerable expenditure that were expended upon establishing new German cultural organizations, rebuilding theatres and concert halls, creating German theatrical ensembles and orchestras and attracting the

---

Polish Radio Station in Poznań, was ousted from Poznań in 1939 and arrested with other 40 people at the cafe "Kawiarnia Plastyków," and executed in Auschwitz on 27 May 1942.

people that are "filled with holy fanaticism to carry German culture to the East and make it their home forever."[100]

Fanatical and unscrupulous men were needed to fulfil the Nazi colonial mission, which in the case of confiscating the Poznań opera house, its cinemas and theatres was presented as a victory of German culture over the Polish "swarming vermin."[101] Thus, Dr. Siegfried Rühle, appointed in 1939 as the new director of the Museum in Posen, which reopened triumphantly on January 24, 1940, vowed to purify its exhibits of "Polish Kitsch" and supplement them with culturally superior German scientific thought. The fact that the previous director of the museum, Nikodem Pajzderski, had been arrested in October 1939 and killed on January 6, 1940, in Fort VII was kept secret.

Parallel to the German takeover of the museum was the transformation of Poznań University into the Reichsuniversität Posen, where only the Germans could study. The founder of Musicological Institute, priest Wacław Gieburowski (1877–1943), conductor of the famous Choir of Poznań Cathedral, had been arrested and sent to the GG, whereas the current director, Łucjan Kamieński, had been arrested by the Gestapo on "anti-German" charges and released thanks to the efforts of his German wife, singer Linda Harder, whom he had married in 1913. Kamieński eventually signed the *Deutsche Volksliste* in 1941 and worked there as an archivist.[102] The Reich Minister for Science, Education and Culture Bernhard Rust to the thus cleansed "vacant post" of director of the Institute of Musicology appointed Walther Vetter (1891–1957). Though he was not an NSDAP member, he was a fervent Nazi; in an homage to Hitler he claimed that it was the "fate which has placed an outstanding and gifted man, the born leader and fulfillment, in the history's circle of light."[103]

---

100 Dr. Peter Gast, "Kultureller Aufbau im Wartheland," in *Ostland Kalender 1941*, 56. Jahrgang des Baltischen Kalenders (Posen: E. Bruhns, 1941), 68. My thanks to Dr. Elżbieta Steinborn for her help in translating German texts.
101 Gast, "Kultureller Aufbau," 69.
102 In September 1946, he was sentenced to three years of prison and loss of property but was acquitted of charges in October the same year.
103 "Das Schicksal den einen überragenden und begnadeten Menschen, den geborenen Führer und Erfüllen in den Lichtkreis der Geschichte stellte" – he pronounced it on the occasion of the Theater-Festwochen in summer 1936. Since 1936 he was also Head of the Department of Musicology in Greifswald and, since 1946, he was a full professor at the Humboldt University in East Berlin and Vice President of the Gesellschaft für Musikforschung (1947–1958). Quoted in Klee, *Personenlexikon*, 640. For a detailed resume of Vetter's career during this period, see Harry Waibel, Diener vieler

Those inhabitants of Warthegau who were classified as Jewish were forced to move to the ghettos.[104] Several musicians who lived in Poznań had to move to the Generalgouvernemt. Nadzieja Padlewska who taught piano at the Poznań conservatory and her husband Leon, professor of microbiology, who was arrested but later released, and their two sons – Roman and Jerzy – went to Warsaw. Roman, an extremely talented composer and violinist was shot by the German soldiers during the Warsaw Uprsing and most of his works, including a Violin Concerto, perished. Jerzy was executed in the Moabit prison in Berlin. Also Stanisław Wiechowicz, composition professor at Poznań Conservatory was forced to move to the GG.

Just like Walther Vetter, a number of other musicians fulfilled the Nazi colonial mission to build up German musical life in the Warthegau. One of the most notable was the Hitler-youth composer Georg Blumensaat, who was appointed Director of the Landesmusikschule Reichsgau Wartheland in Posen. Blumensaat was a prolific writer of political songs, contributing material to such collections as *Unser Kriegs-Liederbuch* (1941), and *Das Neue Soldaten-Liederbuch* (1941). He was also composer and editor of two volumes of the *Posener Chorusbuch* (1941 and 1943) subtitled "aus der praktischen Aufbauarbeit im wiedergewonnenen Osten enstanden" (emerging out of the practical reconstruction of the recovered territories of the East). The Landesmusikschule Gau Wartheland opened on November 15, 1940, with 107 students. It was located in the former convent of the Carmelite Sisters at Graf-Spee-Strasse 23 (renamed from Niegolewskich Street).[105] The modernist building where the Music Conservatory was transferred in 1937, and which belonged to the Polish Bank (PKO) was transformed into a German post office and the square where it was located renamed from Liberty Square to the pre-1918 name Wilhemsplatz. During the III. Posener Musikwoche, on September 6, 1942, Governor Greiser appointed the institution of the Wartheländische Musikerziehungswerk under his supervision, which was to coordinate music education and create music schools in each district town of the Wartheland.[106]

Herren: Ehemalige NS-Funktionäre in der SBZ/DDR (Frankfurt am Main: Lang, 2011), 349.
104 In 1939 there were c. 2500–3000 Jews in Poznań. In 1941, the synagogue was turned into a swimming pool for the German soldiers.
105 Sylwia Grochowina, *Cultural policy*, 220.
106 Ibid., 221–222. A table reproduced from annual report of the state adviser for music in the Reich District Land of the Warta River (19 May 1944) by Grochowina demonstrates that as of 1 April 1944, in addition tothe Gaumusikschule in Poznań there were

Another musician who came to the Warthegau on the invitation of Arthur Greiser with the mission of Germanising concert and operatic life in Posen was conductor Hanns Roessert. A member of the NSDAP since April 1, 1933, Roessert had been first Kapellmeister in the Opera at Halle, where he had also directed the local Kampfbund für deutsche Kultur Orchestra. In fall 1940 Greiser appointed Roessert to become music director of the newly reconstructed Posen Opera House and establish a symphony orchestra, drawing its personnel from all geographical areas of the Reich. Roessert worked with zeal to fashion the most suitable repertoire for the opera house, appointed the Schoenberg pupil Winfried Zillig as his first Kapellmeister, and planned the forthcoming season of orchestral concerts. Within a few weeks, Roessert had assembled an orchestra of 62 players, which made its concert debut in the Aula of the University on November 7, 1940, with a special concert featuring Maria Greiser, wife of the Governor, as soloist in the Piano Concerto of Hans Pfitzner, a composer to whom she was strongly devoted. Such was the enthusiasm generated by this concert that it raised the considerable sum of 350,000 RM in support of the *Winterhilfswerk*.

Further ostentatious musical celebrations of Germanness took place in Posen over the next two years. The first of these was the Ostdeutsche Kulturtage (March 16 to 23, 1941), which were graced by a visit from Reichspropaganda Minister Joseph Goebbels who officially opened the new Posen Theatre. Special attention was given to the Mozart anniversary, which was commemorated by a staged performance of *Die Entführung aus dem Serail* and a lecture from musicologist Erich Schenk titled "Mozart und der deutsche Osten." Another notable appearance was that of the NS Reichs Sinfonie Orchester which gave two concerts of popular classics to close the Kulturtage.[107] Following this, there came the Second Posener Musikwoche (August 31 to September 7, 1941), the first such festival having taken place around the same time the previous year just before Roessert had fully constituted his orchestra or had been in a position to plan the programme. This time, however, Roessert very much stamped his own authority on the proceedings, with an opening concert that concluded with a performance of Siegmund von Hausegger's rarely heard symphonic poem *Barbarossa*. The decision to revive this proto-nationalist late-Romantic work, whose first and third

---

eighteen municipal music schools in Warthegau, there were eighteen municipal music schools, with 132 teachers and 2964 students.

107 For a comprehensive and resolutely nationalist resume of the musical events taking place at the Ostdeutsche Kulturtage, see Edmund von Temnitschka, 'Ostdeutsche Kulturtage 1941 in Posen', *Zeitschrift für Musik* 108 (1941), 332–33.

movements are entitled "Die Not des Volkes" and "Das Erwachen" respectively, around the same time as the German army was invading the Soviet Union (Operation Barbarossa), was surely no coincidence. Not surprisingly, Hausegger's bombastic music received a rapturous reception, as did a performance later in the week of Reger's *Vaterländisches Ouvertüre*.[108]

Likewise, smaller centres of the region, such as Inowrocław (renamed to Hohensalza), had their new Germans venues – again the article in *Warschauer Zeitung*, triumphantly describing the summer festival Sommergastspiel der Landesbühne Wartheland, with events conducted by Günther Reissert, who previously held the function of director of German venue in Posen,[109] is not mentioning the facts that this cultural activity was preceded by ethnic cleansing (particularly the "Bloody Sunday" on the night of 22/23 October 1939 organized within the scope of the so-called *Intelligenzaktion*) and mass resettlements of Polish and Jewish inhabitants were organized, nor that Hohensalza from 1940 served as a resettlement camp for Poles and an internment camp for Soviet, French, and British POWs.

Undoubtedly the most zealously nationalist music festival to take place in the Warthegau was the third and final Posener Kriegs Musikwoche in September 1942. There is good evidence to suggest that it was Arthur Greiser's wife Maria who urged the organizers of this event to pay lavish homage to Hans Pfitzner. In effect, the whole festival was turned into a cult celebration of the old master's achievement with numerous concerts featuring his music. In addition, composer and critic Hermann Unger travelled from Cologne to deliver a lecture entitled "Die Weltgeltung der deutschen Musik und Hans Pfitzner." The culminating event of the Third Posener Musikwoche was the award of the Warthegau Music Prize of 20,000RM to Pfitzner. The official document nominating Pfitzner for the award and signed by Arthur Greiser describes the composer as "the messenger of the German Soul [a reference to Pfitzner's cantata of the same name], the fighter for German art and fundamental attitudes, and the creator of immortal musical masterpieces."[110] Concurrently with the award, Greiser decreed that Posen

---

108 Walther Vetter, 'Zweite Posener Musikwoche: Rauschender Erfolg des einleitenden Konzerts', *Ostdeutsche Beobachter*, 31 August 1941, 4.
109 'Das neue Stadttheater in Hohensalza', *Warschauer Zeitung* 154, 2 July 1940, 4.
110 'Glanzvoller Höhepunkt der Posener Musikwoche. Musikpreis Reichsgau Wartheland 1942 für Hans Pfitzner' *Ostdeutscher Beobachter*, 7 September 1942, 2. The newspaper carries photos of Pfitzner shaking hands with Arthur Greiser and reports on Pfitzner's contribution as accompanist to Elisabeth Schwarzkopf and conductor in a programme featuring his *Kleine Sinfonie*, the Overture to *Kätchen von Heilbronn* as well as Schumann's Fourth Symphony.

would now have a street named after the composer, and that various local music schools would bear his name. Finally, a Hans Pfitzner Prize would be established to help fund the training for the most promising young German musicians in the region. The first awards of these prizes were announced in the October 1943 issue of the journal *Musik im Kriege*.[111]

In his review of the third Posener Musikwoche, published in the *Zeitschrift für Musik*, Edmund von Temnitschka commended the organizers for having devised such a rich programme of musical events, especially concerning the huge struggle of the German war effort that was unfolding during this period. Temnitschka claimed somewhat brazenly that the fact that between 1941 and 1942 the Wartheland region had paid host to no less than 150 Symphony Orchestra concerts, 89 Chamber Music events, 172 Solo Recitals, 37 Choral Concerts and three Music Weeks spoke volumes for the policies that had been put in place by the occupiers and provided great hope for the future.[112] Inevitably, however, such levels of activity could no longer flourish in Posen, given the increasing problems facing the German army on the Eastern front.

Whereas the major German music periodicals carried regular reports, at least up to 1943, of the varied types of musical events taking place in Posen, less information was gleaned about the cultural situation in Wartheland's second city of Łódź, now renamed Litzmannstadt in tribute to the First World War veteran, General and Nazi party member, Karl Litzmann, who had won a decisive victory for German troops at the Battle of Łódź in 1914. As was the case in Poznań, Łódź's musical institutions were thoroughly Germanized, and a large influx of performers from the Baltic regions were transferred to Litzmannstadt to help establish a German theatre there. Initially, the musical forces employed at the theatre were relatively modest, which meant that only operettas could be performed. However, the local press informed about Kulturtage in Litzmannstadt,[113] combining this with anti-Semitic articles on Jewish influence in theatrical life[114] and German role in developing

---

111 "Verschiedene Mitteilungen," *Musik im Kriege* 1 (1943), 157.
112 Edmund von Temnitschka, "Die Dritte Posener Kriegs-Musikwoche," *Zeitschrift für Musik* 109 (1942), 559.
113 *Warschauer Zeitung* 234, 3 October 1940, 4.
114 Josef Tobias: Warschaus jüdischer Theaterkönig Szyfman, etc. Was sie "Kunst" nannten with photograps of Dora Kalinówna, Aleksander Zelwerowicz, Qui pro quo cabaret, Wesby, Lawiński, mentioning Wiera Gran and Stefania Grodzieńska, Andrzej Włast and other cabaret artists, *Warschauer Zeitung* 23, 5 October 1940, 5–6.

culture.[115]

But from the 1942/43 season, the number of musicians was expanded sufficiently in order to enable operas to be staged. Poor attendance by the German population in Litzmannstadt forced the city authorities to undertake schemes aimed at popularizing the theatre, with subscriptions that drastically reduced ticket prices and established long-standing partnerships with Kraft durch Freude and other Nazi organizations. This explains the theatre's unadventurous operatic repertory, which was confined to such standard fare as d'Albert's *Tiefland* (in 1944), Humperdinck's *Hänsel und Gretel* (in 1942), Nicolai's *Die Lustigen Weiber von Windsor* (in 1943), Verdi's *Otello* (in 1943) and Puccini's *Tosca* (in 1942).

The authorities running the German Theatre played it safe so far as opera repertoire was concerned, whereas the fully funded symphony orchestra, established by Adolf Bautze in August 1940, was a more ambitious undertaking. In stark contrast to almost all other musicians in the Wartheland, Bautze had already moved from Germany to Łódź in the 1920s and for several years had established a reputation as an effective conductor of German choirs in the region. In August 1940, the Mayor of the Liztmannstadt appointed him as the city's local functionary for music (Städtische Musikbeauftragte), a post that he combined with taking on the role of being head of the Reichs Propaganda Office (Leiter des Reichspropagandaamtes. Zweigstelle Litzmannstadt) in the city.

Such elevation gave him considerable power and influence, much beyond his relatively limited abilities as a conductor.[116] Indeed, Bautze managed to convince the Propaganda Ministry in Berlin that the establishment of a full-time symphony orchestra in Litzmannstadt was a vitally important German cultural asset for Wartheland. Accordingly, the Ministry furnished the orchestra with a generous subsidy that amounted to nearly 100,000 RM by 1943.[117] Thanks to this subsidy, Bautze was able to increase the number of musicians in the orchestra

---

115 'Deutsche Arbeit und deutsche Kultur untrennbar. Die deutsche Leistung unwiderlegbares Beweismittel für den deutschen Führungsanspruch im Weischselraum – Die Ausstellungen "Deutsches Erbe in Warchau" und "Das Bild des Krieges durch Präsident Ohlenbusch eröffnet," Warschaus Haus der Deutschen Kultur feierlich eröffnet, *Warschauer Zeitung* 232, 1 October 1940.

116 Anselm Heinrich, 'Germanification, cultural mission, holocaust: theatre in Łódź during World War II', *Theatre History Studies* 33 (2014), 99.

117 Anselm Heinrich, *Theatre in Europe under German Occupation* (Abingdon: Routledge, 2017), 178.

from 52 to 85.[118] The conditions attached to this grant, however, resulted in the Ministry demanding that the orchestra change its policy of only featuring standard repertory in its programmes and that in future it should demonstrate a more tangible commitment to music by living composers officially approved by the regime. Accordingly, the programme planning of the Symphony Orchestra from 1942 onwards was more adventurous. In the few seasons of its existence between 1942 and 1944 many of the concerts given by the Litzmannstadt Symphony Orchestra included at least one contemporary work, and a platform was given to a substantial number of composers including Hans Pfitzner, Helmut Jörns, Gerhard Maas, Richard Trunk, Bruno Stürmer, Ottmar Gerster, Rudolf Petzold, Hermann Grabner, Helmut Fiechtner, Arno Knapp, Werner Trenkner, Johann Nepomuk David, Walter Drwenski, Gottfried Müller, Fred Lohse, Rudolf Peters, Winfried Zillig, and Werner Egk. Another sign of the importance attached to the Symphony Orchestra was the frequent appearance of guest soloists from the Reich and the occasional visit from significant conductors, for example Franz Konwitschny, Peter Raabe, Count Hidemaro Konoye, and Eugen Jochum.[119]

2.3. Soundscape of occupied Poland in witnesses' testimonies

Testimonies of witnesses who survived the war in occupied Poland provide important information on the role of music and sounds in the traumatic situations

---

118 Cf. Grochowina, *Cultural Policy*, 206 ff.: "The orchestra, originally consisting of 28 musicians, performed for the first time on 5 May 1940 in the sports hall at Hitler-Jugend-Park (before the war: the park of Father Józef Poniatowski). The musicians performed the oratorio of Joseph Haydn Jahreszeiten (Seasons) with the participation of singers from Berlin and the Johann Sebastian Bach Choir of Łódź. The seat of the orchestra was the palace of Karol Poznański at Danzigerstr. 32 (32 Gdańska street), because the Łódź Philharmonic building was closed and intended for warehouse use. Regular orchestra concerts began on 17 October, and they usually took place in a sports hall or in the so-called House of the Singers (Sängerhaus) at General-Litzmann-Strasse 21 (21 11 November street). At the end of October 1940, the orchestra had 43 musicians, which could be maximized to 55 people, made up solely of Germans."
119 This chapter stems from work on the chapter "Nazi Musical Imperialism in Occupied Poland," in David Fanning, Erik Levi (eds.), *Routledge Handbook to Music under German Occupation* (Routledge: Oxon –New York 2020). I would like to thank the editors for their support and amazing scholarship.

they experienced and in their memory.[120] The survivors quoted below were in most cases interviewed by the author between 2010 and 2017. The video and audio recordings took place at their homes and were followed in some cases by more meetings and conversations. Part of the below-quoted testimonies was collected by other researchers and has a heterogeneous character – they are either (1) transcripts of interviews with witnesses for the Museum of the Warsaw Uprising or (2) recollections written down by the witnesses themselves. The first type of testimonies enables us to find out which sounds are most often mentioned by the survivors of the Warsaw Uprising, and which are described as the most traumatic ones. This offers a tentative typology of trauma-related sounds in the first place. The second type of testimonies is a source of information on the role of music in warfare trauma. The varied source material from interviews by the author brings more detailed, individual perspectives.

Most of these testimonies refer to Warsaw and the experiences in the last stages of the occupation. The ordeal of Varsovians transported to camps was prolonged often until May 1945, whereas those who managed to escape the transports or slipped out of the city before or after the Warsaw Uprising could return to the city already in January 1945. Finally, there were those rare cases of Varsovians who never left the city. They stayed in hiding among the ruins. Some of them survived, like Władysław Szpilman. Others were murdered by German soldiers leaving the city; this was the tragic case of another outstanding pianist of the interwar era, Róża Etkin-Moszkowska, also of Jewish background. This colleague of Szpilman's was killed (according to Szpilman's testimony) on January 16, 1945, along with her husband, the eminent architect and sculptor Ryszard Moszkowski, in the Żoliborz districst, where she had been hidden by friends during the whole of the occupation.[121]

These chronologies are complicated, when we consider that while in August and September 1944 the left bank of Warsaw was a field of atrocities and cruelty of German and ROA (Russian Liberation Army) soldiers, the right bank (Praga) was captured by the Red Army and the Polish Army commanded by generals Zygmunt Berling and Wojciech Bewziuk between September 10 and 15,

---

120 This chapter is based on research presented in K. Naliwajek, "The sounds of Warsaw in 1945: witness accounts," in: Renata Tańczuk, Sławomir Wieczorek (eds.), *Sounds of War and Peace. Soundscapes of European Cities in 1945*, "Eastern European Studies in Musicology", ed. Maciej Gołąb, Vol. 11 (Frankfurt am Main: Peter Lang Verlag, 2018), 55–80. I am very grateful to both editors for their suggestions and their inspiring ideas.
121 Stanisław Dybowski, *Słownik pianistów polskich*, 161.

1944. Already on September 15, 1944, colonel Marian Spychalski was nominated president of right-bank Warsaw by the Polish Committee of National Liberation (Polski Komitet Wyzwolenia Narodowego, PKWN),[122] who then issued a call to "people of culture" to begin work. On the next day conductor Jerzy Wasiak, who previously worked in German-approved theatres and conducted the popular Radiana Choir, showed up at the Culture and Art Bureau organized in Praga; he soon organized the Symphonic Orchestra of the City of Warsaw.[123] Thus, albeit very limited, a certain cultural life was being organized on the right side of the river, whereas at the same time the left bank was mercilessly destroyed by German forces, with civilians being mercilessly slaughtered.[124]

2.3.1. Trauma-related sounds of violence

Different traumatic sounds as remembered by witnesses are described below, organized by type, reflecting their character and the psychological effect on witnesses. They are collected here to determine what types of traumatic sounds are remembered and what is their importance for the witnesses and their narratives. The ordering of these is chronological when possible. In part, their order reflects the order of the witness's accounts.

Sounds instilling anxiety, fear and panic linked with life threatening conditions had a different character in the three main war-time periods mentioned above, according to the general situation in Warsaw. Several witnesses mention in their testimonies from the time before the Uprising highly traumatic sounds related to arrests and killings of Warsaw inhabitants.

---

122 It was a puppet provisional government of Poland, controlled by the Soviet Union, proclaimed on 22 July 1944, in opposition to the Polish government in exile. See Introduction.

123 Jerzy Wasiak (1904 Warsaw – 1980 Warsaw) – pianist, conductor, pedagogue. His brother, Zygmunt Lednicki (1902 Kozienice – 1982 Warsaw), was violinist and conductor. Their actual name was Lederman. They both studied at the Warsaw Conservatory before the war. During the occupation Zygmunt Lednicki was in the Warsaw ghetto, where he performed as soloist and chamber musician. Before and after the war he played in Polish Radio orchestras and after 1956 he was second conductor of the orchestra. Leon Tadeusz Błaszczyk, *Żydzi w kulturze muzycznej działający na ziemiach polskich w XIX i XX wieku* (Stowarzyszenie Żydowski Instytut Historyczny w Polsce, Warsaw 2014), 153, 270.

124 These facts are quoted in Tomasz Mościcki, *Teatry Warszawy 1944-1945. Kronika* (Warsaw, Fundacja Historia i Kultura, 2012), 426–431.

The soundscape of Gestapo arrests scenes is omnipresent in survivors' accounts. They usually contain similar auditory elements and chronologies: a car stopping in front of the house during the night, the sound of military boots on the staircase, banging at the door, shouting in German. These sounds are combined in the witnesses' memories with a reminiscence of intense apprehension and expectation of arrest, which in some cases is not directly verbalized, just expressed through narration of subsequent sounds. In cases when the Gestapo entered the witnesses' homes, memory preserves also the actually experienced horrifying acts by the perpetrators.

Ludwik Erhardt (born in 1934), who after the war became a musicologist and a music critic,[125] recollected in his memoires such sounds, which signalled a dramatic moment in his family's life during the occupation:

> Another scene, present in my memory to this day: a lound ringing of the bell at the door, uniforms, my mother pale as paper, a search. I understood the meaning of this scene much later. In Okólnik [street], in a small room, "Mr. Zygmunt", who lived with us, a close friend from pre-war times, a senior officer from the Vilnius region, who dropped his uniform and changed his name. Someone gave him up and he was arrested on the street. If the search in his room was more thorough, we would have been lost. There were weapons and important documents under the floor. Mom knew that. Major Zygmunt Bohdanowicz was a member of the AK leadership. He died in Auschwitz.[126]

The hidden violence of the scene – because he was then child unaware of its meaning – is imprinted in his memory and expressed by the violence of the doorbell sound. Like several other survivors, often children at the time, he also remembered the sight and soundscape accompanying a public execution:

> Memory conserves different images from childhood years, like photographs in a computer. With some of them I would like to press the "delete" key. I walked usually between Królewska and Okólnik, also Krakowskie Przedmieście, Nowy Świat and Ordynacka streets. Sometimes it was a difficult route. Once, at the corner of Nowy Świat and Świętokrzyska, I found myself in a crowd of people standing in silence. I was only nine, but I did not have to ask anybody explanations anymore. There were captives there who had been shot in front of a crowd of passers-by. I saw it. There is a [commemorative] plaque there to this day.[127]

---

125 He studied musicology at Warsaw University (1952–1956), since 1957 editor, then editor in Chief (1971–2008) of journal *Ruch Muzyczny*. Author of several books on Schumann, Brahms, Stravinsky and Penderecki, as well as several others.
126 K. Naliwajek, A. Spóz, 109.
127 Execution on 2 December 1943 at Nowy Świat 64, close to Świętokrzyska. Police cordons stopped people passing by between Ordynacka and Krakowskie Przedmieście. Around 50 people prisoners of Pawiak were shot. Only 34 names were published

The strongest recollection in this case was the sound of silence after the atrocity of shooting the victims; silence that could express such different scopes of emotion as horror and fear, suppressed anger, and helplessness, but also the intention to commemorate and mourn the victims.

The traumatic sonority of the German language is mentioned in several testimonies, as it is directly associated with atrocities commited by the Nazi perpetrators. In the testimony of Barbara Hanna Relich-Sielicka (1929–2008, pseudonym "Basia," paramedic in the "Iwo" Batallion during the Uprising, negative posttraumatic emotions linked with the language of the perpetrators are sharply and directly juxtaposed with the expression of Polish identity by the dying victims. In this part of her testimony, she spoke about the time before the Uprising and offered descriptions of street executions by hanging and shooting that she had seen, with one of the persons to be shot shouting "Poland is not yet dead" (first words of the Polish anthem). She also stated: "I could not listen to the German language at all, because I lived through the occupation."[128]

Barbara Hanna Sielicka had a singular auditory memory of the night following the beginning of the Uprising on August 1, 1944:

> At night I heard something as if a storm was coming, something went, something was coming, some noise, something thunderlike. And at some point, from the window, it was warm and all the windows were open, suddenly we heard someone shout "Warsaw is free!" What an amazing impression.[129]

This memory of sound resembling the advent of a storm is associated in the witnesses' memory with the premonition of extreme chaos and omnipresent death during the Uprising, as she retold it in other sections of her account. As unsettling and dangerous as this sound seemed on the one hand, it was also

---

later in a German announcement (*Bekantmachung*). It is known, however, that there were more murdered people there, among them painters Janusz Zoller i Stanisław Haykowski. W. Bartoszewski, *Warszawski pierścień śmierci 1939–1944* (Wydawnictwo Interpress, Warsaw 1970), 288–291, 300–301, 316–317. The account of Ludwik Erhardt is quoted in K. Naliwajek, A Spóz, *Okupacyjne losy muzyków*, 108.

128 Interview in Warsaw, on 25 February 2005, held by Magdalena Czoch https://www.1944.pl/archiwum-historii-mowionej/barbara-hanna-sielicka,323.html. It reminds the posttraumatic reaction to Lithuanian language of the Holocaust survivor, whose testimony is quoted by Robert N. Kraft, 'Emotional memory in survivors of the Holocaust: A qualitative study of oral testimony', in Daniel Reisberg and Paula Hertel (eds.), *Memory and Emotion* (Oxford: Oxford University Press 2004).

129 Interview of 2006, quoted above.

extraordinary and reflected the excitement of first days of the Uprising and the joyful feeling of liberty, vividly remembered by most survivors.

Accounts of traumatic sounds of destruction by the German military are often combined with descriptions of the effects of such attacks on inhabitants of Warsaw. Andrzej Kazimierz Olszewski, born in 1931, who after the war became an eminent art historian, remembered the apocalyptic scene of the Warsaw Uprising, and the high-vibration sound of a tank shooting in his direction. Violent images contrast in his memory with the fragility of his father's violin, rescued from the destroyed house, and the narration seems to have an impressive, evocative character of core memory, where events are bundled together rather than ordered:

> A young man is walking through the corridor, with his intestines completely out, shouting: "I am dying!". A medic runs to him: "Bronek – (…) – save him!" It was impossible. Our custodian, mister Sierzputowski, a wonderful veteran of the Russian-Japanese war (greatly resembling Piłsudski), is saying: "My dears, here at the Mokotowskie Field [park] there is a heavy machine gun and you won't pass through the main corridor of the gate, it is out of the question. You have to pass through the cellar and run away through Polna 34 to Mokotowska 3, to the yard!". (…) Everybody had his own load, a bit of food, something precious, father [put] some books of poetry into his pocket, I kept father's violin, which was his beloved instrument. When everybody had already left, I dropped in for the last package. At this moment a roar, so horrible, not a roar, but a sound of high vibration. The tank fired once more, I saw dust and the sky, but I was saved by a chest [filled] with sand, which was standing next to the cellar window. It fell apart, but I was saved. But simply this sound of vibration in the ears, the dust… awful. Escape, we got there, the injured were lying there, blood, slippery [floor].[130]

Among the varied types of warfare sounds described by survivors of the Warsaw Uprising, which in itself was a horrifically loud soundscape, the most specific and most traumatic sound of destruction and death, omnipresent in their accounts, is the sound of huge German rockets referred to by the Wehrmacht with the cryptonym *Nebelwerfer*. This name, suggesting smoke or chemical warfare (ger. *Nebel* means fog), served disinformation goals, as in fact the rocket launcher carried high explosives bringing disastrous effects. They were used by the German army against civilian targets in Warsaw in August and September 1944, as well as on several military fronts in Europe. The type used in Warsaw, sWuR 40 was called by the Germans *Stuka-zu-Fuß*. It referred to the dive bomber and ground-attack

---

130 **Interview led by Joanna Rozwoda, 12 December 2011 and 4 January 2012,** Archive of Oral History of the Warsaw Uprising Museum, http://www.1944.pl/archiwum-histo rii-mowionej/andrzej-kazimierz-olszewski,2805.html.

aircraft Stuka, which by the way had its own characteristic frightening sound, mentioned by several Warsaw Uprising survivors – in this case it would be its stationary variant, "on foot". Warsaw inhabitants quickly came to recognize this rocket by the characteristic terrifyingly loud noise it emitted. They called it with the slightly ironic and dismissive names "cow" or "wardrobe," reflecting their sound characteristics. Horrifying descriptions of *Nebelwerfer* effects on civilian targets are pervasive in testimonies of the time.[131] Bogdan Horoszowski (born in 1930, pseudonym "Komar", a rifleman from the "Krybar" group) explained why they aroused such fear:

> Worst of all, I was afraid of "cows." (…) As soon as I heard that the German soldiers were preparing the cows for the shot – it was as if they were moving a wardrobe – then, I never went to the shelter, but when I heard the firing moment, I was scramming to the cellar because when one got a splinter, he was burning and there was no remedy for it.[132]

Another witness, Wiesław Depczyk (born in 1926, pseudonym "Drohojemski III", corporal army cadet), thus explained the traumatic impact of this rockets' sound:

> On the other side of the alley, they set their hellish roaring "wardrobes" or "cows" (…). The sound of launching of the missiles worked the most on the nerves, more than the bursting missiles themselves. A roar – and you already knew that the missiles would be flying. These missiles were hellish, there was a substance that, when it exploded, it burned, and it was not possible to extinguish it.[133]

It was again Barbara Hanna Sielicka who had vivid memories of these and other warfare sounds; her description of the huge mortar and her survival during a bombing also has the characteristics of core memory:

> We suddenly heard that the planes were flying, and the Germans had already begun to bombard more, because [we heard] "cows", it was "the fat Bertha". One heard the "cow" as it was winded up, it's what we called them, or as if a wardrobe was creaking, the

---

131 This sound made American soldiers call them "screaming Mimi" or "moaning Mimi". The American Intelligence Report on Nebelwerfer 41 from November 1943 issue of the Intelligence Bulletin signalled in the article entitled "Six-Barrel Rocket Weapon (The Nebelwerfer 41)" that "Its name (…) is extremely misleading. In the first place, the Nebelwerfer 41 is not a mortar at all, and, in the second place, it can accommodate both gas-charged and high-explosive projectiles, as well as smoke projectiles." Article available on http://www.lonesentry.com/articles/nebelwerfer/index.html.

132 **Warsaw, 9 August 2006, conversation led by Tomek Żylski.** https://www.1944.pl/archiwum-historii-mowionej/bogdan-horoszowski,874.html.

133 **Warsaw, 7 March 2006, conversation led by Iwona Brandt, https://www.1944.pl/archiwum-historii-mowionej/wieslaw-depczyk,659.html.**

creaking was heard, and everyone was sitting hunched and there was a boom – it was not on us. Because if we heard the boom, it meant it was not on us. And "fat Bertha" was a huge howitzer, set up somewhere near Warsaw sending such huge missiles. Then we heard how this missile was flying, a whistling sound was heard, and after a while there was a very loud explosion. During this period this quadrangle between Hoża, Marszałkowska and Skorupki was very much, very much bombarded. (…) As these bombs dropped, I was blown into the basement through the stairs to the inside, the dust was terrible, terrible dust, nothing could be seen at all. But we lived.

She speaks here of infamous "Big Bertha" (from German *Dicke Bertha*), which was a heavy howitzer used by the German army in the First World War. She was not the only witness to use this name, quite accurately, as years later it was nicknamed "Bertha's Big Brother" by the author of a publication about it. [134] It was in fact a much more modernized super-heavy self-propelled siege mortar, called "Karl-Gerät," originally designed to destroy the Maginot line, but finally the first six (of seven total) were produced only later, from November 1940 to August 1941. It is telling that the first six ones had characteristic nicknames engraved on them, which ennobled them as a truly German "cultural product" by referring to Nordic mythology, so crucial for the foundation of Nazi ideology and aesthetics. The first two, originally named "Adam" and "Eva" were later renamed as "Baldur" and "Wotan,"[135] erasing the unwanted associations with the less noble feminine figure of the Judaeo-Christian tradition. The German nationalist traits introduced by Wagner in his mythological music dramas were much further expanded and developed by his follower, the extreme nationalist Cyrill Kistler in his opera *Baldurs Tod*.[136] The remaining four nicknames were names of Germanic gods: "Thor", "Odin", "Loki", and "Ziu". They were used in Sevastopol and then in Warsaw, where they were transported, one by one, after initial successful tests with "Ziu."[137]

---

134 Thomas Jentz, *Bertha's Big Brother: Karl-Geraet (60 cm & 54 cm)* (Panzer Tracts, 2001).
135 "Wotan" was used already in the name of German tanker in WWI ("MV Wotan") and in the WWII German radio navigation projects were called "Wotan I" (X-Gerät) and "Wotan II" (Y-Gerät).
136 See the analysis of his silhouette and his opera *Baldurs Tod* by Barbara Eichner, History in Mighty Sounds: Musical Constructions of German National Identity, 1848–1914 (Boydell & Brewer, 2012), 147 ff.
137 One of the mortars which did not explode hit the Philharmonic Hall and was defused by Warsaw Uprising sappers; another one was found recently, in 2012, also in the city centre.

2.3.2. Traumatic sound as creativity inception factor

A particularly important account of traumatic sounds of special importance in a survivor's subsequent biography was given by Halina Paszkowska-Turska (1927–2017), who became an outstanding film sound engineer in the post-war era.[138] Imprisoned in the ghetto in Warsaw during the occupation, she then survived in hiding under an assumed name, which she used for the rest of her life. She took part in the Warsaw Uprising in 1944 with the "Rafałki" storming platoon that belonged to the "Konrad" group in Powiśle (in Warsaw, close to the Vistula River). In an interview recorded at her home in November 2016, she gave the following account, beginning with the description of the post-war landscape:

> Yes, one walked on the ruins. People worked from the beginning. They were commencing the reconstruction of Warsaw. After all, it was incredible. I cannot imagine it even today that such a city as Warsaw rose from such ruins! At the time of the Uprising, I was in Powiśle. Between my window and the street there was a big gate that separated us from the Germans. At some point, my colleagues burst into the room, because there was a German attack on Powiśle; they attacked the gate and the boys got in my room with me and smashed the windows with their guns; they told me to get away immediately. (…) But what I wanted to tell you concerns a completely different situation. The armoured train which passed through the nearby bridge made terrible havoc, shooting with machine guns. So we got a message that there was something going on out there at the [National] Museum, next to Smolna street. They apparently arrested all the men, took them to the Museum and shot them. We didn't have a good orientation of where the Germans were and where something needed to be done so that these streets would not be fired on, at this Smolna street – who were out there – Poles or Germans. Our commander sent a group of five or so – we were four or five boys and me – during the night we went up through the streets next to St. Elizabeth cloister. We were supposed to go through Smolna street to find ourselves in the buildings vis-à-vis the Museum. Because this street was under fire we couldn't just march there all together, but you had to simply slip through. And each of us, separately, went fast to slip through the gate. And I was also there, I had to do it. And I found myself in such a situation, that as I entered that

---

138 She worked as sound engineer in ca. 20 drama films, among others the famous *Knife in the Water* [*Nóż w wodzie*, 1962] directed by Roman Polański, nominated for Best Foreign Language Film at the Academy Awards in 1963, *The First Day of Freedom* [*Pierwszy dzień wolności*, 1964] directed by Aleksander Ford and entered into the 1965 Cannes Film Festival, and in over 200 documentary films directed by such outstanding artists as Kazimierz Karabasz (*The Musicians*, 1960, among others) or Marcel Łoziński: *Zderzenie czołowe* (*Frontal Collision*, 1975), *Wszystko może się przytrafić* (*Anything can happen*, 1995), among others. In 2010 she received the Prize of Polish Film Association.

gate, it was filled with debris, glass. And every step of mine was like a shot. Otherwise, it was complete silence. We wanted to go to these houses to see what was happening out there, who was there, whether there were Germans there. And at some point, moving on this broken glass, on this rubble, I came upon an open door and a view of the Museum! Because these houses had two entries from both sides; the other street had before the war been called Third May Avenue. And at one point I was standing, preparing to go and I see smoke as if from a cigarette, in this passage there. It could only have been a German, so I stopped, I froze completely, I stopped breathing. And I stood like that for a couple of minutes. And, of course, I had everything on my head; I was wearing a helmet, strap, and all these things, so there was no doubt who I was. So I was standing still, not to awake this satan. And it was a horrible moment, because I knew that this may be the last moment of my life. But it took quite a long time, so I came to the conclusion that this was not a cigarette, that these are smoking ashes, so I began to breathe a little. So this is the sound, so dramatic, that stayed in my head. And I was thinking then that if I survive, I would like to once yield the drama of these steps, the drama of this sound that plunged me into this completely paralyzing state of threat. And I was thinking then about telling about it to someone one day. And then it turned out that I went into sound engineering and film and for my entire life later on I did nothing else but sounds![139]

The most poignant and impressive response is the choice of Halina Paszkowska, who although she could return to her original name Penczyna after the war, decided to preserve the name Paszkowska, which was suggested to her by an unknown young woman, so that she could survive under a new identity as "Aryan". This girl probably perished during the occupation, because one day she disappeared from the tram route where they used to meet, and thus Halina Paszkowska decided to keep the name also after the war ended as a token of memory and gratitude. Her original name did not sound Jewish, and she needn't have done this even if she wanted to hide her Jewish ancestry in the post-war period.[140] In this symbolic way she also created her "new self." Still, another aspect of high importance, which may have served to help reintegrate the self and regain cultural coherence, was her creativity, which permitted her to mould a traumatic sonic memory into her passion to tell complex artistic narrations with sound. Her highly intuitive way of working with less-than-sophisticated recording equipment brought striking auditory results, which played important, often crucial roles in the film narratives.

---

139 Interview by the author, November 2016.
140 Information provided during a commemorative celebration of her anniversary, which was held on 22 June 2017 at Kultura Cinema in Warsaw, with speeches held by Marcel Łoziński among others.

2.3.3. Sounds of being shot at

Tragic experiences of being shot at were described by Włodzimierz Kotoński (1925–2014), who after the war became an eminent composer and composition teacher. During the occupation he was active in the underground and had lessons with the well-known composer and critic Piotr Rytel, who taught him for free, because of the pupil's precarious situation. He received a clandestine high school diploma in 1944. During the Warsaw Uprising, he was arrested by the German army and deported to the Stutthof camp. He managed to escape from the Death March during which hundreds of Stutthof camp prisoners perished. However, he was subsequently arrested:

> As the front grew nearer, German gendarmes unexpectedly caught me without documents and took me to Kościerzyna. I tried to pass for a civil worker. They questioned me, asked where I was going. (…) They had to return me to Gdańsk, but at night they received an order of quick evacuation and the commander of this small detachment commanded [his soldiers] to liquidate [me] and to run away. The one who was to liquidate me turned out to be a Kashubian. He said to me, "Don't move or I'll shoot you". And he shot into the wall. And they fled.[141]

In the interview, Włodzimierz Kotoński did not comment on the sonority of the shooting, one can only imagine it from his account, which gives only a concise description of the event. When asked if he ever referred to his sound memories in his electronic music, which seems to be the most suitable medium to express such sonorities, he denied this with a characteristic detachment from his war-time experiences and his enthusiasm for life. He returned to his war-time experiences only many years later.

A similar situation was experienced by a young girl, later to become Władysław Szpilman's wife, Halina Grzecznarowska, who lived in Warsaw after the war, but during the occupation lived in her native Radom, 100 kilometres from Warsaw. When the front was approaching, at the turn of 1945, a German army doctor, angry at her mother who gave some tea to a group of forced laborers, shot in her direction on the stairs in front of her house where she was sweeping the stairs. He failed to kill her, shooting just above the head. Before he tried again, she was saved by another German soldier, who had been stationed at this villa and where for two months they had lived together with a Jewish woman and child in hiding. For several years the trace of the shooting remained on the

---

[141] Fragments of interview conducted by the author with Professor Włodzimierz Kotoński, 2014.

wall.[142] Also in this account, no mention of actual sounds of the shooting was given by Halina Szpilman; she simply described the order of events.

2.3.4. Music as a tool of counteracting traumatic sounds

The majority of witnesses who evoke music during the Warsaw Uprising speak of the great importance of music in uplifting the morale of civilians and those who were trapped in the city under destruction. This points to the positive functions of music in traumatic circumstances, with its anaesthetic power and healing properties.

An example of such an account is contained in recollections of doctors and nurses, who – describing the extreme suffering of the wounded, and the medical aid that could be offered to them – spoke about the positive effects of music in these extreme circumstances. In her testimony about the events of August 5–18, 1944, one of the paramedics wrote:

> Soldier's Feast. In the yard of the house at Konopczyńskiego Street 5/7 a solemn mass is held, in the evening – a concert at the Conservatory building at Okólnik Street. The hall is filled to the brim, although the shooting [outside] continues and the air is full of dust from the falling plaster. Patriotic poems were recited by the actress Karolina Łubieńska.[143] Janina Godlewska[144] sang, her beautiful voice of a metallic tone resounded in this hall filled with dust. A man who looked like an artist, perhaps a composer or conductor, taught us all the song "Warsaw children, we are going to fight...".[145] In this hell there were people who tried to bring moments of respite. The Conservatory held concerts, and, among others, Mieczysław Fogg and Barbara Kostrzewska performed there.[146] Songs of the uprising were sung, patriotic poems were recited, Chopin's works were played. Often, the entire hall was involved, catching up with words known to everybody. On that day a wounded person was brought to the hospital in Napoleon Square, burned by a fire missile – a burning "cow." (…) He was all black, his face covered with

---

142 Interview of November 2016.
143 She was a famous actress before the war. Her husband, Zbigniew Rakowiecki (1913–1944), the talented film actor and singer, was killed during the Warsaw Uprising.
144 Janina Godlewska, well known singer, was the person who saved Władysław Szpilman and with her husband, the singer and actor, Andrzej Bogucki, they received Yad Vashem title of RIghtous Among Nations on request of Szpilman.
145 Song *Warszawskie dzieci* written by composer Andrzej Panufnik in occupied Warsaw for the underground to words by Stanisław Ryszard Dobrowolski. One of the most known songs of the Warsaw Uprising.
146 Stars of pre-war and post-war scenes.

carbon crystals (...). His bed in the hall was surrounded by a screen, so frightening was the sight of this agonized man (...)[147]

Different reactions to music and its functions in these hellish circumstances were described by another paramedic – Wanda Siedlanowska (pseudonyms "Wanda" and "244") in her account of a hospital arranged at 25 Podwale Street in the Old City in the cellars of a still undamaged building, where cafe bar "Under the Crooked Lantern" previously functioned:

> Sometimes I brought there a professor of music. At "The Crooked Lantern", on the old stage stood a piano, which served us as a preparatory table to the operating table which was placed next to it. At night, sitting on the steps of the stage, leaning against the legs of the piano, paramedics found a moment of rest during the heavy duty hours. The arrival of the professor was a great celebration for "The Crooked Lantern". With music we forgot where we were, a mood of serenity and calm was returning to "The Crooked Lantern". At the bar doctor "Bogdan" (a surgeon unknown to me by name and surname) with the operative staff sipped the wine from stock we had in the cellars of the bar. The wounded were lying quietly, forgetting their pain. Nurses took the opportunity for this short moment of respite. Detonations outside the window did not irritate us, the music made us forget about the horrors of yesterday, today and of the coming uncertain tomorrow. (...) I remember that date exactly. It was August 24. The professor of music came and started his concert, so we had a short rest. I was sitting in my corner with "Tadeusz" (Tadeusz Tan, a corporal army cadet from Company "Aniela") whose vulnus sclopetaria [actually sclopetarium, gunshot wound] of the right arm did not want to heal at all, when suddenly the music stopped mid-phrase. Two wounded were brought in. We all jumped up. (...) The doctor raises his head and cries to the nurses gathered around the table: "More light, operation!" (...) The wounded summons me with a nod of his hand – "Hold me by the head" – he asks. And then, when I lean over him, he asks, "Let him keep playing." The doctor agrees, it won't disturb him. He is already fully concentrated, moving his finger slowly down the thigh, as if marking the way he is going to run the scalpel in a moment. (...) It lasts all eternity, or maybe only a moment. You can hear the bright, joyous voice of the doctor: "Sister, dressing!" He holds a small, short bullet in his fingers, probably of a machine gun. He is very pleased with himself: "I did not miss it by even a millimetre," he says. And turning to the wounded: "Did it hurt, hm?". The fingers clenched on my shoulder slowly relax, the muscles of my face are sagging: "It's fine now" – he is speaking with an effort, then [saying] to the doctor, professor, and all of us: "Thank you." I have tears in my eyes. This is music that makes me fall apart. Zdzisław [the second wounded]

---

147 Teresa Łubek-Luboradzka, Krystyna Mieczkowska, Barbara Gleb, *Sanitariuszki Batalionów AK Gustaw i Harnaś w szpitalach powstańczych. Wybór wspomnień sierpień–wrzesień 1944* (Warsaw 1994), 46–47.

died half an hour later, without regaining consciousness. Over his grave late that night we sang the "Rota" with strong voices.[148]

2.3.5. Singing as method to counteract traumatic warfare sounds

Another witness who took part in the fighting is Wanda Traczyk-Stawska (born in 1927 in Warsaw), active during the occupation under pseudonyms "Pączek" and "Atma" (her rank in the Uprising was platoon leader, and her unit was General "Monter's" Shield Division of the underground Military Publishing Company – Oddział Osłonowy Wojskowych Zakładów Wydawniczych generała "Montera"). She spoke about the special role of loud group singing as a means blotting out the sounds of German bombardments. The following event took place on 6 September 1944:

> There was a horrible bombardment. Boys and girls who did not take part in the fight were singing as loud as they could so that the bombardment would not be heard. It was at this time that I heard for the first time *Gaudeamus igitur*. How they sang it! It was a gymnastic hall at this gymnasium [Smolna Street]. For the whole time I could not sit anywhere, could not stop because the commander either rushed me to the high building, where there was a light machine gun and the III platoon crew who shooting at the attackers from the escarpment, or I had to run to the post of "'Żaba" [another military unit's cryptonym].[149]

One of the Holocaust child survivors, Halina, recollected the significance of music in the last months of 1944 outside of Warsaw, which constituted an effort to return to a more normal life and to recreate an identity for homeless Varsovians:

> When after the surrender [of the Uprising] we were going to Pruszków, we managed to escape. Some people in Szczęśliwice helped us in this escape. They took us for a night— then stole our things. With our neighbours' friends we went to Milanówek where an acquaintance of these neighbours took us to his villa. The villa was full of people, but there was room to sleep on the kitchen floor. The house was very welcoming, and the cultural life was flourishing. Professor Rączkowski (a famous organist) played piano, several

---

148 Ibid., 28–30. *Rota* (The Oath) with words (1908) by writer Maria Konopnicka and music (1910) composed by Feliks Nowowiejski is treated as sort of anthem speaking of Polish fight for independence against Germans.
149 Interview held in Warsaw, 8 July 2009, by Mariusz Kudła, https://www.1944.pl/archiwum-historii-mowionej/wanda-traczyk-stawska,60.html.

children – already teenagers – sang patriotic songs and chants, poetry was recited. I even attended concerts which were held in Milanówek, of course in private houses.[150]

2.3.6. Imagined music: Musical memory as survival technique

Wacław Gluth Nowowiejski (born in June 1926 in Warsaw), Polish writer and journalist, took part in the Warsaw Uprising as commanding officer of one of the "Żmija" ["Viper"] group squads in Żoliborz (northern quarter of Warsaw). His two brothers were shot in July 1944 in a public execution. One of them, Janusz,[151] was a pianist, who studied before the war with professor Bolesław Woytowicz at the Warsaw Conservatory, and during the war he worked with his brother as a cloakroom attendant at the famous musical cafe led by Professor Woytowicz. Both brothers belonged to the underground. The third brother Jerzy (pseudonym "Pigi") perished as a soldier of the Uprising (corporal army cadet) on September 9 at the Church of St. Joseph of the Visitationists in Warsaw. The only survivor among the four brothers, Wacław Gluth-Nowowiejski, was first wounded on September 14. He was taken to a field hospital at 12 Rajszewska Street. There German soldiers massacred the wounded with hand grenades and killed them one by one with machine guns. They also shot all the nurses, although the girls had visible Red Cross bands on their arms. Wacław Gluth-Nowowiejski was shot in the head and was lying wounded among his killed friends. He was presumed dead by the Germans. Despite lack of food and his severe wounds, he survived until mid-November 1944 hiding in a cellar of a house at 6 Warszawska Street, lying on a bunk and taken for dead whenever discovered by Germans or Russian soldiers. He was rescued by a Polish woman who found him there. After the war, in November 1948, he was arrested for being a member of the Home Army. Imprisoned after cruel interrogations, he was released in 1953.

While lying half-conscious in the cellar he imagined music:

> First of all, I lost track of time, I did not know (…) how we got here and I did not think about it. I stopped thinking. I knew that it was cold, that there was a gale, snow outside (…). And yet, I was lying there and there were moments of complete sobriety. I would say that it is quite a strange thing, and today for me personally it is extraordinary – because I loved and love music, so all of a sudden I began to recall different classical

---

150 Katarzyna Meloch, Halina Szostkiewicz (eds.), *Dzieci Holocaustu mówią…* [Children of the Holocaust talk…), Vol. 3 (Warsaw, Biblioteka Midrasza, Stowarzyszenie Dzieci Holocaustu w Polsce, 2008), 154.
151 This was explained to the author by Wacław Gluth-Nowowiejski in telephone conversation of 3 November 2014.

musical works, as I attended a music school a little during the occupation. Something completely out of this world.[152]

In another conversation,[153] he explained that the sounds he then imagined were Schumann's piano music and some opera music his brother Janusz liked to sing at home. There was no Chopin in his musical memory at the time, just as if the ban to play Chopin was also working somewhere in his unconscious. This may seem paradoxical, all the more so because the only instance when this ban was lifted, for Professor Woytowicz's cafe, was such an emotional and memorable concert, attended by Wacław Gluth-Nowowiejski, when almost everybody was crying.[154]

This psychological mechanism of imagination, resembling Władysław Szpilman's experience when he was in hiding, is a fascinating example of survival strategies. As Szpilman wrote about the same time as Wacław Gluth-Nowowiejski, the beginning of November 1944, when he was in a building at Niepodległości Alley:

> I lay motionless all day long to conserve what little strength I had left, putting out my hand only once, around midday, to fortify myself with a rusk and a mug of water sparingly portioned out. From early in the morning until I took this meal, as I lay there with my eyes closed, I went over in my mind all the compositions I had ever played, bar by bar. Later, this mental refresher course turned out to have been useful: when I went back to work I still knew my repertory and had almost all of it in my head, as if I had been practising all through the war.[155]

Szpilman's specific experience of someone in hiding and guessing what was happening outside by the sounds he could hear, gives his testimony a vivid soundscape character, where military changes are reflected in his perception of the decreasing volume of warfare. Between June and July he remembered that "Soviet raids on Warsaw came more and more frequently; I could see the fireworks

---

152 Wacław Gluth-Nowowiejski in interview of 20 February 2007, led by Małgorzata Brama, for the Archive of Oral History of the Warsaw Uprising, http://www.1944.pl/archiwum-historii-mowionej/waclaw-gluth-nowowiejski,1054.html. He also narrated his experiences in several books: *Śmierć poczeka, Rzeczpospolita gruzów, Nie umieraj do jutra, Stolica jaskiń: z pamięci warszawskiego Robinsona.*
153 Conversation with the author in 2017.
154 This account was narrated by Bolesław Woytowicz himself in his text *W okupowanej Warszawie*, see: annotated version in: Elżbieta Markowska, K. Naliwajek, *Okupacyjne losy muzyków, Warsaw 1939–1945*, Vol. 1 (Warsaw 2014).
155 Władysław Szpilman, *The Pianist. The Extraordinary True Story of One Man's Survival in Warsaw, 1939–1945*, translated by Anthea Bell (Picador, New York, 1999), 168.

display from my window. There was a growling noise in the east scarcely audible at first, then growing stronger and stronger: Soviet artillery." On August 1, 1944, it changed: "the thunder of the Soviet artillery, so close a few nights earlier, was now clearly moving away from the city and becoming weaker."[156]

2.3.7. Sounds of the ruined city

It is evident that the soundscape of the post-war deathly silent, ruined Warsaw vividly contrasts in witnesses' memories, both with sonic reminiscences of the noisy city, still partially "alive" before August 1944, and with the horrifying soundscape dominated by German artillery and bombings during the Warsaw Uprising.

Some of the remembered sounds from the first days after January 17 still possess the alarming quality linked with its life-threatening meaning. The wife of the composer Włodzimierz Kotoński, the harpist Jadwiga Kotońska, among her experiences upon her return to Warsaw in 1945, described specific sounds of a rifle which probably belonged to a Wehrmacht soldier:

> We arrived at the West of Warsaw on January 17, it was totally empty. And suddenly we see a German, he is walking, looking poorly, and [imitations of sounds of rifle hitting the rails]. And my mother said, Listen, let's get away, for he could pick up the rifle and shoot at us. We went back and returned the next day.[157]

The actor Witold Sadowy (born in 1920 in Warsaw) described the contrast between occupied Warsaw as noisy, full of sounds of tramways and rickshaws, and the ruined city immersed in darkness and silence, which he found when he came back to Warsaw on January 19, 1945. In his account of his most tragic experiences upon his return to Warsaw, when he had to exhume the bodies of his father and brother, there are no sounds, although we can imagine them from his narrative:

> My father was lying in a collective grave. So we rented a cart and a guy who helped. And we were digging out this grave. There lay the bodies, massacred, covered with mud. We had to throw these corpses aside. It was horrible. When I think of it now, one cannot imagine that a man could have seen and gone through that much. I finally recognized my father by his jacket. We put [him] in a wooden box, there was no more room left on the cart, so we walked with my mother behind it…

---

156 Ibid., 149 and 151.
157 The above-quoted interview with composer and his wife in 2014.

The city was a desert. And before long, we arrived at the Powązki [cemetery] and buried him and then returned alone... The city was totally empty, people lived crammed together in the ruins of houses. Only afterwards did we clear the rubble, we enjoyed that the lamp could be lit, that there was water, lighting was installed. All people worked, dug out bricks, handed them to others. And thus we rebuilt our city. Some houses were torn down unnecessarily, because they could have been rebuilt...[158]

He vividly remembers concerts and theatre performances, which began to take place in the ruined city. When at a small theatre in Marszałkowska street an opera performance was organized in December 1945, "it was such an incredible event that foreign press wrote about it; that in the ruins of Warsaw operas were performed."[159]

There were many musicians in the streets during the occupation – whereas after January 1945 there was initially no life in the streets and no night life, except for the cafe established by the singer Mieczysław Fogg. However, Andrzej Olszewski mentioned that street musicians playing on the saw returned to the city in 1945.[160]

The musicologist Władysław Malinowski, who was 8 when the war began and 13 when the war ended, remembers first wandering in post-war Warsaw, in a mountain-like landscape filled with snow and silence. This changed in spring when surrealistic Chagall-like images emerged. The first music he heard was from long-play records, which he bought in a store, that opened already in 1945 – Beethoven played by Kreisler.[161]

Memories composed of sounds, among other phenomenal experiences connected traumatic environment, have indeed this vivid, immediate character of core memory. What is more, they might acquire a special, creative character, as Jenny Edkins suggested:

> Events of the sort we call traumatic are overwhelming but they are also a revelation. (...) They question our settled assumptions about who we might be as humans and what we might be capable of. Those who survive often feel compelled to bear witness to these discoveries.[162]

---

158 Interview of November 2016.
159 Ibid.
160 In conversation with author, 2017.
161 Ibid.
162 Jenny Edkins, *Trauma and the Memory of Politics* (Cambridge: Cambridge University Press, 2003), 5.

On the other hand, this overview of sound memories, although very incomplete, gives an idea of the effectiveness of the sound violence of German warfare in Warsaw and how it was intentionally employed as an ideological occupation of symbolic spaces. These testimonies demonstrate cases of individuals who succeeded in transforming their victimized identity to one of survivors. The question to what extent their verbalized memory was useful in the process is open to debate; it seems plausible, however, that the ability to transform a traumatic sound event into a potent creativity-stirring factor might serve as a motivational agent to overcome the trauma and build a new identity, integrating positive and negative experiences into a creative whole.

Chapter Three: The functions of music within the Nazi system of genocide in occupied Poland

Some of the fundamental questions that arise when one attempts to define the roles of music within a genocidal context, can partly be answered by investigating the functions fulfilled by music in the multifarious Nazi system of genocide implemented from September 1939 on the territory of occupied Poland. Music was used and exploited by the Nazis in various ways in these formerly Polish territories.

It is, however, the omnipresence of music and the complexity of roles it played at the sites of mass-murder and maltreatment such as Nazi prisons, ghettos, concentration and death camps, which poses the most challenging questions for the researcher. If we adhere to the purely aesthetic concept of music conceived primarily as art form, with its own intrinsic or historically attributed ethical qualities, the possibility of a relation between mass killing and music seems unfathomable.

In most accounts from these sites of detention, torture, and genocide, the topic of music might seem marginal, and it often does not surface at all, remaining hidden under the more salient descriptions of suffering and extermination. Nonetheless, high importance attached to music both by prisoners and by the Nazi authorities, has drawn the attention of scholars, particularly during the recent two decades, and has subjected the question of the use of music in these circumstances to intense research. An in-depth examination of source material consisting of testimonies of the witnesses, may help to coax this phenomenon out of the shadows, yet a more comprehensive survey can be achieved only through the use of diversified methods exploring its social, psychological, ethical, and historical aspects.

Vast Nazi system of detention and genocide was organized all over the formerly Polish territories in just five years of occupation. The presence of music in camps so far has been described mainly with a focus on Sachsenhausen and other camps in Germany, as well as on Auschwitz, along with its net of subcamps serving as concentration, slave labour and death camps.[1] While the phenomenon

---

1   See literature quoted in the introduction to this book. This chapter is largely based on the research presented in article published in journal *The world of music* of the

of forced singing, the existence of musical ensembles and clandestine music-making by inmates in concentration camps have been described and analysed to some degree, the place of music in the death camps, built during *Operation Reinhard* in order to exterminate the Jews, demands further analysis.[2] Apart from their function as the death camps, Auschwitz-Birkenau and Majdanek also functioned as forced labour camps. Bełżec, Sobibor, and Treblinka were constructed and functioned with a single goal: to efficiently kill and plunder the European Jews. In most Nazi camps, prisoners who were not killed immediately after their arrival, were used as slave labour. They worked in extreme conditions, mostly outside the camps (as road, construction, field, and factory workers) or in *Kommandos* needed inside the camp.

Already before the establishment of ghettos and camps, German policy was aimed at liquidating the Polish "Führerschicht," a "leading class" in Nazi terminology. It constituted a part of so-called *Ausserordentlische Befriedungsaktion* directed against the representatives of the intelligentsia and local Polish authorities. It was meant to minimise the risk of resistance and establishing underground structures, to terrorise the inhabitants and leave them without the prominent figures who could lead them against the occupiers or lend moral and intellectual support, including teachers, lawyers, or directors of important institutions, etc. Similar actions were also undertaken by the Soviet Union in the Eastern part of Poland, which was delineated by the Ribbentrop-Molotov pact. In this case, however, the cleansing was achieved mainly by deportations to Siberia.

Department of musicology at the Georg August University Göttingen *Music and Torture | Music and Punishment*, edited by Morag J. Grant and Anna Papaeti. See Naliwajek: "Music and Torture in Nazi Sites of Persecution and Genocide in Occupied Poland 1939-1945," in *The world of music* (new series), Vol. 2 (1) (Berlin: Verlag für Wissenschaft und Bildung 2013), 31-50.

2 Operation Reinhard (in German *Aktion Reinhard*) was the code name under which the Nazis realized their plan to murder citizens of European countries occupied by the Third Reich, considered by them as Jews according to the Nuremberg Laws. It took place between October 1941 and November 1943 in the General Government on the territory of occupied Poland. Conceived as the method of *Endlösung der Judenfrage* (Final Solution of the Jewish Question), it was implemented even before the Wannsee conference in January 1942; already in October 1941, Reichsführer-SS Heinrich Himmler gave order to SS and Police Leader Odilo Globocnik in Lublin to start construction work of first of the extermination camps in Bełżec. It is estimated that more than two million people were murdered and their property worth approximately 178m German Reichsmark (approximate value: €550m Euro) was stolen by the Third Reich. See: Louis Leo Snyder, *Encyclopedia of the Third Reich* (Wordsworth Editions, 1998).

Among the multiple roles that music played in the death camps, both for the oppressors and the oppressed, there is one that is particularly striking and demanding a closer examination. Why was music used by the Nazis as an important element of torture and how was it intertwined with genocidal actions? What types of music were being used and in which circumstances?

The analysis of testimonies from Polish-Jewish and Polish survivors of different types of detention sites: the death camps, such as Auschwitz-Birkenau, Treblinka, Sobibor, forced labour camps for Jews (Skarżysko-Kamienna, Kurowice, Jaktorów) and prisons (Pawiak Warsaw, Montelupi in Krakow) provides some answers to these questions. Specific cases of physical and psychological torture and the roles ascribed to music in the process of degrading the victims were reported in written and oral testimonies of survivors. They were also gathered for the sake of the prosecution of German commandants as well as German and Ukrainian staff members.

3.1. Psychopathology of the ritual

The Nazis perfectly understood the intricacies of leadership. The perverted interconnection between the dominating leader and the one that was subjugated constituted an essential element of the Nazi system as such. Music became one of the most vital elements of this socio-psychological mechanism, nurturing it with deep and intrinsic emotional energy. Therefore, the various roles of music at the sites of detention and extermination epitomise the relations between the victims and their perpetrators. Still, the seemingly paradoxical uses of music by both groups make the task of analysing and understanding these mechanisms of power very challenging. The fundamental question is the following: what were the reasons for the two groups for using music, and what kind of needs did it fulfil and how?

The goal of physical and psychological abuse inflicted on the victims by the guards was 1) to gain total control over the prisoners and 2) to make them lose their identity and thus to annihilate them psychologically before exterminating them physically. To achieve these ends, the guards used terror and torture. Music was an important part of this strategy, as confirmed by numerous reports. These goals were in line with the oppressors' constant need to strengthen their authoritarian roles. Their psyche was thoroughly permeated by the profound narcissistic urge for power.[3] Music, used in its military, "decorative" or ceremonial

---

3   "Narcissism is defined by a series of factors (American Psychiatric Association, 1994). These begin with favourable or even grandiose self-regard, including a strong sense

aspect – was a particularly effective means of such an empowerment. Everyday usage of music in camps was modelled on its role in the Nazi mass meetings, so popular in Nazi Germany.[4] A camp commandant longed for the grandiose, lofty feeling of a mass festival, a feeling of excitement that he remembered from the Nazi party ceremonies. Back then, he used to be an insignificant member of the masses, and now his social status, in his own view, has "elevated," as he became the "lord of life and death." Music being played during roll calls was meant to fulfil this need for an emotional fix. The quasi-religious aura surrounding it constituted a sort of narcotic to which the Nazis were accustomed to and which they constantly needed.

In the extermination camps, such as Treblinka, the typically sadistic sense of satisfaction achieved by humiliation of others was considerably enhanced by the sight of degraded prisoners, who would be forced to play music for the guards or sing a "cheerful" march at their orders. The prisoners had to play for people who they knew to be responsible for murdering their children, sisters, brothers, parents, and wives.

The Nazi perpetrators used music in the genocidal system, which they built, mainly for psychological torture, debasement, manipulation, and victimization of "their" prisoners. However, it served also for their own personal enjoyment and recreation during or after the genocidal acts, often combined with the physical torture of the victims.

On the other hand, for the prisoners music was a method of keeping their identity by referring to the profoundly ethical, lyrical or – perhaps more superficial but nevertheless powerful – its satirical aspects.[5] Not surprisingly, this type

---

of superiority over others, arrogance, fantasies of greatness, and a belief that oneself is unique. The German Nazis fancied themselves a 'master race' superior to all others, and they clearly regarded their dream of continental, if not world, domination to be an achievable goal. Their self-declared Third Reich signified a pretentious claim to be the successor to the Holy Roman Empire that had once dominated the civilised world." L.S. Newman, R. Erber, *Understanding Genocide: The Social Psychology of the Holocaust* (Oxford: 2002, 263).

4   "The Nazis made systematic use of the media. Simultaneously, Hitler was able to create a 'corporate identity' for his movement, often by borrowing ideas from religion, by means of uniforms, flags, songs, torches, special music, and, of course, the swastika. Finally, he managed to organize his members and sympathisers in mass demonstrations. Here they came into direct contact with the leader, the symbols, the music, and so on." (Newman, Erber, 202).

5   See the description of "Majdanek Radio," a fake radio broadcast created by Majdanek women prisoners, which was in fact a cyclic quasi theatrical form with programmes

of music was illegal and repressed by the Nazi authorities as a threat to their dominance. These two main aspects of music contain in fact a much more complex network of mechanisms operating within the relations between the persecuted and the perpetrators.

Thus, the functions of music at the sites of genocide seem at first glance to be diametrically opposite for the oppressors and for the oppressed, just as the roles of the two groups were opposed to each other. In order to fully understand both aspects of music in the genocidal system – its criminal use by the Nazis as a tool for the degradation of prisoners and its ethical power for the prisoners themselves – one needs to read through the testimonies by the former prisoners, one the one hand, and to analyze the perpetrators' perspetives, on the other.

Some of Nazi concepts are helpful in understanding the role of music in the camps, as they were part of Nazi self-perception in general. *Arbeitsmaterial,* "work material," referred to the available workers capable of performing productive work before being killed.[6] They were also called *Menschenmaterial* – "human material." The function of a human being was to follow the directives of Führer and the Nazi Party, not their own personal goals. The Nazis would say about themselves: "Wir sind alle Stahl und Eisen. Wir sind alle prima Material" ("We are steel and iron. All of us are first-rate material").[7] *Menschentum* meant for the Nazis "humanity" and "German race," and the so-called *menschliche Architektur,* "human architecture," referred to the Nuremberg rallies, where "the celebrants were organised and shaped into regularised block formations."[8] Still, even if prisoners were not perceived as *Menschen* but as *Untermenschen,* there was a sense of an "Untermenschliche Architektur" in the camps. The prisoners were being forcefully arranged into columns and military-style formations that marched to music. It constituted a sort of a distant, distorted reflection of the rallies, where crematoriums were burning instead of torches, and where a sense of ritual could nevertheless be regained.

In her book *Reading the Holocaust,* Inga Clendinnen pointed out that ritual conduct is based on an established script and stated that "the rounds of

---

including choral singing and acting. The group of women which created it was composed of "qualified actresses, poets and radio announcers." It existed until May 1943 when most women who participated in it were transferred to Ravensbrück and other camps. Posłuszny, Posłuszna, *The Aural Landscape in Majdanek,* 111.

6   See: Karin Doerr and Robert Michael, *Nazi-Deutsch / Nazi-German: An English Lexicon of the Language of the Third Reich* (Westport, Connecticut: Greenwood Press, 2002), 70.
7   Ibid., 275.
8   Ibid.

disciplinary procedures so ardently enforced by the Auschwitz SS not only met cultural criteria of discipline and punishment, but were also consciously theatrical, and that these pieces of SS theatre, constructed and enacted daily, reanimated the SS sense of high purpose and invincibility, authenticated the realism of their absurd ideology, and sustained both morale and self-image in what was, indubitably but inadmissibly, psychologically a hardship post."[9]

James Waller in his book *Becoming Evil: How Ordinary People Commit Genocide and Mass Killing* quoted the above-cited statements from Clendinnen, aiming at reconstructing the founding elements of what he termed "a culture of cruelty." He characterized it by three features: professional socialization, the binding factors of the group, and the merger of role and person. Professional socialization is composed of three elements: escalating commitments, ritual conduct, and repression of conscience. Of these elements, "ritual conduct" is the most salient for the examination of the role of music at the sites of genocide. The second feature, binding factors of the group, consists of three elements: diffusion of responsibility, deindividuation, and conformity to peer pressure. The third feature, described as "the merger of role and person, that helps us understand how evildoing organizations change the people within them" is also important when we consider the links between music and genocidal acts. The "theatrical" or "artificial" role of the oppressor merging with his "real" personality, demands more stimuli and it is therefore extremely difficult to undo the interlacing threads of personality as such and the elements of a role. This is how Waller explains the meaning of ritual for the perpetrators:

> A significant aspect of professional socialisation into a culture of cruelty is what anthropologists have identified as ritual conduct. Ritual conduct refers to behaviours that are apparently excessive or unproductive but which nonetheless are persistent. (...) Such behaviours, however theatrical they may seem to outsiders, carry significant meaning and rewards for those who perform them in a culture of cruelty. In short, they are rituals – often repeatable, choreographed experiences – enacted for the psychological benefit of the perpetrators rather than as instrumental exercises in discipline. In Nazi concentration and death camps, for instance, ritual conduct included the roll calls, camp parades, meaningless physical exercises, and the stripping and beating of victims already marked for death.[10]

---

9   I. Clendinnen, *Reading the Holocaust* (New York 1999), 141–142.
10 J. Waller, *Becoming Evil: How Ordinary People Commit Genocide and Mass Killing* (New York: Oxford University Press, 2002), 20, 207.

Music was an important component of this ritual and thus it was valued by the perpetrators as something completely indispensable for the daily functioning of concentration and death camps.

3.2. Music as torture and as deception

The process of the physical degradation of prisoners could be enhanced further by a psychological deterioration; physical torture was intensified by additional factors. Music proved to be a particularly useful tool. In some cases, the role of music, designed to increase the already unbearable suffering, was combined with the function of drowning out the sounds of torture during mass-killings. This was the case of *Aktion Erntefest* – the extermination of Jews in Majdanek, Poniatowa, Trawniki and other camps in the Lublin District on 3 November 1943, which was ordered by Reichsführer-SS Heinrich Himmler. The killing took place to the sound of Johann Strauss' waltzes.

Among the Polish-Jewish musicians killed at that time, there was Pola Braun (? –1943) – a songwriter and poet who lived in Warsaw and was transported to Majdanek in May 1943, after the Warsaw Ghetto Uprising. Her best-known songs, sung by Diana Blumenfeld in the Warsaw ghetto, include: *Tsurik aheym* (*Back Home*), *Hot rahmones* (*Have Mercy*) and *A holem* (*A Dream*). Her poetry and songs written at Majdanek were well known among the Polish inmates who remembered her singing and playing the piano:

> Pola Braun's fingers ran nervously over the keyboard, and (…) it was not singing but the desperate scream from the heart of an unhappy Jewish woman, and her tears dripped down the black and white keys, making the melody even more tearful. She sang tragic songs from the ghetto. The first of them recounted the people who sat in cellars like rats, hungry, depressed, exhausted, and are aware of their impending death. The next son, performed to the poet of Władysław Szlengel, referred to a small station called Treblinka, and spoke about people, their fear and screaming before their terrible end.[11]

Another victim was Dawid Zajderman (? –1943), a popular operetta singer, performer of Jewish songs and actor active in the musical life of the Warsaw Ghetto.[12]

---

11 The testimony of K. Tarasiewicz is quoted in an important article on sound in Majdanek: Posłuszna, Joanna, Posłuszny, Łukasz, "The Aural Landscape of Majdanek," in: *Music and Genocide*, eds. Wojciech Klimczyk and Agata Świerzowska (Frankfurt am Main: Peter Lang Edition, 2015), 105–120.

12 Isachar Fater, *Muzyka żydowska w Polsce w okresie międzywojennym* (Warsaw: RYTM, 1997).

Music from loudspeakers was played during the deportations of Jewish children from Płaszów camp in Krakow to the death camps. Children's songs were emitted through loudspeaker systems exactly at the moment when children were being separated from their parents. The goal of this operation was twofold: it served to drown out the sounds of crying and despair, as well as to mock the tragedy being experienced the families and children.

Radio music was often being played during interrogations in Gestapo prisons as it was described in several accounts by prisoners of the Pawiak prison in Warsaw and Montelupi prison in Krakow. Maria Zieleniewska-Ginter, who spent almost a year in Pawiak (between November 26, 1940, and July 15, 1941), managed to notate some of her experiences from behind bars. She mentioned fellow women prisoners being tortured ("her body was looking more like raw animal meat than human body"[13]), executed or sent to Ravensbrück or Auschwitz. While she waited to be interrogated in Gestapo prison cellars at Szucha Alley, the radio was playing dance melodies all day to drown out the sounds of torture. In short breaks between the music, one could hear the sounds of beatings, the moans of prisoners and the shouts of Germans coming from the prison courtyard. She also saw a boy who almost fainted as he was forced to stand with his hands raised above is head. Another one was forced to jump for an hour, while being whipped. She also described cases of mental breakdown among women prisoners. One of them was Jadwiga Litwinowicz, later executed in Ravensbrück (on April 29, 1943), who sang in full voice Polish national anthem and patriotic songs.

Through the windows of Pawiak's prison, which was next to the Ghetto wall, prisoners witnessed Jews being tortured and murdered, which was accompanied by sadistic games played by Zander, Bürckl, Albert Müller, Brockmann, Frühwirth, Wyppenbeck, and other SS-men. They forced victims to crawl on hot cement clinker and to perform various "gymnastic" exercises. Some victims were immediately murdered by hanging, shooting, strangling or killed by dogs. A special "game" of the SS-men was boxing (popular also among Sobibor camp staff) – Jews were forced to partly undress, smear themselves with black paste and to hit each other. One who failed to hit hard enough, was whipped. Sometimes the orchestra from the Ghetto was brought and ordered to play during this "entertainment."

Tramwaje, Aleja Szucha, a poem written under the occupation by Elżbieta Popowska (1887–1965)[14] contains only descriptions of sounds: we cannot see

---

13 Maria Zieleniewska-Ginter, 208–209.
14 See Konrad Strzelewicz, *Polskie wiersze obozowe i więzienne 1939–1945 w archiwum Aleksandra Kulisiewicza* (Krakow: Krajowa Agencja Wydawnicza, 1984), 194–195.

but we can hear. In this, it evokes the experience of incarcerated people. The lyrical subject sits somewhere in Gestapo prison where prisoners wait for a cruel interrogation. The juxtaposition of contrasting auditory sensations (terrible – lovely) reflects the incoherence of the perceived sounds. This leads to a tragic discovery:

Jęki, westchnienia, urwane słowa,	Moans, sighs, interrupted words,
Twarda, złowroga niemiecka mowa,	Stiff, ominous German speech,
Krzyk straszny... dusza się wzdryga...	A terrible cry... soul shudders...
Radio gra cudny "Poranek" Griega....	Radio playing lovely "Morning" by Grieg....
Zgrzyty.... Coś niby obroty kół,	Grindings... As if some wheels rotated,
Ktoś jęczy głucho....	Someone groans hollowly...
Ktoś pięścią w stół Wali ze złością... Uderzeń grad...	Someone's fist hits The table angrily... Hail of blows...
Krzyki nieludzkie... Boże! mój brat?!...	Inhuman screams... Oh God! my brother?!...

Music was not only a narcissistic-sadistic satisfaction booster for the perpetrators, it also had more practical functions, such as enforcing control and domination over the prisoners. Social psychology confirms that the perpetrators were not insane, as it had been suggested before. It seems more plausible that methods which could seem an "insane" sadistic manipulation, in fact were a conscious method of subduing the prisoners. This makes genocidal crimes committed with the usage of music even more appalling. The diagnosis of a non-psychopathological character of the perpetrators – apart from the book by James Waller – was confirmed by other researchers:

> One conclusion that can be firmly drawn from these analyses is related to the myth that the Nazis were highly disturbed and clinically deranged individuals. The current analysis clearly suggests that a majority of the Nazis were not deranged in the clinical sense and that the above-described common personality characteristics, while undesirable to many, are not pathological in and of themselves and are actually frequently found in the U.S. population. Thus, as a group, the Nazis were not the hostile sadists many made them out to be. Yet, they were not a collection of random humans either.[15]

---

15 E.A. Zillmer et al., *The Quest for the Nazi Personality: A Psychological Investigation of Nazi War Criminals* (Hillsdale, NJ 1995), 181.

These authors quote earlier findings by E. A. Megargee:

> Although a variety of functional and organic disturbances can lead to aggression and violent behavior, most violence is committed by people suffering from no diagnosable impairment. Even if we exclude legal, socially condoned forms of violence such as warfare, we find criminal violence is often performed by normal people for rational motives.[16]

They also quote C. R. Browning and his conclusion, "that the members of the Police Battalion did not act out of frenzy, bitterness, or frustration, but with calculation."[17] Lifton cited former Nazi doctors in Auschwitz, confirming that the mass killing was executed as a "normal job":

> The selections became simply "a part of their life," as a prisoner doctor, Jacob R., commented to me. And Dr. B., too, noted that, whatever reservations SS doctors had at first, they soon viewed selections as "normal duty," as "a regular job." Indeed, within the Auschwitz context, as another survivor testified, "to kill a man was nothing, not worth talking about": a doctor who was perfectly polite and decent most of the time "felt no compunction about sending people into the gas."[18]

Some of these physicians, such as Adolf Wahlmann, were earlier "trained" as "euthanasia doctors." Thanks to this kind of training, they had been already accustomed not only to killing patients, but also to celebrating it with music, which is confirmed by the following account:

> The ten thousandth victim at Hadamar had been celebrated as a milestone, as reported by an employee. Invited by a T4 doctor named Berner, the employees gathered that evening. Each was given a bottle of beer, and they adjourned to the basement. There on a stretcher lay a naked male corpse with a huge hydrocephalic head. (…) I am certain that it was a real dead person and not a paper corpse. The dead person was put by the cremation personnel on a sort of trough and shoved into the cremation oven. Hereupon [the administrator] Märkle, who had made himself look like a sort of minister, held a burial sermon. Another witness reported that the celebration, which included music, degenerated further into a drunken procession through the institution grounds.[19]

---

16 E.A. Megargee, "Aggression and Violence," [in:] H.E. Adams, P.B. Sutker (eds.), *Comprehensive handbook of psychopathology* (New York 1984), 523, quoted in: E.A. Zillmer et al., 183.
17 Ch.R. Browning, *Ordinary men: Reserve Police Battalion 101 and the final solution in Poland* (New York: Harper, 1992), 164 quoted in: E.A. Zillmer et al., *The Quest for the Nazi Personality*, 184.
18 R.J. Lifton, *The Nazi Doctors: Medical Killing and the Psychology of Genocide* (New York: Basic Books, 2000), 175–176.
19 Ibid., 100.

According to a testimony of a former Auschwitz prisoner, quoted by Lifton,

> ...the corrupting of all human and ethical standards took place so rapidly... that one had to be very stern to prevent the somewhat stronger prisoners hastening the death of the weaker fellow prisoners. One extreme example was the behaviour of hardened criminal psychopaths who joined the SS personnel in killing people on work Kommandos, after which prisoners would be sent out to bring back the corpses to fill in the necessary "rows of five" and obtain the proper count – sometimes taking place while the prisoner orchestra played the tune of 'That's How We Live Every Day' (*So leben wir alle Tage*).[20]

Another prisoner described her exposure to twice-daily selections (January to May or June 1943):

> The day – you got up at four o'clock, and it was pitch dark, I mean in winter (...) then roll call, and you stood, and stood, and stood (...) sometimes two hours or more in lines of five until the roll call tallied. And that – to this day I don't know – I can't figure out how it was tallied. I mean how the numbers were supposed to tally, because bunches of people died overnight, the people that were beaten to death as they didn't want to crawl out [of their bunks to come out for the selection]. I mean, I never could figure out what their mathematics were. But it had to be very precise mathematics, because sometimes if the roll call didn't tally, we stood till seven or even eight o'clock! And then, as soon as you were through with the roll call, you always marched out. (...) Orchestra on the left, [playing] rousing marches. On the right, the doctor and the *Arbeitsführer* [chief of work] – and selection.[21]

However, the instrumental attitude towards music adopted and enforced by the perpetrators in the camps, is most fully confirmed by another testimony by a prisoner doctor, who, as Lifton put it:

> ...expressed the anguish of being manipulated by Mengele in a series of cruel deceptions. (...) An example of what she called Mengele's "diabolic" attitude was his appearing on a Jewish holiday and announcing, "This is *Tishah b'av* [the commemoration of the destruction of the First and Second Temples]," and "We will have a concert." There was a concert, then a roll call, and then an enormous selection, causing her to ask bitterly, "Why should we listen to music while we are being cremated?"

She stressed that Mengele's behaviour was carefully planned: "He must have scripted it: music; sit down; *Zählappell* [roll call]; crematorium." All this was part of his "sadistic game," she believed, because "every step Mengele [took] was a psychological basis for torture." And compared with other SS doctors, Mengele

---

20 Ibid., 224.
21 Ibid., 182.

was "more sadistic, (...) more *raffiniert* ['sophisticated, tricky, sly']. He [was] more elaborate (...) because he must have known psychology."[22]

This attitude towards music is confirmed further by another testimony from Auschwitz by Dr. Ella Lingens-Reiner, who played in women's orchestra and was haunted by the image of this orchestra playing concerts at the Auschwitz-Birkenau hospital while at the same time trucks filled with naked women selected for gas chambers were passing by. In her book, tellingly entitled *Prisoners of Fear*, she recollected:

> That we went on playing and listening to music, that we never shouted to those in the trucks to jump out, run, or resist, is something I cannot understand to this day. How was it possible for us to be so calm?[23]

Thus, for the orchestra players, the act of playing was also a sort of an automatized activity, which kept them occupied to the point that they were somehow protected from fully witnessing the terrifying conditions of the camp. The musicians of the orchestra were being terrorized just as other prisoners. They were also tortured by the fact of being forced to play and stay alive, while being incapable of helping fellow prisoners from being tortured and murdered.

Helena Dunicz-Niwińska, a violinist in women's orchestra of Birkenau, described this predicament as follows:

> While playing or in the short breaks between numbers, we did of course plainly see the ranks of enervated, exhausted people passing on the far side of the barbed wire. We were witnesses, and we were aware of what was happening, and of what would happen in the nearby gas chambers and crematoria within the coming hours. The consciousness of that criminal act, which beggared the human imagination, filled us with dread and with a sense of helplessness and hopelessness. This was the basis for our inner conundrum: should we protect our lives and play, or refuse to play and doom ourselves to a harder life, or even to death?[24]

Extreme cases of physical and psychological torture with the use of music were witnessed by Leopold Kozłowski, the only survivor of the famous klezmer family of Kleinmanns. His father, Hermann Kleinman, was an eminent violinist and ran his own klezmer orchestra. Leopold studied piano at the Lwów Conservatoire with composer Tadeusz Majerski. At the end of 1939, Kozłowski

---

22 Ibid., 373–374.
23 E. Lingens-Reiner, *Prisoners of Fear*, London 1948, quoted in Newman, Kirtley, *Alma Rosé: Vienna to Auschwitz*, 269.
24 Helena Dunicz-Niwińska, *One of the Girls in the Band*, transcribed by Maria Szewczyk, translated by William Brand (Oświęcim: Auschwitz-Birkenau State Museum, 2014), 83.

established an 11-member strong orchestra in Przemyślany. It was composed of his colleagues from the local secondary school. Among its members, there was Leopold's brother, Dolko (diminutive for Adolf), a gifted violinist. After the Nazis entered Przemyślany in June 1941, the Kleinmans – father and sons – fled into Russia. They reached the town of Zhmerinka, but two days later the Nazis conquered that area as well. Mr. Kleinman decided to return to Przemyślany, where his wife had remained. As described in the biography, on their way back, they were stopped at night by a patrol of Wehrmacht soldiers. When one of the soldiers asked whether they were Jewish, and their father answered, the soldiers reloaded their guns and were ready to shoot them. At this moment Hermann Kleinmann began to play his violin and his sons joined him with a second violin and an accordion. Leopold commented that the Nazis "didn't have the courage to shoot music."

Leopold's father was murdered on November 5, 1941 during a mass execution of Jews in Przemyślany. In August 1942, Leopold, along with his mother and brother, who was a gifted violinist, was confined to the Przemyślany ghetto. After the liquidation of the ghetto, they became prisoners of the *SS- und Polizeiführers Zwangsarbeitslager* (forced labour camp) in Jaktorów. There, they worked on road construction and back in their camp, they played music. As Leopold said in the 2012 interview, "they played for those who were alive, for the dying, and for the dead."[25] They were also forced to play for the drunken SS soldiers during their orgies. The camp's commander called upon Leopold and ordered him to teach him to play *The Blue Danube* waltz on a pillaged Hohner accordion, threatening him that if he fails to do so, he will be tortured in the most atrocious way. Both Kleinmanns and their mother were transferred to the *SS- und Polizeiführers Zwangsarbeitslager* camp in Kurowice, by the order of the camp commandant, SS-*Scharführer* Karl Kempke. Leopold and his brother played music inside the camp. On more "solemn" occasions, they were accompanied by two other inmates playing the clarinet and double bass. In this camp, their mother was killed. Leopold was also forced to play and was tortured during the frequent orgies organized by the SS soldiers. He described a particular case of torture interrelated with music:

> I played after three days of fasting, I was not even allowed to wash myself, so that I would not drink any water, nothing at all.

---

25 The interview took place in April 2012 in Klezmerhojs, his favourite palce in Krakow, where he could recreate parts of Jewish culture, and was filmed by Łukasz Korwin with whom we could record this testimony.

> I was guarded by a Kapo, a very decent man, by the way, but he had to do it. After three days they brought me to the *Lagerführer*. Tables were covered with food, everything was there, because it was after the "hunting." They ate and I was so hungry that my mouth was bubbling as if I was chewing on soap.
> I saw the food but I was not allowed to touch anything. Yes, they poured mayonnaise on me, there was some herring they threw in my direction.
> I was allowed to eat only what stayed on my chest, food which fell on the ground was for cats, dogs, not for me.
> I played naked; the accordion was almost heavier than me, so I had to bend over. Then one of those bandits, those murderers, came up with this idea and put a candle into my anus. He lit it and they were lighting their cigarettes from it.
> And I had to play "Es geht alles vorüber, es geht alles vorbei, auf jeden Dezember folgt wieder ein Mai." – Everything passes, after each December there comes May. Everything is beautiful, everything is happy.[26]

With the help of Tadeusz Klimko, a Polish resistance fighter from Lvov, Leopold and his brother escaped from the camp. They joined a Jewish resistance unit that was incorporated into the 1st Company of 40th Infantry Regiment of the Polish Home Army. In 1944, they participated in the defence of the town of Hanaczów against an UPA (Ukrainian Insurgent Army) assault. During that time, Leopold's brother Dolko was murdered. After of the Lvov area liberation from the Nazi occupation, Leopold enrolled in the People's Army of Poland. As a soldier of the 6th Pomeranian Infantry Division, he accompanied the entire campaign from Przemyśl to the river of Elba. In 1945, he returned with his division to Krakow. There, he graduated from the Music Academy's Instrumental and Vocal Conducting Department. In the meantime, he had founded the professional Song and Dance Ensembles of Military Division, first in Krakow and then in Warsaw.

3.3. Music and management in Treblinka

In the ghastly conditions of the death camps, among killings and physical torture, prisoners were not only forced to listen to the camp's musical ensemble but also to sing and even dance. Music was undoubtedly considered by the Nazis to be an ideal tool for the psychological torture of the victims in sites of extermination, as confirmed in numerous reports, e.g. concerning the Płaszów camp in Krakow or the Janowska camp in Lvov.[27]

---

26 Ibid.
27 See Naliwajek, *Music and its Emotional Aspects*, 219–220.

In Treblinka, the use of music had two main interlinked goals: to provide entertainment for the perpetrators, while also ridiculing the victims, and to function as a psychological torture for the prisoners. All torture is undoubtedly destined to induce mind-control mechanisms; it seems that this type of torture was considered by the Nazis in some respects even more efficient than the intimidating effect of physical torture. Different uses of music in the Treblinka camp can be found in the testimonies of the witnesses. This allows us to evaluate the nature of the interrelationship between music and torture in the Nazi genocidal system.

Among the written sources, testimonies by Jewish survivors of the Treblinka and Sobibor camps are of particular importance. As witnesses of the unimaginable atrocities, survivors were highly aware of the necessity of giving a testimony, after escaping from the camp. With the exception of Abraham Krzepicki, they all managed to escape after the prisoners' revolts, which took place in Treblinka on August 2, 1943, and in Sobibor on October 14 of the same year. Thus, some of these accounts were written already during the war – as Abraham Krzepicki's account, notated in Yiddish for the Emanuel Ringelblum archive being kept in the Warsaw Ghetto – or even clandestinely published in Warsaw in 1944, as in the case of Jankiel Wiernik's testimony. Others – as in the case of Samuel Willenberg and Richard Glazar – were written after the war, as soon as the living conditions of the authors made it possible. To the perspicuity and the sense of responsibility of these men, we owe the most poignant accounts of the extermination system and of music's functions within it.

The prisoners who were temporarily kept alive in death camps, such as Treblinka, were forced to "work" as corpse carriers, "hairdressers" who cut girls' and women's hair just before they were killed, "dentists" who extracted gold teeth, bridges, and crowns from corpses, "gold finders" who had to find any valuables in the victims' clothing and belongings, cleaners of gas chambers, and constructors of different camp "facilities." In both types of camps – concentration and death camps – prisoners lived under the constant threat of torture and death and were incessantly tortured by thirst, hunger, and exhaustion. In concentration camps, they were treated as prisoners who could be killed at any moment by the camp staff, but they had more chances to survive. In the extermination camps, they were treated as already condemned to death.

Jechiel Mejer Rajchman (1914 Łódź – 2004 Montevideo, Uruguay) was brought to Treblinka with his younger sister in a transport from Lubartów on October 10, 1942. Samuel Willenberg (born in 1923 in Częstochowa) also arrived there in October 1942, in a transport from Opatów. Both Rajchman and Willenberg were chosen at the ramp for slave "work." Rywka (Rebeka, born ca.

1919) Rajchman was immediately killed with other women and children in the gas chambers. Her brother found her dress among the victims' clothing which he had to sort (once the Star of David badges were removed, this clothing was being sent to Germany). Samuel Willenberg went to Treblinka of his own will, after his two younger sisters had been denounced by Polish neighbours in Częstochowa. He also found the coat of his sister Tamara among the clothing he had to sort; only at this moment did he learn her fate. Richard Glazar (1920–1997) was also brought to Treblinka on October 8, 1942, from Theresienstadt. Jankiel (Yankel) Wiernik (1889 in Biała Podlaska – 1972 in Rishon Lezion, Israel) was transported from the Warsaw ghetto to Treblinka on August 23, 1942. All four of them escaped from the camp during the prisoners' revolt of August 2, 1943.

Rajchman wrote his reminiscences in Yiddish, perhaps still during the war, when he was hiding in Warsaw (although probably not during the few months when he had to spend some eighteen hours per day in a hide-out under his Polish friends' bed). After the war, such as many other Polish-Jewish survivors, he continued to use his "Aryan" name, Henryk Romanowski, that appeared in the forged documents that he had received from his Polish friend, Wacław Jarosz in 1943.[28] Richard Glazar wrote his account in Czech immediately after the end of

---

28 He later used the first name Yehiel and the diminutive Chil. His memoirs – if effectively written around the first half of 1944 – were probably lost during the 1944 Warsaw Uprising and the destruction of the city which followed. After the war, he rewrote them with the help of Yiddish poet and writer Mosze Bomze. The original Yiddish title of his memoirs is *Zichrojnes fun Jechiel Mejer Rajchman (Henryk Romanowski)*. The book was, however, first published in 1998 in Uruguay in Spanish. In 2009 it was followed by the French translation (*Je suis le dernier Juif. Treblinka (1942–43)*, Éditions Les Arènes), with major changes. Then a German translation was published *(Ich bin der letzte Jude: Treblinka 1942*, München: Piper, 2009), and a Swedish one (*Jag är den sista juden: Treblinka (1942–1943)*, Stockholm, Norstedt, 2010). In 2011, an English (*Treblinka: a Survivor's Memory, 1942–1943*, London: MacLehose, 2011) and a Polish translation were published. However, quotations used in this article are translated by the author of the article and are based on the 2011 Polish version: Rajchman, Jechiel Mejer, *Ocalałem z Treblinki*, trans. by Bella Szwarcman-Czarnota, Warsaw: Spółdzielnia Wydawnicza Czytelnik, 2011. The footnotes and the epilogue to the Polish translation were provided by Ewa Koźmińska-Frejlak, who tried to find out when exactly Rajchman's memories were written. In her preface, the translator B. Szwarcman-Czarnota points out to Rajchman's consistent use of the present tense (which makes readers of his memoirs immersed in the "here and now" of the author) and his choice of vocabulary denoting the oppressors and the oppressed; the staff of Treblinka camp are always referred to as "murderers," "bandits," "criminals," while the Jews brought

the war, before he returned to Prague from Germany, but it remained unpublished until 1993.[29] Jankiel Wiernik's memoirs were the first ones to be written and published. After his escape from Treblinka, Wiernik sought the help of his former employers, the Krzywoszewski family, who provided him with a false *Kennkarte*. Thanks to the Polish acquaintances and his "Aryan" appearance, he survived by assuming false names. Like Samuel Willenberg, Jankiel Wiernik fought in the Warsaw Uprising in 1944. His memoirs from Treblinka were clandestinely published under the title *Rok w Treblince* (*A Year in Treblinka*) in 1944 by the Jewish National Committee and the Polish Council to Aid Jews Żegota (there were about 2000 copies). They were also microfilmed, sent to London by the Polish underground, translated into English and Yiddish and printed in New York probably as early as 1944 by the American Representation of the General Jewish Workers Union of Poland (Ogólny Żydowski Związek Robotniczy "Bund" w Polsce. Amerykańska Reprezentacja).[30] Each of the reminiscences quoted below is strikingly different, filtered through a different type of personality. Accordingly, even if the information provided is similar, we gain a different insight into the barely comprehensible world of this camp, dehumanized yet created by humans.

The genocidal system was thought out and organized by the Nazis in a way meant to minimize the costs and effort and to maximize profits. That is why the plundering of the Jews was organized in subsequent stages – from dispossessing them of their houses and apartments, bank accounts, factories, shops, art collections, musical instruments, and books, to the pillage of their last valuables and belongings, their clothing, and their hair just before the moment of their death. Meticulously planned methods of deception constituted an important, sometimes even crucial, element of this plan. Musical ensembles in the death camps were often used as a part of this strategy. This is confirmed by Rajchman when he spoke about transports of Jews from Skopje that arrived on March 29 and 31, and

---

to Treblinka are called "victims" (Yiddish "korbanes" from Hebrew "korbanot", which denotes martyrdom).
29 I have quoted here from the Polish edition (Richard Glazar, *Stacja Treblinka*. Warsaw: Ośrodek Karta, Dom Spotkań z Historią 2011). Other editions have been published in German (*Die Falle mit dem grünen Zaun: Überleben in Treblinka*. Frankfurt am Main: Fischer Taschenbuch Verlag, 1993), Czech (*Treblinka, slovo jak z dětské říkanky*. Praha: Ústav pro soudobé dějiny, 1994), and English (*Trap with a Green Fence: Survival in Treblinka*. Evanston, Ill: Northwestern Univ. Press, 1995). In 1997, Glazar committed suicide after his wife Zdenka died.
30 Władysław Bartoszewski: 'Historia Jankiela Wiernika', *Polska* 1964 (8), 633–634.

April 5, 1943. Those in the transports were completely unaware of what awaited them in Treblinka, and they had even brought their furniture with them:

> The murderers knew, however, to whom these things will belong – to the *Herrenvolk*. We heard from the workers in Camp I that when the Bulgarian Jews arrived, the orchestra was playing. The Jews were convinced that nothing bad will happen to them. Getting out of the train, they kept asking if it is here, this big plant in Treblinka... SS-man Karl Spezinger appears and warns us, the "dentists", that we must be very careful, because almost every Bulgarian Jew has artificial teeth. (...) A few minutes past four, thousands of young, beautiful Bulgarian Jews are no longer there and not even a memory of them is left.[31]

3.4. Sadistic domination: forced music-making

As confirmed in the several of the testimonies quoted above, prisoners selected from the transport in Treblinka to be used as slave labour were forced to listen to music and forced to sing themselves, especially at roll calls. According to Rajchman, the roll call in Treblinka extermination camp took place exactly at six in the afternoon. He remembered that on his first day in the camp, precisely at six in the afternoon, a trumpet signal for a roll call sounded and during the roll call itself the orchestra was playing.[32] Prisoners were herded to the *Appell* (roll call) after a day of carrying and throwing corpses into large ditches. During this work they were whipped and tortured. They also witnessed executions and suicides of their fellow prisoners.[33] In such an evil environment, hearing the sounds of music only augmented the sense of degradation and guilt among those people, forced to participate in the extermination of their families and constantly reminded by their executioners that they could only consider themselves temporary survivors.

---

31 Rajchman, *Ocalałem*, 70.
32 In various testimonies from Treblinka the term "orchestra" is used even though – as E. Koźmińska-Frejlak points out in the footnote to Rajchman's text (*Ocalałem*, 24–25) – since October 1942 only two musicians chosen by the Germans (among them Jerzy Rajgrodzki) played during roll call in the *Totenlager* (death camp); only later they were joined by a third musician. From spring of 1943 on there was a band which could be called an "orchestra" in the 'lower camp' in Treblinka II, where 700 to 1500 Jewish prisoners lived. It was composed of some 10 professional musicians from the Warsaw ghetto under direction of Artur Gold and gave performances in special clothes. See: Jacek Andrzej Młynarczyk: "Treblinka – obóz śmierci 'akcji Reinhardt'" in: Dariusz Libionka (ed.), *Akcja Reinhardt. Zagłada Żydów w Generalnym Gubernatorstwie* (Warsaw: IPN, 2004).
33 Rajchman, *Ocalałem*, 24.

Rajchman described a day on which transports containing 18,000 people arrived and *Kommandos* worked incessantly. One of these brigades, called *Schlauch* (hose) – named after the curved path leading to the gas chambers – had to clean all traces of blood from this path as well as from the gas chamber walls, which were being washed and painted anew to receive new victims. Another brigade carried corpses; "every now and then one of the carriers drops the stretchers and commits suicide by jumping into to the deep pool next to the gas chambers and thus ends his damned life. Finally the clock strikes six in the evening. A call: '*Antreten!*' ('Report!') Everybody stands in a line and our *Scharführer* Matias [Matthes][34] orders us to sing a nice song. Everybody has to sing. This lasts almost for an hour; only then we can go to the barracks."[35]

Forced singing added another dimension to the humiliation and torture of prisoners. Samuel Willenberg described torture by singing combined with torture by beating, which took place after the tally during *Appell*:

> Then came the Polish folksong which the Germans loved to hear as chant: "Aren't you sad, mountain man?" [Polish traditional song *Góralu, czy ci nie żal*]. Whenever they thought we had not put feeling into the rendition, they had us repeat it several times. I have no idea why they loved this song so much as to force us to sing it day by day, sometimes several times in succession. Perhaps they wanted the villagers in the vicinity to hear the heart-gladdening things; perhaps, it was another way of camouflaging the atrocities of Treblinka.
>
> Having finished the song in the usual manner, the Germans called the warehouseman – a prisoner form Warsaw called Małpa (Polish for "monkey") because he was so ugly and ordered him to bring a stool from his storeroom. (…) It was my turn. (…) As the Ukrainian lashed me with his whip, I had to count off in German; each blow turned my innards upside down. In dread and terror, I anticipated each additional stroke, and after each I thought I would no longer survive.[36]

---

34 Heinrich Arthur Matthes (1902–?) had been in the SA from 1934, and later in the NSDAP. He took part in the *Wehrmacht*'s military campaign in Poland and France, and then participated in the Nazi euthanasia program Action T4. In August 1942, he was ordered to Lublin and became SS Scharführer (Sergeant) assigned to Operation Reinhard. In the Treblinka extermination camp, he was appointed chief officer commanding Camp II, which consisted of the extermination area and the gas chambers. Matthes himself shot many prisoners, e.g. for not properly cleaning the stretcher used to transport corpses, for drinking some water etc. In Autumn 1943, after the Treblinka rebellion, he was transferred to the Sobibor extermination camp. He was later a policeman in Trieste till the end of war. He was sentenced to life imprisonment in the 1965 Düsseldorf trial.
35 Rajchman, *Ocalałem*, 46–48.
36 Samuel Willenberg: *Revolt in Treblinka* (Tel Aviv, 2009), 125–126, 141.

After the punishment, he was additionally humiliated: like everyone else he had to say "Ich danke." Because of the beating, the wound which he had received in September 1939, while fighting in the Polish army, reopened and he eventually survived only thanks to a fellow prisoner who incised for him the inflamed skin.

As Wiernik wrote, although physical torture was very hard to endure, it was less haunting than the psychological torture – the torture of seeing the infinite yet personalized suffering of victims:

> We had to work from dawn to dusk under the ceaseless threat of beatings from whips and rifle butts. One of the guards, Woronkov, tortured us savagely, killing some of the workers each day. Although our physical suffering surpassed the imagination of normal human beings, our spiritual agonies were far worse. New transports of victims arrived each day. They were immediately ordered to disrobe and were led to the three old gas chambers, passing us on the way.[37]

This agonizing thought of the anonymity of the victims, killed without leaving any traces, motivated the witnesses to carefully remember the particular individuals and the ways they were killed, as well as the identity of their killers.[38]

Glazar described the forced singing of the Treblinka anthem (not mentioned by Rajchman) during the morning and evening roll calls, as well as during the march to and from work; he also mentioned Ukrainian guards ordering prisoners to sing it.[39] After the roll call, prisoners also had to sing songs which the guards like, such as the Polish traditional song *Góralu, czy ci nie żal*. According to Glazar and the others, commandant Kurt Franz came up with the idea of

---

37 Wiernik, *One Year in Treblinka*. New York: American Representation of the General Jewish Workers Union of Poland, 1944 [?], 18.
38 "One of the Germans, a man named Sepp, was a vile and savage beast, who took special delight in torturing children. When he pushed women around and they begged him to stop because they had children with them, he would frequently snatch a child from the woman's arms and either tear the child in half or grab it by the legs, smash its head against a wall and throw the body away. Such incidents were by no means isolated. Tragic scenes of this kind occurred all the time.... Suddenly, I saw a live, nude woman in the distance. She was entirely nude; she was young and beautiful, but there was a demented look in her eyes. She was saying something to us, but we could not understand what she was saying and could not help her. She had wrapped herself in a bed sheet under which she was hiding a little child, and she was frantically looking for shelter. Just then one of the Germans saw her, ordered her to get into a ditch and shot her and the child. It was the first shooting I had ever seen." Wiernik, *One Year in Treblinka...*, 10.
39 Glazar, *Stacja...*, 121–123.

a Treblinka march ('Hymn' in original). Franz was known for his sadism and the cruelty with which he publicly tortured prisoners or killed newly arrived babies.[40] Glazar wrote that Franz ordered a prisoner to write a text to the melody, which was to be – also on his order – composed by prisoner Artur Gold (1897–1943), a famous composer of popular songs and a violinist). In fact, the melody had already been composed in the Buchenwald concentration camp by the prisoner Hermann Leopoldi (1888–1959) for the camp official march *Buchenwaldlied*. It was Kurt Franz who brought it from Buchenwald where he had worked as a guard, and who ordered to write new words for the official song of Treblinka. The text was probably written by Walter Hirsch. Artur Gold may have "arranged" it for the ensemble which played in the camp.[41] Another hypothesis is that Kurt Franz himself wrote the words. This was stated by *Unterscharführer* Franz Suchomel who was part of the Treblinka personnel. He also explained that "new Jews who arrived in the morning [those selected for work and not killed] had to learn it and sing it already during the evening roll call."[42] The anthem's

---

40 Kurt Franz (1914–1998) worked at the Buchenwald camp from 1939, when the former Treblinka commandant Franz Paul Stangl (1908–1971) and most of the Treblinka German personnel took part in the euthanasia Aktion T4. Since April 1942, he was the commandant of the death camp in Bełżec. Four months later he was appointed deputy commandant of Treblinka camp. Nickhamed "Lalka" ("Doll") by the prisoners because of his appearance, his favourite pastime was to mutilate prisoners by ordering his dog Barry to bite their genitals. When he was arrested in 1959, a photo album from Treblinka was found in his house, entitled *Beautiful Years*. He was sentenced to life imprisonment in the Düsseldorf Treblinka trail in 1965 and released for health reasons in 1993.
41 I extend my thanks to Bret Werb, music curator at the United States Memorial Holocaust Museum, who provided me with this information.
42 Since March 1941, SS-*Unterscharführer* (Corporal) Franz Suchomel (1907–1979), like most of the German Treblinka staff, had taken part in Action T4 as a photographer at the Hadamar Euthanasia Centre in Berlin, taking photographs of euthanasia victims before their death. Suchomel was a good singer. After 1949, he worked as tailor, played in five amateur orchestras, and sang in the Catholic church choir in Altötting, Bavaria, where he lived. He was sentenced to six years in prison in 1965 (Klee 2007:615). In a (secretly recorded) interview with Claude Lanzmann, he not only stated that Franz wrote the words of the "anthem," but also sang it (in B-major). Ending the song with a glad smile, he added proudly, pointing his finger forward: "Sind Sie zufrieden?" – "Are you satisfied? This is unique. No Jews know it today anymore!" He seems, however, slightly embarrassed after thus disclosing his true sentiments. Earlier on he asked Claude Lanzmann: "You want history? Here you have history." The interviews by Claude Lanzman are part of Claude Lanzmann Shoah Collection and in part are

words bitterly mock the tragic situation of the prisoners, speaking of the column marching to work, and of duly following not only the orders and all gestures of the commandant, but also the whole Nazi "sacrosanct" ideals of obedience and duty. Held in a major key, it ends with a triumphant and happy "Hurra":[43]

Fester Schritt und Tritt	Steadily keeping pace
Und der Blick gerade aus	And eyes focused straight ahead
Immer mutig und treu	Always bravely and loyally
In die Welt geschaut	We do face the world
Marschieren Kolonnen zur Arbeit	The columns march to work
Darum sind wir heute in Treblinka	That's why we're in Treblinka today
Dass unser Schicksal ist tara-ra	Because our fate is tara-ra
Darum sind wir heute in Treblinka	That's why we're in Treblinka today
Und gestellt in kurzer Frist	And sent here for this short time.
Wir hören auf den Ton des Kommandanten	We obey the voice of the commandant And follow his every cue
Und folgen ihm auf seinen Wink	We march together in strict time
Wir gehen jeden Schritt um Schritt zusammen	For everything that duty demands of us
Für alle, was die Pflicht von uns verlangt	Work is to mean everything here
Die Arbeit soll alles hier bedeuten	And obedience and duty as well
Und auch Gehorsamkeit und Pflicht;	We will work, and work
Wir werden weiter, weiter leisten,	Till that little source of happiness
Bis das kleine Glück gibt einmal einen Wink	gives us a sign
Hurra!	Hurra!

---

available at the United States Memorial Holocaust Museum page. The interview with Franz Suchomel is available on YouTube.
43 Translation edited by Morag J. Grant in the volume edited by her. See: K. Naliwajek-Mazurek, Music and Torture in Nazi Sites of Persecution and Genocide in Occupied Poland 1939–1945, in: the world of music (new series) 2013, Vol. 2, Issue 1, Music and Torture | Music and Punishment, Göttingen: Department of Music at Georg August University.

3.5. Music as entertainment for the guards

Music performed by prisoners was also intended to provide entertainment for the camp personnel. Musicians were widely used to entertain the camp staff, as in the case of Artur Gold in the Treblinka death camp, where the elite of the Jewish musicians perished, including members of the Warsaw Philharmonic and other ensembles from before the war, as well as popular music composers and performers. Artur Gold, a true star of Polish popular music, was degraded to the role of prisoner-entertainer. The power of the perpetrators to force the musicians to provide entertainment, virtually on the ashes of murdered people, constituted an act of sadistic domination. Samuel Willenberg described in his heartbreaking account the day when Artur Gold was brought to Treblinka:

> A new transport from Warsaw provided us with the fifty men needed to round off the prisoner contingent in the camp, which had dwindled greatly as a result of the many on-site executions carried oput by the guard. Amont the new men was the famous Warsaw musicians Artur Gold. (…) That day after roll call, Lalka shouted: *Kappellmeister raus!* – The conductor: out! At the sound of this, Gold and two other prisoners stepped out of line and faced us. Even before this we had thought it strange that they had not ordered us to sing *Mountain Man* [Polish traditional song *Góralu czy ci nie żal*], which we chanted every day after roll call, and the camp anthem *Fester Schritt*. Artur Gold and the other two prisoners formed a violin trio grotesquely dressed in the standard prisoner uniform of rags and high-cut boots procured in the sorting yard. Now they mounted a small wooden platform which was hardly big enough for them. (…) The trio of musicians began to play popular prewar tunes, which, reminding us of years gone by, left us depressed and sore of heart. The Germans were pleased with themselves: they had succeeded in organizing an orchestra in the death camp. As we stood at roll call, Artur Gold entranced us with the old melodies he produced with his violin – amidst the sweet, nauseating stench of decomposing bodies which clung to us as if never wanting to part. The odor had become part of our very being; it was all that remained of our families and loved ones, a last remembrance of the Jewish people, exterminated in the gas chambers. (…) After one of these concerts the Germans decided that the maestros did not look good. Their clothes were too big, held up by all kinds of belts, and their boots were high and heavy. They ordered our tailors to sew jackets of shiny, loud blue cloth, and to attach giant gow ties to the collars. Dressed not as prisoners any longer but as clowns, they provided entraintainment after roll call, day in, day out. However spent we might have been after a twelve-hour workday, we had to stand in ranks and take in a concert. The musuci was usually accompanied by the tenor of the crane engine. The diligent machine kept on exhuming and relocating corpses in the death camp even after 6:00 p.m., for the Germans had decided to expedite the matter of covering the traces and burning the bodies. The moment the concert ended, the SS-men ordered us to march toward the entrance to the hut, even as we remained in roll-call formation. Our groups were organized by blocks, and each block *Kommandant* marched at the head of this group. Lalka of the SS

stood at the fence, arms folded across his chest, regarding us with a smirk. He felt like a lord with powers of life and death over us (...) We were very careful to take no chance with this monster named Lalka, whose cruelty was all too well-known to us. His career in brutality had begun even before the Treblinka camp was established; as early as 1939 he had participated in exterminating chronically ill or insane Germans.[44]

Glazar gave the most vivid accounts of music as entertainment in Treblinka and described the moment when the orchestra was enlarged:

> SS-men needed some entertainment, the most resourceful of them was "Lalka" [Kurt Franz]. Everybody knew he liked music and when he learned about the famous composer and violinist Artur Gold, who came with one of the last transports from the Warsaw ghetto, [he] chose him and ordered him to create a small orchestra in Treblinka. There were many musicians to choose from: two red-haired brothers Schermann (the only siblings in Treblinka), a tenor Salwe, small Edek with his accordion and others. Our masters and commandants brought from their holidays different instruments, trumpets, and clarinets, among others. The violins from transports were there already. Küttner even got scores with German songs and marches. But he was outdone by Franz – he procured percussion from somewhere and ordered everybody to sing with the accompaniment of the band.[45]

As Rajchman observed, music for the camp personnel, e.g. Karl Pötzinger (whom he names "Spetzinger"),[46] the deputy commandant in Treblinka, was a pleasurable pastime as well as a method used to control the prisoners. After the outbreak of typhoid fever in December 1942, thirteen prisoners, still very weak, declared themselves to be healthy; they knew that otherwise the camp staff would kill them – all the other ninety ill prisoners had been shot. The thirteen who were still alive were ordered to stand at roll call for an hour and sing. Rajchman ironically reported:

> It is the murderer Karl Spezinger who is such a music-lover. He likes declamation as well. Our colleague Szpigel, a well-known artist from Warsaw, has to recite and the orchestra accompanies him. After the roll call, the order: *Abtreten! Rechts um!* We have to march on the square. SS-man Gustav,[47] noticing that some of my colleagues move

---

44 Samuel Willenberg, *Revolt in Treblinka*, 132–134.
45 Glazar, *Stacja...*, 122–123.
46 Karl Pötzinger (1908–1944), SA member, took part in the euthanasia program in Brangenburg and Bernburg. He was transferred to Treblinka; as SS-*Scharführer* he was Matthes' deputy, supervised the gas chambers, and later was transferred to Sobibor and then to Italy.
47 Probably Gustav Münzberger (1933–1977), member of the SS since 1938, and the NSDAP since 1940. From 1940 he participated in the T4 Action of euthanasia in Sonnenstein. As *Unterscharführer* he was made a member of the Treblinka staff from

with difficulty, orders them to stand out and gratifies them with a few bullets. (...). I try to raise my legs as much as I can, and with a song on our lips we are marching – half-dead – to the barracks.[48]

In Sobibor, where Jews were murdered between April 1942 and October 1943, music was exploited even more by the Nazi functionaries as an element of psychological degradation of prisoners. Eda Lichtman, who was herself beaten almost to death by the Germans and the Ukrainian guards in Sobibor, described in her account the executions of prisoners after they attempted to escape or on occasions when such plans had been denounced by co-prisoners to the German authorities of the camp. At one such denunciation, by Jozef Kohn, all the Dutch prisoners, 72 men, were taken on the orders of Gustav Wagner to camp III where after a few minutes they were executed:

> During all this time we had to stand in a row. The execution lasted maybe for half an hour. At this time Frenzel[49] appeared and ordered the Dutch women to sing songs. A series of shots cut the silence, intermingling with the tones of forced songs. It distorted with agony the faces of the sisters and wives of victims being murdered at the same time. Suddenly Frenzel ordered to arrange planks which were to serve as a dancefloor. He organized an orchestra and we all had to dance and sing, though our faces were wet with tears and lips contorted with pain. When the Germans came back from the execution, their uniforms were spattered with blood. They won over 72 defenseless Jews.[50]

September 1942 to November 1943. Sentenced in Düsseldorf in 1965 to 12 years in prison, he was released already in 1971. Münzberger had earlier beaten Rajchman almost to death for not noticing that there are still teeth in one corpse's mouth. As Rajchman reported: "This time I received some seventy strokes. He had beaten me on my back with all his strength, almost all the time in the same place. He had nearly broken my vertebral column. When I got up with great difficulty, blood guttered in streams all over my body, dripping to my trousers." His life was eventually saved by a fellow prisoner, the medical doctor Cymerman, who cleaned his inflamed wound. Rajchman, *Ocalałem*, 56.

48 Ibid., 82.
49 Karl Frenzel (1911–1996) was a commandant of Camp I (forced labour camp) at Sobibor, one of the most brutal members of the camp staff. Frenzel was arrested by the US army but eventually released. Then he worked in Frankfurt. In 1966, he was sentenced to life for personally murdering six Jews, and for his participation in the mass murder of a further 150,000 Jews. In 1982, after serving sixteen and a half years, he was released on appeal. He was again sentenced to life imprisonment on 4 October 1985. Due to his advanced age and poor health, the sentence was not imposed. He was released and spent the last years of his life in a retirement home in Garbsen near Hannover.
50 Eda Lichtman's account was given in Polish, in Holon, Israel, in May 1959. Quoted in Bem, Marek (ed.): *Sobibór* Warsaw: Ośrodek Karta, Dom Spotkań z Historią

Lichtman also described another humiliating action involving music:

> One day, after the evening roll call (*Appell*), Otto Weiss, the SS-man, gave orders for a long wooden chest to be brought to him. He directed one of the camp inmates to don a black silk *kaftan* and a *shtreimel*, and to lie down in the chest. Weiss dropped the lid and broke into song, "I'm a Jew with a long snout!" Weiss half-opened the chest lid and ordered the prostate man to salute those who had gathered and repeat his words. Then he continued, "Beloved God, hearken to our song, stop up the Jews' voices so that mankind will have relief. Amen!" The SS men sang the song in a chorus. They ordered the *"Hassid"* to sway back and forth as if praying and made us say "amen" over and over again. They had such a good time.

One day they took a Jew, who had just arrived, from the platform. He had black hair and swarthy skin. The SS immediately dubbed him "der Neger" (the Negro). Wagner ordered him to sing. The fellow improvised in Yiddish, looking at the wonderful pine forest that surrounded the camp:

> Vi lustig ist de unser lebn,
> Man tut unz tsu essen gebn,
> Vi lustig ist im grynen vald
> Vo ich mich ofhalt..."
>
> How joyful is our life here
> They give us food;
> How happy it is for me in the green forest,
> Where I am!

Wagner liked the song. He instructed us to learn it by heart and to sing it after roll call. This "Negro", a cobbler from Kalisz, was a very decent fellow, a soul mate to us all.[51]

Trying to analyse the type of relations between prisoners and personnel, and the place of music within these relations, Glazar wrote: "One could use the term 'masters and slaves' to describe all bipedal creatures in Treblinka. ... But it is not that simple in Treblinka. ... Everybody sings and everybody is being sung

---

2010, 31–32. Original source: Archiv Zentrale Stelle der Landesjustizverwaltungen Ludwigsburg, sign. 208AR-Z/251/59, copy in the collection of Muzeum Pojezierza Łęczyńskiego-Włodawskiego, which holds the memorial for Sobibor camp.

51 Ibid. The testimony of Eda Lichtman was given at the legal proceedings in Hagen, West Germany, and completed by Miriam Novitch (1965) at the *Ghetto Fighters' House*. Thanks to the shared initiative of Judy Cohen and Ada Holtzman, the testimony was translated from Hebrew to English in January 2005 and was edited by Ada Holtzman. Source of the English version of the testimony: www.zchor.org.

of – Germans sing *Heimat, deine Sterne,* Ukrainians *Oy pri luchku, prishirokim poli,* Jews *Shtetele Belz, mayn gelibtes Belz* or *Yidishe mame* or *Eli, Eli...*"[52]

3.6. The interrelationship of torture and music from a psychoanalytical perspective

It is a demanding task to comprehend the reasons for the constant presence of music at the sites of mass killings and its relationship to the torture of prisoners, just as it is difficult to grasp the reality of an extermination site itself. Musical activities such as singing, normally associated with pleasure and joy, were forced upon prisoners immersed in utter despair, clearly for sadistic reasons.

To answer the initial questions – Why was music used as an important element of torture by the Nazis? How was it intertwined with genocidal actions? – it seems that music was considered by the Nazis as a perfect tool for additional psychological torture, torture destined to induce mechanisms of mind-control.

Forced singing in the concentration camps, especially those which operated in Nazi Germany since 1933, was among other things aimed at the "re-education" of political prisoners. The songs used there were meant to humiliate prisoners and to offend their personal beliefs. In the extermination camps, on the other hand, songs served only as moral torture for the prisoners, and – at the same and more importantly – for the entertainment of the guards. Watching Franz Suchomel, who sings the Treblinka "anthem" to Claude Lanzmann, unaware that he is being filmed, one cannot help feeling that he not only actually likes the song, but that he is also proud that no Jew remembers this song anymore.

The sociopsychological motivations of the Nazi SS war criminals for using music in the connection with torture are undoubtedly rooted in the sadistic personalities of the perpetrators. Sadism in a broad sense is defined as a "characterological tendency to enjoy hurting others; this is seen in association with 'malignant narcissism,' paranoid personality disorder, antisocial disorder, and in its most macabre form, serial killing."[53] Pleasure is achieved by personally inflicting pain, cruelty, degradation, or humiliation, or by watching such behaviour. The link between pleasure derived from victims' suffering is only being enhanced by the enjoyment provided by music. The humiliation of victims – being forced to sing the offensive and/or satirical texts in the tragic conditions of the death camp – augments the pleasurable sensations of the perpetrators

---

52 Glazar, *Stacja...*, 50.
53 Akhtar, *Comprehensive Dictionary of Psychoanalysis*, 251.

even more. Another term, "messianic sadism," coined by Salman Akhtar (2007), seems even more appropriate to describe the ideologically and racially motivated sadism of the Nazi camps and prisons personnel. The psychoanalytical definition reads as follows:

> [C]ruelty towards others that in the internal world of the perpetrator seems morally justified. "Messianic sadism" is a facet of extreme ethnoracial and religious prejudice. As the extreme end of hateful prejudice is approached, the raw aggression of the id begins to flow in the veins of the superego. An idealized self-image and an ego syntonic sadistic ideology begins to rationalize antisocial behavior. Thinking becomes dangerously stilted and all capacity for empathy with others is lost. When such a state of mind receives encouragement from politico-religious exhortations, violence appears to be guilt-free and even "divinely" sanctioned. Killing others becomes a means of buttressing one's own callous megalomania and also merging with an idealized deity or leader who comes to embody an archaic and omnipotent superego.[54]

In the psychopathology of Nazi criminals, the torture of large groups of prisoners at roll calls merged with the process of idealizing this very situation as something "divinely" sanctioned by the repetitive, ceremonial-like character of musical performances.[55] These "rituals" provided a powerful boost to the megalomaniac personalities of camp commandants, whose urge for power was limitless, and whose ranks and careers depended on the effectiveness of their genocidal actions. From their pre-war status of average men they were elevated to the status of leaders. It put them in a position to somehow compare themselves to their idealized deity, namely *der Führer*. Glazar recalled what happened when Kurt Franz returned from a vacation, freshly appointed a deputy commandant, and, at the same, time promoted to an *Untersturmführer* (he had earlier left as *Oberscharführer*). Franz shouted: "I want to hear singing here, a powerful choir of all your plucked nobs!"[56]

This is the reson that the album with horrific photographs from Treblinka found upon Kurt Franz's arrest was entitled "The Beautiful Years." He was unable to dispose of this precious souvenir even though it made important evidence in his criminal case, as it evoked his personal glory years, when the sound of music augmented his personal power.

---

54 Ibid., 171.
55 For the discussion of links between music and ideology of Nazi officials cf. Naliwajek, "Music and its Emotional Aspects," 223–224.
56 Glazar, *Stacja*, 122.

3.7. Mass Killings and the Sound of Music

Music seemed to be omnipresent at this horrific site of mass killings and it was thus remembered, especially by Glazar, who mentioned, in an interview with Lanzmann, that one could not hear any birds singing in Treblinka but that it was nevertheless filled with sounds: of yelling, of moaning, of crying and also with the sounds of music.[57]

Unauthorized music-making was repressed by the camp guards because it could have revealed the genuine human condition, the utmost suffering inflicted on the prisoners and their despair. It seems that the human capacity to reflect, to mourn was a threat to the Nazi system, to the totalitarian "propaganda of success". Even the cruellest of acts, such as murdering the innocent victims, had to be committed with a smile. This "good mood" was meant to be provided by the sound of music. Thus, in the Nazi use of music in concentration and death camps in occupied Poland, we can observe an intrinsic connection between the displaced aestheticization, which was characteristic of Nazi beliefs, and which made one of the essential components of Nazi social life, on one hand, and their criminal actions, on the other. Among the various conclusions which stem from the analysis of the roles that music played in the Nazi genocide system, there one that seems especially worthy further examination.

What happened to the ethical component of music when it was being used by the Nazis in military marches or genocidal practices? Did it disappear? Or maybe it was just disfigured or displaced in order to fit into the specific "ethics" or "ethos" of Nazi genocide functionaries?

We should also consider the case when a more ambitious, artistic repertoire is concerned. This psychological and ethical displacement of music in Nazi "culture" still awaits a closer examination.

Jechiel Rajchman began to "work" on the second day after his arrival in Treblinka, i.e. on October 11, 1942, between six and eight in the morning. He was assigned to the group which sorted the clothes of the victims. There he found his sister's dress and kept a piece of it in his clothing till the end of his stay in the camp. After eight o'clock he had to cut the hair of women who were to be killed in the gas chambers, just as his sister had been the day before. This happened under the supervision of Ukrainians with whips and rifles and the camp commandant Franz Stangl, who ordered the prisoners to work quickly. Rajchman

---

57 Richard Glazar in the interview in Claude Lanzmann, Shoah Collection available at the United States Memorial Holocaust Museum webpage.

quotes that they shouted "Los! Schneller die Haare schneiden!" ("Hurry! Cut the hair faster!"), while amongst the cries, beatings and suffering of the women their hair was cut and packed tightly into suitcases. When the gas chamber was already filled with victims, there was a half hour break. At this moment

> Soon a few murderers enter, they order us to sing. A nice song. (…) We have to sing, to cheer up the murderers and so that they feel nice. (…) Every now and then one of them goes out to the corridor and peeks through a little window to check if the victims are already dead.[58]

Rajchman described his feelings: "I am aghast: they choke people with gas there, in the chamber, and we are to sing."[59] Experienced prisoners already knew that they would be beaten up if they do not comply with this order. Rajchman was threatened by a guard, who noticed that his lips were closed, so, against his own will, he opened his mouth as if to sing. After half an hour the next group of naked women appeared, and the prisoners had to cut the victims' hair again.[60]

During four weeks of his work as a corpse carrier, Rajchman became a "dentist" and cleaner of gas chambers. Even in short moments when one chamber was being cleaned and in the other one there were still people who were showing signs of life, "the beasts made us dance and sing songs to the accompaniment of the Jewish orchestra playing next to our barrack."[61]

In his ironic style, Abraham Jacob Krzepicki, who spent just 18 days in Treblinka and managed to escape, described how music performed by prisoners on the days of mass killings was intended to entertain the camp personnel:

> The Open-Air Concert at the Death Camp. As I stood before the door of the Treblinka "bathhouse," I made a new discovery. Earlier, it had seemed to me that I heard sounds of music. I had thought it was a radio loudspeaker which the Germans had installed in order not to be isolated, God forbid, from their Fatherland's Kultur out here in the sticks. I was now to learn that their concern for musical culture went even further. Under a tree, about 40 meters from the bathhouse, not far from the path on which the Jews were driven into the "bath," there was a small orchestra consisting of three Jews with yellow patches and three Jewish musicians from Stoczek (who were later joined by another, better musician from Warsaw). There they stood, playing their instruments. I don't know why, but I was particularly impressed by a long reed instrument, a sort of fife or flute. In addition, there was a violin and, I believe, a mandolin. The musicians were standing there and raising a ruckus for all they were worth. They were probably playing the latest

---

58 Rajchman, *Ocalałem…*, 32–33.
59 Ibid., 33.
60 See: ibid., 32–33.
61 Ibid., 58–59.

hits which were popular with the Germans and Ukrainians, for whom they also used to play at shindigs in the guard stations. The Jews would play while the Gentiles danced.

A musical people, these Ukrainians. On the eve of the anniversary of the outbreak of the war – the night between 31 August and 1 September – the SS-men arranged a musical entertainment for the Jews. The musicians were taken to the roll call square and ordered to play Jewish tunes. Several young Jews were ordered to come forward and start to dance. An elderly Ukrainian corporal directed the show. The Germans thoroughly enjoyed the show; they were clapping and rolling with laughter...

Later on, when I made more detailed inquiries, I found out that this sort of Jewish open-air concert was held also whenever new transports arrived. No doubt the Jewish tunes merged with the shouts and screams of the Jewish men, women, and children who were being driven into the death bath.

There they would stand and play all the time, the Jewish musicians, near the narrow path along which other Jews ran their last race, opposite the open ditches where tens of thousands of Jews lay in their last sleep. There, they stood and played. They were playing for the right to remain alive a few more weeks.[62]

If we compare the "scenario" described above to the history of Maks Rosenfeld Library members from Nowy Sącz, who, just a night before their execution, were forced to play and dance at a show for the wives and children of SS-men, we can observe that the rules of the "SS theatre," described by Inga Clendinnen, were appallingly similar in many cases. At the Janovska Camp in Lvov, some distinguished musicians, such as the composer Jakub Mund, the conductor Leon Striks, and the famous pianist Artur Hermelin, were forced to play in the camp

---

62 Abraham Jacob Krzepicki was drafted into the Polish army in 1939, and taken prisoner by the Germans. After release, he lived in Warsaw. On August 25, 1943, he was deported to Treblinka from *Umschlagplatz* (a point in the Warsaw Ghetto where people were gathered for transportation to extermination camps.) After a successful escape from Treblinka, he returned to the Warsaw Ghetto, joined the Żydowska Organizacja Bojowa (Jewish Combat Organization), was a member of the Hanoar-Hatzioni group headed by Jacob Praszker, and was killed in the Ghetto Uprising of April 1943. His testimony was written down between December 1942 and January 1943 for the Ghetto underground archives kept by the historian Emanuel Ringelblum. The manuscript in Yiddish, buried in the ruins of the Ghetto, was discovered on December 1, 1950 by the Polish construction workers in the ruins of the building at 68 Nowolipki Street. The manuscript is preserved at the Jewish Historical Institute in Warsaw. It was published in Warsaw in *Bleter far Geshikhte* 1956, Vol. XI (1–2). Quoted from the English version: Abraham Krzepicki, *Eighteen Days in Treblinka* in: Alexander Donat (ed.), *The Death Camp Treblinka. A Documentary*, New York 1979, 77–144.

orchestra.⁶³ SS-Obersturmführer Richard Rokita, a former café musician, forced them to play during executions and ordered them to perform a special song, the *Death Tango*, for the other prisoners, just before their execution. It was a well-known tango, entitled *Tango Plegaria*, with music composed by Eduardo Bianco.⁶⁴ In the new Nazi version, the title was changed to the "Death Tango," which was meant to be explicit and mocking at the same time, such as the rest of the lyrics:

---

63 See the research done by Hanna Palmon, a descendant of Artur Hermelin: "The Polish Pianist Artur Hermelin," https://demusica.edu.pl/muzykalia-xiii-judaica-4/. Warsaw: Stowarzyszenie De Musica, 2012; "Jewish Musicians of Lwów," *The Galitzianer. The Quaterly Research Journal of Gesher Galicia* (23 / 2) 2016, 10–15.

64 The account of the subsequent steps of mass extermination and sadistic tortures of Jews from Lvov was given by Filip Friedman, *Zagłada Żydów lwowskich*, Wydawnictwa Centralnej Żydowskiej Komisji Historycznej przy Centralnym Komitecie Żydów Polskich«" No. 4, Łódź 1945. Cf. also Der Prozeß gegen die Hauptkriegsverbrecher vor dem Internationalen Gerichtshof Nürnberg. Nürnberg 1947, Vol. 7, 496 ff. On p. 497, the orchestra is thus described: "Die Deutschen führten ihre Folterungen, Mißhandlungen und Erschießungen bei Musikbegleitung aus. Zu diesem Zweck errichteten sie ein besonderes Orchester, das aus Gefangenen bestand. Sie zwangen Professor Stricks und den bekannten Dirigenten Mund, dieses Orchester zu leiten. Sie forderten Komponisten auf, eine besondere Melodie zu komponieren, die sie den Todestango nannten. Kurz vor der Auflösung des Lagers erschossen die Deutschen sämtliche Mitglieder des Orchesters."

Hörst du wie die Geige schluchzend spielt?	Do you hear how the violin plays sobbing?
Blutig klingen ihre Töne	Bloody sound its notes
Hörst du wie dein Herz sein Ende fühlt?	Do you hear how your heart feels its end?
Das Todestango spielt	It is the tango of death playing
Hab' kein Angst, mein Lieb'.	Have no fear, my love.
Sand wird deine Leiche decken	Sand will cover your corpse
Sternenkerze dient als Brenner	The candles of stars will serve as torches
Und als Polster dient dir nur ein Stein	
Doch glücklich wirst du sein so ganz allein.	And a stone will serve as a cushion But you'll be happy all alone.
Schüsse fallen, Kugeln knallen,	Shots are fired, bullets are fired,
Segregieren! Gift! Nur spielen	Segregation! Poison! Just playing
Und der Tod packt dich in Hand	And death grabs you with its hand
Drum sei fertig und bereit.	So be ready and be prepared.

Similar acts, meant to deprive the prisoners of dignity right before killing them, were widespread among the Nazi personnel. Let us return to the fundamental question concerning the omnipresence of music at the sites of extreme violence: why did the perpetrators need music there? Leopold Kozłowski, in an interview given to me, answered as follows:

> It was their aim. They did not treat music as music. They were happy that they can shoot to the sound of music. This was an accompaniment to their murders. Shootings sounded nice to them with music in the background. They did not treat music as we did – with a capital M – for them it was a game, a hideous game. But in my case it saved my life. Not only mine – Szpilman's too…[65]

3.8. Music as self-defense, resistance, survival, and mourning

For prisoners in detention sites music could constitute a weapon, as well as a measure of self-defence. Singing, whistling, playing harmonica, and other forms of musical expression often constituted a clandestine activity. It was considered illegal by the guards and cruelly punished, especially if somebody sang or played a song of protest, containing patriotic, religious, or political lyrics. Sometimes

---

65 See fn. 357. I quoted this testimony in: Naliwajek, "Music and Torture," 44.

even a suspicion of such intentions could lead to a severe punishment. Music played by the prisoners was also a method of reconstructing one's identity, often in relation to religion or the patriotic tradition. It was a way of transgressing the suffering and death. It helped to mock the living conditions in a camp or a prison and to make life in such places less hopeless. Numerous testimonies of inmates provide evidence of such functions of music. For instance, a group of women upon their arrival to Auschwitz began to sing a satirical song and to dance with the intention described by the witness as follows: "Let's save ourselves. We are laughing (…) We are beginning to sing: Hey ho, ha hey / This cell is so gay…". As the witness recollected:

> The German [women] functionaries are bewildered. They are staring at us like we're crazy, coming from another world. One of them laughed, quite happy about the unexpected entertainment, and she slapped me hard on my back. But the other one took care of the German order, shouting: Du blinde Kuh! Du lustige Mistbiene! Du alte Zitron! [You blind cow! You funny dung bee! You old lemon!] – she kicked Wanda, who was dancing, and she hit Zosia on her back with a stick: *Ordnung muss sein*.[66]

Two examples of music reconstructed by prisoners who were conductors of musical ensembles in Auschwitz-Birkenau prove the ability of musicians to counteract the dehumanization and express their resistance.

Chopin's Étude in E major Op. 10, No. 3 in Auschwitz-Birkenau

Arranging Chopin's Étude in E major Op. 10, No. 3 for the women orchestra in Birkenau, Alma Rosé referred to the popular pre-war song that utilized its musical material. It was *In mir klingt ein Lied* by Alois Melichar (1896 Vienna – 1976 Munich). He was an Austrian composer, ten years older than Alma Rosé, and the author of film scores for Nazi propaganda films. Chopin's *Étude* is composed in the ABA form, with the middle section *con bravura*, full of dramatic force and in Chopin's idiomatic style. It brings a stark contrast to the calm and melodious sections A. The fact that these sections carry a dreamy and poetic mood, while the central part is turbulent and full of dramatic expression, is essential for the way this music functioned in Auschwitz. Melichar made use only of the melodious material contained in sections A, to write his purposefully sentimental song. The author of the German lyrics was Ernst Marischka. Performed and recorded in

---

66 Krystyna Żywulska, *Przeżyłam Oświęcim*, Warsaw: DoM wYdawniczy tCHu, Państwowe Muzeum Auschwitz-Birkenau, 2008. See also Barbara Milewski, "Krystyna Żywulska: The Making Of A Satirist And Songwriter In Auschwitz-Birkenau Is Discovered Through Camp Mementos," *Swarthmore College Bulletin* 2009, 20–23.

various language versions, the song had gained vast popularity before the war. The song took its title from the first words in his version – "In mir klingt ein Lied" ("A song sounds inside me"). Until this very day Melichar's song is being performed both in German and English (titled *So Deep in the Night*). The conductor of the women's orchestra in Birkenau knew this song well from before the war. She most probably performed it with "Die Wiener Walzermädeln" (The Waltzing Girls of Vienna), the all-women ensemble that she had established in 1932, and conducted it during their several concert tours in Europe. The peculiar arrangement she created in Birkenau was written for voice with the accompaniment of instruments that were available there: 1 transverse flute, 2 recorders, 2 mandolins, guitar, cymbal, accordion, 5 first violins, 3 second violins, cello and double bass.

She also introduced significant changes into the banal text by Marischka. She kept the title unchanged so that she could explain herself to the guards that she was conducting just a popular prewar song and not Chopin's music. Nonetheless, title aside, Marischka's sentimental lyrics were changed completely. She replaced all the sentimental (such as "dream of quiet love") with her own words referring to the past ("reminiscences permeat my soul").

Alma Rosé's lyrics	Alma Rosé's lyrics in English translation	Ernst Marischka's lyrics	Ernst Marischka's lyrics in Enligh translation
In mir klingt ein Lied	A song sounds inside me	In mir klingt ein Lied,	A song sounds inside me,
Ein schönes Lied,	A beautiful song,	Ein kleines Lied,	A little song,
Und durch die Seele mir Erinnern zieht	And reminiscences permeate my soul	In dem ein Traum von stiller Liebe blüht.	In which a dream of quiet love blooms.
Mein Herz war still.	My heart was still.	Für dich allein!	For you alone!
Nun erklingen wieder zarte Töne	Now tender tones resound again	Eine heisse, ungestillte Sehnsucht	With burning, unfulfilled yearning
Ruft in mir alles auf.	Calls up everything in me.	Schreib die Melodie!	Write the melody!

Alma Rosé's lyrics	Alma Rosé's lyrics in English translation	Ernst Marischka's lyrics	Ernst Marischka's lyrics in Enligh translation
[Das] Leben war fern,	Life was far away,	In mir klingt ein Lied	There's a song inside me
Und Wünsche fremd.	And dreams became foreign.	Ein kleines Lied,	A little song,
Mein Herz! Wie ruhig warst du, lange Zeit.	My heart! How quiet you were? how long?	In dem ein Wunsch von tausend Stunden glüht.	Inside it a dream of a thousand hours glows
Doch nun kam nah	But now it came near	Bei dir zu sein!	All spent with you!
All mein Glück und mein Verlangen	All my happiness and my desire,	Sollst mit mir im Himmel leben,	You shall live with me in heaven,
Tieftes Sehnen, Schlaflos Bangen.	Deep longing, sleepless fear.	träumend über Sterne schweben,	Dreaming of the stars
Alles, alles lebt jetz wieder auf	Everything, everything is alive again	ewig scheint die Sonne für uns zwei,	The sun will shine forever for the two of us
Ich will doch nur	All I want is	sehn dich herbei	We'll look for you
Frieden für mein Herz,	Peace for my heart,	und mit dir mein Glück.	And with you my happiness.
Nicht denken wieder mehr	Thinking no more	Hörst du die Musik,	Do you hear the music,
An ein schönes Lied.	Of a beautiful song.	zärtliche Musik...	Tender music...

In the last two stanzas, Alma Rosé made her own attempt at describing her spiritual state. Words by Marischka ("There's a song inside me / A little song, / Inside it a wish of thousand hours glows / All spent with you!") were substituted by Alma Rosé with an entirely different text: "Life was far away, and dreams became foreign. / My heart! How quiet you were? how long? / But now it came near / All my happiness and my desire, / Deep longing, sleepless fear. / Everything,

everything is alive again / All I want is / Peace for my heart, / Thinking no more / Of a beautiful song."

Chopin's E major Étude, also known under the "poetic" French title *Tristesse* or *Żal* in Polish, was played in Auschwitz yet in other circumstances. Jerzy Vogel, the youngest of the men's *Kapelle*, was arrested in Warsaw along with his father, Ryszard, a retired officer of the Polish Army. The Germans offered them a grim choice: to sign the *Volksliste* or to be sent to a concentration camp. Having refused to comply, they were sent to Auschwitz. One day he was called by an SS man and taken to the luxurious office of SS-Unterscharführer Wilhelm Emmerich, who was already heavily drunk.[67] He was ordered by him: *Spiel*! (Play!). In Vogel's account:

> There is a piano. Should I play? Now? But what? I cannot gather my thoughts. What should I play to him while he is in such a state? A march? A tango? A waltz? Everything may turn out to be bad. He may shoot me right here, right now, the son of a bitch. (…)
> These sons of bitches, these thugs are romantics after all – I think – and begin to play Liszt's *Love Dream* (*Liebestraum*). And I look at him to see if it works. It does. He's completely dreamy, red-faced, satisfied. So now I know that I need to play sentimental pieces. So I play and I play. And suddenly I don't know what happened to me: I'm playing Chopin's "Sorrow" Etude. What am I doing?! I'm done for. But I can't stop. At one point I hear him humming under his breath, because I'm playing a very melodious, catchy part. But the second part is a virtuoso piece, that is what he will not be able hum to anymore. He will realize it's Chopin, and I already know what is going to happen.
> I am approaching the end of the first part, making various technical tricks, and play the same thing again.
> He's not humming anymore. Well, damn it, I think to myself… But at one point the door opens, and an SS-man enters. He approaches Emmerich and whispers something in his ear. And I am still playing the piano, I can't stop without an order. I hear him calmly saying: "Raus." I thought it was directed to that other German, because they always used to shout at me. So I keep playing, but he jumps up! Comes at me, hits me in the face and kicks me. I fall under the piano, quickly gather myself. He kicks me one more time and pushes me through the door (...) I huddle and wait to see what will happen next. (…) Later it turned out that a transport came and Emmerich was called to the ramp. He knew beforehand that there would be a selection and it was his way of getting ready.[68]

---

67 Wilhelm Emmerich was SS-Unterscharführer (01.01.1940 – 22.04.1943) promoted to SS-Oberscharführer (12.02.1944–15.02.1945). See the IPN webpage https://truthabo utcamps.eu/th/form/r42415236,EMMERICH.html.
68 Ignacy Szczepański, *Häftlings-kapelle* (Warsaw: Książka i Wiedza, 1990), 51–54.

Three Warsaw Polonaises by Szymon Laks

Szymon Laks – a composer, a Pole and a Varsovia – was arrested in Paris as a Jew by the French collaborative police. Then he was transported to Auschwitz-Birkenau where he became the conductor of the male orchestra. In his book written after the war he recalled a very special discovery. One day, he found a piece of paper covered in mud that turned out to be a handwritten music sheet. As he wrote:

> It was just a melody with neither harmonization nor accompaniment. It was entitled *Three Warsaw Polonaises from the 18th century, author: Anonymous*. I washed the precious document as carefully as possible and hung it in a discreet place in the music room to let it dry overnight. Over the next few days, I harmonized all three polonaises for a small chamber ensemble. Then, when circumstances allowed, I began to rehearse them inside the block. They turned out to be real gems of Polish 18th-century music. Some of my fellow Polish inmates congratulated me on this "stunt," considering it an act of resistance. It surprised me a bit, because I was doing it purely for musical satisfaction, even though it was enhanced by the fact that the music was Polish.[69]

After the war, he reconstructed the *Three Warsaw Polonaises* from memory.[70]

One can only presume what a combination of circumstances caused these scraps of Polish musical tradition to end up in the bloody soil of Birkenau. Perhaps, these three polonaises were carefully transcribed by some musicologist, musician, librarian or an archive employee and they ended up in the camp along with this person. Many people undertook a heroic struggle to save library and museum collections from being plundered by the occupiers. The fact that these works were not printed but handwritten means that they were probably copied from the original documents.

The *Three Warsaw Polonaises* are very diverse in terms of style, tempo, character, and internal structure. The first one, a polonaise in D-major, set in the majestic and lively *Allegro maestoso*, full of charm, ornament, and light figurations, is essentially bipartite (12 + 16 bars), containing a repetition of each of these two sections. However, it also possesses some features of a tripartite form, namely the introduction of the second theme in the final section and contrasting material in the middle section. The second polonaise has similar proportions (10 + 16

---

69 See Szymon Laks, *Gry oświęcimskie* (Oświęcim: Wydawnictwo PMAB), 1998.
70 The research on Warsaw Polonaises by Szymon Laks came from the idea of Renata Koszyk, to reconstruct the orchestral version of these pieces. Szymon Bywalec reconstructed orchestral score and conducted the recording effectuated by Beata Jankowska-Burzyńska and Wojciech Marzec. See the website https://forbiddenmusic.info/en.

bars, with both parts repeated), and it contrasts the first one in terms of key (E minor), tempo (*Andantino con espressione*) and expression. It is turbulent, pre-romantic in style, with broken phrases, slightly capricious, as if breathless, that seem to circulate around the note E. The third polonaise is the most vivid one (*Allegro energico*) and also the most complex in its tripartite structure (ABA). Its middle section, the *Trio*, written in the subdominant key of C major, contrasts with the first and the last. The opening motif of the third polonaise is reminiscent of the four opening notes of the Polish anthem. Indeed, both melody and the characteristic punctuated rhythm are identical. However, they elude attention, being immediately "covered" by an entirely different rhythm and melody – the descending sixteenth notes.

Only the third one has been so far identified in primary sources.[71] This confirms its Varsovian character. In the 1920s the eminent musicologist Łucjan Kamieński (1885–1964) discovered a collection of "various dances for violin". He enthusiastically described his significant finding in 1928.[72] According to him, this collection was "compiled in Poland, most likely in Warsaw, by an anonymous German collector at the behest of a certain Mr. Nahke in Leipzig in 1800."[73] The third of the *Warsaw Polonaises* discovered by Szymon Laks in Birkenau is included in this collection. This discovery is the more important that this polonaise is linked with the genesis of the Polish anthem, the *Dąbrowski's Mazurka*.[74]

Szymon Laks's discovery is not just another example of "cannons hidden among flowers" – as Robert Schumann wrote about Chopin's music. Picked

---

71 We owe the discovery to Ilona Lewandowska who is the curator of the Music Department of the Toruń University Library and to whom I extend my thanks. After my inquiries begun in 2020, she identified the third of the *Warsaw Polonaises* in the famous catalog prepared by Stefan Burhardt (S. Burhardt, *Polonez: katalog tematyczny*, Volume 2, *1792–1830*, edited and supplemented by Maria Prokopowicz and Andrzej Spóz, 579). She found this polonaise there under the item 3303, in a group containing ten anonymous polonaises (items 3297–3306).
72 Łucjan Kamieński, "O polonezie staropolskim" [On the old Polish polonaise], *Muzyka* 1928 No. 3, 99–103.
73 "No: 76–85. Polonoise" in *Diverses Danses pour le Violon pour Monsieur Nahke à Leipzig 1800*, 4. The original is in DSB, Berlin, Mus. Ms. 38048–missing. The Toruń University Library is in possession of a photocopy of a copy of this manuscript made by Łucjan Kamieński, under the reference number Fot. BOOT V 1224; mf. BUT 216.
74 According to Tomasz Nowak, Kamieński provided the most compelling arguments regarding the genesis of Dąbrowski's Mazurka. T. Nowak, *Taniec narodowy w polskim kanonie kultury. Źródła, geneza, przemiany*, (Warsaw: BEL, 2016), 150.

up from the dust, pulled out of the mud soaked with the blood and despair of the victims, the old polonaises could be treated as a means of cultural resistance. From the power contained in them – the cultural essence resounding with the first notes of the Polish national anthem – Szymon Laks constructed a new weapon of similar meaning – bolstering the strength and courage of the community of prisoner-musicians. These polonaises are not only "little masterpieces," but they are also an important part of Polish history, and their genetic threads and filiations are still waiting for future discoveries.

Music as mourning

Music became an expression of mourning and prayer in the ghastly realities of the death camps. Witnesses from Treblinka remembered Izaak Salwe, a well-known tenor and actor, transported to Treblinka from the Warsaw Ghetto, singing *Shema Yisrael* for his fellow prisoners. This prayer, traditionally recited as the last words of a dying person, was sung by Jewish men on their way to the gas chambers, as remembered by witnesses.

Traditional songs, secretly played by the prisoners, usually in places where they slept, triggered imaginary processes taking the musicians and their listeners back to their past. It could have a soothing effect for some but for others it could have been unbearable, as it would make them suffer even more. A fourteen-year-old boy, remembered only by his first name Edek, was kept alive because he could play the accordion. His parents and siblings were killed immediately after their arrival in Treblinka. As Glazar observed bitterly, "they could not play any musical instrument." Edek had a "sad face with sad eyes," divested of "any childlike features." He accompanied Salwe who sang *Mayne yiddishe mame*. To him, playing these songs could be both torture and the only way to bring back the memories of his home. He later played an important part in the Treblinka revolt and was killed during it. Willenberg remembered a moment when this kind of music-making was interrupted by one of the prisoners. A Czech, who came with a transport from Theresienstadt, played old prewar songs on his harmonica and thus revived other prisoners' memories. As Willenberg described it:

> The Czech was an intermittent guest at our feasts. He approached our corner, stepping around prisoners who had already gone to sleep. Following him like a shadow sneaked a prisoner from a little town in Poland. Between his fingers he clutched two spoons which he manipulated dexterously against each other and his thigh to produce pleasant melodies. One of his favourite tunes was *The Last Sunday*, a popular ditty from before the war.
>
> Each of us allowed his memories to return to distant prewar years. Its sad melody and evocative lyrics – "I'll make you a bed and wait for you patiently for this last

Sunday" – transported us to another world; for a few moments we forgot where we were. (…) Each of us in his own mind's eye beheld his personal "last Sunday" of freedom. We had absolutely nothing to look forward to, we were sure. No one was waiting for us; everything we had left was utterly gone.[75]

The Last Sunday (in the original Polish version: *Ta ostatnia niedziela*) was in fact one of the greatest hits, which reached enormous popularity in different language versions just before the war. This tango composed by Jerzy Petersburski to the words by Witor Friedwald was recorded by the Polish recording company Odeon in 1936. During the war its meaning evolved into a more explicit one – it no longer denoted the loss of love itself, but rather the sense of impending death. Wiktor Friedwald who was a lawyer and worked at the Society of Authors and Stage Composers ZAIKS was shot by German soldiers in the ghetto on August 12, 1942. It happened in the presence of his wife and his daughter Krystyna in a flat where after the establishment of the Warsaw Ghetto they were forcibly moved from their apartment in Poznańska Street 3. After her mother was taken to Auschwitz, Krystyna Friedwald survived with the help of her school friend, Lubomira Karwowska (1925–2009) and her parents, who managed to get a false *Kennkarte* for her. Krystyna, who was born in 1926 in Lvov, took part in clandestine underground activity and in the Warsaw Uprising in 1944, under the pseudonym "Mewa." After the Warsaw Uprising, they both left the city with the civilians and as prisoners were in a camp and worked in a factory in Berlin.[76]

Pre-war hits, such as the famous *Ta ostatnia niedziela* were also sung by camp prisoners as musical material, sometimes with altered words. Its mournful expression is close to an even more depressing *The Gloomy Sunday*, composed by the Hungarian composer Rezső Seress, the tango known for driving people to suicide, which is why it was eventually forbidden. The strategy of transforming old songs and known melodies by adding new words was widely used in the cities, in ghettos and camps. The composer David Bajgelman wrote his lullabies commemorating deaths of children in the Łódź ghetto. A lullaby of this type was memorised and preserved by Aleksander Kulisiewicz who sang and recorded it in Polish. Aaron Liebeskind, whom Kulisiewicz met in Sachsenhausen and who later perished in Auschwitz, sang it in Yiddish in Treblinka in 1942, to the

---

75 Willenberg, *Revolt*, 155–157.
76 In conversation with Jan Radziukiewicz, December 11, 2013, Eastchester, USA, https://www.1944.pl/powstancze-biogramy/krystyna-friedwald,55895.html; https://www.1944.pl/powstancze-biogramy/lubomira-karwowska,55896.html. Lubomira Karwowska and her parents received the title of the Righteous Among the Nations in 2007.

well-known melody by Alexander Vertinsky.[77] He was mourning his child whose body was soon to be burned:

Krematorium czarne, głuche	A dark, deaf crematorium
Bramy piekieł, trupów stos	Gates of hell, heaps of corpses
Śliskie, sztywne ciała wlokę	I drag the slippery, stiff bodies
Osiwiałem w jedną noc	Went grey overnight
Oto synek leży, synek mój,	There he lies, my little boy,
Małe piąstki w usta wgryzł,	Biting on his little fists,
Jakżeż ciebie w ogień wrzucę tu!	How can I throw you into this fire here!
Złote włoski śliczne twe	Your beautiful golden locks
Lulaj, lulaj – synku mój Lulaj, lulaj – synku mój Synku mój	Hush, hush – my son My little son
Blade słońce, czemu milczysz? Wszak widziałem wszystko tu. Główkę jego roztrzaskali o kamienny, zimny mur. Patrzą w niebo ciemne oczka twe i zastygłe krzyczą łzy. Synku! Wszędzie twoja krew! A przeżyłeś lata – trzy.	Pale sun, why are you silent? After all, I saw everything here. They smashed his head Against a stone, cold wall. Your dark little eyes look up into heaven and your frozen tears cry. Sonny! Everywhere your blood! And it is three years that you've lived.
Lulaj, lulaj – synku mój Lulaj, lulaj – synku mój Synku mój	Hush, hush – my son My little son

Kaczerginski included in his *Lider fun di getos un lagern* (1948) another mournful lullaby for a three-old child, created by Leah Rudnitsky, the young poet and teacher, born in 1916. After the Vilna ghetto liquidation Leah Rudnitsky was

---

77 It was published by the Polish Association of the Former Political Prisoners of Nazi Prisons and Concentration Camps in Koszalin: Anna Marcinek-Drozdalska (ed.), *Ocalone we wspomnieniach. Wspomnienia byłych więźniów politycznych, hitlerowskich więzień i obozów koncentracyjnych* (Koszalin: Koszalińska Biblioteka Publiczna im. Joachima Lelewela, 2011), 122.

herself murdered in Majdanek or Treblinka. The lullaby, which she wrote after the execution of 4,000 Jews at Ponary on April 5, 1943, depicts the scenery of child's death cradle in the first stanza – "Dremlen feygl oyf di tsvaygn, / Shlof, mayn tayer kind, / Bay dayn vigl oyf dayn nare / Zitst a fremde un zingt. Lyulyu, lyulyu, lyyu" ("Birdies slumber on the branches, / Sleep my precious child, / At your cradle in the dugout / Sits a stranger crooning: hushabye.") and that of her father's death in the third.[78] Ruth Rubin quoted this, and other Yiddish lullabies and songs devoted to children's suffering. The second stanza of another song from Kaczerginski collection, *Shlof mayn zun mayn kleyner* (*Sleep my little son*), is bitterly ironic: "Dayn zind iz gor a groyse – / Du host gebrakht tsum krig. / Du lozt nit tsu di arier / Dergreykhn zeyer zig. Lyulyulyu" ("They say your crime is great – For you have brought the war. You prevent the Aryans / From achieving their victory. Hushabye").[79]

Children themselves used games and musical expression to cope with their suffering and to strengthen their spirit. They were described by Georges Eisen in his book *Children and Play in the Holocaust. Games among the Shadows*.[80] Such accounts and poetry written by the children were sometimes preserved in the form of diaries while their authors were killed. Music occasionally appears in these harrowing chronicles. In the diary of Dawid Rubinowicz (1927–1942), a twelve-years-old boy from Bodzentyn, a small town near Kielce, music it is mentioned only once, in the last entry of his diary on June 1, 1942. On that day he wrote that "it was a day of happiness" because his father returned from Skarżysko-Kamienna labour camp; at first, he heard a truck coming and people singing, and he thought: the Jews are coming back from the camp. He commented that all of this was happening as if in a film. Soon the diary suddenly breaks off with the words "blood" and "who."[81]

"It is with particular pleasure that I have taken note of your announcement that for 14 days now a train with 5,000 members of the chosen people has been running daily to Treblinka" – these words were written on August 13, 1942 by the *SS-Obergruppenführer* Karl Wolff (1900–1984) to Albert Ganzenmüller

---

78 Rubin, *Voices*, 438 and 459 after Kaczerginski, 87.
79 Rubin, *Voices*, 437 after Kaczerginski, 100.
80 Georges Eisen in his book *Children and Play in the Holocaust. Games among the Shadows*, 1988.
81 Dawid Rubinowicz, *Pamiętnik* (Warsaw: Książka i Wiedza, 1987). This diary is translated to several languages. The editors suppose that perhaps the diary could have been continued in another notebook which got lost, as the preserved notebook is filled up.

(1905–1996) who was the deputy director of the Deutsche Reichsbahn (German National Railway), responsible for transports to the extermination camps[82] The Jews from Bodzentyn were transported from Suchedniów to Treblinka on September 21 and arriving in the camp on the next day.

The children often transformed old lullabies or ditties into lullabies of death, trying to find some comfort in the last days and hours of their life. A short death lullaby remains the only trace of an anonymous girl and her lonely death at the Majdanek camp. She sang it to the melody of the traditional, melancholy Polish lullaby *Na Wojtusia z popielnika iskiereczka mruga* about a boy who is listening to tale told by a spark dying in the hearth. We do not know whether she was Jewish or Polish (the former is more likely, although there were also Polish girls among the prisoners). The only thing that we know about her (from a short note which she left at the bottom of the manuscript) is that she was nine. The piece of paper she kept in her shoe was found in a transport of prisoners' clothing in Wałcz (*Deutsch Krone* in German) in Western Pomerania. The lyrics succinctly express the anguish of millions:

> "Była sobie raz Elżunia / Umierała sama / bo jej ojciec na Majdanku, / w Oświęcimiu mama." – "There once was a girl named Lizzy / Dying alone / Cause her dad was in Majdanek / And her ma' in Auschwitz gone..."[83]

---

82 They were both members of NSDAP since 1931. Wolff was a General of Waffen-SS, the chief adjutant of Himmler, since 1936 the Chief of the Personal Staff Reichsführer-SS, since 1939 a liaison officer of between the SS and the Führer. He was Himmler's coordinator of the planning of IG Farben's Buna plant in Auschwitz. In summer 1940 he had a meeting with Bütefisch and Ambros in Auschwitz, as he justified it: "The IG Farbenindustrie was one of the largest donors within the Freundeskreis Reichsführer-SS." This "Circle of Friends," formerly "Freundeskreis der Wirtschaft beim Reichsführer SS Himmler," also known as the Keppler-Kreis – Keppler's Circle) was a group of German industrialists whose aim was to strengthen ties between the NSDAP and German business and industry. The group was formed and coordinated by Wilhelm Keppler, one of Adolf Hitler's close economic advisers. Since September 1943 Wolff was a Higher SS and Police Leader in Italy. After 1945, he worked as a representative for a publishing house in Kempfenhausen by the Starnberger lake. In 1964 he was sentenced in Munich to 15 years of imprisonment for aiding and abetting murder in at least 300,000 cases (deportations to Treblinka). Klee, *Personenlexicon*, 173–174; 686.

83 It was published in the book which contained poems by Majdanek's prisoners: Zofia Murawska-Gryń (ed.), *Pieśni zza drutów: wiersze, pieśni i piosenki powstałe w obozie koncentracyjnym na Majdanku* (Lublin: Towarzystwo Opieki nad Majdankiem, 1985), 142; 82. Halina Birenbaum translated it from Polish to Hebrew (*Wiersze sprzed i z czasu*

Acknowledgments

The tortuous path towards understanding the incredibly complex world of music in occupied Poland would have been impossible to fathom without the help of many generous people, the witnesses of the tragic epoch who not only shared their memories, perceptions, beliefs, and some of their most excruciating experiences with me but also offered their friendship and support. Their courage and integrity have been an everlasting inspiration. I am grateful to Dr. Halina Szpilman, Helena Dunicz-Niwińska, Leopold Kozłowski, Witold Sadowy, Professor Wanda Wiłkomirska, and her brother Józef Wiłkomirski. Samuel Willenberg and his wife Krystyna sent me Artur Gold's recordings and the map of Treblinka. I am honoured that they agreed to be my guides through the darkest paths of music history. Several outstanding people helped me to understand various aspects of their lives under German occupation and its aftermath: Dr. Stefan Carter from Montreal, Aureliusz Dembiński, soldier in the "Gustaw" batallion during the Warsaw Uprising, Barbara Drzewiecka, Elżbieta Dziębowska, Professor Jan Ekier, Professor Marian Fuks, Wacław Gluth-Nowowiejski, Professor Michał Głowiński, Leszek Izmajłow, Professor Witold Kieżun, Jan Kossakowski, Jadwiga Kotońska, Professor Włodzimierz Kotoński, Professor Andrzej Olszewski, Halina Paszkowska-Turska, Kordian Tarasewicz, Marian Turski, Professor Mirosław Perz, Dr. Władysław Malinowski. Halina Sander-Janowska helped me to understand the intricacies of the identity of a young girl in Łódź who had a Jewish mother and a German father, killed by the communists just after the war. The books by Halina Birenbaum published in the early 1990s opened my eyes to the tragedy of the Holocaust, and the letters and poetry we exchanged have been an important inspiration.

I dedicate this book to my parents, Kinga Szczepkowska-Naliwajek (1945–2006), art historian, and Zbigniew Naliwajek, professor of French literature, who have spent their entire lives working on what they believed in, the task of promoting new generations of young researchers, communicating, and exchanging ideas between scholars of different backgrounds, German historians of art and French literature specialists. Thanks to them I was lucky enough to grow up in an inspiring intellectual milieu, free of any bias, as they were true role models,

---

potopu. Ma'ariv Book Guild, 1990) and published it also on her webpage, http://www.zchor.org/birenbaum/poemy.htm.

offering others their respect, support, and curiosity. I am also thankful to Elżbieta Sikora, who with her unremitting bravery and creativity is a powerful inspiration. With my father, they have kept encouraging me on this difficult path.

I am grateful to all friends and colleagues who have supported me with their wisdom at different stages of my inquiries. The late Elżbieta Markowska, Professor Maciej Gołab, Frank Harders Wuthenow, Lady Camilla Panufnik, Professor Michał Bristiger and his wife Barbara, colleagues from the Witold Lutosławski Association, Maria Burchard, Grzegorz Michalski, Elżbieta Szczepańska-Lange, Grażyna and Krzysztof Teodorowicz, Marek Żebrowski from the Polish Information Centre at UCLA.

I am indebted to Holocaust Memorial Museum in Washington for being able to attend the workshop on International Tracking Service and to Dr. Christine Schmidt from the Wiener Library for the Study of the Holocaust and Genocide.

I extend my thanks to the international family of scholars and colleagues who at various points of my life helped me with their insights, knowledge and experience. I am sure that I would not have been able to complete this book without the patient assistance and criticism of these outstanding researchers – Professor Erik Levi, Morag Grant, Anna Papaeti, Pauline Fairclough, Lisa Jakelski, Nicholas Reyland, Renata Tańczuk, Sławomir Wieczorek who discussed and edited my articles partly incorporated in this book.

All these colleagues and friends have helped and inspired me: Andrea Bohlman with her inspiring book, Professor Michael Custodis, Dr. Danuta Drywa from the Stutthof Museum, Dr. Albrecht Goetze, Danuta Gwizdalanka and Krzysztof Meyer who gave me information on music in occupied Krakow, Renata Koszyk, Hanna Palmon, Jean-Yves Potel, Harvey Sachs, Carla Shaperau, Andrzej Szpilman, Sylwia Zabieglińska, who encouraged me and read the preliminary version of this book, Karol Laskowski and Karol Perepłyś from Studio 27, Barbara Milewski, Dr. Lyudmila Sholokhova, the director of the library at the YIVO Institute, Dr. Violetta Rezler-Wasilewska, the director of Central Museum of Prisoners-of-War in Łambinowice (Lamsdorf).

I am thankful to my son Stanisław who helped me to transcribe the interviews and to my daughter Zofia for her support. I am also grateful to all friends who had supported me: Magda Bańkowska-Romańska, Anna and Paweł Szymański, Monika Janiszewska, Małgorzata Wyszyńska, Maciej Goss, Joanna Połeć, Maciej Grzybowski, Krzysztof Chorzelski, Karina Klimaszewska, Justyna Rekść-Raubo, colleagues from Nowy Teatr in Warsaw and the Warsaw Autumn Festival programming commitee.

In the final months of the editing process, I was lucky to be offered help by friends. Without their assistance this task would have been impossible. I am very grateful to Robert Elias, the former director of the Orel Foundation, who was the first reader of this book and edited its first version. His faith and friendship kept me going on. I also extend my thanks to Bret Werb for reviewing the script and his valuable suggestions.I am also thankful to Jan Burzyński, the editor, who perfectly understood the difficulties of the author's path and made it possible to bring it into existence.

Mikołaj Wiśniewski, Professor of English studies at the SWPS University of Social Sciences and Humanities, invented the title of the book and transformed the text into actual English.

Marcin Rychter, editor of *Eidos. A Journal for Philosophy of Culture*, not only patiently read and edited the manuscript at different stages, transforming awkward sentences into more clear ones, but also encouraged and inspired me during our long discussions.

Going through the process of completing this book, I have more acutely realized that we all share a specific memory and that all of us have to cope with troubling images which continue to haunt us. We carry the posttraumatic burden inherited from the previous generations – the memory of the genocide which touched our families and is imprinted in our DNA. Bob as the son of Hungarian Jews, survivors of Auschwitz. Mikołaj as the grandson of Seweryna Szmaglewska, the author of *Smoke over Birkenau*, the first account of the genocide in Auschwitz, where she spent three years. Marcin as the great-grandson of Stanisław Rychter who coordinated clandestine education in Southern Poland during the war and was beaten to death during SB interrogations after the war. And finally – me, the great-granddaughter of the historian of art Nikodem Pajzderski, arrested in October 1939 and killed on January 6, 1940, in Fort VII in Poznań – most probably because, being the director of the National Museum in Poznań, he represented to the Third Reich functionaries the idea of Polish national identity in an area which was meant to be thoroughly Germanized.

Last but not least, I would like to thank all my colleagues, friends and mentors from the Institute of Musicology at the University of Warsaw who supported me in various ways: Professors Piotr Dahlig, Agnieszka Leszczyńska, Szymon Paczkowski, Irena Poniatowska, Zbigniew Skowron, Sławomira Żerańska-Kominek, Alina Żórawska-Witkowska, Tomasz Nowak, as well as Dr. Mariusz Gradowski and Anastasya Niakraseva. I extend my thanks to the director of the Institute Professor Iwona Lindstedt for her constant encouragement and for funding this publication.

Epilogue

This book is an attempt at combining two very different perspectives – the one of the victims and the one of the perpetrators – it is an attempt at listening to their voices in order to understand what separates them. It took me more than fifteen years of research and my own personal dilemmas, to understand that it is propaganda which coerces both the designated victims and the perpetrators to adopt their roles.

Persuasion through songs and other rhymed verse, as well as books of fiction, along with images and speeches broadcast on radio and with the help of all other available hi-tech media, constitutes one of the most effective tools of propaganda. As such, propaganda aims at proving the superiority of a given culture and the necessity of either conquering and appropriating or destroying other cultures which – in order to legitimize such actions – are presented as hostile, sick, malevolent, or inhuman. These techniques are often directed at children and young people in order to make them believe in the regime and prepare them for the roles of its future functionaries. Songs are used with the intention of influencing both the general audiences and specific social groups, such as soldiers, party members, pupils, etc.

Already in the 1920s, the propaganda experts discovered what components and methods are useful for effective persuasion and marketing. One of them, Freud's nephew Edward Bernays, described this "mechanics" in his *Propaganda* (1928)[1] where he used an expression strikingly resembling the above quoted opinion of a German witness: "A man who is able to inject an idea, rules."[2] Later Hitler, Stalin, Goebbels, and other practitioners of totalitarian propaganda,

---

1 See also Edward Bernays' earlier publication, *Crystallizing Public Opinion* (1923). Among more recent literature on the topic two excellent books explain these topics in depth: Victoria O'Donnell, Garth S. Jowett, *Propaganda and Persuasion*, 3rd ed. (Thousand Oaks, CA: Sage Publications, 1999); Anthony R. Pratkanis and Elliot Aronson, *Age of propaganda: the everyday use and abuse of persuasion*, rev. ed. (New York: Henry Holt and Company, 2002).

2 "The man who injected this idea into the shoe industry was ruling women in one department of their social lives. Different men rule us in the various departments of our lives. There may be one power behind the throne in politics, another in the manipulation of the Federal discount rate, and still another in the dictation of next season's dances." Edward Bernays, *Propaganda* (New York: Horace Liveright), 1928, 36.

simply developed and used these techniques consistently and on a global scale. They have been globally used ever since, most recently in Putin's Russia.

A song for young people dedicated to "our dear friend" Stalin, *Let's sing, comrades, let's sing* (*Spoem, tovarishchi, spoem,* 1940), written by an experienced Soviet propagandist Vasily Lebedev-Kumach, aims at evoking precisely this sense of security: "let the song resound for our dear friend beneath the thatched roofs of our houses. / It is thanks to his will and his thought that everyone can work and live today. / He loves us all, you and me, and has all our hearts at the."[3] The chorus of a contemporary children song, *Uncle Vova*, repeats the declaration that at the command of the leader (Putin), the collective subject is ready to fight in the war, and even to undertake suicide missions: "We wish peace to everybody but if the Chief commander calls us for the last battle, uncle Vova, we are with you."[4]

In recent decades, mainly after the Rwanda genocide, researchers have realized that the stages of genocide were analogous in all the cases.[5] All genocides are preceded by a critical turning moment in which one group is being effectively persuaded by a multifaceted propaganda claiming not only that the other group – presented as substantially different and unjustly privileged – is potentially dangerous, but also that it intentionally acts in a pernicious way. This propaganda is also meant to instil a physical sense of disgust and fear mixed with a potentially murderous contempt and hatred towards the incriminated group. The latter is being gradually stripped of human traits and provided with dehumanizing masks. These derogatory masks are made up of degrading adjectives,

---

3 This song, *Spoem, tovarišči* with music by Dmitry Kabalevsky, was published, among other Stalinist songs of this type in Polish translation (in this case by Jan Brzechwa), under the title *Niech dźwięczy śpiew*, with the subtitle "youth songs about Stalin." It was edited by Zofia Lissa (Warsaw: Czytelnik, first edition 1949, second edition 1950). Lebedev-Kumach worked in the press office of the Revolutionary Military Council in 1919–1921. He is known for his song *The Holy War* (*Священная война*), published by the Soviet propagandist newspaper *Pravda* and Red Army newspaper *The Red Star*, written after the German invasion on the Soviet Union in June 1941, set to music by A. Alexandrov to become the "war anthem of the Soviet Union."
4 The song *Дядя Вова* with English subtitles available at: https://www.youtube.com/watch?v=mrBOxEVducM. The video with schoolchildren from Volgograd singing it in uniforms was "produced on the initiative of State Duma Deputy Anna Kuvychko of the ruling United Russia party." See Alexey Timofeychev, "'Uncle Vova, we are with you!' Russian songs about Vladimir Putin", in web journal *Russia beyond*, dated 14 December 2017, https://www.rbth.com/arts/327015-uncle-vova-we-are-with-you.
5 See: Morag J. Grant et al., "Music, the 'Third Reich', and 'The 8 Stages of Genocide'".

epithets, and nouns, and their aim is to prove that those accused do not deserve the same rights as the ones enjoyed by those who deem themselves superior and just. The process of dehumanizing future victims always precedes actual genocide. Beyond this point everything previously unimaginable, such as the killing of neighbours, becomes possible. Thus, bearing in mind that it is actually propaganda that is the most decisive tool in persuading people to "voluntarily" kill others, the propaganda makers are those who bear the greatest responsibility. The United Nations International Criminal Tribunal for the Rwandan genocide decided to sentence to fifteen years of imprisonment the popular singer Simon Bikindi, a Hutu, who in his patriotic and seemingly innocuous songs, referred to the Tutsis as "snakes" (while the Hutu Radio Télévision Libre des Mille Collines, RTLM, called Tutsis "cockroaches") and made his listeners believe that it was their task to get rid of them.

Simon Bikindi, who went into hiding, was eventually found, arrested, and judged by the International Tribunal. The Chamber found Bikindi guilty of direct and public incitement to committing genocide.[6] Sentenced for incitement to genocide, he died in prison. What was the purpose of sentencing a singer while the majority of actual killers were never tried? He was clearly responsible for designating and dehumanizing the victims in his lyrics, as they were depicted in a way that was compelling for the perpetrators.

Before the actual killings took place, the future killers had been brainwashed with a universal compound made up of several ingredients: the pleasure of singing together, the sense of camaraderie, the joy of shared adventure, the *jouissance*, the sense of purpose, power, economic status, glory – and the most engaging – messianic sadism ("we will save our world by being cruel to the 'enemies of our world' and by eliminating them"). All of the above and much more is both propagated and legitimized by the songs of hatred.

The authors of the songs that dehumanized victims and incited to genocide, as well as those who marketed them – the Nazi musicians and musicologists – were just as responsible as the operators of gas chambers. Composers of Nazi cantatas, who glorified the criminal state and its leaders, were similarly responsible.

---

6 "The Chamber found that towards the end of June 1994, in Gisenyi Prefecture, while travelling as part of an Interahamwe convoy, Bikindi was in a vehicle outfitted with public address systems broadcasting songs including Bikindi's, and he used the public address system to state that the Hutus should arise and exterminate the Tutsis," https://unictr.irmct.org/sites/unictr.org/files/cases/ictr-01-72/public-information/en/profile-bikindi.pdf.

Denunciators of Jewish musicians, such as Gerigk, were responsible directly. None of them have been punished in court.

All those who used to debase others, taking advantage of their socially privileged position and their authority that enabled them to propagate malicious and highly detrimental messages on a mass level, all those who propagated hatred of any kind – the journalists, clergymen, politicians, authors of lyrics, music, and scholarly writers – are responsible for inciting violence against the victims. The Action Française author, Leon Daudet, and his Polish follower Adolf Nowaczyński, as well as Louis-Ferdinand Céline, Houston Stewart Chamberlain and Richard Wagner with his *Judentum in der Musik* are fine examples of such influential personalities who had prepared the ground for genocide.

In this light, the responsibilty for the mass killings of children, women, men, and elderly people falls not only on Wehrmacht soldiers, SS functionaries and all those who "just followed orders", not only on leaders, such as Goebbels, but also all on all those who dehumanized others by exploiting music. This group includes the authors of hundreds of Nazis songs, Nazi doctors who legitimized their atrocities by evoking the idea of *Rassenhygiene*, and Nazi musicologists, such as Gotthold Frotscher who wrote in 1938: "Thus, the contemplation of art becomes a question of biological knowledge, style criticism becomes racial style research... *Völkisch* music must be demanded, so that, according to the words of the Führer, blood and race once again will become a source of artistic intuition."[7] Another example of a Nazi musicologist is Wilhelm Heinitz (1883–1963). In 1937, he applied for NSDAP membership, and in 1938 he published *Die Erforschung rassischer Eigenschaften aus der Volksmusik* ("The exploration of racial characteristics of folk music") where he stated: "The stranger (southern or non-Nordic man) wears only a spiritual mask of a will which is alien to him. But eventually he needs to be subjected to the laws of nature."[8] After 1945, he

---

7 "Damit wird die Kunstbetrachtung zu einer Frage der biologischen Erkenntnis, die Stilkritik zur Rassestilforschung... Völkische Musik muß gefordert werden, damit nach den Worten des Führers Blut and Rasse wieder zur Quelle der künstlerischen Intuition werden." Frotscher (1897–1967) was Professor in Gdańsk since 1930 and Professor at the University of Berlin since 1936. After 1945, he continued his work as professor of musicology in Berlin. Eva Weissweiler: *Ausgemerzt! Das Lexikon der Juden in der Musik und seine mörderischen Folgen* (Eliminated! The Encyclopedia of Jews in Music and its Murderous Consequences, Köln 1999). Quoted in Klee, *Das Personenlexikon zum Dritten Reich*, 170.
8 Quoted in Klee, *Personenlexikon*, after Eckart Krause et al. (eds.), *Hochschulalltag im 'Dritten Reich.' Die Hamburger Universität 1933–1945* (3 Bände. Berlin 1991).

was appointed chairman of the Landesverband der Tonkünstler und Musiklehrer Hamburgs ("National Association of Music Artists and Music Teachers in Hamburg") and "recognized as a victim (sic!) of the Nazi regime."[9]

Another musicologist, Friedrich Blume (1893–1975), was a professor in Berlin from 1933. In May 1938, he gave a lecture *Music and Race* (*Musik und Rasse: Grundfragen einer musikalischen Rassenforschung bei den Reichsmusiklagen der Reichsmusikkammer in Düsseldorf*) and in 1939 he authored *The Race Problem in Music* (*Das Rasseprohlem [sic] in der Musik*) and *German Musicology in the commemorative publication for the 50th birthday of the Führer* (*Deutsche Musikwissenschaft in der Festschrift zum 50. Geburtstag des Führers*). After 1945, he continued to hold the function of the director of the Kiel Institute of Musicology. In 1949, he was appointed editor of the prestigious Music Encyclopaedia *Die Musik in Geschichte und Gegenwart – Allgemeine Enzyklopädie der Musik* at the Bärenreiter Verlag.[10]

It could be said that, in the General Government, music itself was exploited and victimised. Cultural and musical policies were used as a method of mind control intended to exert control over psychological domains in which even the toughest police methods failed. It also served as a means of subjugating conquered whole ethnicities.

At the same time, however, it is the song repertoire created during these six years of extreme suffering, marked by terror and mass extermination of Poland's citizens by the Third Reich, which reflects most vividly the desire to overcome the horror, to protest against it, and to fight the occupiers. I shall continue the analysis of music composed and performed during that time in another volume. The investigation of social, psychological, and political functions that music played in Poland during the time of Nazi occupation and the Holocaust, still requires more source material to be both disclosed and preserved, while the witnesses are still amongst us.

---

9   Klee, *Personenlexikon*, 239.
10 Ibid., 54–55.

List of abbreviations

AAN	The Central Archives of Modern Records (Archiwum Akt Nowych)
AK	Home Army (Armia Krajowa)
BN	Biblioteka Narodowa, Warsaw, Poland
Gestapo	Nazi Secret State Police (Geheime Staatspolizei)
GKBZN	Main Commission for the Investigation of German Crimes in Poland (Główna Komisja Badania Zbrodni Niemieckich w Polsce)
HA	Haupt Abteilung
IPN	Institute of National Remembrance (Instytut Pamięci Narodowej)
KdF	Strength Through Joy (Kraft durch Freude)
KfdK	Kamfbund für deutsche Kultur
KL	Konzentrationslager
MiJuV	Musik in Jugend und Volk
NKW	Nowy Kurier Warszawski
NKVD	The People's Commissariat for Internal Affairs (Russian: Naródnyy komissariát vnútrennikh del, the interior ministry of the Soviet Union)
NSDAP	Nationalsozialistische Deutsche Arbeiterpartei
NSLB	National Socialist Teachers League (Nationalsozialistischer Lehrerbund)
PWM	Polskie Wydawnictwo Muzyczne
HJ	Hitler Youth (Hitlerjugend)
RJF	National Youth Leader (Reichsjugendführer)
RM	Ruch Muzyczny
RSHA	Reich Security Main Office (Reichssicherheitshauptamt)
SB	Security Service (Służba Bezpieczeństwa)
WTM	Warsaw Musical Society (Warszawskie Towarzystwo Muzyczne)
WZ	Warschauer Zeitung

Archives

AAN	Archiwum Akt Nowych, Warsaw, Poland
AIPN	Archive of the IPN, Warsaw, Poland
IPN	Institute of National Remembrance, Warsaw, Poland
WTM	Warsaw Musical Society, Warsaw, Poland

Bibliography

Agamben, Giorgio: *Remnants of Auschwitz. The Witness and the Archive*. translated by Daniel Heller-Roazen, New York: Zone Books 1999.

Agamben, Giorgio: "Heidegger e il nazismo," in: *La Potenza del pensiero. Saggi e conferenze*, Vicenza: Neri Pozza Editore, 2005.

Anisfeld, Rena: *Gevies Eydes* [Bearing Witness], translated by Maciej Krol, edited by Renee Miller, Yizkor Book Project, 850–860, https://www.jewishgen.org/yizkor/Nowy_sacz/now850.html.

Arad, Yitzhak: *The Operation Reinhard Death Camps*, Revised and Expanded Edition: Belzec, Sobibor, Treblinka. Indiana University Press, 2018.

Arad, Yitzhak: *Plunder of Jewish Property in the Nazi-Occupied Areas Of the Soviet Union*, https://www.yadvashem.org/articles/academic/plunder-of-jewish-property-in-occupied-areas-of-soviet-union.html.

Agatstein-Dormontowa, Dora: "Żydzi w okresie okupacji niemieckiej," in *Krakow w latach okupacji 1939–1945. Studia i materiały, Rocznik Krakowski*, Vol. 31 (1949–1957). Krakow: Nakładem Towarzystwa Miłośników Historii i Zabytków Krakow, 1957.

Akhtar, Salman: "From Unmentalized Xenophobia to Messianic Sadism: Some Reflections on the Phenomenology of Prejudice," in H. Parens, A. Mahfouz, S. W. Twemlow & D.E. Scharff (eds.), *The Future of Prejudice: Psychoanalysis and the Prevention of Prejudice*. Lanham: Rowman & Littlefield, 2007.

Akhtar, Salman: *Comprehensive Dictionary of Psychoanalysis*. London: Karnac Books, 2009.

Arendt, Hannah: *Responsibility and Judgment*. New York: Schocken Books, 2003.

Auerbach, Rachel: "In the fields of Treblinka," in Alexander Donat (ed.), *The Death Camp Treblinka. A Documentary*. New York: Holocaust Library, 1979, 19–74.

Bajer, Hans: "Verbotene Lieder der Bewegung in der Kampfzeit," *Die Musik* 30 (12), September (1938), 800–804.

Bartoszewski, Władysław: 'Historia Jankiela Wiernika', *Polska* 8 (1964), 633–634.

Bartoszewski, Władysław: *Warszawski pierścień śmierci 1939–1944.* Warsaw: Interpress, 1970.

Bartov, Omer: *Anatomy of a Genocide: The Life and Death of a Town Called Buczacz.* New York: Simon and Schuster, 2018.

Basak, Adam: *Eksterminacja inteligencji jako metoda ludobójstwa. Polskie doświadczenia a praktyka kodyfikacyjna i orzecznictwo w sprawach zbrodni hitlerowskich.* Wrocław: Acta Universitatis Wratislaviensis. Studia nad Faszyzmem i Zbrodniami Hitlerowskimi, Karol Jońca (ed.), Vol. 14, 1991.

Beckerman, Michael: "Listening in the Grey Zone," in: Fanning, David, and Levi, Erik (eds.), *The Routledge Handbook to Music under German Occupation, 1938–1945. Propaganda. Myth and Reality*, London / New York: Routledge, 2020, 451–458.

Bem, Marek (ed.): *Sobibór.* Warsaw: Ośrodek Karta, Dom Spotkań z Historią, 2010.

Berenstein, Tatiana, Eisenbach, Artur, Rutkowski, Adam (eds.): *Eksterminacja Żydów na ziemiach polskich w okresie okupacji hitlerowskiej: zbiór dokumentów,* [Extermination of Jews on Polish territory during Nazi occupation: collection of documents] Warsaw: Żydowski Instytut Historyczny, 1957.

Berg, Mary: *Dziennik z getta warszawskiego*, przełożyła Maria Salapska, Warsaw: Czytelnik, 1983.

Berger, Roni: *Stress, Trauma, and Posttraumatic Growth Social Context, Environment, and Identities.* New York: Taylor and Francis, 2015.

Bieńkowska, Barbara: *Losses of Polish libraries during World War II.* Warsaw: Wydawnictwo Reklama Wojciech Wójcicki, 1994.

Birdsall, Carolyn: *Nazi Soundscapes. Sound, Technology and Urban Space in Germany, 1933–1945*, Amsterdam: Amsterdam University Press, 2012.

Biskupski, Mieczysław B. and Piotr Stefan Wandycz:, *Ideology, Politics, and Diplomacy in East Central Europe*, Rochester, 2003.

Błaszczyk, Leon Tadeusz: *Żydzi w kulturze muzycznej ziem polskich w XIX i XX wieku*, Warsaw: Stowarzyszenie Żydowski Instytut Historyczny w Polsce, 2014.

Bohlman, Andrea F.: *Musical Solidarities. Political Action and Music in Late Twentieth Century Poland.* New York: Oxford University Press, 2020.

Bolesławska-Lewandowska, Beata: *The life and works of Andrzej Panufnik (1914-1991)*, translated by Richard Reisner, Ashgate: Farnham, 2015.
Brandwajn-Ziemian, Janina: *Młodość w cieniu śmierci*. Łódź: Oficyna bibliofilów, 1995.
Brauer, Juliane: *Musik im Konzentrationslager Sachsenhausen*. Berlin: Schriftenreihe der Stiftung Brandenburgische Gedenkstätten Vol. 25, 2009.
Brauer, Juliane: "How Can Music Be Torturous? Music in Nazi Concentration and Extermination Camps," *Music & Politics* (10) 2016.
Browning, Christopher R.: *Ordinary men: Reserve Police Battalion 101 and the final solution in Poland*. New York: HarperPerennial, 1992.
Browning, Christopher R.: "An American Historian's Perspective," *German Studies Review* 2012 (35/2), 310–318.
Burhardt, Stefan: *Polonez: katalog tematyczny*, 1792–1830 (Volume 2). Edited and supplemented by Maria Prokopowicz and Andrzej Spóz. Kraków: PWM, 1976.
Chęćka, Anna: *Ucho i umysł: szkice o doświadczaniu muzyki*, Gdańsk: Wydawnictwo Słowo/Obraz Terytoria, 2012.
Cizmic, Maria: *Performing pain: music and trauma in Eastern Europe*, Oxford: Oxford University Press, 2012.
Clendinnen, Inga: *Reading the Holocaust*, New York 1999.
Cohen, Anthony P.: *Self Consciousness: An Alternative Anthropology of Identity*. New York: Routledge, 1994.
Cygan, Jacek: *Klezmer. Opowieść o życiu Leopolda Kozłowskiego-Kleinmana*. Krakow–Budapest: Austeria, 2010.
Czocher, Anna: "Jawne polskie życie kulturalne w okupowanym Krakowie 1939–1945 w świetle wspomnień," *Pamięć i Sprawiedliwość* 4/1, 7 (2005), 227–252.
Czocher, Anna, Dobrochna Kałwa, Barbara Klich-Kluczewska and Beata Łabno (eds.), *Is War Men's Business? Fates of Women in Occupied Krakow in Twelve Scenes*. Krakow: Muzeum Historyczne Miasta Krakowa 2011.
Davis, Norman: *God's Playground. A History of Poland*, New York: Columbia University Press, 1982.
Dąbrowski, Jan et al.: *Krakow under Enemy Rule*. Krakow: Drukarnia Uniwersytetu Jagiellońskiego, 1946.
Doerr Karin and Michael, Robert: *Nazi-Deutsch / Nazi-German: An English Lexicon of the Language of the Third Reich*. Westport, Connecticut: Greenwood Press, 2002.
Drewniak, Bogusław: *Kultura w cieniu swastyki*. Poznań: Wydawnictwo Poznańskie, 1969.

Dunicz-Niwińska, Helena: *One of the Girls in the Band. The Memoirs of a Violinist from Birkenau*, transcribed by Maria Szewczyk, translated by William Brand, Oświęcim: Auschwitz-Birkenau State Museum 2014.
Dunicz-Niwińska, Helena: "Jan Józef Dunicz (1910–1945)," *Muzyka* 2005/2, 121–125.
Dunin-Wąsowicz, Krzysztof, Janina Kaźmierska and Halina Winnicka (eds.): *Warszawa lat wojny i okupacji 1939–1945*. Studia Warszawskie, Vol. 10 (2), Instytut Historii Polskiej Akademii Nauk. Warsaw: Państwowe Wydawnictwo Naukowe, 1972.
Dybowski, Stanisław: *Słownik pianistów polskich*. Warsaw: Selene, 2003.
Ebbinghaus, Angelika: "Introduction: Reflections on the Nuremberg Medical Trial," in: Johannes Eltzschig, Michael Walter (eds.), *The Nuremberg Medical Trial 1946/47. Guide to the Microfiche Edition*, München: K.G. Saur Verlag, 2001, 11–64.
Edkins, Jenny: *Trauma and the Memory of Politics*. Cambridge: Cambridge University Press, 2003.
Egzekucje w Operze, Protokół nr 19/II [Executions at the Opera, protocol], in *Biuletyn Głównej Komisji Badania Zbrodni Niemieckich w Polsce* (I), Poznań: Wydawnictwo GKBZNP, 1946.
Eisen, George: *Children and Play in the Holocaust. Games among the Shadows*. Amherst: University of Massachusetts Press, 1988.
Eischeid, Susan: *The Truth about Fania Fénelon and the Women's Orchestra of Auschwitz-Birkenau*. Department of Music, Valdosta State University, Georgia: Palgrave Macmillan, 2016.
Engelking, Barbara, Leociak, Jacek: *Getto warszawskie. Przewodnik po nieistniejącym mieście*. Warsaw: Wydawnictwo IFiS PAN, 2001.
Epstein, Catherine: *Model Nazi. Arthur Greiser and the Occupation of Western Poland*. Oxford: Oxford University Press, 2010.
Esposito, Robert: *Bíos: Biopolitics and philosophy*, translated by Timothy Campbell, "Posthumanities" 4, Minneapolis, London: University of Minnesota Press, 2008.
Fackler, Guido: *Des Lagers Stimme – Musik im KZ. Alltag und Haftlingskultur in den Konzentrationslagern 1933 bis 1936*, Bremen: Edition Temmen, 2000.
Fackler, Guido: "Music in Concentration Camps 1933–1945," transl. by Peter Logan, *Music & Politics* 2007.
Flam, Gila: *Singing for Survival: Songs of the Lodz Ghetto 1940–45*. Urbana and Chicago: University of Illinois Press, 1992.

Fanning, David, and Levi, Erik (eds.): *The Routledge Handbook to Music under German Occupation, 1938–1945. Propaganda. Myth and Reality*, London, New York: Routledge, 2020.

Fairclough, Pauline: "The Routledge Handbook to Music under German Occupation, 1938–1945: Propaganda. Myth and Reality," *Music and Letters* 101 (4), November 2020, 799–802.

Flam, Gila: *Singing for Survival: Songs of the Lodz Ghetto, 1940–45*. Urbana and Chicage: University of Illinois Press, 1992.

Fater, Isachar: *Muzyka żydowska w Polsce w okresie międzywojennym*, translated to Polish by Ewa Świderska, Warsaw: Oficyna Wydawnicza Rytm, 1997.

Fisher, Atarah, and Gilboa, Avi: "The roles of music amongst musician Holocaust survivors before, during, and after the Holocaust," *Psychology of Music*, 44/6 (2016).

Frołów, Anna: *Życie muzyczne w okupowanej Warszawie w latach 1939–1945*. Warsaw: Akademia Muzyczna im. F. Chopina, 2004.

Fröhlich, Elke (ed.): *Die Tagebücher von Joseph Goebbels. Sämtlische Fragmente*, Vol. 3, München: K. G. Saur, 1987.

Fuks, Marian: "W dzielnicy zamkniętej," *RM* 16 (1981), 16.

Fuks, Marian: "Filharmonia Warszawska w latach okupacji niemieckiej (1939–1945)," in: Maria Bychawska, Henryk Schiller (eds.), *100 lat Filharmonii w Warszawie. 1901–2001*. Fundacja Bankowa im. Leopolda Kronenberga, Filharmonia Narodowa, Warsaw 2001, 119–141.

Gast, Peter: "Kultureller Aufbau im Wartheland," in *Ostland Kalender 1941, Jahrgang des Baltischen Kalenders* 56, Posen: E. Bruhns, 1941.

Gebirtig, Mordecai, Michał Borwicz, Nella Rost, and Józef Wulf: *S'brent: (1939–1942)*. Krakow: Wojewódzka Żydowska Komisja Historyczna, 1946.

Geiss, Imanuel and Jacobmeyer, Wolfgang (eds.): *Deutsche Politik in Polen 1939–1945: aus dem Diensttagebuch von Hans Frank, Generalgouverneur in Polen*. Opladen 1980.

Gieysztor, Aleksander: "Wojna a kultura: propozycje badawcze," in: Czesław Madajczyk (ed.), (1982). *Inter arma non silent Musae. Wojna i kultura 1939–1945*, Warsaw: Państwowy Instytut Wydawniczy, 208–209.

Gilbert, Shirli: "Buried Monuments: Yiddish Songs and Holocaust Memory," *History Workshop Journal*, no. 66 (2008), 107–28.

Gilbert, Shirli: *Music in the Holocaust. Confronting Life in the Nazi Ghettos and Camps*, Oxford: Oxford University Press, 2005.

Glazar, Richard: *Stacja Treblinka*. Warsaw: Ośrodek Karta, Dom Spotkań z Historią, 2011.

Głębocki, Wiesław, Mórawski, Karol: *Kultura walcząca 1939–1945. Z dziejów kultury polskiej w okresie wojny i okupacji*. Warsaw: Wydawnictwa Szkolne i Pedagogiczne, 1979); 2nd ed. Warsaw: Wydawnictwo Interpress, 1985.

Goebbels, Joseph: "Unsterbliche deutsche Kultur. Rede zur Eröffnung der 7. Großen Deutschen Kunstausstellung," in: *Der steile Aufstieg*, Munich, Zentralverlag der NSDAP, 1944.

Goebbels, Joseph: "Der Rundfunk als achte Großmacht" ("The Radio as the Eight Great Power"), *Signale der neuen Zeit. 25 ausgewählte Reden von Dr. Joseph Goebbels* (Munich: Zentralverlag der NSDAP, 1934), 197–207.

Gołąb Maciej: *Józef Koffler*, tr. by Maksymilian Kapelański, Marek Żebrowski and Linda Schubert (Los Angeles: Polish Music Center, 2004).

Gołąb Maciej: *Musical Modernism in the Twentieth Century. Between Continuation, Innovation and Change of Phonosystem*, Eastern European Studies in Musicology, Frankfurt am Main: Peter Lang, 2015, Vol. 6.

Gołąb Maciej: *Mazurek Dąbrowskiego. Muzyczne narodziny hymnu.* Warsaw: Narodowy Instytut Fryderyka Chopina, 2021.

Gollert, Friedrich: *Warschau über deutscher Herrschaft. Deutsche Aufbauarbeit im Distrikt Warschau*. Krakau: Burgverlag Krakau GmbH, 1942.

Good, Byron J., and Hinton, Devon E. (eds.): *Culture and PTSD: Trauma in Global and Historical Perspective* (Philadelphia: University of Pennsylvania Press, 2016).

Grant, Morag. J., Mareike Jacobs, Rebecca Möllemann, Simone Christine Münz, Cornelia Nuxoll: "Music, the 'Third Reich', and 'The 8 Stages of Genocide'" in: W. Klimczyk, A. Świerzowska (eds.): *Music and Genocide*, "Studies in Social Sciences, Philosophy and History of Ideas" Vol. 9, Peter Lang Edition, Frakfurt am Main 2015, 23–68.

Grochowina, Sylwia: *Cultural policy of the Nazi occupying forces in the Reich District Gdańsk-West Prussia, the Reich District Wartheland, and the Reich District of Katowice in the years 1939–1945*. Toruń: Foundation of General Elżbieta Zawacka, 2017.

Gwizdalanka, Danuta: *Muzyka i polityka*. Krakow: PWM, 1999.

Gwizdalanka, Danuta: "Element podejrzany nr 1," *Ruch Muzyczny* (10) 2012.

Haar, Ingo: *German Ostforschung and Anti-Semitism*, in: I. Haar, Michael Fahlbusch (eds.), *German Scholars and Ethnic Cleansing, 1920–1945*, New York: Berghahn Books, 2005.

Haas, Michael: *Forbidden Music: The Jewish Composers Banned by the Nazis.* Yale University Press, 2014.

von Haken, Boris: "How Do We Know What We Know about Hans Heinrich Eggebrecht?," *German Studies Review* 2012 (35/2), 299–309.

Harders-Wuthenow, Frank: "Fate and Identity – Polish-Jewish composers in the 20th Century," https://demusica.edu.pl/muzykalia-xiii-judaica-4/ (Warsaw: Stowarzyszenie De Musica, 2012).

Haußwald, Günter: "Kulturaufbau im deutschen Osten," *Zeitschrift für Musik* 108/3 March (1941), 191–92.

Hennemeyer, Kurt: "Vom deutschen Geist in der polnischen Musik," *Die Musik* 31 No. 12, September (1939–1940), 786–97.

Hilberg, Raul: *The politics of memory: the journey of a Holocaust historian*. Chicago: Ivan R. Dee, 1996.

Hirsch, David D.: "Camp Music and Camp Songs: Szymon Laks and Aleksander Kulisiewicz" in G. Jan Colijn and Marcia Sachs Littell (eds.), *Confronting the Holocaust: A Mandate for the 21st Century, Studies in the Shoah*. Oxford: University Press of America, 1997.

Hitler, Adolf: *Mein Kampf*. Munich: Zentralverlag der NSDAP, 1936.

Hoffmann, Hilmar: *The Triumph of Propaganda: Film and National Socialism, 1933–1945*, trans. John A. Broadwin and V. R. Berghahn, Providence, RI, 1997.

Höss, Rudolf: *Wyznania spod szubienicy: autobiografia Rudolfa Hössa komendanta KL Auschwitz spisana w krakowskim więzieniu Montelupich*, transl. Wiesław Grzymski, annotated by Andrzej Pankowicz. Warsaw: Oficyna Wydawnicza Mireki, 2012.

Idzikowski, Mieczysław: 'Straty wojenne w portretach Fryderyka Chopina', *RM* 20 (1962).

Jakelski, Lisa: *Making new music in Cold War Poland: the Warsaw Autumn Festival, 1956–1968*. Oakland, California: University of California Press, 2017.

Jentz, Thomas: *Bertha's Big Brother: Karl-Geraet (60 cm & 54 cm)*. Boyd, MD: Panzer Tracts, 2001.

Jezierski, Andrzej (ed.): *Historia Polski w liczbach. Ludność. Terytorium*. Warsaw: Główny Urzad Statystyczny, 1994.

Kamieński, Łucjan: "O polonezie staropolskim" [On the old Polish polonaise], *Muzyka* 1928 No. 3, 99–103.

Karzinkin, Leonid: "Pisarz na oddziale (7 X 1941 – 17 I 1943)," in *Wspomnienia więźniów Pawiaka*. Warsaw: Polska Akademia Nauk, 1964, 125–143.

Kater, Michael H.: *The Twisted Muse: Musicians and their Music in the Third Reich*. Oxford: Oxford University Press, 1997.

Kater, Michael H.: *Composers of the Nazi Era: Eight Portraits*. Oxford: Oxford University Press, 2000.
Kater, Michael H.: *Das 'Ahnenerbe' der SS 1935-1945. Ein Beitrag zur Kulturpolitik des Dritten Reiches* (Dissertation, University of Heidelberg, 1966). Studien zur Zeitgeschichte. Vol. 6. Munich: Oldenbourg. 2006.
Kater, Michael H.: *Culture in Nazi Germany*. Yale University Press, 2019.
Kępiński, Antoni: "Z psychopatologii nadludzi." In: *Refleksje oświęcimskie*, Krakow: Wydawnictwo Literackie, 2005, 59-76.
Kempter, Klaus: "'Objective, not neutral:' Joseph Wulf, a documentary historian," *Holocaust Studies*, 21, 1-2 (2015): 38-53.
Kisielewski, Stefan [S. K.]: "Życie muzyczne pod okupacją," *RM* 1 (1945), 12-13.
Kisielewski, Stefan [S. K.]: "Polska twórczość muzyczna pod okupacją," *RM* 1 (1945), 14-16.
"Śmierć Romana Padlewskiego," *RM* 4 (1945), 14-15.
Klee, Ernst: *Das Personenlexikon zum Dritten Reich: wer, war, was vor und nach 1945*. Frankfurt am Main: S. Fischer, 2007.
Klee, Ernst: *Auschwitz: medycyna III Rzeszy i jej ofiary*. Translated by Elżbieta Kalinowska-Styczeń. Krakow: Universitas, 2009.
Knapp, Gabriele: *Das Frauenorchester in Auschwitz: Musikalische Zwangsarbeit und ihre Bewältigung*. Hamburg: von Bockel Verlag, 1996.
Kopeczek-Michalska, Krystyna: "Życie koncertowe w Warszawie w latach okupacji," *Muzyka* 3 (1970), 47-64.
Kostka, Violetta: *Tadeusz Zygfryd Kassern: indywidualne odmiany stylów muzycznych XX wieku*, Poznań: Rhytmos, 2011.
Kostka, Violetta: "An artist as the conscience of humanity: life in emigration and the artistic output of Tadeusz Zygfryd Kassern," *Musicology Today* (2011), published by Institute of Musicology, University of Warsaw, 134-162.
Kraft, Robert N., "Emotional memory in survivors of the Holocaust: A qualitative study of oral testimony," in: Daniel Reisberg and Paula Hertel (eds.), *Memory and Emotion*. Oxford: Oxford University Press, 2004.
Krause, Eckart et al. (eds.): *Hochschulalltag im 'Dritten Reich.' Die Hamburger Universität 1933-1945*. Berlin 1991.
Krzepicki, Abraham Jacob: "Eighteen Days in Treblinka," in: Donat, Alexander (ed.): *The Death Camp Treblinka. A Documentary*. New York: Holocaust Library 1979, 77-144.
Kubalski, Edward: *Niemcy w Krakowie*, ed. Jan Grabowski, Zbigniew R. Grabowski. Krakow - Budapest: Wydawnictwo Austeria, 2010.

Kwiatkowski, Maciej Józef: "Muzyka w Polskim Radiu w czasie II wojny światowej," *RM* 12 (1981), 3–4.
Kwiatkowski, Maciej Józef: *"Tu mówi powstańcza Warszawa"... Dni Powstania w audycjach Polskiego Radia i dokumentach niemieckich*, Warsaw: Państwowy Instytut Wydawniczy 1994.
Kwiek, M.: *Wojenne dzieje zbiorów Warszawskiego Towarzystwa Muzycznego*, *RM* 17–18 (1946), 24–26.
Lacan, Jacques: *Écrits. A Selection*, transl. Alan Sheridan. London: Taylor & Francis edition, 2005.
Lachendro, Jacek: "The Orchestras in KL Auschwitz," *Auschwitz Studies* 27, Auschwitz-Birkenau State Museum 2015.
Stanisław Lachowicz, *Muzyka w okupowanym Krakowie 1939–1945*. Krakow: Wydawnictwo Literackie, 1988.
Laks, Szymon and Coudy, René: Musiques d'un autre monde. Paris: Mercure de France, 1948
Laks, Szymon: *Gry oświęcimskie*, Oświęcim: Państwowe Muzeum Oświęcim-Brzezinka, 1998.
Lasker-Wallfisch, Anita: *Inherit the Truth, 1939–1945: The Documented Experiences of a Survivor of Auschwitz and Belsen*, London, Giles de la Mare, 1996.
Laub, Dori, "From speechlessness to narrative: The cases of Holocaust historians and of psychiatrically hospitalized survivors," *Literature and Medicine*, 24/2 (2005).
Law Reports of Trials of War Criminals, selected and prepared by The United Nations War Crimes Commission, Vol. 14. London: His Majesty's Stationery Office, 1949.
Leder, Andrzej: *Prześniona rewolucja. Ćwiczenie z logiki historycznej*. Warsaw: Wydawnictwo Krytyki Politycznej, 2014.
Lerski, Tomasz: *Syrena Record. Pierwsza polska wytwórnia fonograficzna 1904–1939*, New York – Warsaw: Editions "Karin", 2004.
Lerski, Tomasz: *Encyklopedia Kultury Polskiej XX Wieku: Muzyka-Teatr-Film*, Vol. I, Warsaw: Polskie Wydawnictwo Naukowo-Encyklopedyczne, 2008.
Levi, Erik: *Mozart and the Nazis: How the Third Reich Abused a Cultural Icon* (New Haven, London: Yale University Press, 2010).
Levi, Erik: "Pamela M. Potter, Art of Suppression: Confronting the Nazi Past in Histories of the Visual and Performing Arts," *Transposition. Musique et sciences sociales*, 7, 2018, http://journals.openedition.org/transposition/2323.

Li, Darryl: "Echoes of Violence: Considerations on Radio and Genocide in Rwanda," *Journal of Genocide Research*, 6/1 (2004), 9–27.
Lichtman, Eda: "Praca," in Bem, Marek (ed.): *Sobibór*. Warsaw: Ośrodek Karta, Dom Spotkań z Historią, 2010, 26–38.
Lifton, Robert Jay: *The Nazi Doctors: Medical Killing and the Psychology of Genocide*, New York: Basic Books, 2000.
Lindstedt, Iwona: *Kazimierz Serocki. Piszę tylko muzykę*. Krakow: PWM, 2020.
Lingens-Reiner, Ella: *Prisoners of Fear*, London: Gollancz, 1948.
Lipszyc, Rywka: *Dziennik z getta łódzkiego*, ed. Ewa Wiatr. Krakow-Budapest: Klezmerhojs Wydawnictwo Austeria 2017.
Lukas, Richard C.: *The Forgotten Holocaust. The Poles under German Occupation 1939–1944*. New York: Hippocrene Books 1986.
Łubek-Luboradzka, Teresa, Mieczkowska Krystyna, and Gleb, Barbara (eds.): *Sanitariuszki Batalionów AK Gustaw i Harnaś w szpitalach powstańczych. Wybór wspomnień sierpień–wrzesień 1944*. Warsaw: 1995.
Łuczak, Czesław: *Dyskryminacja Polaków w Wielkopolsce w okresie okupacji hitlerowskiej: wybór źródeł*. Poznań: Wydawnictwo Poznańskie, 1966.
Madajczyk, Czesław (ed.): *Inter arma non silent Musae. Wojna i kultura 1939–1945*, Warsaw: Państwowy Instytut Wydawniczy, 1982.
Majer, Diemut: *'Non-Germans' under the Third Reich. The Nazi Jurisdiction and Administrative System in Germany and Occupied Eastern Europe, with Special Regard to Occupied Poland, 1939–1945*, trans. from German by Peter Thomas Hill, Edward Vance Humphrey, Brian Levin, published in association with the United States Holocaust Memorial Museum (Baltimore: The Johns Hopkins University Press, 2003).
Majewski, Piotr: *Wojna i kultura. Instytucje kultury polskiej w okupacyjnych realiach Generalnego Gubernatorstwa*. Warsaw: Wydawnictwo Trio, 2005.
Marcinek-Drozdalska, Anna (ed.): *Ocalone we wspomnieniach. Wspomnienia byłych więźniów politycznych, hitlerowskich więzień i obozów koncentracyjnych*. Koszalin: Koszalińska Biblioteka Publiczna, 2011.
Markowska, Elżbieta, and Naliwajek, Katarzyna: *Okupacyjne losy muzyków, Warszawa 1939–1945*. Warsaw: Towarzystwo im. Witolda Lutosławskiego, 2014.
Maruzsa, Zoltán: "The Molotov-Ribbentrop Pact and What is Behind." In: *Unknown Clauses: The Background Deals of Totalitarian Systems in the Face of World War II The Molotov-Ribbentrop Pact*, ed. Zoltán Maruzsa. Budapest: Department of Modern and Contemporary Global History, 2010.

Matelski, Dariusz: "Rola muzeów i muzealników polskich w ratowaniu i restytucji utraconego dziedzictwa kultury w XX–XXI wieku (część I – do 1945 r.)," *Rocznik Muzeum Wsi Mazowieckiej w Sierpcu* (2) 2011, 65–106.

Matusak, Piotr: *Edukacja i kultura Polski Podziemnej 1939–1945,* Siedlce: Siedleckie Towarzystwo Naukowe, 1997.

Megargee, Edwin I.: "Aggression and Violence," in Henry E. Adams, Patricia B. Sutker (eds.), *Comprehensive Handbook of Psychopathology,* New York: Plenum Press, 1984, 523–545.

Megargee, Geoffrey P. (ed.): *Ravensbrück Subcamp System* in *The United States Holocaust Memorial Museum Encyclopedia of Camps and Ghettos, 1933–1945,* Vol. I: *Early Camps, Youth Camps, and Concentration Camps and Subcamps under the SS-Business Administration Main Office (WVHA),* Indiana University Press, 2009.

Meloch, Katarzyna, and Szostkiewicz, Haline (eds.), *Dzieci Holocaustu mówią…* Warsaw: Biblioteka Midrasza, Stowarzyszenie Dzieci Holocaustu w Polsce, 2008.

Meyer, Michael: "The Nazi Musicologist as Myth Maker in the Third Reich," *Journal of Contemporary History,* Vol. 10, No. 4 (Oct., 1975), 649–665.

Michael, Robert and Doerr, Karin: *Nazi-Deutsch/Nazi-German: An English Lexicon of the Language of the Third Reich.* Westport, Conn.: Greenwood Press, 2002.

Milewski, Barbara: "Remembering the Concentration Camps: Aleksander Kulisiewicz and his Concerts of Prisoners' Songs in the Federal Republic of Germany." In: *Dislocated Memories: Jews, Music, and Postwar German Culture,* ed. Tina Frühauf and Lily Hirsch. Oxford University Press, 2014.

Milewski, Barbara: "Krystyna Żywulska: The Making of a Satirist and Songwriter in Auschwitz-Birkenau Is Discovered Through Camp Mementos," *Swarthmore College Bulletin* 2009, 20–23.

Milewski, Barbara: "Hidden in Plain View: The Music of Holocaust Survival in Poland's First Post-war Feature Film." In: *Music, Collective Memory, Trauma, and Nostalgia in European Cinema after the Second World War,* ed. Michael Baumgartner, Ewelina Boczkowska. Routledge: New York, 2019.

Młynarczyk, Jacek Andrzej: "Treblinka – obóz śmierci 'akcji Reinhardt.'" In: *Akcja Reinhardt. Zagłada Żydów w Generalnym Gubernatorstwie,* ed. Dariusz Libionka. Warsaw: IPN, 2004.

Morgan, Gareth: *Images of organisation.* Beverly Hills: Sage, 1986.

Müller, Theodor: *Landeskunde des General Gouvernements. Im Auftrage der Hauptabteilung Wissenschaft und Unterricht der Regierung des Generalgouvernements*, bearbeitet von Dr. Theodor Muller. Krakow: Burgverlag Krakau G.m.b.H, 1943.

Naliwajek, Katarzyna: "Music and its Emotional Aspects during the Nazi Occupation of Poland." In: *Besatzungsmacht Musik. Zur Musik- und Emotionsgeschichte im Zeitalter der Weltkriege (1914–1949)*, Histoire, Vol. 30, ed. Sarah Zalfen, Sven Oliver Müller, Iris Törmer. Bielefeld: transcript Verlag, 2012, 207–224.

Naliwajek, Katarzyna: "The Use of Polish Musical Tradition in Nazi Propaganda," *Musicology Today*. 7 (2010), 243–259.

Naliwajek, Katarzyna: "Muzyka jako metoda przetrwania i oporu w mieście dwóch powstań i Zagłady." In: *Warszawa 1939–1945. Okupacyjne losy muzyków*. Vol. 2, ed. Naliwajek, Andrzej Spóz. Warsaw: Towarzystwo im. W. Lutosławskiego, 2015, 8–23.

Naliwajek, Katarzyna: "Music in Nazi Genocide System in Occupied Poland – Facts and Testimonies." In: *Colloque "Musique et camps de concentration", Conseil de l'Europe, Strasbourg 7–8 November 2013*, DVD, ed. Amaury du Closel. Council of Europe: Forum des Voix Étouffées, 2015, 39–50.

Naliwajek, Katarzyna: "The Racialization and Ghettoization of Music in the General Government," in Pauline Fairclough (ed.), *Twentieth-Century Music and Politics*. Farnham: Ashgate, 2013, 191–210.

Naliwajek, Katarzyna: "Music and Torture in Nazi Sites of Persecution and Genocide in Occupied Poland 1939–1945," in: *The world of music (new series)*, Vol. 2, Issue 1, (2013), Music and Torture | Music and Punishment, Göttingen: Department of Music at Georg August University, 31–50.

Naliwajek, Katarzyna: "Nazi Censorship in Music: Warsaw 1941." In: *The Impact of Nazism on Twentieth Century Music*, ed. Erik Levi. Vienna: Boehlau Verlag, 2014, 151–173.

Naliwajek, Katarzyna: "The Functions of Music within the Nazi System of Genocide in Occupied Poland." In: *Music and Genocide*, ed. Wojciech Klimczyk and Agata Świerzowska. Frankfurt am Main: Peter Lang Edition, 2015, 83–103.

Naliwajek, Katarzyna: and Spóz, Andrzej: *Okupacyjne losy muzyków. Warszawa 1939–1945*. Vol. 2, Warsaw: Towarzystwo im. Witolda Lutosławskiego, 2015.

Naliwajek, Katarzyna: "Chopin inter arma," in: Irena Poniatowska, Zofia Chechlińska (eds.), *Chopin 1810-2010: ideas, interpretations, influence: the Third International Chopin Congress, Warsaw, 25 February to 1 March 2010*, Vol. 2. Warsaw: The Fryderyk Chopin Institute, 2017, 399-409.

Naliwajek, Katarzyna: "The sounds of Warsaw in 1945: witness accounts," in: Renata Tańczuk, Sławomir Wieczorek (eds.), *Sounds of War and Peace. Soundscapes of European Cities in 1945*, "Eastern European Studies in Musicology", ed. Maciej Gołąb, Vol. 11, Frankfurt am Main: Peter Lang Verlag, 2018, 55-80.

Naliwajek, Katarzyna: "Nazi Musical Imperialism in Occupied Poland," in: Fanning, David, and Levi, Erik (eds.), *The Routledge Handbook to Music under German Occupation, 1938-1945. Propaganda. Myth and Reality*, London / New York: Routledge, 2020, 61-81.

Nałęcz, Mariola: "Chopiniana z dawnej kolekcji Breitkopfa i Härtla w zbiorze Biblioteki Narodowej w Warszawie;" "Fragmenty korespondencji Fryderyka Chopina," in: M. Kozłowska (ed.), *Ocalone przez BGK: katalog wystawy*, Warsaw: BGK, 2014.

Nałkowska, Zofia: *Dzienniki 1939-1944*. Warsaw: Czytelnik, 1996.

Nawrocki, Stanisław: "Losy inteligencji poznańskiej podczas okupacji," *Kronika Miasta Poznania* 66/2 (1998).

Newman, Leonard S. and Erber, Ralph (eds.): *Understanding Genocide: The Social Psychology of the Holocaust*, Oxford: Oxford University Press 2002.

Newman, Richard and Kirtley, Karen: *Alma Rosé: Vienna to Auschwitz*, Portland: Amadeus Press, 2000.

Niedhart, Gottfried and Broderick, George (eds.): *Lieder in Politik und Alltag des Nationalsozialismus*, Frankfurt am Main: Peter Lang, 1999.

Niezabitowska, Małgorzata: "A Pole who tries to be a Jew" (Polak, który próbuje być Żydem), *Karta* (1980), 55-65.

Ochlewski, Tadeusz: "Muzyka w Warszawie podczas okupacji," *RM* 11 (1970), 16-17.

Olszewski, Andrzej K.: "Moje wspomnienia z życia muzycznego podczas okupacji niemieckiej," *Saeculum Christianum* 9 (2002).

Pallmann, Gerhard: "Das Kriegserlebnis im Spielgel des Soldatenliedes," *Die Musik* 32/2, November (1939-1940), 41-49.

Palmon, Hanna: "The Polish Pianist Artur Hermelin," https://demusica.edu.pl/muzykalia-xiii-judaica-4/. Warsaw: Stowarzyszenie De Musica, 2012.

Palmon, Hanna: "Jewish Musicians of Lwów," *The Galitzianer. The Quaterly Research Journal of Gesher Galicia* (23 / 2) 2016, 10-15.

Panufnik, Andrzej, *Composing myself, and other texts*. London: Toccata Press, 2016.

Pasztaleniec-Jarzyńska, Joanna and Halina Tchórzewska-Kabata: *The National Library in Warsaw: tradition and the present day*. Warsaw: Biblioteka Narodowa, 2000.

Pettyn, Andrzej: "Chopin's Heart," in Kazimierz Sztarbałło and Michał Wardzyński (eds.), *Heart of the city: church of the Holy Cross in Warsaw*, trans. Joanna Holzman, Warsaw: Mazowiecka Jednostka Wdrażania Programów Unijnych, 2011, 148–50.

Polubiec, Zofia (ed.): *Okupacja i ruch oporu w Dzienniku Hansa Franka 1939–1945*, Vol. I, 1939–1942, trans. from German by Danuta Dąbrowska and Mieczysław Tomala, Warszawa 1970.

Posłuszna, Joanna, Posłuszny, Łukasz, "The Aural Landscape of Majdanek." In: *Music and Genocide*, ed. Wojciech Klimczyk and Agata Świerzowska. Frankfurt am Main: Peter Lang Edition, 2015, 105–120.

Pospieszalski, Karol Marian: *Hitlerowskie "prawo" okupacyjne w Polsce*, Poznań: Instytut Zachodni, *Documenta Occupationis 5*, 1952.

Piotrowski, Stanisław: *Hans Franks Tagebuch*. Warsaw: PWN, 1963.

Potter, Pamela: *Trends in German Musicology 1918–1945: The Effects of Methodological, Ideological and Institutional Change on the Writing of Music History*. Ann Arbor, 1991.

Potter, Pamela: "Dismantling a Dystopia: On the Historiography of Music in the Third Reich," *Central European History* 40, (2007), 623–651.

Präg, Werner and Jacobmeyer, Wolfgang (eds.): *Das Diensttagebuch des deutschen Generalgouverneurs in Polen 1939–1945*, Stuttgart, 1975.

Prieberg, Fred K.: *Musik im NS Staat*. Frankfurt am Main: Fischer Taschenbuch Verlag, 1982; second expanded edition: Berlin: Dittrich, 2010.

Prieberg, Fred K.: *Handbuch Deutsche Musiker 1933–45*, CD-R. Kiel 2004.

Rajchman, Jechiel Mejer: *Ocalałem z Treblinki*. Trans. Bella Szwarcman-Czarnota. Warsaw: Spółdzielnia Wydawnicza Czytelnik, 2011.

Raphael, Beverley, and Dobson, Matthew: "Acute posttraumatic interventions," in John P. Wilson, Matthew J. Friedman and Jacob D. Lindy (eds.), *Treating Psychological Trauma and PTSD*. New York: Guilford, 2001.

Regamey, Konstanty: "Muzyka polska pod okupacją niemiecką" (Polish Music under German occupation), *Horyzonty. Miesięcznik poświęcony sprawom kultury. Ilustrowane pismo polskie na emigracji – bezpartyjne i apolityczne* (Horizons. A monthly cultural review. Illustrated Polish Émigrés Review – nonpartisan and unpolitical). Freiburg 1946 (Year I), No. 1.

Reich-Ranicki, Marcel: *Zwischen Diktatur und Literatur: ein Gespräch mit Joachim Fest.* Frankfurt am Main: Fischer Taschenbuch, 1993.

Richie, Alexandra: *Warsaw 1944: the fateful uprising,* London: William Collins – an imprint of Harper Collins Publishers, 2013.

Ringelblum, Emmanuel: *Kronika getta warszawskiego: wrzesień 1939 – styczeń 1943,* trans. from Yiddish by Adam Rutkowski, Warszawa: Czytelnik, 1988.

Rosenberg, Alfred: *Der Mythus des zwanzigsten Jahrhunderts: eine Wertung der seelisch-geistigen Gestaltenkämpfe unserer Zeit.* München: Hocheneichen Verlag, 1934.

Rudzisz, Marian: "My Jewishness" (pseudonym, Moje żydostwo), *Karta* (1980), 66–71.

Rutkowski, Bronisław: "Konserwatorium Muzyczne w Warszawie w latach okupacji," *RM* 24 (1946), 3, 4.

Egzekucje w Operze, Protokół nr 19/II, In: *Biuletyn Głównej Komisji Badania Zbrodni Niemieckich w Polsce (I),* Poznań: Wydawnictwo GKBZNP, 1946.

Rutowska, Maria, Edward Serwański: *Straty osobowe polskiego środowiska muzycznego w l atach 1939–1945,* Warsaw: GKBZH, 1977.

Rutowska, Maria, Edward Serwański: *Losy polskich środowisk artystycznych w latach 1939–1945: architektura, sztuki plastyczne, muzyka i teatr: problemy metodologiczne strat osobowych.* Poznań: Instytut Zachodni, 1987.

Sachs, Harvey: *Music in fascist Italy.* London: Weidenfeld and Nicolson, 1987.

Shapreau, Carla, *Lost Music project: the Nazi-Era Plunder of Music in Europe,* www.carlashapreau.com.

Sheffler, Anne C.: "Musicology, Biography, and National Socialism: The Case of Hans Heinrich Eggebrecht", *German Studies* 2012 (35/2), 290–298.

Schenk, Dieter: *Hans Frank. Hitlers Kronjurist und Generalgouverneur.* Frankfurt am Main: S. Fischer Verlag GmbH, 2006.

Schenk, Dieter: *Hans Frank. Biografia generalnego gubernatora,* tłum. Krzysztof Jachimczak. Krakow: Wydawnictwo Znak, 2009.

Sichergestellte Kunstwerke im Generalgouvernement (Catalogue of looting of works of Polish art "secured" in the General Government). Breslau: Wilh. Gottl. Korn, [ca 1940].

Shore, Marci: *Caviar and Ashes: A Warsaw Generation's Life and Death in Marxism, 1918–1968.* New Haven, London: Yale University Press, 2006.

Sonner, Rudolf: "Aufbau und Kultur seit 1933," *Die Musik* 30/7 April (1938–1939), 435.
Szczęśniak, Hubert: "Muzykalia w zbiorach Państwowego Muzeum Auschwitz-Birkenau," *Kwartalnik Młodych Muzykologów UJ* 1 (2017), 125–175.
Snyder, Louis Leo: *Encyclopedia of the Third Reich*. Ware, Hertfordshire: Wordsworth Editions,1998.
Snyder, Timothy, *Bloodlands: Europe between Hitler and Stalin*, 2nd edn. New York: Basic Books, 2012.
Stanilewicz, Maria: "Muzyka w okupowanej Warszawie," RM 10 (1981), 5.
Stanilewicz, Maria: "Muzyczny ruch wydawniczy," RM 19 (1981), 14– 15.
Stern, Samuel: *Die Schrecken von Auschwitz. Internationaler Suchdienst Arolsen: Pseudo-Medizinische Versuche im KL Auschwitz, Phlegmone-Versuche*, 15.05.1973. Annex I.
Stola, Dariusz: "Jewish Emigration from Communist Poland: The Decline of Polish Jewry in the Aftermath of the Holocaust," *East European Jewish Affairs* 2017 47 (2–3), 172.
Strzelewicz, Konrad: *Polskie wiersze obozowe i więzienne 1939– 1945 w archiwum Aleksandra Kulisiewicza*. Krakow: Krajowa Agencja Wydawnicza, 1984.
Szajnberg, Nathan: "Übertragung, metaphor, and transference in psychoanalytic psychotherapy," *International Journal of Psychoanalytic Psychotherapy* 11 (1985– 1986) Vol. 11, 53– 75.
Szarota, Tomasz: *Okupowanej Warszawy dzień powszedni*. Warsaw: Czytelnik 2010.
Szczepański, Ignacy: *Häftlings-kapelle*. Warsaw: Książka i Wiedza, 1990.
Szewera, Tadeusz and Straszyński, Olgierd: *Niech wiatr ją poniesie: antologia pieśni z lat 1939–1945*. Łódź: Wydawnictwo Łódzkie, 1970.
Szewera, Tadeusz: *Za każdy kamień Twój Stolico... Pieśni i piosenki walczącej Warszawy 1939–1945*. Łódź-Tarnobrzeg: Biblioteka Tarnobrzeskich Zeszytów Historycznych, 1999.
Szmaglewska, Seweryna: *Smoke over Birkenau*, translated by Jadwiga Rynas. Oświęcim: Auschwitz Birkenau State Museum, 2017.
Szpilman, Władysław: *The Pianist. The Extraordinary True Story of One Man's Survival in Warsaw, 1939–1945*, trans. Anthea Bell. New York: Picador, 1999.
Święch, Jerzy: *Literatura polska w latach II wojny światowej*, Warsaw: Wydawnictwo Naukowe PWN, 1997.
Tarnawska-Kaczorowska, Krystyna (ed.): *Muzyka źle obecna*. Warsaw: Sekcja Muzykologów Związku Kompozytorów Polskich, 1989.

Trümpi, Fritz: *The Political Orchestra: the Vienna and Berlin Philharmonics during the Third Reich.* Chicago: University of Chicago Press, 2016.

Tulving, Endel, and Craik, Fergus I. M.: *The Oxford Handbook of Memory.* Oxford: Oxford University Press, 2000.

Turner, Deborah: "Oral documents in concept and in situ, part I: Grounding an exploration of orality and information behavior," *Journal of Documentation*, Vol. 68 No. 6, (2012), 852–863.

Van der Kolk, B. A., and Fisler, R., "Dissociation and the fragmentary nature of traumatic memories: Overview and exploratory study," *Journal of Traumatic Stress*, 8/4 (1995).

Vetter, Walther: "Zweite Posener Musikwoche: Rauschender Erfolg des einleitenden Konzerts," *Ostdeutsche Beobachter*, 31 August 1941.

de Vries, Willem: *Sonderstab Musik: Music confiscations by the Einsatzstab Reichsleiter Rosenberg under the Nazi occupation of Western Europe.* Amsterdam: Amsterdam University Press, 1996.

Waibel, Harry: *Diener vieler Herren: Ehemalige NS-Funktionäre in der SBZ/DDR.* Frankfurt am Main: Lang, 2011.

Waller J., *Becoming Evil: How Ordinary People Commit Genocide and Mass Killing.* New York, 2002.

Weber, Claudia: *Krieg der Täter. Die Massenerschießungen von Katyń.* Hamburg, 2015.

Weissweiler, Eva: *Ausgemerzt! Das Lexikon der Juden in der Musik und seine mörderischen Folgen*, Köln 1999.

Werb, Bret: "Fourteen Shoah Songbooks." *Musica Judaica* 20 (2013), 39–116.

Werb, Bret: "Shmerke Kaczerginski, the Partisan-Troubadour." *Polin: Studies in Polish Jewry.* Volume 20 (2007): *Making Holocaust Memory.* Oxford and Portland: Littman Library of Jewish Civilization, 392–412.

Wieczorek, Sławomir: *On the music front: socialist-realist discourse on music in Poland 1948 to 1955*, translated by Robert Curry, Peter Lang, Berlin, 2020.

Wiernik, Jankiel: *One Year in Treblinka.* New York: American Representation of the General Jewish Workers Union of Poland, 1944 [?].

Wiesel, Elie, Doris L. Bergen, Christopher R. Browning, David Engel, Willard A. Fletcher, Peter Hayes, Michael R. Marrus, and Nechama Tec. "Revensbrück Subcamp System" in *The United States Holocaust Memorial Museum Encyclopedia of Camps and Ghettos, 1933–1945*, Vol. I: Early Camps, Youth Camps, and Concentration Camps and Subcamps under the SS-Business Administration Main Office (WVHA),

edited by Geoffrey P. Megargee, Indiana University Press, 2009, 1192–1228.
Willenberg, Samuel, *"Revolt in Treblinka" In the Death Camp Treblinka. A Documentary*. In Alexander Donat (ed.), New York: Holocaust Library, 1979, 1892–13.
Willenberg, Samuel, *Revolt in Treblinka*. Tel Aviv: Żydowski Instytut Historyczny im. Emanuela Ringelbluma, 2008.
Wilson, John P.: "An overview of clinical considerations and principles in the treatment of PTSD," in John P. Wilson, Matthew J. Friedman and Jacob D. Lindy (eds.), *Treating Psychological Trauma and PTSD* (New York: Guilford, 2001).
Wiłkomirski, Kazimierz: *Wspomnienia*. Krakow: Polskie Wydawnictwo Muzyczne, 1971.
Woźniakowska, Anna: *60 lat Filharmonii im. Karola Szymanowskiego w Krakowie. 1945–2005*. Krakow: Filharmonia im. K. Szymanowskiego w Krakowie, 2004, 22–28.
Wulf, Joseph: *Musik im Dritten Reich: eine Dokumentation*. Gütersloh: Sigbert Mohn Verlag, 1963.
Young, Allan: *The Harmony of Illusions. Inventing Post-Traumatic Stress Disorder*. Princeton, NJ: Princeton University Press, 1997.
Zieleniewska-Ginterowa, Maria: "Z pobytu w celi małoletnich," in *Wspomnienia więźniów Pawiaka*. Warsaw: Polska Akademia Nauk, 1964, 191–214.
Zillmer E.A., M. Harrower, B.A. Ritzler, R.P. Archer: *The Quest for the Nazi Personality: A Psychological Investigation of Nazi War Criminals*, Hillsdale, NJ 1995.
Zog nisht keynmol az du geyst dem letstn veg: a zamlung lider far yugnt tsum 4-tn yortog fun oyfsthtand in varshever geto. Warsaw: Tsentral-komitet fun yidn in poyln, 1947.
Żurawska-Witkowska, Alina: "Straty wojenne," *RM* 14 (1981), 4–7.
Žižek, Slavoj: *The Plague of Fantasies*. London, New York: Verso 2008.

Audiovisual materials
Chopin in Birkenau, CD produced by Renata Koszyk, 2016.

Appendix

Appendix to Introduction

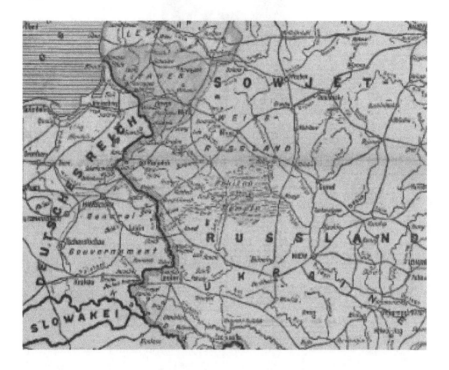

Source: BUW

1939. The aftermath of the Ribbentrop-Molotov Pact and Nazi-Soviet attack on Poland: division of Poland into USSR-annexed territories, Reich-annexed territories and the *Generalgouvernement*.

Fragment of a German map published in the *Kattowitzer Zeitung* No. 215 of August 7, 1941

252 Appendix

Source: Andrzej Straszyński Family Archive

Zofia Rysiówna before her arrest.

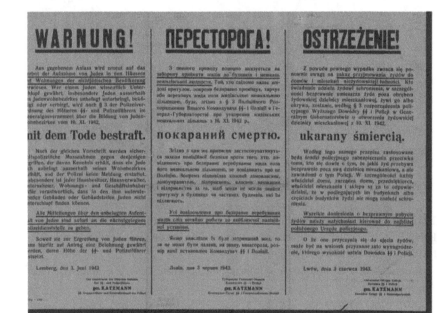

Source: BN

Announcement (in German, Ukrainian and Polish) of June 3, 1943 from Lemberg, signed by governor of the Galizien District, chief of SS and police, Fritz Katzmann,[1] on death penalty for harbouring Jews (written in lower case) and remuneration for catching Jews, based on "Polizeiverordnung" (police regulation) of November 10, 1942, establishing the "Jewish residential district."

BN

---

1 Fritz Katzmann (1906-1957), from 1928 member of SA/NSDAP, from 1930 – of SS. From November 1939 SSPF in Radom, from July 1941 SSPF in Galizien District with headquarters in Lemberg. From 1943 Higher SSPF in Weichsel (Danzig-West Prussia). Member of Reichstag, assessor at the People's Court. Katzmann's report of June 30, 1943: "The district of Galicia is thus free of Jews, except for those who are in the camps under the control of SSPF... Only through the personal sense of duty of every single leader and man has it been possible to get this plague under control in the shortest possible time." ("Der Distrikt Galizien ist damit, bis auf die Juden, die sich in den unter Kontrolle des SS- und Polizeiführers stehenden Lagern befinden, judenfrei... Nur durch persönliches Pflichtbewußtsein jedes einzelnen Führers und Mannes ist es gelungen, dieser Pest in kürzester Frist Herr zu werden.") After 1945 he lived undiscovered under the name Bruno Albrecht in Darmstadt. Quoted after Klee, *Das Personenlexikon*, 230.

Announcement (in German, Ukrainian and Polish) of January 29, 1944 from the Lvov area, signed by the chief of SS and Police for District Galizien.

List of 84 Poles and Ukrainians sentenced to death for harbouring (*Judenbehergergung*) or helping Jews (*Judenbegünstigung*) and other "crimes" ("Bandengruppen" means military resitance; the word "Banditen" is used generally for anyone offering resistance). A conductor from Stanisławów, Alfred Stadler (No. 56 on this list), is sentenced for "participation in forbidden organizations."

Below the list of people sentenced, there is an ultimatum based on blackmail – a typical method of manipulating and terrorizing the population of occupied territories:

> The sentence has already been carried out on the persons named in items 1 to 10.
> The convicts from 11. to 84. have been considered for a pardon.
> Should, however, in the next three months in the area of the city of Lemberg or the district headquarters of Lemberg-Land and Zloczow, acts of violence be committed, in particular attacks on Germans, on members of the states allied with the Greater German Reich, or on non-Germans working in the interests of the reconstruction work in the Generalgouvernement, then – unless the perpetrator is seized immediately – the sentence will also be carried out on the convicts considered for pardon, in such a way that for each act of violence committed against one of the subjects of the Greater German Reich the number of convicts considered for pardon will decrease by at least 10. If the crime is committed by communist elements, then communists from among the abovementioned list will be excluded from pardon; if the crime is committed by other misguided elements, then those of the above-mentioned who were politically close to them will be excluded from pardon.
> It is therefore in the hands of the non-German population,
> by immediately arresting
> or by arranging for the arrest of the perpetrator or perpetrators
> or by influencing misguided elements known to them
> or by reporting suspected persons
> to see to it that the sentence is not carried out on the convicted persons under consideration for pardon.[2]

---

2   Das Urteil ist an zu Ziffer 1, bis 10. Genannten bereits vollstreckt worden.
    Die Verurteilten von Ziffer 11. bis 84. sind für einen Gnadenerweis in Aussicht genommen.
    Sollten jedoch in den nächsten 3 Monaten im Bereich der Stadt Lemberg oder der Kreishaptmannschaften LembergLand und Zloczow Gewalttaten, insbesondere Überfälle auf Deutsche, Angehörige der mit dem Grossdeutschen Reich verbündeten Staaten oder im Interesse der Aufbauwerkes im Generalgouvernement arbeitenden Nichtdeutschen begangen werden, so wird – sofern der Täter nicht sofort ergriffen wird – das Urteil auch an den für einen Gnadenerweis in Aussicht genommenen

Appendix 255

NAC

Alfred Stadler (1899, Stanisławów – February 2, 1944, Lvov) – conductor killed in above-mentioned executions.

Verurteilten vollstreckt werden und zwar in der Form, dass für jede Gewalttat an einem der Schutzbefohlenen des Grossdeutschen Reiches der beabsichtigte Gnadenerweis für mindestens 10 der Verurteilten hinfällig wird. Ist die Tat von kommunistischen Elementen begangen, so warden aus dem Kreise der Obengenannten kommunisten, ist die Tat von sonstigen irregeleiteten Elementen begangen, so warden von den Obengenannten diejenigen, die diesen politisch nahe standen, von dem Gnadenerweis ausgeschlossen.
Es liegt deshalb in der Hand der nichtdeutschen Bevölkerung,
durch sofortige Festnahme
oder Veranlassung der Festnahme des oder der Täter
oder durch Einwirkung auf ihnen bekannte, irregeleitetet Elemente
oder durch Anzeigen verdächtiger Personen
dafür zu sorgen, dass das Urteil an den für einen Gnadenerweis in Aussicht genommenen Verurteilten nicht vollstreckt wird.

256   Appendix

BN

"All Germans of Lemberg are invited to the ceremonial opening of the German Popular Education Center Lemberg-Galicia" ("Alle Deutschen Lembergs geht's an Einladung zur Feierlichen Eröffnung der Deutschen Volksbildungstätte Lemberg-Galizien Freitag, 1 Mai 1942, 20 Uhr im Opernhaus") organized by NSDAP *Distriktstandortführung Galizien*, with a speech by its chief, Dr. Wächter. May 1, 1942, Lvov Opera House. BN

Featured music: "Triumphal March" from *Aida* by Verdi, Marching Song (*Marschlied*) *Vorwärts nach Osten* by Norbert Schultze (published in 1942 in *Lieder Blätter des Reichsarbeitsdienstes 1*, known also as "Russlandlied"), *Deutschland-Lied* and *Horst-Wessel-Lied*. *Bombenfliegermarsch* by Hans Teichman was another march which was also sung in 1939 with different words as *Die Gumbinner Füsiliere: Es hat uns der Führer gerufen*, its second stanza began with the words "We hunted down the Polish hordes" ("Wir jagten die polnischen Horden, wir jagten sie zu Hauf"). Performed by a military band of the Luftwaffe regiment and a soldiers' choir from Lemberg ("Die Musikkorps eines

Luftnachrichtenregiments unter Leitung von Musikleiter Hensel; Ein Soldatenchor des Standortes Lemberg").

BN

Opera House in Lvov, performances for Ukrainians only: *Traviata* on September 7, 1943 at 7 p.m.

258   Appendix

BN

Die Entführung aus dem Serail in Lemberg Opera, on September 3, 5, 6, 1942, at 7:30 PM:
"Comic opera in 3 acts by W. A. Mozart. The performance is held only for Germans and allies (Die Vorstellung findet nur für Deutsche und Verbündete statt).
Guest appearances of German and Austrian singers: Julius Raum – Selim Bassa, Ingeborg v. Streit (Stadttheater Münster) – Konstanze, Elinor Junker (Opernhaus Nürnberg) – Blonde, Werner Schupp (Opernhaus Karlsruhe) – Belmonte, Willam Wenigk (Staatsoper Wien) – Pedrello, Herbert Alsen (Staatsoper Wien) – Osmin.
Conductor: Fritz Weidlich
"The director of the Innsbruck Conservatory, Prof. Fritz Weidlich, known as a conductor of opera and symphony concerts and also as a pianist and a chamber musician, has been appointed by Governor General Dr. Frank as music director of the city of Lemberg. Weidlich will put together a symphony orchestra of Lemberg which will be based primarily on the orchestra of the Lemberg Opera House" (*Deutsche Tonkunst, Lemberg,* "MNN", June 4, 1942). A later article from November 13, 1942,

entitled *Debut*, read "With a performance of Verdi's *Aida*, Fritz Weidlich has inaugurated the German era of the Lemberg Opera" (AMZ 69 / 23, 197).[3]

---

3   Der Leiter des Innsbrucker Konservatoriums, Prof. Fritz Weidlich, als Dirigent von Opern-und Sinfoniekonzerten und auch als Pianist und Kammermusiker bekannt, ist von Generalgouverneur Dr. Frank zum Musikdirektor der Stadt Lemberg berufen worden. Weidlich wird für Lemberg ein Sinfonieorchester zusammenstellen, das sich in erster Linie aug das Orchester des Lemberger Opernhauses stützen wird" ("MNN", June 4, 1942). Quoted after Prieberg, *Handbuch*, 1651.

Appendix

Announcement signed by the SS- and Police chief for Warsaw District, Warsaw, December 3, 1943, informing of the execution of 100 men on Puławska Street 13. As number 28. – Henryk Trzonek, born on October 29, 1912. Next to him, as number 29. – Stefan Bryła, born on August 17, 1886. Trzonek was a talented viola player who played in the string quartet established in occupied Warsaw by Eugenia Umińska. Stefan Bryła was an eminent architect and a specialist in steel bridge construction, who had been arrested along with his whole family for organizing clandestine teaching on November 16, 1943 (he was the dean of the underground Architecture Department of the Warsaw University of Technology).

Original announcement reproduced in *Biuletyn GKBZNP* (Poznań: Wydawnictwo GKBZNP) 1946.

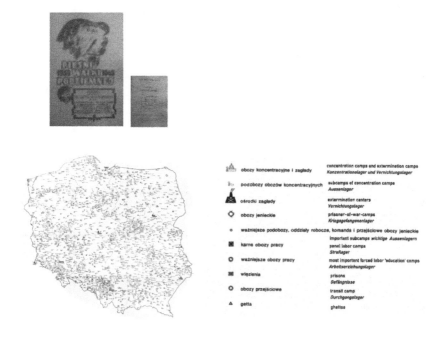

Clandestine songs by Witold Lutosławski published in 1948 (Kraków, PWM)

Map representing different types of German camps and prisons established on the territories of occupied Poland (showing post-war frontiers).

These types include: Concentration camps and extermination camps (*Konzentrationslager und Vernichtungslager*), subcamps (*Aussenlager*), (extermination

Appendix

camps (*Vernichtungslager*), prisoner-of-war camps (*Kriegsgefangenenlager*), important subcamps (*wichtige Aussenlagern*), special work units made of prisoners (*Kommandos*), labor education camps (*Arbeitserziehungslager*), prisons (*Gefängnisse*), penal camps (*Straflager*), ghettos (*Gettos*).

This map was edited by Jan Laskowski based upon research conducted by the Main Commission for the Investigation of Nazi Crimes in Poland (GKBZH). It was published in *Obozy hitlerowskie na ziemiach polskich 1939-1945. Informator encyklopedyczny* (Nazi camps on Polish territories 1939-1945. Encyclopaedic guide, Warsaw: PWN, 1979).

Appendix to Chapter one

German map of museums and private collections in Polish territories as of 1939, marked on the administrative map of the GG, with its five "Distrikts": Warschau, Radom, Lublin, Krakau and Galizien (original title: *Generalgouvernement: Öffentliche und private Museen u. Sammlungen Stand vom J. 1939*, edited by von Till. Published in Cracow in 1942 by the Head Office of the Museums of the Department of Science and Education of the Government of the GG ("Hauptverwaltung der Museen der Hauptabteilung Wissenschaft und Unterrricht der Regierung des Generalgouvernement").

"The Germans did not limit themselves to simply plundering Jewish property. In the first weeks of the invasion they provoked pogroms in nearly all of the cities and towns of Poland. In the presence of forcefully assembled non-Jewish citizens the Germans organized exemplary spectacles in the main squares during which Jews were abused and beaten, mocked and killed. (for example in Siedliszcze, Mińsk Mazowiecki, Węgrów, Radziejów etc.).

In other places Jews were forced to dance and sing to shout and recite absurd self-incriminations (Bełżyce, Bełchatów, Węgrów, Okrza, Zgierz). The Jews were rounded up in the street on the pretext of gathering them for work. They were ordered to show up at a given time and forced to march to a different town or to some hastily arranged camp.

Religious Jews faced special humiliations and abuses. Their beards were either cut or pulled out, sometimes with whole patches of skin. Their beards were also set on fire which they were not allowed to extinguish. For example in the Sejm Parliament Gardens in Warsaw, in Okrza, Zgierz, Węgrów, Piotrków, etc.). Rabbis and orthodox Jews were ordered to dance or sing in public. They were geared at and dragged out into the streets in liturgical vestments. In Cisna the Germans burned liturgical vestments and holy books in the main square. They forced the Jews to set fire to the these themselves, and then ordered them to dance around the fire singing "Wir freuen uns, wie das Dreck brennt" ("We're happy to see to see this filth burn"). Jews were also made to scrub cobble stones and the floors of public restrooms with their liturgical vestments.

In Kalisz Jews were forced to jump over a bonfire in which hand written copies of the Torah were burnt. Synagogues were set on fire or sometimes Jews themselves were forced to do this. (…)

The Germans enjoyed all such atrocities during on Jewish holidays (Włocławek, Płońsk, Bełżyce, Mielec, etc.). In many cases (rather than simply burn them down), the Germans used synagogues as stables (Gniewoszów, Maków), factories (Przemyśl), public swimming pools (Poznań), entertainment venues (Nowy Tomyśl), medical facilites (Góra Kalwaria), prisons (Kalisz) or even public restrooms (Ciechanów)."[4]

---

4   Description of forced singing and dancing, a way of torturing the Jews by the Germans being used since September 1939 in various locations of occupied Poland. *Biuletyn GKBZNP* (Poznań: GKBZNP) 1946, 180-182.

Appendix 263

BN

Poster with Beethoven's death mask, advertising the Opening Concert of the GG Philharmonics in Cracow on October 14, 1940: "Opening ceremony. First Philharmonic Concert. Conductor: Dr. Hanns Rohr. Programme: Johann Sebastian Bach – Overture (Suite No. 3) in D major; Ludwig van Beethoven – Symphony No. 8 in F major; Johannes Brahms – Symphony no. 1 in C minor. Tickets for Zloty 2.-, 6.- and 8.- in the Deutsche Buchhandlung Fritsche at Adolf-Hitler Platz. Preannouncement: Second Philharmonic Concert with soloist Wilhelm Kempff, Monday, November 25, 1940: Pfitzner, Mozart, Tchaikovsky."[5]

---

5   "Philharmonie des Generalgouvernements Krakau, Haus Apollo, Westring 18, Montag, 14. Oktober 1940, Abends 19.30 Uhr Eröffnungsfeier. I. Philharmonisches Konzert. Leitung: Dr. Hanns Rohr. Programme: Johann Sebastian Bach – Ouvertüre (Suite Nr.

264   Appendix

BN

Poster advertising the Opening Concert of the GG Philharmonics in Warsaw ("Philharmonie des Generalgouvernements, Warschau"), at the "Theater der

---

3) in D-Dur Ludwig van Beethoven – 8. Symphonie in F-dur; Johannes Brahms – I. Symphonie in c-moll Karten zu Zloty 2.-, 6.- und 8.- in der Deutschen Buchhandlung Fritsche / Adolf-Hitler Platz Voranzeige: II. Philharmonisches Konzert (Solist: Wilhelm Kempff), Montag 25 November 1940: Pfitzner, Mozart Tschaikovsky."

Appendix 265

Stadt Warschau", Monday, October 28, 1940, at 8 PM. The same programme as two weeks earlier in Cracow.

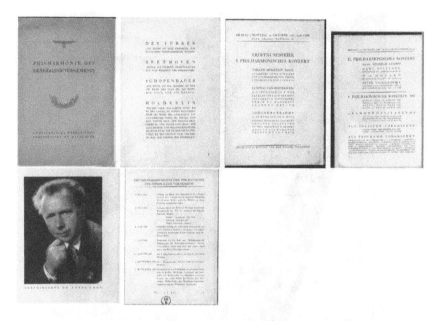

Pages from the programme of the Inauguration of GG Philharmonics. The brochure opens with Hitler's photograph and closes with Hans Frank's photograph. On page 5, there are "inspirational" quotes from 1) Hitler; 2) Beethoven; 3) Schopenhauer; 4) Hölderlin. The following pages contain programmes of the first and second Philharmonic Concert, a photo of the conductor Hanns Rohr, the history of the GG Orchestra, and texts by Hann Rohr.

Appendix to 1.6.

Sculpturer Wacław Szymanowski with Chopin's monument he created at the Barbedienne foundry in Paris, 1926. NAC 1-K-5463

Chopin's statue cut into pieces and transported by train to a German foundry
Nazi correspondence on Chopin collections[6]:

Ernst Krienitz,[7] October 6, 1943:

> The opening of the Chopin collection, prepared in the Cracow City Library, will take place at the end of this month in accordance with the instructions of the Governor General. For this purpose, I ask you to arrange the following.
>
> 1) Exact list of all Chopiniana remaining at the Warsaw State Library or located in other places in Warsaw.
>
> 2) An accurate written account of what has been ascertained so far about the loss of Chopiniana from the Warsaw City Library. These are probably some 20 manuscripts, 11 letters and other Chopin autographs acquired at that time by the publishing house Breitkopf and Härtel for 100,000 Reichsmark.

---

6 Quoted after Prieberg, *Handbuch*, 884-885.
7 Krienitz was one of editor of Deutsche *Militäar-Musiker-Zeitung. Einziges Musik-Fachblatt der deutschen Wehrmacht*, which was published as a weekly since 1933, as a biweekly since 1942 and since 1943 only monthly. Ibid., 1091. See also 1157, 6192.

3) Details of the acquisition of Chopin's 24 Preludes in March 1942; from whom and at what price.

4) I ask Mr. von Pulikowski for an overview of Chopin collections that exist in the world so far."[8]

October 9, 1943:

"1. An 'accurate list of all Chopiniana ... which are located in other places in Warsaw:' Before September 1939, despite all the efforts of the commission for the publication of a critical complete edition of Chopin's works, it was impossible to prepare such a list because many private collectors concealed their ownership of Chopiniana.

– This difficulty only increased significantly after September 1939.

– The following list cannot therefore be described as an 'exact' list of 'all' Chopiniana.

a) Warsaw Archives Office: certain family documents exist.

b) Museum of the City of Warsaw (former National Museum): some Chopin museum pieces, including a piano.

c) Laura Ciechomska (from the line of Chopin's mother), private property: owned autographs, letters, pictorial material, museum pieces before the war. - Current residence and possessions unknown.

d) Jew Leopold Binental (Hoża Street 15), currently allegedly in Switzerland, owned letters, pictures and autographs.

e) F. Chopin Institute owned several Chopiniana, the whereabouts of which are not known. Most of the autographs and photographs were in the hands of Prof. Józef Turczyński, who before the outbreak of the war travelled with these materials to Paderewski and Prof. Ludwik Bronarski in Switzerland to discuss questions of the Urtext. What Prof. Turczyński actually took with him to Switzerland and what he left at home is unknown, since the house in which Professor Turczyński's private apartment was located, burned down completely (September 1939).

– Other Chopiniana were taken over by the President of the Chopin Institute, Minister August Zaleski, because he wanted to organize a small Chopin exhibition there on the occasion of his upcoming visit to New York.

---

8   Source: Regierung des Generalgouvernements (Government of the General Government), Haupt Abteilung Wissenschaft und Unterricht (Science and Education), Hauptverwaltung der Bibliotheken (Main Administration of Libraries), Gustav Abb, to Head of the State Library Warsaw, Library Councillor Dr. Wilhelm Witte, October 6, 1943. Source: Library of the University of Wrocław, shelfmark: 156/IX, HV Libraries, St. 1201 No. 25 c. 80. Provenance: Willem de Vries).

- At the same time as Dr. Gerigk and Dr. Boetticher, having been authorized by the Governor General, confiscated the Elsner manuscripts from the State Library and manuscript No. 52 from the Przeździecki Library, the same gentlemen – without the presence of a member of the Institute – also confiscated, according to the caretaker, two suitcases of materials from the F. Chopin Institute.

- What remained after this confiscation was taken over by Department II of the City Library (Rakowiecka 6) on 3 November 1940: Chopin autographs and the like were not among these items.

2. The 24 Preludes were purchased in March 1942 by Mr. Stanisław Nowicki, Rybno near Sochaczew, for the price of 14,000 złoty. These preludes were offered for 20,000 złoty; only after lengthy negotiations could the price be reduced.

Appendix I to Wilhelm Witte's reply to Gustav Abb, October 9, 1943, with the list by Dr. Julian Pulikowski. Source: Bibliothek der Universität Wrocław. Quoted after Prieberg.

June 3-11 and July 1940:
Dr. Gerigk undertakes a second trip to Poland and, with the help of W. Boetticher, searches in Krakow and Warsaw for German music or music that is to be requisitioned for Germany. With the authorization of the Governor General, the two confiscate from the holdings of the State Library and two other libraries in Warsaw, among other things, manuscripts by Chopin's teacher Joseph Elsner and steal two suitcases of material from the Chopin Institute. Quoted after Prieberg, 2001-2002.[9]

October 7, 1940:
(1) Dr. Gerigk issues a confirmation for Pg. Dr. Wolfgand Boetticher that he is traveling to Warsaw on behalf of "our office" in order to pack and transport the material collected there by Governor General Frank for the "Rosenberg office" (source: BA NS 15/6).

(2) In a second certificate of the same date, Gerigk detailed the work assignment for Dr. Boetticher, namely to inspect the warehouses of Polish branches of

---

9 3. bis 11. Juni und Juli 1940: Dr. Gerigk unternimmt eine zweite Reisen ach Polen und forscht mit Hilfe W. Boettichers in Krakau und Warschau nach deutschen oder für Deutschland zu requierenden Musikalien. Mit Ermächtigung des Generalgouverneurs beschlagnahmen die beiden aus derm Bestand der Staatsbibliothek und zweier anderer Bibliotheken Warschaus u.a. Handschiften von Chopins Lehrer Joseph Elsner und lassen zwei Koffer material aus dem Chopin-Institut mitgehen.

"Columbia" and "His Master's Voice" and search for recordings of Jewish and other harmful music and to confiscate them (source: BA NS 15/6).[10]

Among other things:10. Dr. Boetticher at the church registry in Warsaw. 12? XI/42, because of the denomination (and descent) of the Polish pianist and composer Thekla Badarszewska (1838-1865). 11. Dr. Gerigk to Kielce Registry Office, November 12, 1942, concerning the descent of the musicologist Leopold Binental.[11]

A letter from the AR, Special Staff Musik, Dr. Boetticher, to the Chief of the Military Administrative District of Paris, 13/I/41, stating that the confiscated instruments of Landowska were not French art property but "ownerless Jewish property," for which reason access was given (Source: ACDJC, Document CCXXXI-22).[12]

---

10 Quoted after Prieberg, who on the page 6443 describes Boetticher's doctoral thesis on Schumann, and on the page 8062 quotes the letter of Dr. Boetticher from the Sonderstab Musik to the *Reichsministerium fur die besetzten Ostgebiete*, of July 24, 1943, about delivery of 120 pianos to the SM. "7. Oktober 1940: (1) Dr. Gerigk stellt eine Bestätigung für Pg. Dr. Wolfgand Boetticher aus, dass dieser im Auftrag 'unserer Dienststelle' nach Warschau reise, um das dort von Generalgouverneur Frank für die "Dienststelle Rosenberg" freigegebene Material zu verpacken und abzutransportieren (Quelle: BA NS 15/6).

(2) In einer zweiter Bescheinigung Gleichen Datums detalliert Gerigh den Arbeitsauftrag für Dr. Boetticher, nämlich Durchsicht der Lager der polnischen Zweigfirmen von 'Columbia' und 'His Master's Voice' auf jüdische und zersetzende Schallplatten und deren Beschlagnahme (Quelle BA NS 15/6)".

11 "11. Dr. Gerigk an Standesamt Kielce, November 12, 1942, wegen Abkunft des Musikwissenschaflers Leopold Binental. Prieberg 8066: quotes Verfahren im ARR, (Hauptstelle) Amt Musik, betreffs *Fragen des Lexikon der Juden in der Musik II* (Source: BA NS 15/21 a, unpaginiert)." Ibid.

12 8068: Schreiben des AR, Sonderstab Musk, Dr. Boetticher, an den Chef des ilitärverwaltungsbezirks Paris, 13/I/41, mit dem Hinweis, die beschlagnahmten Instrumente der Landowska seien nicht französischer Kunstbesitz, sondern "herrenloses jüdisches Gut", weshalb der Zugriff gegeben war (Quelle: ACDJC, Document CCXXXI-22).

("Schreiben des Sonderstabes Musik, Dr. Boetticher, an Reichsministerium fur die besetzten Ostgebiete, 24/VII/43, über Abgabe von 120 Klavieren an dieses").

Prieberg 8066: quotes Vorgang im ARR, (Hauptstelle) Amt Musik, betreffs Fragen des Lexikons der Juden in der Musik II (Quelle: BA NS 15/21 a, unpaginiert). Darin u.a.:

10. Dr. Boetticher an Kirchenbuchstelle Warschau. 12/XI/42, wegen Konfession (und Abkunft) der polnischen Pianistin und Komponistin Thekla Badarszewska [original ortograph] (1838-1865).

Appendix to Chapter two

Bibliothèque Cantonale de Lausanne
Erlaubniskarte issued by the Abteilung Propaganda im Amt des Distrikts Warschau for composer and pianist Constantin Regamey

Dr. Friedrich Gollert, *Warschau unter deutsche Herrschaft* ("Warsaw under German rule"), published in Cracow in 1942, for the third anniversary of the outbreak of the war. Preface by Dr. Ludwig Fischer, der Gouverneur des Distrikts Warschau, SA-Gruppenführer.

The *Vorwort* in translation:

On the occasion of the second anniversary of the General Government, I commissioned a report on the work carried out in the Warsaw district. This work was published in a book form under the title „Two years of reconstruction work in the district of Warsaw".

After only a few weeks, 3000 copies of the book were sold out. Numerous orders from the Reich could no longer be fulfilled. In view of the strong interest that arose in the *Generalgouvernement* in general, I have therefore decided to publish a second, greatly expanded and completely revised edition of the book.

This new book is the standard work on German reconstruction work in the Warsaw district. It is a historical document of the quiet work of the German men and women who have been working here since the foundation of the *Generalgouvernement*. It should make them sure that their work, which often had to be carried out under the most difficult conditions and which by its very nature could receive little external recognition, has not been forgotten.

In addition, it should give all those who wish to familiarize themselves with the East, a brief introduction to some of the manifold problems posed by the newly won territories.

Dealing with these questions is one of the socio-political duties of every German today.

The *Generalgouvernement* offers the best illustrative material for this: In it, the redesigning of the eastern region (*Ostraum*) has already been tackled with complete success in the midst of the largest war in world history.

Warsaw, 1 September 1942, on the third anniversary of the beginning of the war.

Ludwig Fischer
Gouverneur

By decree of Dr. Ludwig Fischer, the "governor of the Warsaw district" (*Gouverneur des Distrikts Warschau*), the ghetto in Warsaw was established on October 2, 1940.

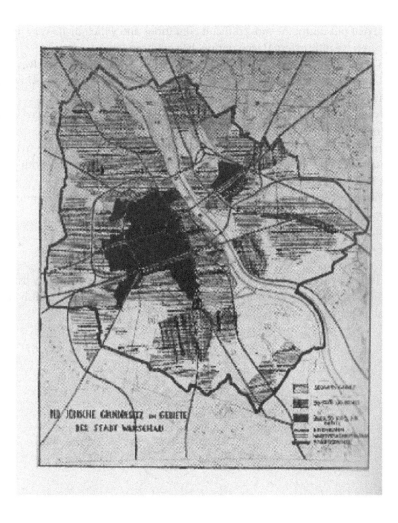

This "Guide through Warsaw" published in 1942 contains a map of "Jewish property in the territory of the city of Warsaw," with areas marked as "30-50% of Jewish property" and "over 50-100% of Jewish property."

BEKANNTMACHUNG

OBWIESZCZENIE

Announcement in German and Polish issued in Warsaw District on September 5, 1942, "Concerning the death penalty for supporting jews [original spelling] who crossed the border of the jewish quarter without authorization."[13] Text of the announcement:

> "Recently, a larger number of jews got out without permission from the district designated for them. They are still within the limits of the Warsaw district.
> I would like to draw your attention to the fact that the third decree of the General Governor dated 15.10.1941 (VBl. GG. S. 595) stipulates that not only jews will be sentenced to death for crossing the border of the jewish quarter, but anyone who in any way assists them in hiding. I point out that not only admitting jews to one's house for the night and providing them with food is considered as abetting them, but also providing whatsoever means of transport, buying whatsoever goods from them, etc.
> I appeal to the population of the Warsaw district to report immediately to the nearest police station or gendarmerie any jew who is outside the boundaries of the jewish district without authorization.
> Whoever aided a jew or is still aiding one, and reports by 9.9. 1942, 4 PM, to the nearest police station or the gendarmerie, will not be held accountable.
> Also those who have purchased any goods from jews and return them by the same time to the address ... will not be held accountable.

---

13 Bekanntmachung: Betr.: Todesstrafe für Unterstützung von Juden, die die jüdischen Wohnbezirke unbefugt verlassen haben [Inc.:] In der letzten Zeit haben sich zahlreiche Juden aus den ihnen zugewiesennen Wohnbezirken unbefugt entfernt [...]: Warschau, den 5. September 1942

Appendix 277

BN

Poster advertising concerts at the famous Café-Bar "U Aktorek" (at Piusa XI street, 12), an establishment founded by actresses who did not want to collaborate and worked there as waitresses. Concert on October 27, 1941 features Eugenia Umińska who performed Beethoven's Violin Concerto with the accompaniment of two pianos (probably played by Witold Lutosławski and Andrzej Panufnik). Below is the information that the piano duo Lutosławski-Panufnik plays there every day.

BN

Poster of April 28, 1944, Friday – W. Lutosławski i A. Panufnik (piano duo) at the SiM (Sztuka i Moda, Art and Fashion) Café in Warsaw at Królewska 11 street, "Composers' Concert"
Visible stamp of German office authorizing texts of such announcements.

BN

Poster advertising the famous piano duo of Władysław Szpilman and Andrzej Goldfeder, which performed in the Warsaw Ghetto. Goldfeder, who graduated from the Warsaw Conservatory in 1924 (he studied with Henryk Melcer-Szczawiński), changed his first name during the war (he replaced Adolf with Andrzej). He escaped the ghetto and survived two years with the help of Michał Gabriel Karski (1895-1978), a translator of poetry and literature and an author of the book *Hitler, podpalacz Europy* (*Hitler, the arsonist of Europe*, Warsaw: Universum, 1932). During the Warsaw Uprising they were separated. Andrzej

Goldfeder was shot by Germans in a small town near Warsaw at the end of 1944, a week before the Soviet army entered this area.[14]

Poster designed by the renowned photographer Benedykt Dorys, ca. 1942.

Benedykt Dorys (1901—1990) survived the war with the help of Czesław Olszewski (1894—1969), eminent Polish photographer, who also held clandestine concerts at his apartment.

Appendix to 2.1.1. Poles for Poles

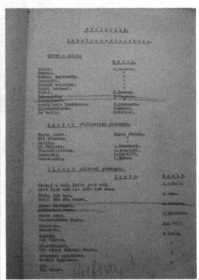

Wójcik Family Archive

Concert café programme with annotations by a Nazi censor.

---

14 Curcumstances of his death are from https://new.getto.pl/pl/Osoby/G/Goldfeder-Adolf-Nieznane.

Roman Padlewski – composer, musicologist and violinist – during the occupation.

German documents – photograph of Andrzej Tokarski (No. 2367) as prisoner in KL Auschwitz, after he was caught in a round-up in Warsaw, and telegram informing on his death in the camp.

Propaganda through music for Poles as presented by the German media

Propagandistic press for Poles: article and photographic material about dancing and music at the Warsaw café Lardelli

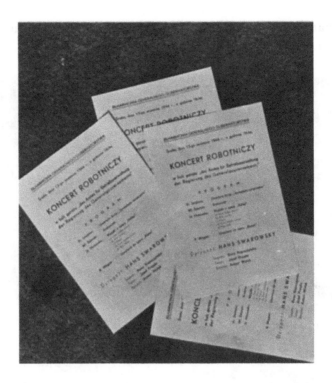

Propagandistic posters advertising music events for Polish workers (in Polish):
"The General Government Philharmonic: Workers concert in the garage hall of the Amt für Betriebsverwaltung der Regierung des Generalgouvernement (Office of Business Administration of the GG Government), Wednesday, September 13, 1944, at 4 p.m.

Programme: Smetana – *Overture to Opera "The Bartered Bride"*; Władysław Żeleński – Krakowiak; Stanisław Moniuszko – Excerpts from the opera *Halka*; Wagner *Overture to opera "Rienzi"*. Conductor: Hans Swarowsky. Soprano Rena Kopaczyńska, tenor: Józef Prząda, Baritone: Antoni Wolak

Appendix to 2.1.2. Germans for Germans

Another propagandistic German publication, Karl Grundmann, "Guide through Warsaw: with numerous illustrations, list of German authorities, public institutions, information about the district and city map with new German street names" (*Führer durch Warschau: mit zahlreichen Abbildungen, Verzeichnis der deutschen Behörden, öffentlichen Einrichtungen, angaben über den Distrikt und Stadtplan mit neuen deutschen Strassenbezeichnungen*) (Krakau: Buchverlag Deutscher Osten, 1942)

Appendix

The publication also contains documentation of German musical life and education. Above: concert at the Wilanów Palace.

A German school in Sokołów

Appendix

NS - Reichssinfonie - Orchester

Die Dresdner Philharmoniker in Warschau

Ernste Bilanz, in ORR Ohlenbusch: *Der kulturelle Aufbau*. In: Max Freiherr du Prel, *Das Generalgouvernement*. Im Auftrage und mit einem Vorwort von Generalgouverneur Reichsminister Dr. Frank. 1942, 142-143:

"Not all public offices were even in place when many German theatres were already giving guest performances in the larger cities, and barely six weeks after the establishment of the General Government, the Vienna Philharmonic Orchestra with Hans Knappertsbusch was already visiting Cracow. In the following years, some of the best theatres from the Reich gave guest performances in the

General Government, the most important orchestras gave concerts, and outstanding artists were welcomed here as soloists or in ensembles. As early as the summer of 1940, large open-air festivals were held in Warsaw, followed by the establishment of a permanent theatre in the fall. On September 1, 1940, exactly one year after the beginning of the memorable campaign, the State Theater of the General Government, built on the personal initiative of the Governor General, opened its doors in Krakow with a festive performance of Hebbel's 'Agnes Bernauer' (...).

Staging of six great classical works, twelve plays and comedies, two operettas and two ensemble guest performances of the Vienna State Opera and the Royal Opera Vittorio Emanuele-Florence is the proud outcome of the past season. The German Orchestra of the State Theater not only performed stage music, but also organized a series of symphonic concerts, which revealed the astonishingly high level of the ensemble, which consisted mostly of young musicians. In the 1941/42 season, the State Theater began to perform opera, operetta and ballet with its own cadre, in addition to plays and concerts."[15]

---

15 "Noch waren gar nicht alle Dienststellen vorhanden, da gastierte bereits manche deutsche Bühne in den grösseren Städten, und kaum sechs Wochen nach Errichtung des Generalgouvernements waren schon die Wiener Philharmoniker mit hans Knappertsbusch in Krakau zu Gast. In der Folgezeit hat manche der ersten Bühnen des Reiches ein Gastpiel im Generalgouvernement absolviert, die bedeutendsten Orchester veranstalteten Konzerte, und hervorragende Künstler konnten als Solisten ode rim Ensemble hier begrüsst warden. Bereits im Sommer 1940 fanden in Warschau grosse Freilicht-Festspiele statt, denen im Herbst die Errichtung eines ständigen Theaters folgte. Am 1. September 1940, auf den Tag genau ein Jahr nach Beginn des denkwürdigen Feldzugs, öffnete in Krakau das Staatstheater des Generalgouvernements, das auf persönliche Anregung des Generalgouverneurs errichtet wurde, mit einer Festaufführung von Hebbels 'Agnes Bernauer' seine Tore (...)
Die Aufführung von sechs grossen klassichen Werken, zwölf Schauspielen und Komödien, zweit Operetten nd zwei Ensemble-Gastspielen der Staatsoper Wien sowie der Kgl. Oper Vittorio Emanuele-Florenz sind die stolze Bilanz der abgelaufenen Spielzeit. Das Deutsche Orchester des Staatstheaters diente nicht zur Besteitung der Bühnenmusik, sondern veranstatete selbst auch eine Reihe von Symphonie-Konzerten, die das erstaunlich hohe Niveau des zum grössten Teil aus junger Musikern bestehenden Klankörpers offenbarten. In der Spielzeit 1941/42 hat das Staatstheater begonnen, nebem Schauspiel und Konzerten auch Oper, Operette und ballet mit eigenen Kräften zur Aufführung zu bringen."

Appendix

"Warschauer Zeitung" of November 1-2, 1940

Advertisement of the "Second Symphonic concert" on November 3, 1930 at the Staats-Theater des GG, featuring among others excerpts from Wagner and the favourite Nazi contemporary composer Pfitzner (*Ouverture to Kleist's "Kätchen von Heilbronn"*), promoted in the GG. On the right advertisements of cafes and "varietés," which were marked by the GG authorities as „nur für Deutsche." In Café Club on the corner of Nowy Świat Street (later, on October 24, 1942 and on July 11, 1943 attacked by the communist underground in revenge for mass executions of prisoners at the Pawiak prison), the "Orchestra" lead by Bronisław Stasiak is advertised. As in the case of several other musicians in occupied Warsaw, playing at the cafes was a cover for this well-known jazz trumpeter who also performed with his big band at Bodega and Swann, other clubs "for Germans only." He is featured on propagandistic German photographs. In April 1942 he was arrested for his underground activity, in March transported to Auschwitz and murdered in Buchenwald.

Appendix to 2.1.3. Music by Jews for Jews

By decree of Dr. Ludwig Fischer, "governor of Warsaw district" (*Gouverneur des Distrikts Warschau*) the ghetto in Warsaw was established on October 2, 1940

File concerning decrees by Heinz Auerswald,[16] Commissar of the "Jewish residential district" (*Kommissar für den jüdischen Wohnbezirk*) in Warsaw.

---

16 Heinz Auerswald (1908-1970), lawyer. Since 1933 SS member, since 1939 – NSDAP. Officer of the *Schutzpolizei* during the Polish campaign. Afterwards Head of the Department of Population and Welfare at the District Chief of Warsaw (*Leiter der Abteitlung Bevölkerungswesen und Fürsorge beim Distriktchef Warschau*). Between April 1940 and November 1942 *Ghettokommissar*. After deportation of the ghetto inhabitants to Treblinka he was appointed district governor in Ostrów. From January 1943 Wehrmacht. After 1945 lawyer in Düsseldorf. Klee, *Das Personenlexikon zum Dritten Reich*, 21.

Akten Auerswald Blatt: 0606	Auerswald Files: Sheet: 0606[17]
Allgemeines. a. Der Obmann des Judenrates hat die Weisung erhalten, versäumt von allen Fällen einen Bericht zu erstatten, in denen der Wasserzufluss im jüdischen Wohnbezirk gesperrt wurde. In Beantwortung der Weisung ist ein Verzeichnis von 62 Häusern vorgelegt worden, darunter 47-wegen Nichtregelung der Gebühren. b. Es ist ein Verzeichnis der Kraftwagen im jüdischen Wohnbezirk übersandt worden. c. Den Behörden wurde das Verzeichnis von 332 gewesenen Offizieren überreicht. d. Die Behörden wurden von der Inbetriebsetzung von 6 Omnibussen auf der behördlich genehmigten Strecke in Kenntnis gesetzt. e. Der Obmann des Judenrates hat die Weisung erhalten, die Ordnungsposten bei den instandgesetzten Mauern Waliców-Ceglanastr. zu verstärken, wo Beschädigungen entstanden sind. f. Die Behörden haben die Weisung erteilt, den Strassenabschnitt Stawki 1-19 für den Verkehr abzusperren und Durchgänge zu diesen Häusern von der Niska - bzw. Pokornastr. zu schaffen. g. Der Obmann des Judenrates hat sich an die Behörden um die Genehmigung gewendet, die Wohnungen im Hause Pawia 21, das von der polnischen Gefängniswache geräumt wurde, in Empfang zu nehmen. h. Die Behörden haben die Weisung erteilt, dass:	General. a. The chairman of the Judenrat has been instructed to report without fail on all cases when the water inflow in the Jewish residential district was blocked. In response to the directive, a list of 62 houses has been submitted, including 47 for failure to pay fees. b. A list of motor vehicles in the Jewish residential district has been sent. c. The authorities were given a list of 332 former officers. d. The authorities have been informed of the entry into service of 6 buses on the officially approved route. e. The chairman of the Judenrat has received instructions to strengthen the order posts at the repaired walls on Waliców and Ceglana streets where damage has occurred. f. The authorities have issued instructions to close the road section Stawki 1-19 to traffic and to create passages to these houses from Niska and Pokorna streets. g. The chairman of the Judenrat has appealed to the authorities for permission to receive the apartments in the house Pawia 21, which was vacated by the Polish prison guard. h. The authorities have issued instructions that:

---

17 Akten Auerswald: Blatt: 0606 (page 2). Administrative measures concerning the Warsaw ghetto (among other things, work deployment inside and outside the ghetto; prosecution, addition of various firms, monthly reports of the Chairman of the Jewish Council in Warsaw. Commissar of the Jewish residential district (files Auerswald). Originally 650 pages have been taken on inventory. Number of directly linked document: 698.

Akten Auerswald Blatt: 0606	Auerswald Files: Sheet: 0606[17]
1. Vorführungen in den Theatern, Kaffeehäusern, Varietés, sowie alle Konzertveranstaltungen einer Genehmigung und Bestätigung des Programms bedürfen, das unmittelbar dem Herrn Kommissar für den jüdischen Wohnbezirk vorzulegen ist; 2. die Ausführung von Musikwerken nicht-jüdischer Komponisten verboten ist; 3. die Inbetriebsetzung von neuen Buchhandlungen oder Leinbüchereien einer Genehmigung bedarf; den Buchhandlungen und Leihbüchereien ist es verboten, Bücher in deutscher Sprache, wie auch fremdspräche zu verkaufen oder auszuleihen.	1. Performances in theatres, coffee houses, variety shows, as well as all concert events require approval and confirmation of the programme, which must be submitted directly to the Commissioner for the Jewish Residential District; 2. the performance of musical works by non-Jewish composers is prohibited; 3. the opening of new bookshops or lending libraries is subject to authorization; bookshops and lending libraries are prohibited from selling or borrowing books in German as well as other foreign languages.

Żydowski Instytut Historyczny im. Emanuela Ringelbluma, 226. Ring. II_121007

Oratorio music concert on October 19, 1941, at the Great Synagogue of Warsaw at Tłomackie. Great Synagogue Choir conducted by its log-time conductor Dawid Ajzensztadt and Jewish Symphonic Orchestra conducted by Marian

---

Immediate source of acquisition or transfer: Zentrale Stelle Ludwigsburg, Received on: 1978-07-07. ITS 1.2.7.7. Reference Code: 9031100.

Neuteich with soloists: soprano Maria Ajzensztadt, violinist H. Reinberg and Israel Fajwiszys on organ.

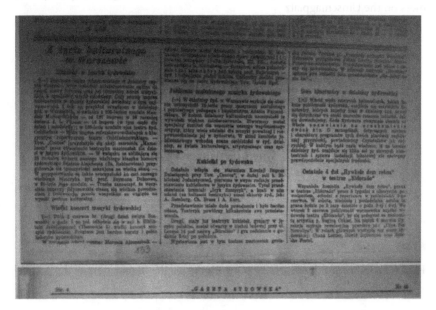

"Gazeta żydowska" and the description of the concert of Josima Feldshuh (1929 – 1943), a prodigy child – piano virtuoso and composer who had her debut in the Warsaw Ghetto and died from tuberculosis when her parents managed to leave the ghetto with her.

Marysia Ajzensztadt, the "Nightingale of the Ghetto", murdered by German soldiers on the Umschlagplatz

NAC

Pianist Leon Boruński murdered in Otwock during the "liquidation" of the hospital

NAC
Andrzej Włast

Photograph reproduced after Isachar Fater, *Muzyka żydowska w Polsce w okresie międzywojennym*, 222.

Jakub Gladsztajn (Jacob Glatstein) (1895-1942) with a children's choir in the Warsaw ghetto. As Reingelblum wrote in his Chronicle, Gladsztajn taught music and singing at the „Yehudyyah" secondary school in Warsaw. He wrote music to ghetto songs with texts by Icchak Kacenelson. His brother Israel authored an opera based on Jewish motives and performed at the "Scala" theatre in the Warsaw Ghetto. The third brother, Josef was a music critic for "Fołks Cajtung" before the war. All the three brothers were murdered in the summer of 1942 in Treblinka (Ringelblum, *Kronika getta*, 598).

296 Appendix

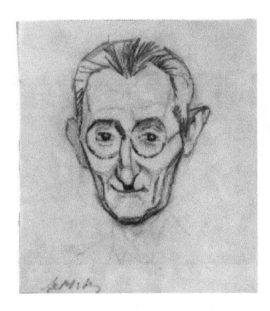

Żydowski Instytut Historyczny im. Emanuela Ringelbluma (ARG 1457 ring. I 1221)

Portrait of Israel Glatstein by Gela Seksztejn (1907-1943)

Appendix

GZ 1942 No.75 of 26 June. Advertisement of Kalman's operetta *Bajadera* adapted and directed by Iwo Wesby who had the function of musical director at the "Femina" theatre, with Helena Ostrowska and Stefania Grodzieńska among main singers. After his escape from the Warsaw Ghetto in September 1942, Iwo Wesby survived in hiding with his daughter and wife Eleonora Singer thanks to the help of the famous singer Mieczysław Fogg.

298 Appendix

> **Kawiarnia – „NOWOCZESNA" – Restauracja**
> NOWOLIPKI 10
>
> Zaprasza na następujące imprezy:
>
> **Czwartek, 6 lutego o godz. 4³⁰ pp.**
> **Wielki Festiwal Romansów Cygańskich**
> w wykonaniu powiększonej orkiestry pod batutą **ARTURA GOLDA**
> Jako soliści wystąpią: Znakomity pianista **Władysław SZPILMAN**
> Słynny skrzypek-wirtuoz **Arkadi FLATO**
> W programie: Najpiękniejsze romanse i czardasze, przeróbki jazzowe ze znanych filmów, utwory własne i inne. W części koncertowej wykonana zostanie II-ga RAPSODIA LISZTA ════ Wejście bezpłatne.
>
> **Sobota, 8 lutego o godz. 12 w pol.**
> **WIELKI PORANEK DZIECIĘCY**
> z udziałem znakomitego zespołu dziecięcego **Haliny Ajzenberżanki**
> Jako soliści wyst.: Polcia Szwarcbard, Irka Rozenfried, Ironka Zylberberg
> oraz fenomenalna 10 letnia śpiewaczka LUSIA CYWIAK
> W programie: Muzyka, Tańce, Śpiewy, Recytacje.
> Zabawę prowadzi ulubieniec milusińskich **MICHAŁ ZNICZ**
> Całkowity dochód przeznaczony na „Doraźną Pomoc Zimową".
>
> **Niedziela, 9 lutego o godz. 12 w pol.**
> WIELKI PORANEK p. t. **»W KRAINIE TANGA«**
> Udział biorą:
> Powiększona orkiestra **Artura Golda** oraz doangażowani
> harmoniści i gitarzyści
> Jako soliści wystąpi: Mistrz bel-canto
> znakomity baryton **Salvatore Kuszes**
> Artysta Opery „Theatro Liriko" w Mediolanie
> W programie: Poraz pierwszy w Warszawie oryginalne tanga
> argentyńskie, brazylijskie i hiszpańskie.
> Ponadto: **WŁADYSŁAW LIN**, mistrz słowa, aktualności i satyry
> **ANNA FISCHERÓWNA**, amerykańskie piosenki jazzowe.
>
> Sala dobrze ogrzana. Prosimy o wczesniejsze rezerwowanie miejsc.
> Bilety do nabycia w kasie Kawiarni „Nowoczesna", Nowolipki 10.
>
> Druk. Melcer i Korlan, Warszawa   1941 r.

Żydowski Instytut Historyczny im. Emanuela Ringelbluma, ARG 392 Ring I 1008.

Advertisements of concerts at the "Nowoczesna" Café at Nowolipki Street 10:
On February 6, 1941, at 4.30 PM, by "Grand Festival of Gypsy Romances performed by a an enlarged orchestra under the baton of Artur Gold," with

Appendix 299

soloists "eminent pianist Władysław Szpilman and famous violinist-virtuoso Arkadi Flato.

Żydowski Instytut Historyczny im. Emanuela Ringelbluma, ARG 394 Ring 777 100002.

Poster of the "Jewish Symphonic Orchestra" in the Warsaw Ghetto, advertising the "Second of the Symphonic Concerts Cycle" with Marian Neuteich (conductor) and Helena Ostrowska (soprano) on August 2, 1941. The concert was played twice: at noon at the Melody Palace hall, on Rymarska Street 12 and at 5 p.m. at the Great Hall on Sienna Street 16.

Żydowski Instytut Historyczny im. Emanuela Ringelbluma

Advertisement of the "Second Symphonic Concert" with Helena Ostrowska (soprano), Marian Neuteich (conductor) and the Jewish Symphonic Orchestra on a wall in the Warsaw Ghetto.

Władysław Szlengel, A Window to the Other side

Mam okno na tamtą stronę,	I have a window to the other side,
bezczelne żydowskie okno	an impudent Jewish window
na piękny park Krasińskiego,	on the beautiful Krasiński park,
gdzie liście jesienne mokną…	full of wet autumn leaves…
A mnie w oknie stanąć nie wolno	And I am not allowed to stand in the window
(bardzo to słuszny przepis),	(a most appropriate ordinance, indeed),
Żydowskie robaki… krety…	Jewish worms… moles…
powinni i muszą być ślepi.	should and have to be blind.
Pod wieczór szaroliliowy	Towards the greylilac evening
składają gałęzie pokłon	branches make a bow
i patrzą się drzewa aryjskie	and Aryan trees stare

w to moje żydowskie okno...	into my Jewish window...
Niech siedzą w barłogach, norach w robotę z utkwionym okiem i wara im od patrzenia i od żydowskich okien...	Let them sit in their pits, burrows eyes fixed on work and away from staring and from their Jewish windows away...
A ja... kiedy noc zapada... by wszystko wyrównać i zatrzeć, dopadam do okna w ciemności i patrzę... żarłocznie patrzę...	And me... when the night is falling... to balance all things and efface them, I stand in the window in darkness and stare... voraciously stare...
i kradnę zgaszoną Warszawę, szumy i gwizdy dalekie, zarysy domów i ulic, kikuty wieżyc kalekie...	and I am stealing the extinguished Warsaw, its distant rustles and whistles, outlines of streets and houses, stumps of its crippled towers...
Kradnę sylwetkę Ratusza, u stóp mam plac Teatralny, pozwala księżyc Wachmeister na szmugiel sentymentalny...	I am stealing the City Hall's silhouette, the Theatre Square at my feet, the Wachmeister moon tolerates a little bit of sentimental smuggling...
Wbijają się oczy żarłocznie, jak ostrza w pierś nocy utkwione, w warszawski wieczór milczący, w miasto me zaciemnione...	My voracious eyes penetrate, like blades, the bosom of night, the silent Warsaw evening, my city blackened throughout...
A kiedy mam dosyć zapasu na jutro, a może i więcej... żegnam milczące miasto, Magicznie podnoszę ręce... zamykam oczy i szepcę: – Warszawo... odezwij się... czekam...	And when the stock is sufficient for tomorrow and maybe more... I bid farewell to the silent city, Magically I raise my hands... I close my eyes and whisper: – Warsaw... speak... I am waiting...
Wnet fortepiany w mieście podnoszą milczące wieka... podnoszą się same na rozkaz ciężkie, smutne, zmęczone... i płynie ze stu fortepianów	Soon pianos in the city lift up their silent lids... raising themselves to the command heavy, somber and tired... and from a hundred pianos there drifts

w noc... Szopenowski polonez...	into the night... Chopin's polonaise...
Wzywają mnie klawikordy,	The clavichords are calling me,
w męką nabrzmiałej ciszy	in anguished swollen silence
płyną nad miastem akordy	chords float over the city
spod trupio białych klawiszy...	from under the dead-white keys...
Koniec... opuszczam ręce...	The end... I lower my hands...
wraca do pudeł polonez...	the polonaise returns to the boxes....
Wracam i myślę, że źle jest	I turn and think that it's bad
mieć okno na tamtą stronę...	to have a window to the other side...

Żydowski Instytut Historyczny im. Emanuela Ringelbluma
Emaciated violinist playing in the Warsaw Ghetto street

Appendix 303

The cover (designed by Mieczysław Berman) to the brochure by Bernard (Ber) Mark, entitled *The Uprising in the Warsaw Ghetto*, Moscow: Nakładem Związku Patriotów Polskich w ZSRR (Published by the Union of Polish Patriots in the USSR), 1944. Fragment of the text, documenting the specific "soundscape" of killings accompanied by a Nazi song (from pages 6-7):

(...) a bullet in the head for teaching children, for praying in forbidden synagogues, for selling books, for talking to a companion in misery at work, for hiding pieces of leather, for making new shoes, for sewing clothes from new material; a bullet in the head for getting married under the age of 28, for providing medical assistance to the elderly and children and patients with infectious diseases. Death mows down people, with a hail of bullets from an armoured car, which – just for fun – is penetrating the ghetto streets. And at the gate – the black, gloomy, heavy gate, blocking the whole world and the life – the Nazi guards strike up conversations with the Jews caught for hard labour and sneer: "You have no shame; your brothers in Germany, in Austria, have honour; deprived of their rights, they took their own lives. And you? Cowards!"
A day in the ghetto.
The night in the ghetto is terrible – muffled moans of smugglers shot at the ghetto wall and the sound of falling bodies, sudden manhunts, restless sleep. But the day is even more terrible. (...) At the end of the ghetto, on the Square of Arms, lies a huge open-air mortuary surrounded by barbed wire. Here lie thousands of corpses of typhus victims – the elderly, children, women. Here piles of corpses are piled up – victims of hunger, exhaustion, beatings.
The sun rises. With an incredible screech, the gate opens. A unit of the auxiliary Nazi police enters the interior, a motley crew of thugs and criminal criminals from Germany and various countries occupied by the swastika knights. They know neither Polish nor Jewish, but holler the *Horst-Wessel-lied*'s words with particular satisfaction:
Und wenn vom Messer spritzt das Judenblut,

Och, ist as wohl und gut.
- And when Jewish blood gushes from under the knife, how good and how pleasant!

Commentary to the Horst-Wessel-lied quoted in the book Powstanie w ghettcie warszawskim:

The German text of the song is closer in fact to the fourth stanza of the "beloved" SA song *War einst ein junger Sturmsoldat* (*There once was a young stormtrooper*) quoted by Hans Bajer in his article in "Die Musik" of 1938 („Wir sind vom Gausturm Groß-Berlin / und haben frohen Mut. / Wenn das Judenblut vom Messer spritzt / dann geht's noch mal so gut). See section 1.1. *Nazi propaganda of German cultural supremacy and racial hatred.*

The *Sturmsoldaten* song, (another version of text: "Wenn der Sturmsoldat ins Feuer geht, ei, dann hat er frohen Mut, / und wenn's Judenblut vom Messer, dann gehts wieder so gut"), which was sung by the SA and which is used now under title *Blut* in the Neo-Nazi German scene (the band which sang it was convicted for incitement to crime), is an anti-Semitic variant of *Das Heckerlied*, a revolutionary song of the Baden Revolution of 1848-1849.

Appendix

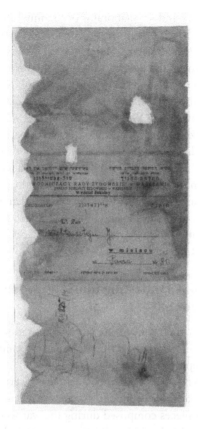

Żydowski Instytut Historyczny im. Emanuela Ringelbluma

Invitation to a school academy organized on December 21, 1941 at the "Femina" hall at 35 Leszno Street (now Aleja "Solidarności") "in connection with the opening of primary schools for Jewish children, with the participation of a children's choir under the direction of Izrael Fajwiszys (1887 Jampol – Poniatowa 1943) and singer Marysia Ajzensztadt (1921 Warsaw – 1942 Warsaw).

Invitation No. 81 issued officially by the Chairman of the Jewish Council in Warsaw, Adam Czerniakow, from the School Department of the Board of the Jewish District in Warsaw. The addressee of the invitation is I. (Izrael) Lichtensztajn who was a publicist (he was active in the Poalej Syjon-Lewica party), a teacher of secret classes and a collaborator of Emanuel Ringelblum; in the Underground Ghetto Archive he dealt with the school department.

On August 3, 1942, he buried some of the documents of the Archive in a shelter in the basement of the Borochów school at 68 Nowolipki Street. He was helped in this by two of his students from this school: Nachum Grzywacz and Dawid Graber. Both they and Lichtensztajn's wife, the outstanding painter Gela Seksztajn (1907 Warsaw – 1943 Warsaw), attached their wills to these documents.

Nachum Grzywacz wrote: "We decided to describe the present time. Yesterday we stayed up late at night because we weren't sure if we would live to this day. Now I'm in the middle of writing, and there's a terrible shooting on the street. One thing I am proud of is that in the days of the greatest calamity I was one of those who buried the treasure. [...] We have hidden these materials so that you could learn about the suffering and murder inflicted by Nazi tyranny."

Quote and information from: Barbara Engelking, Jacek Leociak, *Getto warszawskie*, 534-635, 639; Ringelblum, *Kronika*, 18.

Appendix to 2.1.6. Clandestine music as protest, resistance, and quest for freedom

Faced with a ban of normal concert life and the limitations of the repertoire by the Nazi censorship in café programmes, numerous clandestine concerts were organized in private apartments.

One of the best known private apartments where concerts were played was the one of music lover Stefan Wiśniewski, Boduen Street in Warsaw. Numerous first performances of pieces composed during the war were given there by best musicians, such as pianists Jan Ekier, Zbiegniew Drzewiecki, Andrzej Wąsowski, violinists Irena Dubiska, Eugenia Umińska, composers Konstanty Regamey and Andrzej Panufnik. A Jewish friend in hiding there was disguised as a maid.

Another example of home where concerts for public were held was the apartment of musicians and music lovers Wanda and Czesław Olszewski Polna Street 32, at the corner of Polna and Mokotowska Streets in Warsaw.

In March 1940 a concert in 130th Chopin's birthday anniversary was performed by Jan Ekier.

During the following concerts, held regularly every 2 weeks such outstanding musicians as violinist Irena Dubiska, singer Maria Faryaszewska, pianists Stefania Allinówna, Jerzy Lefeld, Stanisław Staniewicz, Władysław Walentynowicz (later deported as forced labour worker to Germany). Music recordings were also played and recitations by actors were held - among others Mariusz Maszyński (shot with his mother and sisters 6 August 1944 by soldiers of RONA, Russian Liberation Army).

On 31 May 1942 Jan Ekier and Jerzy Lefeld performed here Six Epigraphes antiques by Claude Debussy.

These concerts were held until 1942, then it was impossible anymore to organize them for a bigger amount of listeners, because the situation in the apartment changed.

Pianist and pedagogue Arkadiusz Bukin, who moved to the apartment with his pianos began to give private music lessons. Among the pupils were the hosts' son Andrzej Olszewski and Danuta Dworakowska (after the war professor at the Warsaw conservatory), Misza Iwanow (after the war director of music school in the outskirts of Warsaw), Tadeusz Smogorzewski, Aleksy Siemionow and others. Occasionally they gave children's concerts. At one of them an outstanding talent, pupil named Szymek could not perform anymore - he was murdered in the ghetto.

At this time Wanda and Czesław Olszewski began to hide Jews in the apartment and it became too dangerous to organize concerts there. For the longest period of time (over two years, until the end of the Warsaw Uprising) the excellent photographer-portraitist Benedykt Jerzy Dorys, lived there, with false papers on the name of Jerzy Roszczyk. He also worked with Olszewski at a photographic atelier, where apart from official commissions, false identity cards (Kennkarte) and other documents for the Polish Underground were prepared.

Dorys spoke of his stay at the Olszewskis' home in the book by Stefan Chaskielewicz *Ukrywałem się w Warszawie* [*I was hiding in Warsaw*] (Krakow 1988). They took care of me, because they felt Poles and wanted to save other, who also felt being Poles ".

Source: Andrzej K. Olszewski, *Moje wspomnienia z życia muzycznego podczas okupacji niemieckiej* [My Memories from the music life during the German occupation], „Saeculum Christianum" 9 (2002) No. 2.

Programme of French music concert of 31 May 1942, at the Olszewski's apartment.
Archive of Professor Andrzej Olszewski

Appendix

Armed songs, a clandestine collection of songs, published in 1943, with a fake date on the cover (1938). All the songs are published for obvious reasons anonymously. On page 14 the text by Tadeusz Gajcy, *Uderzenie* (Attack), on page 31 music to this song composed by Jan Ekier (1942).

NAC

Jan Ekier and his sister Halina during a concert before the war

A fragment of the song's text:

On our weapon, cloudy and sharp   Na broni naszej chmurnej i ostrej
we will carry the new shape of our homeland   ojczyzny nowej uniesiemy kształt,

a strike for a strike, a strike for a strike,	ciosem na cios, ciosem na cios,
for injustice an unerring shot will speak!	za krzywdę celny mówić będzie strzał!
Just hit fiercely and firmly	Tylko uderzyć zawzięcie i mocno
— under fist only a rushing march	tylko pod pięścią rozpędzony marsz
Heart like a thunder, heart like a thunder,	serce jak grom, serce jak grom,
Stand alert, face to face with the enemy.	wrogowi czujnie stanąć twarzą w twarz.

Tadeusz Gajcy (pseudonym „Witold Orczyk") 1922-1944

A fragment of another poem by Gajcy:

Śpiew murów	The Song of the Walls
Nocą, gdy miasto odpłynie w sen trzeci, a niebo czarną przewiąże się chmurą, wstań bezszelestnie, jak to czynią dzieci, i konchę ucha tak przyłóż do murów. Zaledwie westchniesz, a już cię doleci z samego dołu pięter klawiaturą w szumach i szmerach skłębionej zamieci minionych istnień bolesny głos chóru. „Bluszczem głosów spod ruin i zgliszcz pniemy się nocą nad dachy i sen, tobie, Warszawo, co w snach naszych śnisz, nucąc wrześniami żałobny nasz tren". (....)	At night, when the city drifts off into its third dream, and the sky is wrapped up in a black cloud, arise quietly, as children do, and press the conch of the ear to the walls. as soon as you sigh, you will hear, from the ground floor ascending the keyboard in rustles and whispers of a tempestuous snow storm of extinguished lives, the painful choir of voices. "In a vine of voices from ruins and carnage we rise at night above roofs and dream the dream of you, Warsaw, in our dreams, humming our mournful September threnody." (...)

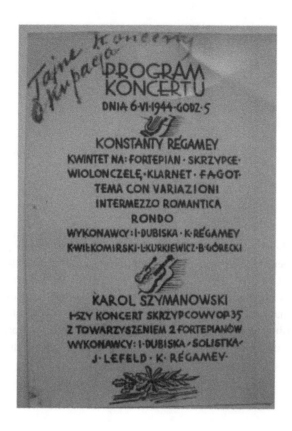

Clandestine concert programme of June 6, 1944 at 5 PM, organized to mark the date of the Normandy Invasion and featuring the performance of a newly composer work by Konstanty (Constantin) Regamey, the *Quintet*, and Karol Szymanowski's First Violin Concerto played by Irena Dubiska with the accompaniment of two pianos (Regamey and Jerzy Lefeld)

Krystyna Krahelska „Danuta" (24 March 1914 - 2 August 1944) – poet, ethnographer, member of the Home Army; author of the famous clandestine songs: *Hej, chłopcy, bagnet na broń* [Hey, lads, fix your bayonets] (1943), *Kołysanka o zakopanej broni* [A Lullaby about Buried Guns] and *Kujawiak konspiracyjny* [Conspiratorial Kujawiak] (1941-1942). Shot while helping the wounded during the Warsaw Uprising. Grażyna Kobylańska – a young coloratura soprano shot in the throat and killed by a sniper during the Warsaw Uprising while she served as a nurse with a red cross armband.

Appendix to 2.1.5. Control of the symbolic spaces

BN

27. Announcement of the City Governor in German. Subject: Seizure and surrender of radio sets
(27. Bekanntmachung des Stadthauptmanns. Betr.: Beschlagnahme und Abgabe von Rundfunkgeräten)
Cracow, January 11, 1940.

> On the basis of the decree of the Governor-General of December 15, 1939, the following is ordered for the district of the city of Kraków:

314 Appendix

All radio sets and accessories as well as all individual parts of such devices, insofar as they are in Polish or Jewish possession, are to be handed over to the city administration (town hall 3rd floor via the stairs at the main entrance) by January 25, 1940.

Citizens of the Reich and persons identifying themselves as ethnic Germans as well as the authorities must register the possession of a radio set with me in writing. The registration is certified by me.

In principle, paragraph 1 applies to the Ukrainian and Goralenvolk populations. (…)

I would point out that infringements of that order are punishable under Paragraph 5 of that regulation. Likewise, anyone who intentionally and maliciously damages a radio subject to seizure before delivery will be punished.

Cracow, 11 January.
The Governor Zörner
Lord Mayor

NAC

Poznań Opera House in November 1939, first German Nazi public meeting

Appendix 315

NAC
Public during the General Governement Philharmonic concert at the Collegium Maius court of the Jagellonian Library (renamed "Stadt Bibliothek"). September 1944
Photographed by Paul Brandner

NAC

Rudolf Hindemith, conductor of the General Government Philharmonic (right) and Paul Haslinde, intendant of the General Government Philharmonic. Cracow, May 1942

Appendix

Musicians killed during the German occupation of Poland – a few portraits

NAC

Artur Gold (1897 Warsaw– 1943 Treblinka) – famous composer of popular songs and a violinist.

Photo made in Katowice in 1933.

NAC
Photograph before 1939

Edward Bender (1903 or 1905 Lvov – 1944 Warsaw) – eminent bass singer.

After his debut at the Warsaw Opera House, he was engaged there starting in 1935. He performed at La Scala in Wagner's *The Rhine Gold* and sang alongside Feodor Chaliapin in *Boris Godunov* by Modest Mussorgsky. He performed at the

Polish Radio and at the Warsaw Philharmonic. Bender was shot on the first day of the Warsaw Uprising. (Lerski).

Róża Etkin-Moszkowska (1908-1945)
Photo she offered to her professor Zbigniew Drzewiecki, 1936
Barbara Drzewiecka Archive

An outstanding pianist, an excellent interpreter of Chopin's music, new music, eg. Alban Berg, as well as contemporary Polish composers.

She began learning to play the piano as a child; at the age of less than ten she became a student of the Fryderyk Chopin Higher School of Music in Warsaw in the class of Aleksander Michałowski – a famous pianist and pedagogue, a student of Moscheles, Tausig, Liszt and Mikuli. She made her debut two years later, in 1920, performing among others the virtuoso Etude in E flat major with Liszt's Grandes études de Paganini.

In 1924, at the age of 16, she played Rachmaninoff's Concerto in D minor with the Warsaw Philharmonic Orchestra conducted by Grzegorz Fitelberg; in 1926 with the same orchestra – Liszt's Concerto in E flat major (in April) and Bach's Concerto in D minor (in October).

She graduated from the Warsaw Conservatory under the direction of Zbigniew Drzewiecki.

In 1927 she received third place at the First Chopin Competition, as the youngest participant; she continued her studies in Berlin at the Konservatorium Klindworth-Scharwenka with Maurycy Mayer-Mahr. In May this year, she performed in Berlin at the well-known Bechstein Hall. Hugo Leichtentritt, an influential critic and musicologist of world renown, wrote about her playing at the time:

Her numerous concerts in Germany and Poland were enthusiastically received by critics. They often had very ambitious programmes, e.g. in 1931 at the Beethovensaal in Berlin Etkin performed Bach's Goldberg Variations arranged by Busoni, Schumann's Fantasy in C major and Chopin's 12 Etudes. She had an extensive piano repertoire. In Warsaw, she often performed in Polish Radio broadcasts, at the Conservatory and Philharmonic, as well as at concerts of the Polish Society for Contemporary Music, performing works by Szymanowski and other contemporary Polish composers. During the last symphonic concert of the 1937-38 season, she performed Brahms' Concerto in B flat major. It was written about her at the time that "among the generation of young Jewish pianists in Poland, the artist should be awarded the first place."

RÓŻA ETKINÓWNA

Her husband was Ryszard Moszkowski, an architect, a well-known sculptor and violin collector, whom she met in Berlin. He was the son of the brother of the composer Maurycy Moszkowski.

She survived the German occupation in Warsaw, hiding all the time because of her Jewish origin in the homes of Polish friends. On January 16, 1945, she was tracked down by the Germans in Warsaw's Żoliborz district and murdered together with her husband.[18]

Marian Neuteich

 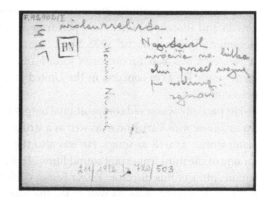

BN

Marian Neuteich, 1930, portrayed by Benedict Jerzy Dorys (1901-1990), Print on silver-gelatin paper, 1962. On the back, a note with the photographer's hand: "He came for a few days before the war to take his family [abroad] and perished."
Published with the consent of the author's heir, professor Ludwik Dobrzyński.

Marian Neuteich (1906 Łódź – 1943) – composer, conductor, cellist, teacher. A graduate of the Warsaw Conservatory, where he studied composition with Kazimierz Sikorski. His cello teacher was Eli Kochański, and his conductors were Grzegorz Fitelberg and Adam Dołżycki.

He was an outstanding musician, much appreciated in musical circles, as evidenced by his functions. Shortly after graduation, he became president and principal conductor of the Symphony Orchestra of the Association of Music Societies. He was a member of the board of the Polish Society for Contemporary

---

18 Dybowski, *Słownik*.

Music and the Trade Union of Musicians. Marian Neuteich served as treasurer of the board elected at the general meeting of PTMW on 18 April 1937. At that time, the board also included Michał Kondracki and Roman Palester, while Zbigniew Drzewiecki was the president, Konstanty Regamey and Bolesław Woytowicz were the vice-presidents, and Barbara Podoska (Palester's wife) was the secretary. At the first concert organized by the Polish Society for Contemporary Music in 1935, a fragment of Marian Neuteich's Quartet, Bolesław Woytowicz's *Little Children's Cantata* for three voices, piano works by Jan Ekier, Piotr Perkowski and Roman Palester were performed, as we learn from a review by K. Regamey ("Prosto z mostu" 1935, No. 4-5, p. 7).

Neuteich was also a member of Józef Kamiński's Warsaw String Quartet for many years. He gave concerts in the United States, Argentina and many European countries.

His partially preserved compositional output includes works for string quartet (m.in *Theme with* Variations), as well as a string trio, cello sonata, orchestral and piano works, as well as songs. He was also the author of film music, including for one of the most important sound films, *Dzikie pola* by Józef Lejtes and other famous films of this director: *Young Forest, Girls from Nowolipki, Border, A Day of Great Adventure, Rose*, as well as for the film *Knights of Darkness* by Bruno Bredschneider and Stefan Szwarc.

During the occupation, he was imprisoned in the ghetto, where he organized a symphony orchestra in the ghetto, together with other outstanding musicians, Szymon Pullman and Adam Furmański. The Jewish Symphony Orchestra played with about 66 musicians, operating in extremely difficult conditions, lacking many instruments, but nevertheless performed works by Beethoven, Mozart, Haendel, Weber, Dvořák, Tchaikovsky and Mendelssohn.[19]

Singer Helena Ostrowska

One of the few surviving documents of Neuteich's conducting activity in the ghetto is a poster announcing his concert with the participation of Helena Ostrowska. She was a talented singer, the wife of a doctor, who – after her husband's death

---

19 Andrzej Kempa and Marek Szukalak in their *Żydzi dawnej Łodzi: Słownik Biograficzny* (Jews of Old Łódź: Biographical Dictionary) (Łódź 2001) state that "Shortly before the outbreak of the Warsaw Ghetto Uprising, Neuteich was deported by the Germans to the camp and armaments plant in Poniatowa in the Lublin region and died there." Another possible place of his death is considered to be the camp in Trawniki. Neuteich's date of birth is given in some sources as 1890.

in the ghetto – hid with her daughter on the "Aryan side" under the name Irena Jabłońska. Arrested on March 17, 1944, she and her daughter were shot in Pawiak. These facts are poignantly described by Stefania Grodzieńska who earlier performed with Ostrowska in the Warsaw Ghettto and who was hiding in the same house of Zofia and Gabriel Kijkowski in Gołąbki:

> A talented singer, a soprano after the conservatory, preparing for an opera career, found herself in the ghetto because of her origin, which was a surprise for her, as for many other Poles and Polish women.
> After one of the liquidation actions, she left the sewers together with her four-year-old daughter. Deceived by a paid guide, she wandered with the child through the sewers until she miraculously managed to get out with the help of unknown people.
> The only child of rich parents living abroad, the wife of a wealthy doctor, murdered by the Germans during the liquidation of the ghetto, pampered and served from birth, found herself among strangers, helpless, desperate, ready to return with her child to where she escaped from.
> "And God created woman..." Well, God created Zosia Kijkowska for such situations. And Zosia Kijkowska brought them both – Helena Ostrowska with her daughter Zosia – to Gołąbki.
> The cultural life of [their home] in Gołąbki was immensely revived. In a large room, next to a stove, stood an ancient piano. In the evenings, Hela sat at the piano and played and sang beautifully.
> Since the beginning of the war, none of us have heard music. We didn't go to concerts, there was no radio (it was buried in the garden). We waited all day for these evenings.
> Hela had a lot of femininity and grace. I see her sitting at the piano, tilting her blonde head with a braided crown towards us, singing opera arias, Moniuszko's songs, playing Chopin. Then we all sang military songs, legion songs, pre-war hits with her, evoking such a recent, lost reality [...]
> They drove up to the house so quietly that no one could hear anything. There were a dozen of them. Eight or nine broke into the apartment, the rest stayed outside. For the time being, they were rummaging around the ground floor, screaming and shoving. It was only from overheard fragments of the conversation with Gabriel that I understood what was going on. They were looking for Zosia. [...]
> The door opened. Two pushed Hela and Joasia. No, we couldn't blame Eli for breaking down right away. She repeated her words senselessly:
> "My name is Irena Jabłońska, I have documents". She had "good looks," she had documents, but once again the theory of Francis [Jarosy] came true, that it is not facial features, but expression that determines the recognition of "origin." With this paleness, terror in her eyes, lowered corners of her mouth, she could not raise any doubts: this was someone condemned to death. If she had been alone, she would have behaved differently and maybe she would have saved herself, but Joanna hugged her tightly and staggered with her. And she almost fell when the Gestapo man punched her mother in the face. The little girl answered questions quietly: "My dad died a long time ago, I don't remember him, my name is Zosia."

(...) On the same day, they died under false names. Hela said nothing. Nor did Joanna. (...)
The next day we learned that the Gestapo was in Gołąbki. They stayed there for a few days. They didn't learn anything. Before they left the house, they called on neighbours to bury Gabriel's corpse in the garden. The house was sealed off.

In the collection of documents edited by Regina Domańska in *Pawiak, więzienie Gestapo* (Pawiak, Gestapo's Prison) on page 436 under the date March 17, 1944, we read: "27 women were brought. Among them (...) Jabłońska Irena Maria with a child. Irena Jabłońska and her child were pulled out of the roll call."[20] They were shot.

Looted Chopin memorabilia from the collection of Leopold Binental (1886–1944), the Polish-Jewish chopinologist murdered by the Germans

---

20 Quoted after Stefania Grodzieńska, *Urodził go „Błękitny Ptak"* (Warszawa: Wydawnictwa Radia i Telewizyjne, 1988). She quotes here Regina Domańska, *Pawiak: więzienie gestapo: kronika 1939-1944*, Warszawa: Książka i Wiedza, 1978.

NAC - National Digital Archives
Leopold Binental before the war
Undated photo

Leopold Binental – musicologist, violinist, pedagogue, music critic, outstanding Chopin scholar, collector, author of seminal publications on Chopin, was a descendant of a prosperous Polish-Jewish family. He was born on January 10, 1886, in Kielce. His father Henryk (originally Haim) Binental, who married Franciszka (née Guranowski), made a fortune on land trading and then on the production of yeast, malt and spirits. He built an impressive factory on the outskirts of Warsaw, which he supervised later on with his three son – Mieczysław, Józef and Aleksander.

Because young Leopold Binental turned out to be musically gifted, his father took care of his education, and sent him to France where he studied music and musicology at the Paris Conservatory. He also studied law at the Sorbonne and graduated with excellent results. It was in Paris that he met young Janina Heilpern, who also came there from Warsaw to study painting. They married very young, in January 1908, after their return to Warsaw—Leopold was only 22 and Janina – 19. In January 1911 their only child, the daughter Krystyna, was born.

After the outbreak of the Polish-Bolshevik war, Binental volunteered for the Polish Army, and afterwards he was confirmed by the Ministry of Military Affairs in the degree of reserve lieutenant. From the end of 1919 he worked as a senior clerk at the Ministry of Culture and Arts for three years, but his vocation was to become an independent scholar and extremely gifted promoter of Polish music. He worked as music critic in „Kurier Warszawski" (1924-1939) and the in illustrated weekly magazine "World, a journal of social life, literature and art" (Świat: pismo tygodniowe ilustowane poświęcone życiu społecznemu, literaturze i sztuce). He also published articles French and German periodicals, e.g. *Documents et souvenirs* (of Chopin) in "La Revue musicale" (December 1931). In 1925 Binental organized the Polish Music Festival in Paris, the successes of which are confirmed by reports in the French press.

He became one of the most important figures at WTM as president of the scientific and publishing section of the Society. He was also professor of violin at the Fryderyk Chopin Music School run by this society and until 1939 taught a chamber music class there.

Binental also collected works of art; his collection comprised precious ancient, Middle Eastern and modern European ceramics, medieval sculpture and tapestries, gold smithery and Judaica, In his Warsaw apartment No. 8 at 15 Hoża Street, full of antiques and works of art, he also kept his valuable collection of Chopin souvenirs.

He was widely respected as a Chopin scholar and became Executive Secretary of the Board of the Fryderyk Chopin National Institute, founded in 1934. He initiated and co-organised exhibitions about Chopin in the National Museum in Warsaw (1932) and the Polish Library in Paris (1932 and 1937), which were recognized as important events, also by the French press.

He is the author of catalogues of exhibitions he created:

- Catalogue of the First Exhibition of Chopin Documents and Souvenirs (Katalog I Wystawy Dokumentów i Pamiątek Chopinowskich, organized by the WTM and the National Museum in Warsaw in 1932, published under the auspices of the Committee of the Second International Chopin Piano Competition (Warsaw, M. Garasiński, 1932);
- Catalogue of the exhibition organized at the Polish Library in Paris *Frédéric Chopin, George Sand et leurs amis* (Paris: Bibliothèque polonaise, 1937). His position as Chopin specialist was firmly established, especially from the moment when he published his monograph on Chopin, the first one in Polish (1930), and then in German (1932) and French (1934), and his subsequent works only augmented his stature. He included in his works reproductions of Chopin's notes, prints, drawings, musical manuscripts, letters and other memorabilia, which were in part owned by himself.

Chopin. W 120-tą rocznicę urodzin. Dokumenty i pamiątki (Chopin. On the 120th anniversary of his birth. Documents and mementoes). Warsaw, 1930.

Chopin: Dokumente und Erinnerungen aus seiner Heimatstadt, translated by Aleksander Guttry, Breitkopf & Härtel, Leipzig 1932. The French translation of this book – Chopin (Paris, Les Éditions Rieder, Imprimerie des Presses Universitaires de France, 1934) was awarded a prize by the French Academy.

Unfortunately all the items from Leopold Binental's Chopin collection, which he reproduced and documented in his books are now considered lost.

Drawings:

- by Fryderyk Chopin, not dated:
  - a fragment of a castle; in the background a small church surrounded by trees, pencil drawing with the composer' signature and a note: in the 2nd week of boredom [w 2-im tygodniu nudów]
  - two caricatures drawn in pencil; among them figures of two men, one in a military uniform

Appendix 327

- Teofil Kwiatkowski, Salon in the last apartment of Fryderyk Chopin at Place Vendôme 12 in Paris, watercolour; on its reverse was a note by Jane Wilhelmina Stirling, composer's student: Salon de Chopin, 12, Place Vendôme. Paris 1849

Manuscript of Chopin's song Wish [Życzenie, op. 74, No. 1] to the words of poet Adam Mickiewicz

Letters:

- 2 letters from Hector Berlioz to Fryderyk Chopin in Paris [Paris, first before May 5, 1834; second after April 1, 1839]
- letter from Frederic Chopin to Solange Clésinger in Paris, [London], 30 June [18]48.
- letter of Fryderyk Chopin to Józef Elsner in Warsaw (with address), Paris, December 14, 1831; acquired by Binental from Maria Ciechomska (granddaughter of Chopin's sister Ludwika Jędrzejewiczowa), probably before 1930.
- Chopin's card with his text written to Julian Fontana in Paris, [Paris, presumably in December 1836]
- Fryderyk Chopin to Julian Fontana in Paris, [Nohant, November 1841]
- Fryderyk Chopin to his family in Warsaw, [Calder House], 19 August 1848
- Eugène Delacroix to Fryderyk Chopin, [Paris, probably in March 1845]
- Franz Liszt to Fryderyk Chopin in Paris, [Eilsen], 26 February 1843
- Felix Mendelssohn-Bartholdy to Fryderyk Chopin in Paris with a note by Robert Schumann, Leipzig, 28 March 1836
- Robert Schumann to Fryderyk Chopin in Dresden, Leipzig, 8 September 1836 (with address)

Prints:

- Program of the first public concert of Chopin in Paris, of 25 February 1832 at the Salle Pleyel
- Franz Liszt concert program with the participation of Fryderyk Chopin, Paris, 9 April 1837
- Program of the last concert of Fryderyk Chopin in Paris, Salle Pleyel, 16 February 1848
- Notification of the funeral of Fryderyk Chopin on 30 October 1849 at the church of St. Magdalena in Paris

The Plunder of the Binental Collection

The Frederic Chopin Museum in Warsaw, mainly Hanna Wróblewska-Straus – historian of art, for many years curator and director of the Museum of the Fryderyk Chopin Association – did all they could to trace and document the unknown fate of Leopold Binental and his Chopin collection. Wróblewska-Straus also established lists of lost Chopin memorabilia. In 1966 the museum acquired the account of medical doctor Krystyna Iłowiecka-Hoffman, whose parents were friends with the Binentals. From the affidavit she gave to the museum on 15 June 1966 we know that at the beginning of the occupation the Germans harassed Binental four times (at least), breaking into his apartment, taking the manuscripts and works of art that they considered most valuable. Zbigniew Drzewiecki, who was harassed by the Gestapo himself, mentions this in his memoirs: "After the outbreak of the last war, Binental was going through the whole ordeal of Gestapo persecution, and finally succeeded to escape to France. "

At the turn of February and March 1940, Leopold Binental and his wife were waiting for Swiss visas, which were obtained by Ignacy Jan Paderewski, who was then 80 years old, shortly before his death in 1941. At the time, according to an account by doctor Iłowiecka-Hoffman, "they made a fictitious sale of their apartment in order to protect their property from being completely plundered by the Germans. When the visas arrived in April 1940, the professor and his wife received permission from the German authorities to leave the General Government, along with a strictly defined list of personal belongings that they were allowed to take. In April 1940 they left the main station by train in the direction of Vienna, full of fears whether they would actually be able to get to Switzerland and anticipating the worst harassments from the Germans during the journey. […] They were heading to Paris to meet their daughter Krystyna, a student at the Academy of Fine Arts in Paris. […] After about two months we received a card from Geneva via the Swiss Red Cross with more or less this text: 'We arrived happily, we are going to Krysia tomorrow'. A few days after receiving this card Germany occupied France." On June 14, Paris was taken over by the German army. In the meantime his book Chopin – *The Artist's Life and his Art* (*Chopin – Życiorys twórcy i jego sztuka*, published in Warsaw, F. Hoesick, in 1937), appeared in a Swedish translation (Knut-Olof Falk) under title *Chopin: hans liv och konst* published by the Stockholm edition house Seelig & Co in 1940.

The Binentals arrived in France in May 1940 and they lived with their daughter in a shelter run by the Polish Red Cross. After the fall of France, a network of shelters was created, and after the liquidation of the Polish Red Cross by the German authorities, they came under the management of the Society for the Care of Poles in France. The Society was headed by prof. Zygmunt Lubicz Zalewski, historian and literary critic, friend of Binental. Thanks to the research results contained in the doctoral thesis by Henri Gielec, *Le lycée polonais Cyprian Norwid de Villard-de-Lans (1940-1946): articulation des liens historiques franco-polonais* it was possible to determine that at least for some time after the fall of France Leopold Bienental lived in exile with other members of the Polish intelligentsia and former officials of the Polish government, among them his colleague, director of the Bibliotheque polonaise in Paris, Czesław Chowaniec, at the Grand Hôtel in Grenoble.

Only when Germany attacked the territories of Val d'Isère and Vercors, and especially from the beginning of 1944, the Germans carried out searches on the premises of GAPF (Groupement d'Aide au Polonais de France) – and arrested the people hiding in exile: "Deportations to Germany for work and in concentration camps are more and more frequent. In March, 5 people were arrested at the Lasalle refuge (in the Gard), a dozen others in the Polish institutions in Toulouse, 2 people in Challes-les-Eaux. But it was the Isère department that clearly became the center of the arrests of Poles. In March, all the men from the Sappey refuge were deported to Grenoble for interrogation and torture. In the capital of the department, around fifteen people were arrested, including Feliks Chrzanowski, Jan Głębocki, Leopold Binental, Rudolf Tarczyński" (Gielec, *Le lycée polonais*, 219).

According to information from the Auschwitz-Birkenau State Museum, a transport from Drancy set off on March 27, 1944, and it arrived at KL Auschwitz on March 30, 1944. This was the 70th transport of Jews from Drancy to the extermination camps, it contained 1003 prisoners; there were seven more transports to Auschwitz-Birkenau (the last one was sent on July 21, 1944).

Leopold Binental was designated there as number 176137. In the period from April 12 to June 11, 1944, he was listed in the files of the KL Auschwitz III-Buna hospital, dated October 15 and 25, 1944. Then he was transferred to the subcamp KL Auschwitz III – Fürstengrube, where he was listed in the files of the SS "Hygiene Institut" - (Hygiene Institut der Waffen-SS und Polizei Auschwitz O / S).

No information on his wife is extant.

In the meantime the Chopin Museum which contained the Eduard Ganche collection bought by Hans Frank was triumphantly opened in Cracow. Even though this event was used as effective propagandistic material, processed from the same repeated photographs and texts and the well-known propagandistic film, we do not know if any of Binental's objects could be found there or elsewhere. According to the account of Krystyna Iłowiecka-Hofman, Binental was able to deposit his art collections at the National Museum. This was confirmed by the before-mentioned recent research by Dubiński and Świetlicka.

Krystyna Binental who was in Paris after the war before moving to the United States, found in the documents brought by her parents from Warsaw, which were extant, a depositary receipt from September 1939 issued by the National Museum in Warsaw. On December 2, 1947, she wrote to the director of the National Museum in Warsaw asking for information on "what collections of my late father Leopold Binental were found at the National Museum in Warsaw." In the letter she described the fate of her family after leaving Poland: "My late parents came to France in May 40. Then they stayed with me at the shelter of the Polish Red Cross four years. In 194(?) we were chased to the mountains to another small shelter and in March 1944 arrested by the gestapo. I survived thanks to the sacrifice of my mother and my Parents were deported to Poland and murdered in Oświęcim". In fact, it turned out that Binental managed to deposit at the National Museum in Warsaw the non-musical part of his collection in March 1940, and this in major part survived, whereas his Chopin collection perished. According to historians of art and persons specializing in the restitution of Chopin's memorabilia, precious historical documents from Leopold Binental's collection might still be extant, which requires further investigation.

List of items related to Chopin lost or stolen during the German occupation of Poland[21]

Six oil portraits of the Chopin family by painter Ambroży Mieroszewski (1829), known only from reproductions in the books of Leopold Binental, belonging to the lost personal items from the collection of Laura Ciechomska (1862–1939, Warsaw), grand-daughter of Chopin's sister, Ludwika Jędrzejewiczowa

> Mikołaj (Nicolas) Chopin and Tekla Justyna (née Krzyżanowska), Fryderyk Chopin's parents
> Fryderyk Chopin
> Izabella, Chopin's sister, married Barcińska
> Ludwika, Chopin's sister, married Jędrzejewicz
> Wojciech Żywny, Chopin's piano teacher

---

21 **List based upon research by** Hanna Wróblewska-Straus. Translated by Wojciech Bońkowski, edited by Andrea F. Bohlman for the Exhibition *Muisc in Occupied Poland* (2010).

Reproductions from: Leopold Binental, *Chopin. W 120-tą rocznicę jego urodzin. Dokumenty i pamiątki* [Chopin. On the Occasion of his 120th Birthday: Documents and memorabilia], Warszawa 1930; Leopold Binental, Czesław Chowaniec, *Frédéric Chopin, George Sand et leurs amis. Exposition à la Bibliothèque Polonaise*, exhibition catalogue, Paris 1937

Other items from the same collection were lost, such as manuscripts and letters, including:
Portraits

- Two copies of a lithograph of Maria Wodzińska, based upon her own watercolour (1836) with dedications to Chopin's parents and his younger sister Izabella
- Two pencil portraits of Chopin by George Sand (ca. 1841)
- Chopin's living room at the Square d'Orléans in Paris, unsigned watercolour (1842–1849)
- A daguerreotype of Ludwika Jędrzejewiczowa (Paris 1849)

Musical manuscripts:

- Fryderyk Chopin, piano exercises written (according to Leopold Binental) for his niece Ludwika, daughter of Ludwika Jędrzejewiczowa, autograph
- Felix Mendelssohn-Bartholdy and Fryderyk Chopin (bass part), three-voice canon; autograph dated *Paris 16 avril* [18]*32*

Letters:

- General Józef Bem to Fryderyk Chopin in Paris, Paris, 5 December 1835. Written on Société Politechnique Polonaise paper
- Two personal cards of Fryderyk Chopin with his Paris address: *9, Place d'Orléans, rue St. Lazare* [1842-1849], and his London address: *4. St James's Place* [1848]
- Justyna Chopin to her son in Paris [Paris, February 1848]
- Nicolas Chopin to his son in Tetschen (currently Děčín). Letter written in Polish and French, probably in Rumburk (currently the Czech Republic), 14 September [1835]
- Eugène Delacroix to Ludwika Jędrzejewiczowa in Paris, Paris, 2 November 1849
- Jacques Halévy to Fryderyk Chopin in Paris, letter written in Paris, probably 1836-1837
- Ferdinand Hiller to Fryderyk Chopin in Paris, Frankfurt, 30 May 1836
- Ignaz Moscheles to Fryderyk Chopin in London, Leipzig, 3 May 1848
- George Sand to Ludwika Jędrzejewiczowa, [Nohant, 18 September 1844]
- Last known letter of Maria Wodzińska to Fryderyk Chopin in Paris, [Służewo, autumn 1836]
- Small package from Maria Wodzińska and her family to Fryderyk Chopin, with a note in the composer's hand: *Moja bieda* [My misery]
- 29 letters to Fryderyk Chopin from his parents and sisters (Ludwika, later married Jędrzejewicz, and Izabella, later married Barcińska) with occasional notes by Chopin's brothers-in-law and Michał Skarbek
- A dozen letters from George Sand to Ludwika Jędrzejewiczowa and from Solange and Auguste Clésinger to Fryderyk Chopin
- The majority of letters written to Chopin by eminent musicians, writers, Polish, French and German poets, the composer's pupils, diplomats, as well as a part of the correspondence of Ludwika Jędrzejewiczowa and Izabella Barcińska with Julian Fontana, concerning the posthumous publication of Chopin's works.

History of the Fryderyk Chopin Institute Collection

Chopin's autographs, purchased or otherwise obtained by the Fryderyk Chopin Institute (IFC) in the years 1935-1939 (a total of thirteen items), fortunately survived the period of Nazi occupation, thanks to the foresight and personal courage of Mieczysław Idzikowski (1898-1974), publisher and co-founder of the

IFC in 1934. A selection of the autographs, held until 1939 at the Handlowy Bank at Czacki St in Warsaw, were hidden by Idzikowski at the bookshop of his father, Leon Idzikowski (at 19 Jerozolimskie Ave) and later at the apartment of his mother-in-law, Maria Kotkowska (19 Marszałkowska St). After the Warsaw Uprising, these autographs were moved out of Warsaw under Idzikowski's guidance. In 1945, they were returned to the collections of the IFC. The other autographs held at the Handlowy Bank remained there until early 1945. Fleeing Warsaw in January 1945, the Nazis opened the bank's safes and scattered the autographs on the floor. Recovered by the bank's employees in October 1945, the autographs were returned to the first seat of the reactivated IFC on Zgoda St (which would later become the Chopin Society, TiFC).

Lost paintings, documents, and memorabilia from other collections:

- Two unsigned miniatures (oil on copper and watercolour) representing Jan Matuszyński, from the collection of Wanda Pawłowicz-Pstrąg
- First editions from the collection of Roman Ziffer: 1) F. Chopin, first edition of the *Rondo in C minor* dedicated to Louise Linde, née Nussbaum, Warsaw, published by Antoni Brzezina in 1825 (the work was later given opus number 1); 2) F. Chopin, first edition of the *Rondo à la Mazur in F major* dedicated to Alexandrine de Moriolles, Warsaw, published by Antoni Brzezina in 1825 (later Op. 5).
- Two letters from Chopin to Jan Matuszyński: 1) from Szafarnia (early September 1825); 2) from Vienna (early January 1831), from the collection of Prince Włodzimierz Feliks Czetwertyński

Collections of the Warsaw Music Society:

- Oil portrait of Fryderyk Chopin by Antoni Kolberg, 1848
- *The Chopin Family's Salon at the Krasiński Palace in Warsaw*. Sketch by Antoni Kolberg (penned and coloured in ink, some details watercoloured), 1832
- *Chopin's Last Moment*, oil on wooden board by Teofil Kwiatkowski, signed *T. Kwiatkowski*. Other versions of this painting are now held at the Fryderyk Chopin Museum
- F. Chopin, autograph of the *Mazurka in A flat major* Op. 24 No. 3, dedicated *à Mme Linde*, signed *FChopin* and dated *22 Sept Dresde 1835*
- Autograph of a letter from Chopin to Julian Fontana in Paris, [Paris, 1832–1833]

Lost Chopin collections from the Central Archives of Historical Records in Warsaw:

- Letter from Nicolas Chopin to Stanisław Grabowski (Minister of Religion and Public Education) in Warsaw, requesting a government scholarship for his son Fryderyk, Warsaw, 13 April 1829, autograph
- 13 letters from Fryderyk Chopin to Jan Białobłocki from the years 1825–1827; only some excerpts were reproduced in the publications of Stanisław Pereświet Sołtan (1926) and Leopold Binental (1930).

Archives of the Government Commission of Religion and Public Education relevant to the Higher School of Music:

- Last page of a report by Józef Elsner, dean and professor at the Higher School of Music (Fine Arts Department of the Royal University of Warsaw), dated 20 July 1829, which includes an appreciation of Chopin's genius: *Szopen Friderik Szczególna zdatność geniusz muzyczny* [Fryderyk Chopin, particular aptitude, a musical genius]

Chopin's music manuscripts from the collections of the Directorship of State Art Collections in Warsaw:

- autographs presented to Maria Wodzińska: *Etude in A flat major* Op. 25 No. 1 and *Etude in F minor* Op. 25 No. 2 dated *Ch / Drezno / 1836*; *Waltz in A flat major* Op. 69 No. 1 dated *Drezno Sept. 1835*; *The Ring*, song to words by Stefan Witwicki [
- Op. 74 No. 14] dated *Drezno 8 7bre 1836*; and *The Messenger*, song [Op. 74 No. 7] (Ludwika Jędrzejewiczowa's copy)
- *Lento con gran espressione in C sharp minor* [*Nocturne*], copy of Ludwika Jędrzejewiczowa based upon an autograph sent to her by Chopin in 1830, probably destroyed after 19th September 1863.
- Pencil portrait of teenage Maria Wodzińska, undated
- A ticket signed *FFChopin*, dated *22 Sept. Drezno 1835* and including the text *Soyez heureuse* as well as a fragment of the first two bars of the *Nocturne in E flat major* Op. 9 No. 2.

Appendix 335

Chopin Family Portraits

Mikołaj Chopin, Fryderyk Chopin's father

Justyna Chopin née Krzyżanowska, Fryderyk Chopin's mother

Appendix

Emilja and Ludwika Chopin, Fryderyk Chopin's sisters

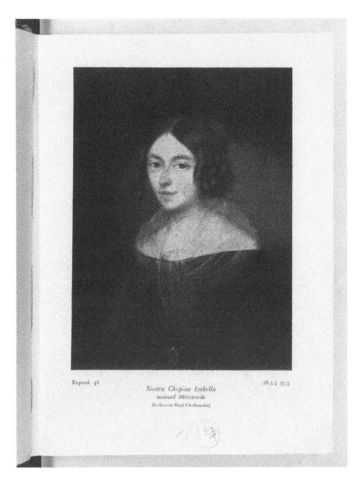

Izabella Chopin, Fryderyk Chopin's sister

Appendix

Fryderyk Chopin in his adolescence

Wojciech Żywny, Fryderyk Chopin's piano teacher

Index of Names

Abb, G. 90, 268, 269
Abendroth, H. 113
Adams, H.E. 186, 241
Agamben, G. 19, 49, 232
Agatstein-Dormont, D. 126, 127
Ajzensztadt, M. 137, 293, 294, 305
Akavia, M. 27
Akhtar, S. 47, 203, 204
Albert d', E. 157
Alexander, L. 13
Alexandrov, A. 226
Alicki, A. 141
Ambros, O. 220
Anders, W. 25
Anisfeld, A. 17
Anisfeld, C. 17
Anisfeld, Ch. 17
Anisfeld, I. 17
Anisfeld, J. 17
Anisfeld, R. 17, 20
Arad, Y. 62
Aronson, E. 225
Arendt, H. 50, 51
Asnyk, A. 126
Auerswald, H. 290

Bacewicz, K. 31
Bach, J.S. 158, 263
Bajer, H. 60, 304
Bajgelman, D. 217
Balint, M. 14
Ball, E. R. 109
Bańkowska-Romańska, M. 222
Barbacki, B. 17
Bartoszewski, W. 26, 135, 162, 193
Bartz-Borodin (Bartsch?),? 112
Baumgartner, M. 41, 242

Bautze, A. 157
Beckerman, M. 19, 233
Beethoven, L. Van 28, 67, 88, 101, 104-106, 113, 114, 116, 119, 120, 175, 263-265, 277, 322
Bekker, P. 68
Belina-Skupiewski, S. 16
Bell, A. 173
Bellini, V. 106
Bem, M. 201
Bemberg, H. 110
Berenstein, T. 99
Berg, M. 43, 120
Berghahn, V. R. 73
Berling, Z. 159
Berman, M. 303
Bernatzky, R. 106
Bernays, E. 225
Berner, F. 186
Bertram, H. 73
Bewziuk, W. 159
Bianco, E. 208
Bikel, T. 23
Bikindi, S. 227
Bilica, K. 42
Bilińska-Riegerowa, M. 130
Binental, L. 79, 268, 270, 325, 326, 328-331
Birdsall, C. 48, 127, 128
Birenbaum, H. 220, 221
Biskupski, M. B. 73
Bizet, G. 105
Błaszczyk, L. T. 43, 160
Blume, F. 229
Blumenfeld, D. 183
Blumensaat, G. 153
Bock, F. Von 76

Boczkowska, E. 41
Boetticher 269, 270
Bogucki, A. 112, 169
Bohdanowicz, Z. 161
Bohlman, A. 26, 222, 330
Bohm, C. 109
Bolesławska-Lewandowska, B. 30
Bömer, K. 59
Bomze, M. 192
Borgmann, H.-O. 140
Boruński, L. 122, 294
Borwicz, M. 28
Böttcher, V. 147
Brahms, J. 263, 264
Brama, M. 173
Brandt, I. 164
Brandt, K. 15
Brandwajn, H. 123
Brandwajn-Ziemian, J. 122, 123
Brandwein, P. 33
Branwajn, Z. 123
Brauer, J., 42
Braun, P. 183
Bristiger, M. 40
Broadwin, John A. 73
Broderick, G. 53
Bronarski, L. 268
Browning, C. R. 28, 186
Bryła, S. 260
Brzechwa, J. 226
Buczkowski, K. 129
Bühler, J. 77, 130
Burchard, M. 222
Burhardt, S. 215
Burzyński, J. 223
Buzzi, A. 108
Bütefisch, H. 220
Bywalec, S. 19, 41, 214

Campbell, T. 15
Carstens, P. 145
Carter, S. 221

Catalani, A. 105, 108
Chęćka, A. 46
Chopin, F. 12, 18, 19, 31, 62, 79, 84, 87-95, 107, 116, 120, 122, 126, 133, 135-137, 145, 146, 150, 169, 173, 210, 211, 213, 215, 266-269, 302, 319, 320, 323, 325-334
Chopin, N. 332, 334
Chorzelski, K. 222
Ciechomska, L. 268, 330
Cizmic, M. 30
Clendinnen, I. 181, 182, 207
Clewing, C. 94
Cohen, A. P. 48, 49
Cohen, J. 202
Coudy, R. 29
Custodis, M. 42, 222
Cygan, J. 33
Cymerman,? 201
Czarkowska, H. 131
Czoch, M. 162
Czocher, A. 27, 130

Dąbrowska, D. 83, 112
Dąbrowski, J. 85, 124, 127, 129
Dahlig, P. 223
Damzog, E. 151
Daniłowski, W. 103
David, J. N. 158
Davies, N. 11
DeCormier. R. 23
Dejmek, K. 35
dem Bach, E. von 92, 136
Dembiński, A. 221
Depczyk, W. 164
der Kolk, A. van 29
Dirlewanger, O. 92, 93
Dobrowolski, S. R. 138, 169
Doerr, K. 181
Dołżycki, A. 104, 107, 321
Donat, A. 207
Donizetti, G. 106

Index of Names

Drabik, Z. 130
Drescher, H. 62, 63
Drewniak, B. 38
Drwenski, W. 158
Drywa, D. 222
Drzewiecka, B. 221, 319
Drzewiecki, Z. 306, 319, 322, 328
Dubiska, I. 30, 306, 311
Duhamel, G. 29
Dunicz, J. J 31, 32
Dunicz, L. 32
Dunicz-Niwińska, H. 19, 31, 32, 42, 44, 188, 221
Dunin- Wąsowicz, K. 37
Dunin-Wąsowicz, J. 140
Dusza,? 133
Dvořák, A. 322
Dybowski, S. 43, 109, 159
Dziębowska, E. 37, 221
Dzieduszycki, W. 130

Ebbinghaus, A. 14
Eberl, I. 15
Edkins, J. 175
Eggebrecht, H. H. 28
Egk, W. 158
Ehrenberg, C. 106
Eichner, B. 165
Eischeid, S. 42
Eisen, G. 219
Eisenbach, A. 99
Ekielski, M. 130
Ekier, H. 129, 130, 131
Ekier, J. 106, 130, 131, 138, 221, 306-308, 322
Ekier, K. 129
Elias, R. 223
Elsner, J. 62, 63, 269,
Eltzschig, J. 14, 235
Emmerich, W. 213
Engelking, B. 40
Enoch, F. 23

Epstein, C. 144, 147-149
Erb, R. 101
Erber, R. 180
Erhardt, L. 161, 162
Esposito, R. 14, 15
Etkin-Moszkowska, R. 122, 159

Fackler, G. 43
Fahlbusch, M. 76
Fairclough, P. 36, 222
Familier-Hepner, J. 122
Fanning, D. 19, 36, 58, 158
Fater, I. 43, 183, 295
Fedyczkowa, Z. 104
Feldshuh, J. 293
Fénelon, F. 42
Fiechtner, H. 158
Filip, F. 88
Fink, H. 62, 63
Fischer, L. 71, 93, 99, 100, 272, 273, 290
Fisler, R. 29
Flam, G. 41, 142
Flex, W. 60
Fliederbaum, L. 123
Fogg, M. 110, 169, 175, 297
Frank, H. 77-83, 86, 90, 91, 98, 101, 105, 112, 125, 130, 132, 265, 269, 270, 287, 329
Frank, N. 52
Franz Joseph 33
Franz, K. H. 47
Fredro, A. 126
Freiherr du Prel, M. 78, 287
Frenzel, K. 201
Friedberg, M. 129
Friedwald, W. 217
Friedwald, K. 217
Friemann, W. 109
Fritz, G. 57
Fröhlich, E. 143
Frołów, A. 40

Frotscher, G. 63, 228
Frühauf, T. 29
Fuks, M. 38, 40, 221
Furmański, A. 118, 322

Gaczek, J. 130
Gadomski, H. 98, 99
Gajcy, T. 138, 308, 309
Gall, J. 109
Ganche, E. 90, 329
Ganzenmüller, A. 219
Garfunkel, L. 62
Gast, P. 151, 152
Gebhardt. K. 13, 16
Gebirtig, M. 28, 41, 127
Geiss, I. 83
Gerigk, H. 58
Gerster, O. 158
Gieburowski, W. 146, 152
Gierek, E. 32
Gieysztor, A. 38
Gilbert, S. 19, 41, 142
Gimpel, B. 34
Glatstein, J. 137, 295
Glazar, R. 191-193, 196, 197, 200, 202-205, 216
Głębocki, W. 38
Globocnik, O. 178
Gluck, C. W. 113
Gluth-Nowowiejski, Janusz 172
Gluth-Nowowiejski, Jerzy 172
Gluth-Nowowiejski, W. 172, 173, 221
Głowiński, M. 221
Godlewska, J. 112, 136, 169
Goebbels, J. 58, 59, 70, 71, 77-80, 113, 143, 154, 225, 228
Gold, A. 118, 194, 197, 199, 200, 221, 298, 317
Goldfeder, A. 103
Goetze, A. 222
Gollert, F. 71, 72, 85, 100, 101, 272
Gołąb, M. 39, 159

Gomułka, W. 32
Gordon, K. 88
Goss, M. 222
Göring, E. 94
Górka, M.? 17
Gounod, C. 109
Grabner, H. 158
Grabowski, Jan 131
Grabowski, Z. R. 131
Gran, W. 156
Grant, M. J. 46, 178, 198, 226
Grechaninov, A. 110
Greiser, A. 143, 154
Greiser, M. 154
Grenet, E. 88
Grieg, E. 104, 105, 110, 120
Grochowina, S. 42, 153
Grodzieńska, S. 156, 297, 323, 324
Grzecznarowska, H. see Szpilman, H.
Grzybowski, M. 222
Grzymski, W. 47
Guttreich, M. 17
Guzy-Pasiak, J. 30
Gwizdalanka, D. 31, 39, 222

Haar, I. 57, 76
Haas, M. 36
Hahn, J. 16
Haken, Boris von 28
Hamann, H. 16, 17
Harder, L. 152
Harders-Wuthenow, F. 40, 44, 222
Hausegger, S. von 154
Haydn, J. 158
Haykowski, S. 162
Hecht, G. 77
Heidegger, M. 49
Heinrich, A. 157
Heinitz, W. 228
Heller-Roazen, D. 19
Hennemeyer, K. 62, 89
Heraclitus 49

Hermelin, A. 40, 207, 208
Hertel, P. 162
Hesse, A. 57
Heydrich, R. 13
Himmler, H. 16, 178, 183
Hindemith, R. 132, 316
Hippler, F. 73
Hirsch, L. 29, 36
Hirsch, W. 197
Hitler, A. 135, 263, 264
Hoffman,? 31
Hoffmann, H. 73
Holtzman, A. 43, 202
Holzman, J. 94
Horoszowski, B. 164
Horszowski, M. 118
Hösl, A. 99, 114, 142
Höss, R. 47-49, 52
Humperdinck, E. 157
Husadel, H. F. 94

Ilnicka, J. 130
Izmajłow, L. 221

Jacobmeyer, W. 83
Jacobs, M. 46
Jakelski, L. 26, 30, 222
Janiszewska, M. 222
Jarosz, M. 17, 192
Jarosz, W. 192
Jarzębski, J. 110
Jentz, T. 165
Jezierski, A. 21
Jochum, E. 158
Jolles, N. 129
Jowett, G. S. 225
Jörns, H. 158

Kabalevsky, D. 226
Kaczerginski, S. 23, 29, 32, 218, 219, 248
Kaczmarek, T. 17

Kalinówna, D. 156
Kalinowska-Styczeń, E. 13
Kalmanowicz, H. 122
Kałwa, D. 27
Kamieński, Ł. 152, 215
Kapelański, M. 39
Karabasz, K. 166
Karasiński, A. 110
Karasiński, Z. 110
Karłowicz, M. 62
Karski, J. 16, 86
Karwowska, L. 217
Kaschub, H. 13
Kaszak, M. 150
Kataszek, S. 110
Kater, M. H. 36
Kaźmierska, J. 37
Kazuro, S. 43
Keitl, W. 76
Kempa, A. 117, 322
Kempke, K. 189
Kempter, K. 27
Keppler, W. 220
Kietliński, M. 141
Kieżun, W. 221
Kirtley, K. 18, 188
Kiryk, F. 17
Kisielewski, S. 36
Kistler, C. 165
Klee, E. 13, 14, 58
Kleinman, A. 189
Kleinman, H. 33, 188, 189
Klich-Kluczewska, B. 27
Klimaszewska, K. 222
Klimczyk, W. 46, 65, 183
Klimko, T. 33, 190
Kloza, D. 141
Knapp, A. 158
Knapp, G. 42
Kodály, Z. 105
Koffler, J. 39
Konopnicka, M. 171

Konoye, H. 158
Konwitschny, F. 158
Kopeczek- Michalska, E. 37
Kopera, F. 129
Korngold, E. W. 68
Korwin, Ł. 189
Kościuszko, T. 126
Kossakowski, J. 221
Kostrzewska, B. 169
Koszyk, R. 19, 214, 222
Kotońska, J. 174, 221
Kotoński, W. 168, 174, 221
Kozaczko,? 17
Kozłowska, M. 43
Kozłowski-Kleinman, L. 31, 33
Koźmińska- Frejlak, E. 192, 194
Kraft, R. N. 162
Krahelska, K. 138, 312
Krause, E. 228
Kreisler, F. 175
Křenek, E. 68
Kreuder, D. 88
Krienitz, E. 89, 267
Król, E. C. 59
Kruk, H. 62
Krzepicki, A. J. 191, 206, 207
Krzeptowski, W. 94
Krzyształowicz, K. 129
Kubalski, E. 131
Kudła, M. 171
Kulisiewicz, A. 29, 184, 217
Kupershmid, S. 24
Kutschera, F. 37
Kuvychko, A. 226
Küttner, K. 200
Kwiatkowski, M. J. 38
Kwiek, M. 36

Łabno, B. 27
Lacan, J. 14
Lachendro, J. 42
Lachowicz, S. 39, 128, 131, 132

Laks, S. 29, 40, 41, 214-216
Lange, H. 146, 151
Lanzman, C. 197, 203, 205
Laskowski, K. 222
Latoszewski, Z. 104, 115, 136
Laub, D. 29
Laubert, M. 57
Lawiński, L. 156
Lebedev-Kumach, V. 226
Lednicki (Lederman), Z. 160
Lefeld, J. 306, 307, 311
Leociak, J. 40, 306
Leopoldi, H.197
Lerski, T. 43
Leszczyńska, A. 223
Levi, E. 19, 36, 44, 58, 89, 108, 113, 158, 222
Lewandowska, I. 215
Lewińska, I. 131
Ley, R. 68, 69
Li, D. 46
Libionka, D. 194
Lichtenstein,? 68
Lichtman, E. 201, 202
Lifton, R. J. 186
Liebeskind, A. 217
Lindstedt, I. 39, 223
Lingens- Reiner, E. 188
Lipski, J. 59
Lissa, Z. 226
Liszt, F. 327
Litwinowicz, J. 184
Litzmann, K. 156
Lohse, F. 158
Łoziński, M. 166, 167
Łubek-Luboradzka, T. 170
Łubieńska, K. 169
Łuczak, C. 147, 148
Lukas, R. C. 83
Łukasiewicz, F. 131
Lurie, W. 93

Lutosławski, W. 17, 30, 31, 35, 38, 41, 99, 103, 136, 137, 222, 243, 260, 277, 278

Maas, G. 158
Mączka, Z. 14
Madajczyk, C. 38, 82, 113
Madeja, J. 130
Madeyska, K. 130
Mahfouz, A. 47
Mahler, G. 18
Majer, D. 55
Majerski, T. 33, 88
Majewski, P. 39
Malinowski, W. 175, 221
Mankiewiczówna, T. 110
Marchesi, S. 109
Marcinek-Drozdalska, A. 218
Marczak- Oborski, S. 38
Marischka, E. 210-212
Mark, B. 303
Markiewiczówna, W. 130
Markowska, E. 30, 173, 222
Markowski, A. 34
Maruzsa, Z. 74
Mascagni, P. 108
Massenet, J. 110
Matelski, D. 150
Matthes, H. A. 195
Matusak, P. 39
Mayski, I. 25
Mayzner, T. 43
McLuhan, M. 128
Megargee, G. P. 16
Melichar, A. 210
Meloch, K. 172
Mengele, J. 187
Meyer, K. 222
Meyer, M. 88
Meyerowa, I. 131
Michael, R. 181
Michalski, D. 111

Michalski, G. 222
Mickiewicz, A. 35, 126, 327
Mieczkowska, K. 170
Miklaszewski, W. 16
Mikulski, J. 106, 132
Mikuszewski, M. 130
Milewski, B. 29, 41, 210, 222
Milhaud, D. 68
Młynarczyk, J. A. 194
Młynarski, E. 118
Möllemann, R. 46
Molotov, V. 11
Moniuszko, S. 284
Mórawski, K. 38
Morbitzerowa, M. 130
Morgan, G. 49, 52
Moś, K. 19
Moś-Wdowik, M. 19
Mozart, W. A. 258
Mrugowski, J. 15
Murphy, J. 69
Mund, J. 207
Murawska-Gryń, Z. 220
Müller, G. 158
Müller, S. O. 20
Münz, S. C. 46
Münzberger, G. 200

Nachtstern, A. 132
Nahke,? 215
Nałęcz, M. 43
Naliwajek, K. 17, 20, 30, 31, 44, 159, 161, 162, 173, 178, 190, 198, 204, 209
Naliwajek, Z. 221
Nawrocki, S. 109, 150
Negri, P. 140
Neumann, A. 127
Neumann, E. 146
Neuteich, M. 117, 119, 293, 299, 300, 321, 322
Newman, L.S. 180

Newman, R. 18
Ney, E. 113, 114
Niakraseva, A. 223
Nicolai, O. 157
Niedhart, G. 53
Niezabitowska, M. 35
Noskowski, W. 150
Noskowski, Z. 106
Nowaczyński, A. 136, 228
Nowak, 215, 223
Novitch, M. 202
Nowowiejski, F. 171-173, 221
Nuxoll, C. 46

Obidowicz, W. 131
Ochlewski, T. 40
O'Donnell, V. 225
Okulicki, L. 25
Olszewski, A. 95, 163, 175, 221, 307
Ottman, W. 130

Paczkowski, S. 223
Paderewski, I. J. 149, 328
Padlewska, N. 153
Padlewski, J. 104
Padlewski, R. 30, 36, 104, 281
Paganini, N. 104, 105
Pajzderski, N. 146, 152, 223
Palitzsch, G. 46
Pallavicini, S. 16
Pallmann, G. 60, 61, 64
Palmon, H. 40, 208, 222
Pankowicz, A. 47
Panufnik, A. 41, 103, 169, 277, 278, 306
Panufnik, C. 222
Parens, H. 47
Paszkowska-Turska, H. 27, 166, 167, 221
Paulsen, P. 150

Perepłyś, K. 222
Perkowski, P. 34, 35, 112, 135, 136, 322
Perz, M. 221
Peters, R. 158
Petersburski, J. 110, 217
Pettyn, A. 94
Petzold, R. 158
Pfitzner, H. 68, 154-156, 158
Piasecka, I. 135
Piasecki, S. 135
Piłsudski 33, 135, 163
Piłsudski, J. 33
Piotrowski, S. 78
Piwarski, K. 129
Platówna(-Rotter), F. 130
Polański, R. 166
Polubiec, Z. 83, 112
Połeć, J. 222
Ponce, M. 109
Poniatowska, I. 223, 243
Poniatowski, J. 135, 158
Popowska, E. 184
Posłuszna, J. 181, 183
Posłuszny, Ł. 181, 183
Pospieszalski, K. M. 82, 148
Pote, J.-Y. 222
Potter, P. 28
Pötzinger, K. 200
Praszker, J. 207
Pratkanis, A. R. 225
Präg, W. 83
Prieberg, F. K. 42, 63
Prokopowicz, M. 215
Przerwa-Tetmajer, K. 109
Puccini, G. 104, 108, 157
Puget, L. 130, 131
Pulikowski, J. Von 90, 269
Pullman, S. 119, 322
Putin, V. 226

Index of Names

Quignard, P. 46
Raabe, P. 158
Rachmaninov, S. 106
Rączkowski, F. 171
Raczyński, E. 86
Radzymińska, J. 140
Rajchman, J. M. ("Henryk Romanowski") 191-196, 200, 201, 205, 206
Rajgrodzki, J. 194
Rakowiecki, Z. 169
Rapaport, E. 34
Rauschenberger, W. 89
Regamey, C. 30, 40, 83, 271, 306, 311, 322
Reger, M. 106, 155
Reich-Ranicki, M. ("Wiktor Hart") 123, 124
Reisberg, D. 162
Reissert, G. 155
Rekść-Raubo, J. 222
Relich-Sielicka, B. H. 162
Respighi, O. 109
Reyland, N. 30, 222
Rezler-Wasilewska, V. 222
Ribbentrop, J. 12, 74
Richie, A. 92
Rieger, A. 130
Rimsky-Korsakov, N. 106
Ringelblum, E. 117-120, 191, 207, 296, 298-300, 302, 305, 306
Roessert, H. 154
Roessner, Z. 131
Rohr, H. 101, 132, 263, 265
Rokita, R. 208
Rosé, A. 18, 19, 188, 210-212
Rosenbaum, I. 122
Rosenberg, A. 64-66, 70
Rossini, G. 106
Rost, M. 28
Rozwoda, J. 163

Różycki, L. 104, 109
Różycki, S. 119
Rubczak, M. 130
Rubin, R. 22, 23, 32, 219
Rubinowicz, D. 219
Rudzisz, M. 35
Rudzka-Cybisowa. H. 131
Rudnitsky, L. 218
Rühle, S. 152
Rust, R. 152
Rutkowski, A. 99, 120
Rutkowski, B. 36
Rutkowski, N. 109
Rutowska, M. 39
Rychter, M. 223
Rychter, S. 223
Ryś, Zbigniew 16, 17
Ryś, Zofia 15, 17, 18
Rytel, P. 168

Sachs, H. 36, 42, 222
Sadowy, W. 174, 221
Salacz, J. 132
Salapska, M. 43
Salwano, S. 110
Salwe, I. 216
Sander-Janowska, H. 221
Sari, A. 104, 106
Sauer, M. 150
Scharff, D. E. 47
Schenk, D. 90
Schenk, E. 154
Scher, P. 60
Schermann, ? 200
Scherner, J. 127
Schieder, S. 88
Schlengel, W. 120
Schmid, K. 133
Schmidt, C. 222
Schön, W. 99
Schönberg, A. 68
Schreker, F. 68

Schröder, R. A. 61
Schubert, F. 67, 106, 107, 109, 114, 119
Schubert, L. 39
Schultze, N. 73, 256
Schumann, R. 87, 215, 327
Schwarzkopf, E. 155
Sekles, B. 68
Seress, R. 217
Serwański, E. 39
Seyss-Inquart, A. 77
Shapreau, C. 56
Sheridan, A. 14
Sholokhova, L. 222
Shore, M. 26, 35
Shreffler, A. C. 28
Siedlanowska, W. 170
Sikorski, K. 142, 321
Skowron, Z. 223
Skriabin, A. 104
Skrzywan, W. 129
Smetana, B. 106
Smolik,? 17
Snyder, L. L. 178
Snyder, T. D. 11
Sonner, R. 68
Sonnleitner, F. 132
Spendiarov, A. 105
Spitta, H. 61
Spóz, A. 17, 30, 31, 38, 161, 162, 215
Spychalski, M. 160
Stalin, J. 11, 25, 32, 33, 225, 226
Stadler, A. 254, 255
Stangl, F. 205
Stanilewicz-Kamionka, M. 38
Stefańska, H. 130
Stern, S. 13
Stojka, J. 132
Stola, D. 33
Stolfowa, J. 130
Stolfowa, O. 130
Straszyński, O. 16, 41, 116, 117

Straszyński, A. 252
Strauss, J. 104, 106, 183
Strauss, R. 68
Striks, L. 207
Stromberg, H. 118
Strzałkowski, H. 140
Strzelewicz, K. 29, 184
Stürmer, B. 158
Suchomel, F. 197, 198, 203
Sutker, P.B. 186
Sym, I. 105, 116
Syrewicz, W. 130
Szablowski, J. 31
Szamotulska 31
Szatkowski, H. 94
Szczepańska-Lange, E. 222
Szczepański, I. 213
Szczepkowska-Naliwajek, K. 221
Szczęśniak, H. 42
Szewera, T. 41, 140
Szigetthi,? 13
Szlagowski, A. 92, 93
Szlemińska, A. 130
Szmaglewska, S. 223
Szostak, L. 127
Szostak, Z. 127
Szostkiewicz, H. 172
Szpilman, A. 222
Szpilman, H. 169, 221
Szpilman, S. 103
Szpilman, W. 33, 35, 38, 103, 112, 118, 136, 159, 168, 169, 173, 279, 299
Sztarbałło, K. 94
Szukalak, M. 117
Szulc, T. 132
Szwarcman-Czarnota, B. 192
Szyfman, A. 156
Szymala, J. 19
Szymański, A. 222
Szymański, P. 222
Szymanowski, K. 132
Szymanowski, W. 147, 266

Index of Names

Śmidowicz, J. 105, 106
Świderska, E. 43
Święch, J. 38
Świerzowska, A. 46, 65, 183
Świętońska, B. 141

Tan, T. 170
Tańczuk, R. 159, 222
Tarasewicz, K. 221
Tarnawska-Kaczorowska, K. 39
Tchaikovsky, P. 104
Tcherepnin, N. 110
Teichman, H. 256
Temnitschka, E. von 154, 156
Teodorowicz, G. 222
Teodorowicz, K. 222
Teutsch, O. 132
Timofeychev, A. 226
Tobias, J. 156
Tomala, M.
Törmer, I. 20
Toselli, E. 109
Traczyk-Stawska, W. 171
Trenkner, W. 158
Treterowa, K. 129-131
Troczyński, K. 150
Trunk, R. 158
Trzonek, H. 30, 260
Tuchowski, A. 39
Turski, M. 27, 221
Twemlow, S. W. 47

Uebersberger, H. 57
Umińska, E. 30, 260, 277, 306
Unger, H. 155

Verdi, G. 106, 119
Vertinsky, A. 218
Vetter, W. 152, 153, 155
Vogel, J. 213
Vogel, R. 213
Vries, W. De 56, 90, 268

Wagner, G. F. 289
Wagner, R. 64, 65, 228
Wahlmann, A. 186
Waibel, H. 152
Wajda, A. 35
Waldman, G. 63
Walentynowicz, W. 109, 306
Wallek-Walewski, B. 106
Waller, J. 182, 185
Walter, M. 14
Wandycz, P. S. 73
Wardzyński, M. 94
Wasiak, J. (Lederman) 160
Wächter, O. 80, 256
Wąsowski, A. 131, 306
Weill, K. 68
Weiner, W.? 130
Weintraub, K. 78
Weiss, O. 202
Weissmann, A. 68
Weissweiler, E. 228
Werb, B. 24, 28, 29, 32, 197, 223
Wesby, I. 297
Wetzel, E. 77
Wiechowicz, S. 31, 153
Wieczorek, S. 26, 159, 222
Wielhorski, A. 109
Wiernik, J. 191, 193
Wiłkomirski, J. 221
Wiłkomirski, K. 34, 35, 132
Willenberg, S. 191-193, 195, 199, 200, 221
Windt, H. 73
Winnicka, H. 37
Wiśniewski, M. 223
Witte, W. 90, 268, 269
Włast, A. (Gustaw Baumritter) 69, 110, 159, 294
Wójcik, B. 108
Wójcik, J. 108
Wolff, K. 219
Wolska-Stefanowicz, J. 52

Woronkov,? 196
Woytowicz, B. 106, 172, 173, 322
Wróblewska-Strauss, H. 79, 328, 330
Wulf, J. 27, 28, 41, 89
Wyspiański, S. 126
Wyszyńska, M. 222

Zabieglińska, S. 222
Zajderman, D. 183
Zaleski, A. 268
Zalfen, S. 20
Żebrowski, M. 39, 222
Żeleński, W. 126, 129, 284
Zelwerowicz, A. 156
Zeyland-Kapuścińska, Z. 108
Zieleniewska-Ginter, M. 184

Zillig, W. 154, 158
Zillmer, E.A. 186
Zimińska, M. 136
Zoller, J. 162
Zörner, E. 128, 314
Żerańska-Kominek, S. 223
Żmudziński, T. 131
Żórawska-Witkowska, A. 223
Żuk, A. 141
Żurawlew, J. 106
Żylski, T. 164
Žižek, S. 50
Edek 200, 216
Elżunia 220

Eastern European Studies in Musicology

Edited by Maciej Gołąb

Vol. 1 Paweł Gancarczyk / Lenka Hlávková-Mráčková / Remigiusz Pośpiech (eds.): The Musical Culture of Silesia before 1742. New Contexts – New Perspectives. 2013.

Vol. 2 Laura Vasiliu/Florin Luchian/Loredana Iaţeşen/Diana-Beatrice Andron (eds.): Musical Romania and the Neighbouring Cultures. Traditions–Influences–Identities. Proceedings of the International Musicological Conference July 4–7, 2013, Iaşi (Romania). 2014.

Vol. 3 Barbara Przybyszewska-Jarmińska: Marcin Mielczewski and Music under the Patronage of the Polish Vasas. Translated by John Comber. 2014.

Vol. 4 Tomasz Jasiński: The Musical Rhetoric of the Polish Baroque. Translated by Wojciech Bońkowski. 2015.

Vol. 5 Bogusław Raba: Between Romanticism and Modernism. Ignacy Jan Paderewski´s Compositional Œuvre. Translated by John Comber. 2015.

Vol. 6 Maciej Gołąb: Musical Modernism in the Twentieth Century. Translated by Wojciech Bońkowski. 2015.

Vol. 7 Wojciech Bońkowski: Editions of Chopin's Works in the Nineteenth Century. Aspects of Reception History. 2016.

Vol. 8 Ivana Perković / Franco Fabbri (eds.): Musical Identities and European Perspective. An Interdisciplinary Approach. 2017.

Vol. 9 Bożena Muszkalska (ed.): The Kolbergs of Eastern Europe. 2018.

Vol. 10 Renata Tańczuk / Sławomir Wieczorek (eds.): Sounds of War and Peace. Soundscapes of European Cities in 1945. 2018.

Vol. 11 Tomasz Jeż: The Musical Culture of the Jesuits in Silesia and the Kłodzko County (1581–1776). 2019.

Vol. 12 Magdalena Walter-Mazur: Musical Culture of Polish Benedictine Nuns in the 17th and 18th Centuries. 2018.

Vol. 13 Danuta Popinigis: Carillons and Carillon Music in Old Gdańsk. 2019

Vol. 14 Andrzej Tuchowski: Nationalism, Chauvinism and Racism as Reflected in European Musical Thought and in Compositions from the Interwar Period. 2019.

Vol. 15 Ludwik Bielawski: Time in Music and Culture. 2019.

Vol. 16 Barbara Literska: Nineteenth-Century Transcriptions of Works by Fryderyk Chopin. Translated by John Comber. 2019

Vol.	17	Barbara Literska: Tadeusz Baird. The Composer, His Work, and Its Reception. 2019.
Vol.	18	Sławomir Wieczorek: On the Music Front. Socialist-Realist Discourse on Music in Poland, 1948 to 1955. 2020.
Vol.	19	Alicja Jarzębska: Strawinski – Thoughts and Music. 2020.
Vol.	20	Małgorzata Sieradz: The Beginnings of Polish Musicology. Translated by Lindsay Davidson. 2020.
Vol.	21	Piotr Wilk: The Venetian Instrumental Concerto During Vivaldi's Time. Translated by John Comber. 2020.
Vol.	22	Aneta Markuszewska: Festa and Music at the Court of Marie Casimire Sobieska in Rome (1699–1714). Translated by Anna Gutowska and Tomasz Zymer. 2021.
Vol.	23	Julia R. Adams: Musical Humor and Antonín Dvořák's Comic Operas. 2022.
Vol.	24	Pawel Strzelecki: "New Romanticism" in the Works of Polish Composers After 1975. 2022.
Vol.	25	Katarzyna Naliwajek: Sounds of Apocalypse. Music in Poland under German Occupation. 2022.

www.peterlang.com